Thunder Over Zion

Willis W. Ritter, ca. 1950. Courtesy Special Collections,
J. Willard Marriott Library, University of Utah.

THUNDER OVER ZION

The Life of Chief Judge WILLIS W. RITTER

PATRICIA F. COWLEY

&

PARKER M. NIELSON

THE UNIVERSITY OF UTAH PRESS
Salt Lake City

The Defiance House Man colophon is a registered trademark of the University of Utah Press. It is based upon a four-foot-tall, Ancient Puebloan pictograph (late PIII) near Glen Canyon, Utah.

10 09 08 07 06   5 4 3 2 1

LIBRARY OF CONGRESS CATALOGING-IN-PUBLICATION DATA

Cowley, Patricia F., 1934-

Thunder over Zion : the life of chief judge Willis W. Ritter / by Patricia F. Cowley and Parker M. Nielson.

p. cm.

Includes bibliographical references and index.

ISBN-13: 978-0-87480-876-6 (cloth : alk. paper)

ISBN-10: 0-87480-876-6 (cloth : alk. paper) 1. Ritter, Willis W., 1899- 2. United States. District Court (Utah)—Biography. 3. Judges—Utah—Biography. 4. Judges—United States—Biography. I. Nielson, Parker M., 1932- II. Title.

KF373.R52 C69 2006

347.73'14092—dc22

[B]

2006023889

This biography is dedicated to Patty, whose tireless, resourceful efforts and scholarship, prior to her affliction with Alzheimer's, made it possible.

Was there ever such a profession as ours, anyhow? We speak of ourselves as practicing law, as teaching it, as deciding it; and not one of us can say what law means.

—Benjamin N. Cardozo

CONTENTS

PREFACE

Willis William Ritter, United States District Judge for the District of Utah from October 21, 1949, until the date of his death, on March 4, 1978, was the one judge whose name was familiar among those who had little or no idea of the difference between one judge's jurisdiction and that of another; did not follow the news, politics, and the law or other public issues; didn't pay much attention to the names of public officials below the rank of president or governor. They might have never known of him but for some broad gesture in which he challenged bureaucracies, and the federal government itself, or some other vested authority, religious or secular, bringing them down a notch or two.

He was enigmatic, even to those who knew him best, and a folk hero of sorts to many who felt that he had struck a blow for them. They would have been right, in a way. Willis Ritter saw himself as a champion of the "little people." Those who knew him, worked with him, and observed him in the court year after year saw him the same way, though not always approvingly.

"Ritter," as he was referred to by friend and foe alike, could be the stereotypical judge—white hair, judicial robes, serious-looking disciplinarian—when he chose. Almost anyone can look like a judge if he or she wears a judicial robe, but Ritter never wore robes on the bench—just a suit and tie, sleeves rolled up like the people who work the soil, the mines, factories, or refineries—except for special occasions such as when he sat on a three-judge panel convened by the Court of Appeals for the Tenth Circuit. Ritter didn't need a robe. When people saw him on the bench, they knew they were looking at a judge, one fully in command of court and matters brought before him. His eyes—the rigidly direct way he could look at people—had an effect something like a child feels when his parent looks at him with deep concern. He was the people's judge, of one heart, perhaps, with truck drivers, waitresses, and janitorial workers, and when he took the bench he demonstrated the power of the federal court as no one else could. He had the guts to wield his power when others lacked the courage. He made the federal court into something special. He gave juveniles, with whom he typically was most fatherly, the oppressed, and minorities relief when they couldn't get it elsewhere. He stood up under pressure doing so—pressure that would have wilted others.

Ritter ruled decisively and consistently, usually orally and from the bench. He was well ahead of his times on matters such as civil rights and right to counsel. He was a buffer between the people and those in most rigid authority.

But he had a capacity for bias and dislike that a judge ought not have. We're all human. He was not sneaky about it, like others who might just sit there going through the motions of politeness and civility, only to let you have it in the end. His enormous capacity for resentment and bias hurt him, bruising his judicial flesh. Few who ever appeared before him, including his most ardent critics and opponents, did not agree that he was brilliant and that if he could have controlled his personal conduct and biases, harnessed his enormous talent along positive lines, he would have been one of the giants of the federal bench.

His personal behavior, womanizing, and tendency to be boorish, particularly when under the influence of alcohol, turned many against him. In the end, they included even his trusted aides. Scarcely a friend was left at his death. He had become the object of ridicule, outrage, pity, and contempt.

Patricia F. "Patty" Cowley, born Patricia Faye Kimball in 1934, was married to James P. "Phil" Cowley in the 1960s and was acquainted with many leaders of the day in the Democratic Party, nationally and in Utah. Most of them, including her husband, were lawyers, and many had been students of Willis W. Ritter at the University of Utah College of Law and had appeared before him as United States District Judge for the District of Utah. While engaged in ad hoc meetings, dinner parties, and brainstorming sessions with party notables of the day, often in her home, Patty heard Ritter praised, scorned, ridiculed, admired, cussed, cursed, adored, damned, and argued about incessantly. She became fascinated with this man Ritter, whom she heard so much about but had never met, this intellectual giant or despicable fat mouse—take your pick—the truth was hard to discern.

Overcome with curiosity and intellectual determination to "plumb the depths" of Willis W. Ritter, she began by researching his family history. She visited Wasatch County and the site of the early Ritter home, searched the county records for information about him and his beginnings, visited the sites associated with Ritter in Salt Lake County. Patty befriended Ritter's daughter Nancy and went with her to the Ritter family place on the Snake River. Scores of people were interviewed who had some connection, knowledge, or incident with Ritter, both favorable and unfavorable. Nancy made it possible for Patty to have access to the Willis W. Ritter Papers, deposited after his death at the J. Willard Marriott Library, University of Utah, with access limited to Nancy and Patty. He was, as Patty would say, "hard to get your arms around."

As she was completing her research in the 1980s, Patty was overcome with an early onset of Alzheimer's. She boxed her notes and drafts and put them away for a better day, which never came. While she still had the faculties to do so, she and her family asked me, Parker M. Nielson, an old acquaintance and friend, to undertake completion of Patty's work.

I have experience writing on law-related subjects and extensive litigation and practice before Willis W. Ritter. I agreed to undertake the project and the many boxes of notes, research, and drafts were delivered to me. Joy Sanders Clegg Lowham, the daughter of Nancy, who was then deceased, arranged for me to have access to the Ritter Papers, which are heavily relied upon in this biography and were indispensable to completion of Patty's work.

Ritter's papers include substantially all of the files related to his judicial office. They also include the papers related to his years as a professor of law, his study of law, and his college years, together with many documents concerning his personal life. This biography attempts to go beyond those matters, however, and deal with the politics of the times in which Ritter had his origins and the interaction of both himself and his confederates with the Church of Jesus Christ of Latter-day Saints and its leaders, who were dominant in the politics of Utah during the Ritter years.

—Parker M. Nielson

ACKNOWLEDGMENTS

With a work like this one—several decades in the production, begun by one author now afflicted with Alzheimer's and concluded by another; inspired and encouraged by a daughter of Willis W. Ritter, in the person of Nancy, who is now deceased; and encouraged by a granddaughter, in the person of a Joy Sanders Lowham—it would be impossible to even reconstruct all of the persons who have afforded valuable assistance, after knowledge of them has expired into the ethereal or Elysian realm where providence, or biology, consigns them in such an incident. It seems inappropriate, and inadequate, to merely recite the cliché "You know who you are, and your help is appreciated." Still, at least *some* of the more obvious will be named, with apology to those who cannot, for the reasons cited, be identified. Joy Sanders Lowham and her mother, Nancy, before her are extended special recognition for having secured access to the important sites to the life of Willis W. Ritter and the Ritter Papers, without which this biography would be seriously deficient. In that connection are the personnel at the Nature Conservancy, which now operates the Thousand Springs farm, which provided access and documents located there important to this biography.

There are, of course, the many acquaintances and colleagues of Ritter who have furnished interviews. They are identified in the notes. Their assistance is acknowledged and appreciated.

Phil Cowley, David and Pam Winder, Bernie Rhodes, Linda Nielson, Pamela Blomquist, Glen Richman, and Lavina Fielding Anderson are given special thanks for having read early versions of the manuscript, offering helpful constructive criticism, and encouraging completion of the project begun by Patty.

1

BEGINNINGS

Historic continuity with the past is not a duty, it is only a necessity.

—Oliver Wendell Holmes Jr.

On Sunday evening, January 8, 1978, CBS's *60 Minutes* displayed clandestine video of tired seventy-nine-year-old United States District Judge Willis William Ritter leaving by the side door of his courthouse, crimson faced, collar turned up, battered leather briefcase he had carried for twenty-eight years in his right hand, and crumpled fedora on his head. It was in the evening at perhaps nine o'clock, and he was on his way to a desolate room at the Hotel Newhouse directly across the intersection from his court, where he led a lonely existence. The lights blazed, the cameras rolled, and the startled jurist nearly stumbled on the steps, grasped the arborvitae to steady himself, and almost fell over into the bushes. The reporter, Mike Wallace, making no excuse for his film crew's ill breeding, claimed the judge had been drinking and having an affair with his secretary.

Titillating as that may have been, it surely would not have rated an installment of *60 Minutes.* Other judges have had affairs, and more prominent public officials have acquitted themselves worse. What was it about this particular judge that merited a story on prime-time national television titled "The USA vs. Judge Ritter"? What about him had attracted the combined power of those trying to get rid of him, or curb his power and authority, including the president of the bar association, the attorney general of the State of Utah, the United States Justice Department, Solicitor General Robert Bork, the United States Attorney for the District of Utah, the Judiciary Committee of the United States House of Representatives, both senators from Utah, and several subcommittees of the United States Senate—urged on by the news media collectively, its reporters, cameramen, and courtroom artists who had run afoul the powers of Ritter (as he was commonly known and is referred to herein), the "chief" federal judge (as he insisted he be called)? They were all represented, in a sense, by Mike Wallace and *60 Minutes.*

Ritter's problems did not begin that night on *60 Minutes.* They began much earlier, with his confirmation hearings, and perhaps even before that, with his service during World War II in the Office of Price Administration (OPA). The story of Willis William Ritter, so contentious that it was featured on national television during the last days of his life, even as he lay on his deathbed, is the saga that follows.

He was the first Utah native to occupy the office of United States District Judge for the District of Utah. The power of a federal judge is considerable, and everyone who knew Willis W. Ritter or appeared before him knew that, if he did not revel in possessing it, he knew how to wield it as well as anyone who ever lived. He was the sole federal judge in the district, at least initially, which magnified the importance of the office. His appointment was only the second time since statehood that the office had changed hands, the first coming in the early days when distrust of Mormons almost required that a non-Mormon and outsider be appointed. Ritter was not Mormon, contrary to the openly expressed wishes of church officials to at long last have one of their faith in the office. That frustrated desire of church leaders was expressed during the process of his nomination and confirmation, no doubt leaving him bitter over apparent opposition to him by religious authorities. Many said that he disliked Mormons. The truth is probably that he resented those who wielded and abused power, which in Utah was centered in the Mormon Church, leaders of which were sometimes blatant about it. His feelings about those who tried to control society and public opinion were strong and undoubtedly affected his behavior adversely on occasion.

Ritter was by nature a shrewd man. He had a way of looking at you that made you feel as if he were seeing right through your skin, that he knew exactly what was in your mind. His was a piercing intellect that grasped the essence of a matter long before discourse or even a brief statement had reached its conclusion. And, of course, he was a lawyer, a calling that conditions one to constantly question the motives of other human beings.

Though he often seemed a practical, hard man, Ritter held ideals. Among the most clearly visible were those reflected in his political attitudes, which were those of the Democratic Party as incorporated in the New Deal and Fair Deal of Presidents Franklin Delano Roosevelt and Harry S Truman.

Ritter found in Roosevelt's politics and ideas an effective representation of his own concerns and values, centered on the needs and rights of ordinary people, people with little power of their own to defend them against forces of government and business. Ritter idolized Roosevelt, perhaps above any other public figure, and approved highly of Harry S. Truman and John F. Kennedy.

Ritter was born in 1899, to parents resident in a mining town, with grandparents who were miners, and he spent his childhood and got his primary and secondary education in a second mining community. As a youth he worked in the mines. Mining was to be a major influence in the life of Willis W. Ritter. A biography of Ritter must therefore begin with the story of mining in Utah, Park City in particular.

His early childhood was spent in Heber Valley, on the other side of the mountains from Parleys Park, established by Mormon leader Parley P. Pratt in 1848, flanking a rich store of mineral deposits. The Mormons knew Utah Territory contained mineral wealth almost from the time of their arrival, but Brigham Young admonished them not to exploit it:

> I can stand in my door and see where there are untold millions in rich treasures of the earth, both gold and silver. But the time has not come for the Saints to dig gold. It is our duty first to develop the agricultural resources of this country. As for gold and silver and other rich minerals of the earth, there is no country that equals this, but let them alone, let others seek them, and we will cultivate the soil, for if the mines are opened first, the people would rush in here in such great numbers that they would breed a famine, and we would be overwhelmed.

The Mormons heeded the advice of their prophet and stayed on their farms, at least until the 1860s.[1]

Soldiers were sent to the territory in 1862, however, under the command of Colonel Patrick Edward Connor, to secure the overland mail route—and, incidentally, keep an eye on the Mormons. Connor was hostile to the Mormons. He refused to take his troops to Camp Floyd, established by Johnston's army in 1858, a comfortable thirty-five miles south of Salt Lake City.[2] Instead, Connor established Camp (later Fort) Douglas, on the east bench of Salt Lake Valley, overlooking Young and the Mormon capital. In open defiance of Young's wishes, Connor prospected for minerals and encouraged his soldiers to use their idle time, of which they had plenty, to do so.[3]

About 1868 one of these soldier-prospectors climbed over the Wasatch Range east of Salt Lake City from Little Cottonwood Canyon, where Connor had recently discovered the Emma Mine, the first silver discovery in the Wasatch.[4] He found himself on a steep hillside overlooking Parleys Park, later known as Snyderville, where there was a stagecoach stop. Samuel Snyder had a sawmill there, and members of his family were growing potatoes, peas, beans, corn, and melons. As the prospector lunched on jerky, he dug his heels into the loose rocks of the steep mountainside, to avoid sliding down the slope, and scraped away the overburden concealing a rich vein of silver. It was the first discovery of what would become the Park City Mining District.[5] Many of the soldiers did not return to the places from which they came when their tour of duty ended, but stayed in Utah, prospecting or working in the mines.

By the time of discovery of minerals between Heber Valley and Parleys Park, nearly one hundred thousand Mormons had emigrated to Utah Territory and contiguous areas in the Great Basin. They began arriving in California by steamship, rather than crossing the continent by wagon or on foot, pulling handcarts. They were met in San Francisco by wagon trains that transported them to Salt Lake Valley. Meanwhile, Brigham Young agreed to provide labor for the transcontinental railroad then under construction; the Union Pacific Railroad agreed to transport laborers, tools, and supplies to the western end of its line; and the Mormons prospered by the exchange. They had the opportunity to import needed machinery and supplies and hard cash with which to do so from the sale of surplus cattle and cotton to the workmen building the railroad or from additional income generated by their employment as laborers.[6]

The transcontinental railroad was completed in 1869, ending the pioneer period with the driving of the golden spike at Promontory Summit, west of the railroad-wagon road terminus established at Corinne, near present-day Ogden. Mining was made more profitable in the process by the fast, low-cost transportation of large quantities of ore provided by the railroad. Mormons, no longer feeling bound by Young's dictum against mining, were freed from railroad labor to join the soldiers in prospecting for minerals.

By 1870, several mines were operating in and around Parleys Park. The mining camps that sprang up seven miles to the south, at the confluence of Silver Creek and Deer Valley, had a population of 164. The federal mining law of May 10, 1872, was enacted, declaring "all valuable mineral deposits in lands belonging to the United States...shall be free and open to exploration and purchase." Exploitation of the mineral discoveries thus became possible. Members of the mining camps adopted the name Parleys Park City, later dropped the name of the Mormon leader, and Park City was founded.[7]

The narrow-gauge Summit County Railroad between Echo City and Coalville was converted to standard gauge and extended from the east to Park City in 1880. In 1881, the line was sold under foreclosure to the Echo and Park City Railroad, a Union Pacific subsidiary. Also in 1881, Salt Lake and Eastern Railroad and the Salt Lake and Fort Douglas Railroad both began construction of a grade from the west, up Parleys Canyon. Due to the difficulty of the terrain, it was not completed until 1890, by which time the two companies had merged into the Utah Central Railroad, establishing a narrow-gauge grade to Salt Lake City with a high trestle at Lamb's Canyon.[8] The combined effect of opening the mineral deposits of the United States to exploitation and the coming of the railroads produced fortunes in Park City, Utah, and in the West.

A mining promoter named George Hearst came to Park City in 1881. Hearst purchased the Ontario claim in 1872, with profits from the Comstock lode in Nevada. It was the Ontario that made him wealthy and was the basis for the great Hearst fortune that eventually included the Homestake Mine in South Dakota, the Cerro de Pasco Mine in Peru, the famous Hearst Castle, and the influential Hearst newspaper chain that became prominent under his son, William Randolph Hearst.[9]

Thomas Kearns came to Park City penniless in 1883. After working as a laborer at the Ontario for more than six years, doing shift shaft work, he teamed up with David Keith in 1889 and began developing the Mayflower Mine. The Mayflower made him a millionaire in less than a year.[10] With his profits Kearns leased the Silver King claim in 1890, discovered silver at eight hundred feet, touching his own Mayflower property, and with his partners he purchased the Silver King and the adjoining Park City Mining Company. Silver King was incorporated for three million dollars in 1892, with David Keith as president and Thomas Kearns vice president.[11]

By Willis W. Ritter's account, "My father and his line named Ritter came over from Bavaria in 1701," the first of his progenitors to arrive in America, "and I happen to know that because Dad had a cousin in Chicago who wanted to join the Sons of the American Revolution and he ran down the genealogy on it. My ancestors fought in the Civil War and in the Revolutionary War and I was in the service in 2 wars myself."[12]

Several generations after the first Ritter arrived, a descendant named William Ritter, Willis W. Ritter's paternal grandfather and perhaps one of those who fought in the Civil War, was born in Pennsylvania in 1831.[13]

Emma Chamberlain, Ritter's paternal grandmother, was born in 1850, the youngest of seven children born to William and Mary Chamberlain, who were born in Benson, Oxford, England. After the birth of four of Emma's brothers and sisters, William and Mary Chamberlain emigrated to the Cape of Good Hope, South Africa, where Emma was born. There they encountered Mormon missionaries, who persuaded them to join the new church and migrate to Utah and join the rapidly growing religious community dedicated to establishing a new "Zion."

The Chamberlain family was directed by the Mormon Church to go to Charleston, around 1859, with other newcomers, and homestead land. It was the practice of the church in those days to assign, or "call," newcomers to particular areas, either to establish new communities or to join those already established and help build the new "Zion."

Charleston was one of the more auspicious locations the Chamberlains might have been assigned. With rich soil, and near steaming hot springs, it was situated at the southwest corner of the lush alpine valley of the cold, fish-laden Provo River. The valley, later named Heber Valley, was about a day's wagon ride east from Salt Lake City, with Parley's Park along the route. Towering peaks, crowned by Mount Timpanogos, border the western edge of the valley, and the majestic, game-rich Uinta Mountains, the only major mountain range in the United States running east-west, among the highest in the state of Utah and headwaters of the Provo River, stretch to the east, the entire way to Colorado.

About 1867, Emma Chamberlain of Charleston, Utah Territory, married William Ritter, newly arrived in the Great Basin. Little is known of William Ritter before then. Their union marks the start of the Ritter line, or at least that portion of it about which we have specific knowledge. When they married, William Ritter was thirty-seven and Emma Chamberlain seventeen. Mining fever—or, at least, the perception that mining was more rewarding, or interesting, or remunerative than farming—had overcome some of the Mormons by that time, which probably explains why they were in Nevada in 1868 when their first child, a boy they named William Wolfe Ritter, was born on July 17, 1868.[14] There was little reason at that time, other than mining, to live in Nevada.[15] William and Emma had a daughter later and named her Emma.

Emma eventually left William Ritter, returned to Heber Valley, and married Peter Krälla of Midway, a few miles east of Charleston. Krälla, called "Dutch" Pete Kraller, was Swiss, as were many of Midway's early settlers, and became owner and proprietor of a small resort established at the hot springs near Charleston known as Schneitter's Hot Pots. Emma died in 1885, at age thirty-five, and was buried in the Chamberlain family plot at Charleston. William died in 1895, at sixty-four, and is buried next to Emma.

When he reached maturity, William Wolfe Ritter was also employed in mining. That pursuit brought him to Park City in about 1896 or '97. While walking down Park City's Main Street one day, he looked in the window of Adams' Photography, established in 1895, where Willis Adams presented fine tinted photographs for viewing by passers-by.[16] What caught the eye of William, however, was not the photographs, but a comely woman he was seeing for the first time. They would marry, she would become the mother of his children, including one named Willis, and eventually leave him. "My dad saw her standing, looking out of the studio window," according to the family tradition explained by Willis's sister, Min. "He saw her and said he never saw anyone who looked so sad. They were engaged after that."[17]

William Wolfe learned that the comely woman he was attracted to was Martha May Sykes. She and Mary Dye Adams, Willis Adams's wife, were half sisters, daughters of the same mother and different fathers. Their mother, Minnie May, was born in Tennessee.[18] Her first husband, Mary's father, who abandoned her after Mary's birth, was named Dye. Minnie May Dye was thus unmarried when she met John Sykes, during, or soon after, the Civil War in the early or mid-1860s. According to Ritter family lore, Sykes was a Union soldier who had been wounded, imprisoned by the Confederate Army in West Virginia, and fell victim to malaria. Minnie May was John's nurse during his recovery. They married, and when he was ordered to duty at Fort Douglas, Utah Territory, on the east bench of Salt Lake City, she and her three children went with him.[19]

Sykes appears to be one of the soldiers who stayed in Utah to prospect or work in the mines. Whatever the facts, he worked in the mines and married Minnie May, and they had several children, the eldest of whom was Martha May, born at Fort Douglas in 1878.

Martha May Sykes was living with the Adamses in their apartment above the studio because her mother had recently left John Sykes. She was left with the Adamses when her mother took her younger brothers to Idaho, where they were to remain. Minnie May said she would be back for Martha May when she got settled, but when she returned Mary Adams refused to let Martha May go. She and her husband, Willis, would look after Martha May, Mary said.

Martha May Sykes (who preferred to be called May) and William Wolfe Ritter were married in 1897. William was thirty years old, and May was twenty. It was the year following Utah's admission to the Union, after many years of strife and misunderstanding between the Mormons and the federal government over polygamy and Brigham Young's ambition to establish an independent State of Deseret. It was also the year of a diphtheria epidemic in Park City and severe economic upset resulting from a change in the national currency standard from silver to gold.[20]

Statehood and the diphtheria epidemic affected May and William only indirectly. The change in the currency standard was their more direct concern, for it affected the economy of Park City. The city was founded to exploit the rich silver deposits surrounding it. If the demand for silver or its price declined, Park City's decline would follow. Those effects appeared almost immediately: mines were closed, large numbers of workers were let go, and the wages of those remaining were drastically reduced. Merchants found themselves with more and more unpaid accounts. Individuals and families left town to find work elsewhere.

May and William were among those who left. They went to Silver City, near Eureka, in the then booming Tintic Mining District of Juab County. The Tintic District was also predominantly silver, lead, and zinc, but quartz was present in association with those minerals, and high concentrations of gold were bound in the quartz. The extension of the Salt Lake and Western Railroad to nearby Mammoth Mills in 1882 and completion of a branch to serve Silver City a year later, and a branch to serve Eureka in 1889, made many otherwise marginal mines profitable operations.[21]

William and May had a house of their own, and John Sykes, May's fifty-eight-year-old father, rented in a boardinghouse next door and worked in the quartz mines.[22] Within two years May and William were expecting their first child. May felt unwell during most of her pregnancy. The cause of her discomfort was apparently not serious, but William, worried about her and the expected child, insisted on taking her to Salt Lake City for the delivery, just in case she needed medical care. So May and William Wolfe Ritter boarded a train in January 1899 at Silver City and traveled seventy-five miles to Salt Lake City for the birth of their first child.

May's "laying-in" took place in a two-story adobe building at 122 South 300 East in Salt Lake City. The building is long gone and its use uncertain, but it appears to have been a hospice or boarding place owned by the Park City Miners' Union.[23] It evidently provided adequately, for May regained her health and her child, named Willis William Ritter, was born there in good health on January 24, 1899, at 2:15 PM.

May and William's second child, a girl, was born in Silver City in October 1900. They named her Minnie May after her grandmother and called her Min. William worked in a quartz mine and staked a profitable claim of his own. William "had 'pay dirt,'" Min recalled. "He was making a little bit. But a little money went a long way then."[24]

May was pregnant for the third time about a year and a half later when word arrived that William's stepfather, "Dutch" Pete Kraller, had died, leaving to William and his sister, Emma, the small hot-springs resort in Midway known as Schneitter's Hot Pots. So William and May Ritter took what was transportable of the first few years of their lives as a family and left Silver City behind to take up a new and different life in Midway, a few miles from Charleston, where Willis's paternal grandmother and the Chamberlains had settled in 1859 as Mormon converts. "Schneitter's Hot Pots were known throughout the entire mountain area. The most discriminating people praised the wonderful food prepared under the direction of Mrs. Fannie Schneitter. Mr. and Mrs. Schneitter were noted for their warmth and hospitality."[25] Thousands of people thronged to the resort.

Early pioneer journals describe cone-shaped pots of various sizes on the grounds of the resort that formed around the area's hot mineral springs. The water ranged in temperature from 70 to 112 degrees Fahrenheit. High concentrations of lime in the water formed the cones, which filled with water, then flowed over the top. Some were 15 feet in depth, and others appeared to be bottomless. The largest cone was 200 feet in diameter and 100 feet high. A weight was lowered into the large cone, and no bottom was found at 150 feet. The country around these pots appeared to be hollow, indicated by rumbling sounds when wagons passed over it.[26]

When dry, the cones became craters. It was reported that between 400 and 500 rattlesnakes were killed in one crater in a single day. In the spring they appeared on the outside of the crater, gathered in knots, with heads sticking out in all directions. The creek that fed water to the springs was named Snake Creek, and the crater was known as Snake Creek Den.[27]

The boundaries of the Park City Mining District were about eight miles north of Midway. For more than thirty years the mining district had served as the major market center for the farmers of Midway and Heber Valley. The mines furnished employment for many men from Midway, and Park City was a major source of patrons for the hot pots. They also came from Salt Lake City, for a day, or longer, for an outing or to enjoy the baths throughout the year.[28]

Swiss-born Simon Schneitter, and his wife, Louiza, farmed the acreage and discovered pot rock, the debris of the troublesome warm spring that made his alfalfa soggy. His neighbors began dropping in to "bathe," and their numbers grew until it was necessary to build a board-enclosed pool into which Schneitter piped the warm water. Simon opened the area as a resort. "According to an authentic 'fable,'" Kraller acquired title to the hot pots in a poker game held in Park City in 1897.[29]

The hot pots had changed hands several times since its original owner homesteaded it in 1875.[30] Kraller had recently taken title to it from Jacob Schneitter, paid the mortgage in February 1902, and died shortly thereafter. Emma wanted nothing to do with the resort itself and wanted only to turn her half of the inheritance into cash, so Mary Adams agreed to buy Emma's share. The resort was conveyed to William Ritter and Mary Adams out of the Kraller estate in July 1903.[31]

May and Mary, though half sisters and close in a way, were different in appearance and temperament and didn't always get along. Minnie May Sykes had been Catholic, and May Ritter and all of her and William's family became Catholics, while Mary Adams was a devout Christian Scientist. May was dark, friendly, gay, and willful, conveying personal warmth and charm. Mary, ten years her senior, was of pale complexion, solemn, and taciturn and seemed to be in perpetual mourning. It was as if Mary was in penance for the whole sinful world. May believed Mary really was in mourning, in a sense. It began, May thought, when her first husband left her. Mary always dressed in black, with high, starched white collars, had no children of her own, and told May that people should be able to get babies by picking them off trees the way you pick apples. She was known as a good woman who cooked and cleaned, carried coal for the stove, stoked the fire, and made quilts for her cats. Mary also arranged subjects for her husband's portraits, and arranged the lives of people around her, to the degree they would let her do so. Conflict with May's personality resulted, for May would not allow Mary to control her. Mary reacted by siding with William in any dispute between them.

William and May lived at the resort, managed it, and looked after the details. Mary continued to live in Park City, fifteen miles away, but true to her character, Mary checked carefully on what William and May were doing.[32] May, William, and the children lived in the main house, a two-story colonial style building with twelve rooms known as Virginia House. There was a separate kitchen building, a milk house, and a vegetable storehouse.

It was an ideal setting for children. Willis recalled going with family and friends by bobsled to Kamas, Charleston, Heber, or Park City, snuggled under quilts and surrounded by hay, and being greeted by a crackling fire and home-cooked meal prepared by May on their return. Winter fun was matched by the delights of summer, when young Willis frolicked among waterwheels in the ditch, the tall alfalfa, and his many pets, especially rabbits.[33] May and William's third child, John Henry, was born at the resort on June 27, 1902, their first summer at the hot pots. Their fourth and last child, Russell Benjamin, was also born there, in September 1905.

The steaming springs and limestone craters were objects of childhood imagination, mystery, and intrigue, as they had been for the first pioneers to enter the valley and the American Indians before them, giving rise to much investigation, speculation, and amazing stories. Min claimed the pools were bottomless and told an old story of an Indian jumping in and drowning, but his body was never found. "They had two hot pools, a big 'plunge,' and a small pool. The big plunge was lots more fun than jumping in the little pool," according to Min. "My mother served the meals—trout dinners and fried chicken. Of course, we had some hired help. Some people liked to come in the winter too. One fellow came from Salt Lake City and stayed quite a lot. He gave me a doll with a kid body and a china face."

The children spent their days tagging after their father and mother or on ventures of their own. The boys "liked mountain climbing and would go and take their lunch and spend the day exploring," Min explained. "Willis didn't like me to tag along." William was "strict with our raising. We were polite, walked just so and would say the right thing and be in the right places. … We stood at attention. He'd read books to us. He read *Uncle Tom's Cabin.* I was learning to read then, and made sure he read the words correct."

Willis was ill with diphtheria when he was about six or seven.

> Dad closed off one of the bedrooms and stayed in there with Willis all through that sickness. Mom would bring the meals to the door and leave them outside and bring anything they wanted. I was standing and watching the doctor [Russell Wherritt, for whom May and William's fourth child, Russell Benjamin was named] sterilize his hand in the basin. On the shelf above—he was using carbolic acid to sterilize, I guess—the bottle dropped and splintered. My little eyes were right there and it missed me, barely. No one else got diphtheria.[34]

Under its new ownership, the resort became known as "Ritter's Hot Pots."[35] Stationery was printed with the new name: "Ritter's Hot Pots, W. W. RITTER, PROP. Good bathing. First class hotel. Bar connection. May be reached via RGW RR through Provo Canyon or by stage from Park City."[36] May did the cooking. Overnight guests stayed in Virginia House, which accommodated up to twelve.

John Sykes followed his daughter to Midway. Grandpa Sykes's left eye drooped, the effect of some illness, but if he got angry, that eye would pop open. The children remember him sitting by the coal stove in the big house and that he chiseled steps to the top of the large cone, or "volcano," as the children called it. William oversaw the general operations and acted as host. Liquor was available, and there was a certain amount of gambling, no doubt involving William.

Financial affairs at the resort were shaky, possibly connected with the gambling. In February 1903 William and May executed a warranty deed for the property to Andrew Lunnen, in connection with a mortgage to the Bank of Heber, in the amount of twenty-five hundred dollars. Also in February 1903, there was a warranty deed of a portion of the property to Anton Anderson for ninety dollars.

After five years, the idyllic lifestyle ended, in 1906. Willis was seven and Min six when the family left the hot pots to move to Park City. Mary's penance for the whole sinful world led to a dispute over management of the resort. "[Aunt Mary] insisted they didn't cater to a fast crowd," Min explained, "but they are the ones that spend money. Father didn't agree. That's why they sold."

The place, consisting of 26.10 acres that remained and nine shares of stock in Midway Irrigation, was conveyed back to Jake Schneitter, of Eureka, the son of Simon Schneitter, in September 1907 for five thousand dollars. "I remember how sick I was about leaving," Min remembered. "We pulled out the lane and I said, 'I'm going to buy this place someday.' Willis felt bad too."[37]

Simultaneous with "Dutch" Pete Kraller acquiring the hot pots, down the road in Midway lived Arthur Vivian Watkins. Born December 18, 1886, Watkins would become the arch opponent of Willis W. Ritter when he became a nominee for United States District Judge for the District of Utah. It is ironic that they both had their beginnings in Midway, well-nigh neighbors. Vivian, as he was known to his family, was Arthur, or Art, to his political supporters. In later years, after becoming judge, Ritter would refer to his critic, with all the derision his voice could project, as Arthur *Vivian* Watkins.

When he was ten years of age, while William and May met and wed in Park City, Watkins left Midway with his parents, who relocated in Vernal, where they farmed and he went to high school. As the Ritters were leaving the hot pots, Watkins was completing his prep school education at Brigham Young Academy in Provo, where he enrolled at the age of seventeen.[38] The paths of Arthur Vivian Watkins and Willis W. Ritter, both formerly of Midway, would not cross again until 1949, when Ritter was nominated to become United States District Judge for the District of Utah. When they did, their clash would become the defining event in the life and career of Willis W. Ritter.

2

PARK CITY II

> It is said that famous men are usually the product of unhappy childhood. The stern compression of circumstances, the twinges of adversity, the spur of slights and taunts in early years, are needed to evoke that ruthless fixity of purpose and tenacious mother-wit without which great actions are seldom accomplished.
>
> —Winston S. Churchill

When May and William Ritter left the hot pots with their family in 1907 to move back to Park City, they found it bigger, having almost doubled in population, to about seven thousand, and looking more substantial than in 1897 when they met, married, and left for Silver City.[1] The move to Park City made it possible for Willis and Min to attend a formal school, which may have been a reason for the move, in addition to disagreements with Aunt Mary over management of the resort.

Wealth produced by the mines, the basis for Park City's establishment, had increased with improvement of its railroad facilities. In addition to the standard-gauge Summit County Railroad between Echo City and Coalville, a Union Pacific subsidiary, Rio Grande Western Railroad (RGWRR) gained control of Utah Central Railroad's narrow-gauge grade, which afforded access through Parley's Canyon to Salt Lake City, and converted it to standard gauge. RGWRR's first standard-gauge engine puffed into Park City on August 4, 1897. After realigning and rebuilding the worst parts of the grade, it merged with Utah Eastern in 1898.[2]

The Spanish-American War, declared on April 23, 1898, forced the price of silver up, at least temporarily. With continued improvement of the railroads, higher prices increased the speculative opportunities. The Hearst properties were purchased in 1899, after their closure caused by water problems, and were reopened by Utah financiers Jacob and Simon Bamberger. In 1907 the Silver King Consolidated Mining Company, owning property jointly with the Silver King Mine, was founded, with Samuel Newhouse its president. Newhouse came to Utah from Colorado in 1896, where he was a mining speculator and promoter, and developed the Highland Boy and other mines in Bingham Canyon. In 1905 Newhouse acquired mining property in the San Francisco Mountains of Beaver County, where he developed the mine, mill, and town of Newhouse, then became a developer of the Park City mines.[3] A new group of entrepreneurs had thus arrived in the city since William and May left in 1897. They were to have an influence in the life of young Willis.

There were also obvious physical changes. A devastating fire had swept through the city in 1898, destroying many of the old clapboard buildings, including Willis Adams's photography shop. With the incentive of a rejuvenated economy, Park City was rebuilt quickly. Willis Adams's shop was one of the early buildings reconstructed, more substantially than before. By 1900 there were about seventy new Main Street buildings in the area gutted by the fire. The first of them were wood-frame structures, but after the initial haste to rebuild subsided, more substantial, fire-resistant brick and stone structures became common. New places were added—another high school, more boardinghouses, a new town meeting-dance hall, and a new and grandly styled saloon called the Oak, in addition to the dozen or so existing before the fire.[4] There was a new bandstand—a gift to the town from the Oak.

After the fire, the town acquired fire engines, and a new high-pressure water system was installed with fire hydrants in little houses, like outhouses with hoses in them, every half mile up and down the street. William A. Gidley, who was nearly deaf and carried a horn for you to speak into, was fire chief.[5]

Winter, always harsh in Park City with its elevation of more than seven thousand feet, was fierce that year. Telephone poles between Park City and Salt Lake City were buried or blown down, and men working at the mines were unable to get to work for days at a time. Park City historians George A. Thompson and Fraser Buck relate that in later years, the operator of a filling station near the Spiro Tunnel, W. D. "Tommy" St. Jeor, formerly city marshall, claimed that the snow used to cover the pines. Reminded that the pines were shorter then, Tommy reflected for a moment and replied: "Well, maybe so, but it used to cover those telephone poles over there, and they ain't growed an inch."[6]

The Ritters' new home was at 628 Park Avenue, on the corner of Park Avenue and Heber Avenue, at the entrance to the business district. It had thirteen rooms, a concrete exterior, and was commonly referred to as the "cement house." One of the rooms was set aside for injured people, usually victims of accidents in the mines.[7] They were brought to May, who gave them emergency care for a day or two, until they could go home or be put on a train for Salt Lake City, where they could get medical care in a hospital.[8]

Water problems had plagued the Park City mines from their inception, causing periodic closures. In 1907 a cave-in at the Ontario drain tunnel, several miles in length and draining the mines in Ontario Canyon to Keetley above Heber City in the Provo River drainage, resulted in another closure. Only the upper levels could be worked, and the best ore at the Daly-West and Daly-Judge Mines was under water. Smaller mines like the American Flag were also flooded.[9]

The economic situation was harsh enough to earn the title "panic of 1907." It was the result, according to some authorities, of too much money in the hands of too few people—the Rockefellers and Morgans, in particular.[10] The price of silver, between $1.15 and $1.29 per ounce in the 1880s, always subjected to frequent fluctuations, crashed after the repeal of the Sherman Silver Purchase Act in 1893, spiked as a result of the Spanish-American War, then declined from $1 an ounce to 52¢, followed quickly by cuts in the number of workers employed and reduced wages for those lucky enough to have a job. Money became so scarce that script, which had no value other than the word of the company issuing it, was used by some of the mines. Most merchants refused it, and before long the banks and business houses announced that they would deal in hard money only.

With money so scarce, an evangelistic fervor grew, led by those who were appalled that the miners would spend what little money they had in saloons and gambling halls. A get-tough city administration was voted in, resulting in gambling houses going out of business and the "red light district" being confined to a location on the edge of town.[11]

Rather than take in boarders, as many in Park City did, May supplemented the family income by working as a nurse and midwife. She went to the homes of expectant mothers to deliver babies and, of course, cared for the injured in her own home. William Ritter worked in the mines as a mill man and on the concentrator. Eventually, he became foreman.[12]

Hard times appeared to be over in Park City when the price of silver reached 65.9¢ per ounce by the end of 1907. In 1908 the Spiro Tunnel was opened, and draining of the mines began. A parade was held on May 13, 1908, to celebrate, with sporting events and dances until early morning. "Merchants began buying new stock... stores that had announced closing dates decided to stay open.... and speeches, sports, free shows, and barbeques were the order of the day." The euphoria was premature, for the price of silver again declined to 54.4¢ per ounce, then after a long, low ebb, saw another rise in 1914.[13]

Youth remembered nearly always seems idyllic, but Park City in those days probably was, as Min recalled it, one of the best places to grow up. The town's small size, setting, mix of people, and an innocence since vanished allowed youngsters a lot of freedom, a range of activity—planned and spontaneous—the availability of many companions, and a sense of being important. Everyone knew everyone else and his or her family connections. The ethnic and national backgrounds of the population were richly diverse—Irish, Cornish ("the world's best miners"), English, Scots, Chinese (always gardeners, cooks, waiters, restaurateurs, and laundry proprietors, and never counted in the population census), and Scandinavians.[14] The religions represented were several as well, among which Mormons numbered the fewest.

Parents who worked in the mines rode horses to work, and horses were used in the mines for hauling ore and other purposes. The children took the horses to the top of Main Street when their parents got off work, where there was a water trough and hay in piano boxes used as mangers. Shadow Lake was above Deer Valley.[15] Young people would go from there, on company horses that they were allowed to use on Sundays; cross the pass above the Silver King Mine, now known as Guardsman Pass; and drop down into Big Cottonwood Canyon. They could go to the Cardiff Mine in Brighton and have a meal at the boardinghouse.

There were dances and picnics in the meadows where, in the late twentieth century, the ski tram was located. The boys would ride bobsleds, starting on Park Avenue above where condominiums were eventually built, and raise bumps in the street a few feet apart. Couples would take walks to Moonlight Bridge, where the fire department was, or walk the tracks. The last train left at 2:00 PM. Everyone knew there would be no trains after that, so walking the tracks became a peculiar Park City pastime. A horn sounded whenever there was an emergency and at the 8:00 PM curfew, after which the children would go home.

At school the boys always wore long black stockings, black shoes, navy-blue knickerbockers, and a jacket with a box pleat on either side, with a belt, white shirt, collar, and necktie. When they came home, most of the boys would change to coveralls, but Willis always dressed up. When he became stout during middle age, those who knew him in Park City could never make the connection with the little boy Willis.[16]

Chafing Min's sensibilities were the occasions when her parents would go out and leave Willis in charge, as the eldest. "We made candy in the evenings sometimes, molasses taffy. We pulled it 'til it was just beautiful, almost white. On the nights when Willis was boss he would say, 'there will be no candy made in this house tonight,' and the [younger] children would argue, and cry and holler. Willis never did anything he did not want to do."[17]

One of the few times Min detected a hint of vulnerability in Willis was when they were in their teens and posed for a studio photograph with their younger brothers. Min wore high heels, her first. They gave her enough added height to stand a little taller than Willis, who never mentioned it but spent the entire picture-taking session standing on tiptoe.

There were occasions when Willis misbehaved and got in trouble. Min remembers when Willis went hiking in the mountains with the other kids, including Tom Martin, who was his age. "I came in and here was Tom Martin sitting in a chair in the kitchen. 'What's the matter here?' my mother asked him. He wouldn't speak. The boys had stolen the kid's lunch. He [eventually] told my mother and father. Willis gets walloped." Min noted, "It was not Dad's custom to give swats, but I'd rather have swats than the lectures."[18]

The horse and wagon were still the backbone of transportation when the Ritters returned to Park City, but automobiles were appearing in ever increasing numbers. The coming of the Model T Ford in 1909 ended the horse's monopoly. Before that the road up Parleys Canyon was so bad that the few automobiles there were sometimes had to travel on the railroad grade. The Model T placed the automobile within the price range of nearly everyone, and before long the streets were busy with "tin lizzies." The roads were improved, and by 1914 there was regular stage service between Park City and Salt Lake City, at least in the summer.[19]

Childhood memories notwithstanding, life in a mining town was not paradise, exactly. Mills and smelters of the time were crude affairs. The Marsac Mill, located in Park City proper, right along Main Street, and others located nearby belched noxious fumes and clouds of yellow smoke that drifted over the town and produced tailings that polluted the streams. Farmers as far away as Snyderville, Coalville, and Heber City complained that fouled waters affected their livestock. Silver Creek, named in 1848 by Parley Pratt for its bucolic beauty and out of which early residents could catch a fine mess of trout, was crossed by the romantic Moonlight Bridge and flowed past the Marsac Mill, after which it was renamed and remains known today as "Poison Creek." Above town, also in the Silver Creek watershed, were several other large mining operations with associated mills, including the Ontario, Daly, Daly-West, and Silver King. Just below town, on the banks of Silver (or Poison) Creek, was the Park City Smelting Company and a concentrator owned by the Crescent Mining Company.[20]

Women in Ontario Canyon complained that when they hung their wash out to dry, the smoke would eat holes in the cloth. In 1913 two hundred residents signed a petition urging the city council to compel the operators of the Ontario Mill to control the fumes. An investigation ordered by the council reported that "wires on pianos were corroded, sewing machines put out of commission by the needles [being] made useless, clothing [was] rotted by the fumes and carpets, rugs, etc., ruined."[21]

The reality of ethnic strife calls into further doubt recollections of idyllic harmony. Park City's saloons, of which there were about two dozen, were gathering places for various nationalities. There were saloons that catered only to the "Cousin Jacks," the "Micks," the "Bohunks," the "Swedes" and the "Finns." As the evening wore on, if someone decided to intrude on another group, a fight was sure to break out.[22]

According to the Reverend French Oliver, who left Park City in disgust in 1901, it was "only 40 rods from Hell." In addition to the saloons, there were gambling halls and the house of ill-repute that seemed to follow every mining town, referred to by respectable citizens as "the shirt-tail factory." The city's finances were kept in the black by levying periodic fines of forty dollars for the madam and twenty dollars for each of the brothel's "soiled doves," which seemed to satisfy the critics.[23]

Aside from taunting his sister, Willis seems to have been that rare young man who simultaneously excelled scholastically, took part in school activities of all kinds, and entered with his fellows into the activity of the moment. Willis and Min went to school for the first time that first year in Park City at Washington Elementary.[24] Min thought they would be in the same grade, because they had the same level of education at home by their father. Willis was pleased that the principal put him right into the second grade because he was older.

Min was already tired of being runner-up to her brother: "It was just myself and Willis, the only two left. I was taking Latin. Willis took German. The teacher who gave us the spelling bee was my Latin teacher. The word was 'cessation.' I never heard it in my life. I told her Willis was studying Caesar. Willis and I stood back and forth for awhile and finally, he beat me on 'cessation.' The teacher said I should know that. I told her, 'no, he studied Caesar; that's how he knew it.'" Later on, in her teens, Min gained a sense of herself that freed her from being runner-up. But until then she suffered many a defeat. By the eighth grade Willis was thin, but not tall, had established himself as a fine, brilliant student, and was already attractive to girls his age.[25]

William and May divorced in about 1916. May left and married a man named William Sams, and they went to Ely, Nevada. Willis was depressed following the divorce, appears to have had little contact with his natural mother, if any at all, and in later years refused to even talk about her. May then settled in Maywood, California, where she died at about the age of sixty-two, in 1939 or 1940, and is buried in Englewood.[26]

Min and Willis's two brothers went with May. Min married shortly after they left, when she was sixteen. William Ritter remained in Park City, working in the mines. Willis, who was old enough to make his own decision in the matter, remained with his father, at least initially.

Willis was fond of William Ritter, whom he recalled as a compassionate, caring man with whom he worked in the mines after high school was dismissed. Willis also recalled that William liked to lift a glass or two at a bar on Main Street called the Club, managed by Heinie Herndon, and to play "sluff," which may have been a habit brought with him from his days operating Ritter's Hot Pots.[27] He was apparently among the miners who appalled evangelical critics like the Reverend French Oliver by spending what little money they had in saloons and gambling halls.[28] In any event, William, for whatever reason, was unable to provide support for Willis. Before 1917, when he entered his senior year of high school, Willis had been taken into the home of Willis and Mary Adams. The Adamses had no children, judged Willis the brightest of the children of Mary's half sister, May, and were willing to take him in. From the time of William and May's divorce, Mary Adams assumed the role of mother to Willis. She and Willis Adams are sometimes listed as his parents on public records.[29]

William Ritter continued to live in Park City until he went to the home of Mary and Willis Adams, ill with miner's consumption, or silicosis, a product of his days in the mines, and he died at their home in the winter of 1925. William was buried at the old Park City cemetery. His coffin was moved on runners in the snow. The ground was "frozen so hard they could hardly dig a grave," so "he was buried in a bowl, of sorts, rather than in a casket," Min recalled.[30]

When Willis entered Park High School, he established a large presence:

president of the Sports Club for two years, debater for three, engaged in dramatics and extemporaneous speaking, and assistant editor of the yearbook as a freshman. "Willis was an amiable person at the time," according to Sister Marie Camille. "I used to dance with him at the high school dances," Myrtle Buck recalled. "He was a fine fellow, a beautiful young man. He was very brilliant."[31]

Among a class of eighteen, to describe Willis's peers as outstanding would not fairly state the case. There was Leif Anderson, who became a lawyer in Park City, and Tom Welch, who became a medical doctor. Willis's friend and lifelong rival was Roger Traynor, who served as justice on the California Supreme Court for thirty years and was considered by some the most outstanding judge in the United States.[32] And, of course, there was the eventual Sister Marie Camille, and her brother, Roger McDonough, who was four years older but acted as one of their teachers and later became an outstanding justice of the Utah Supreme Court.

When the United States entered World War I in 1917, during Willis's senior year, McDonough enlisted in the United States Army, missing the graduation ceremony. The school sent him off with a grand farewell party and presented him with a wristwatch and Kodak camera. He returned from the war and became a significant influence in the lives of his former students, Willis and Traynor in particular, who continued to solicit the counsel and advice of McDonough as their careers developed.[33]

Willis was business manager for the yearbook his senior year and composed a senior history, in which he declared that "the members of our class who will carry their high scholastic standards into the colleges of our land need not enter timidly as 'Freshies,' for they have Park High's training to support them." Willis presided as student-body judge, and it may have been prophetic that the yearbook declared: "He gives five demerits without thinking sometimes."

Roger Traynor, rather than Willis Ritter, was named valedictorian. Years later, after he had become United States District Judge, Ritter's friend and justice of the Utah Supreme Court D. Frank Wilkins found the 1918 graduation program listing Ritter as salutatorian. Wilkins took it to Ritter. "I see where Traynor graduated valedictorian," Wilkins teased. Ritter greeted the good-natured gibe with chilly silence. An hour or so later, when Ritter appeared in a better mood, Wilkins asked: "What is a salutatorian?" "Salutatorian," Ritter replied, "that means second."[34]

The most important influence in shaping the life of the young Willis Ritter may have been his uncle after whom he was named, Willis Adams. From the time he was taken into the home of the Adamses, he effectively had two fathers. Willis Adams, his foster father, though lacking formal education, loved books, learning, and ideas. Fond of both natural and foster fathers, Willis acquired many of his attitudes and skills from Adams. A fantasy written for the 1918 yearbook by B. A. Fowler, principal and social science teacher at Park High, projected Ritter as a future White House photographer, in seeming acknowledgment of the influence of Adams, the premier Park City photographer.[35]

Adams was also an artist. Born in Indiana in 1854, Adams grew up on his parents' farm, but showed no interest in farming. At an early age he spent his time finding out-of-the-way places to sketch. An interest in a farm-implement business was acquired by his father, to give his son a means of livelihood, but failed. With adulthood fast upon him, and having no interest in the obvious options of farming or store keeping, Adams came up with the idea of photography, and went to work for a Goshen, Indiana, photographer named Dowdy. Photography was a respectable occupation that would keep him in food and shelter—perhaps more—and provide an outlet for his artistic inclination.

Like George Ottinger, and many other painters of the time, Adams became a photographic tinter. He studied at the Art Institute of Chicago, then came west almost ten years to the day after completion of the transcontinental railroad, in 1869, with his brother, Charles, to take pictures of the frontier, as had W. H. Jackson and other artists of the period. Willis and Charles Adams opened a photographic studio in Ogden, known as Adams Brothers Photography, and in 1895 Willis Adams moved on to Park City to open another one under the same name.

While employed as a photographer, Adams also pursued his painting. He produced more than four hundred works of art, including oils, watercolors, pastels, pencil, and chalk drawings.[36] Years later, many of Adams's paintings and drawings adorned Ritter's judicial chambers in Salt Lake City. Ritter would walk around the room, pointing to one picture and then another, telling stories about the time and place where it was painted and how he and Adams had gone to the scene, sometimes by wagon.[37] Adams also left a large legacy of photographs of Park City taken before the 1898 fire.

Willis Adams became more than a foster father to Ritter, and the two spent valuable time together. During Ritter's teens he and Adams became close companions. In addition to family outings, they hiked together in the mountains—observing, taking photos, and sketching—and they "walked the track," a pastime peculiar to Park City. Adams found few in Park City with whom to share his interests, other than his nephew and foster son, Willis. Willis Adams and Willis Ritter had a truly symbiotic relationship, as their names implied, with Adams, the teacher, being inspired by Willis Ritter, the willing student. They spent hours together, sharing a sense of the beauty and wonder of nature and their mutual intelligence and love of learning. Adams's personal diaries are laced with entries about the wildflowers, berries, and plants; of the arrival and leave-taking of robins; of going to the meadow to greet songbirds or blackbirds; and of the seasonal, daily, or hourly changing hue of the sky.

Nor was Adams's thinking and sense of ethics imparted to his foster son limited to art and nature. Willis Ritter's personal papers contain a dissertation on the League of Nations, in which Adams denounced "war" as "a cry in our blood from our cave forbears [*sic*]. Business men have long since thrown the club into the discard for the more civilized methods of diplomacy and the fair deal, because they have found that these produce better and surer results," he continued, but "not so the nations." He concluded, "Columbia, your duty lies straight before you. Your future efforts will be directed toward the demonstration of your advansed [*sic*] theory of Democracy throughout the whole world."[38]

In Adams's diary entry for September 10, 1910, he explains "My Creed," composed of seven paragraphs or articles. Adams wrote: "1st, Whatever happens. Be happy. Let nothing rob you of this God given birthright." Second, he wrote, "Always be contented in mind," and third, "Despise no man. At the earthly feast at which you and others are the guests." "Be not afraid" was number four, and "in the great lexicon of 'Truth,'" he declared at number five, "there is no such word as: Hate." "As God is love," he wrote at number six, "as we do toward our fellow man, so will it be with us. Let PRINCIPAL [*sic*] be our guide and the Golden rule our motto," and he concluded with his indictment of "ANGER" at number seven: "In truth there can be no anger. Anger is the antithesis of Love. Swearing, without anger, is far more harmless than anger without profanity. Anger is a return to the brutal condition from which man should have long since risen."

"Willis idolized Uncle Willis," Min recalled. "They took long walks. First, they would buy a little sack of lemon drops. They would stay for hours and eat lemon drops. What they talked about I don't know."[39] Whatever they discussed, Ritter was exposed to his uncle's learning, sense of ethics, and an artist's perspectives on life—an ability to see the deeper meaning of things, people, and events surrounding him.

Adams taught him to see in the way that an artist sees—not the way most of us do, but in a concentrated way and beneath the surface. Ritter translated this to the way he saw people. You had the feeling often that he could look at someone, at you, and see right through the person, know everything about him. He learned to perceive and concentrate in all areas from Adams.[40]

Willis's personal appearance was also modeled after Adams, at least during his early adult and academic life. Adams looked refined, more like a professor or minister than a businessman. Ritter had the same appearance when he became a law professor.

In Willis's senior year at Park High, the worldwide influenza pandemic of 1918 struck Park City. The "greatest mass death" since the plague of the Middle Ages, it "killed maybe 2 per cent of all people in the world." The United States "lost somewhere from half a million and 650,000 people—more souls than...lost in every war" fought in the century put together.[41] Microbiology was poorly understood at the time and immunization still in the future, but contagion was known and feared. A quarantine was imposed requiring everyone on the streets to wear a gauze mask at least six layers thick and to boil it at least twice a day. Persons leaving town were not allowed to return unless first quarantined. Dr. Edward P. LeCompte, who served with Colonel George Custer's Seventh Cavalry right up to the Battle of Little Bighorn in 1876, had come to Park City and controlled the quarantine and other precautions.[42]

With graduation from Park High approaching, Mary Adams went to one of the mine supervisors and asked him for a job for her foster son. Willis had already worked underground in the mines with William during vacations, mostly at the Judge Mine.[43] In April 1918 he was given a job as roustabout, running the compressor at the Daly-West Mine, and that summer he worked as a laborer for Park City Consolidated Mining Company. Following graduation he worked again at the Daly-West Mine, underground at the nine hundred-foot level as a mucker and ore-car pusher and in the zinc smelter, until September.[44] Beginning in 1920, Willis worked for approximately a year and a half at Silver King Coalition Mines as a laborer and handyman at the mill, where he befriended James Ivers Jr., its president. Willis became known in the community as industrious and of good reputation, and the mining companies found him to be a clean-living boy of excellent morals and character whose work record was good.

The young Willis certainly knew of, and was influenced by, the vast disparity in means and opportunity so obvious in turn-of-the-century Park City. George Hearst, Samuel Newhouse, Thomas Kearns, David Keith, John Judge, W. H. Dodge, Albion Emery, and the legendary Susanah Bransford Emery Holmes, "the silver queen," were among those who took fortunes out of the mines in Park City during the period of the Ritter family's domicile.[45]

Willis knew of the Hearst fortune. The Thomas Kearns fortune was amassed during a period of rapidly declining silver prices, while the men working in the mines were forced to accept a fifty-cent- to one-dollar-per-day pay cut together with a ten-cent-a-day cut in board. Meanwhile, Silver King Mine paid a dividend of thirty-seven thousand dollars in 1893. James Ivers Jr., Willis's friend and president of the mine, was a business partner and confidant and privy to the affairs of the celebrated icons of Park City and the state of Utah and no doubt shared much information concerning them with Willis. The companies had a reputation for paying good wages when the price of metal was high, but without labor unions to represent them, the miners were forced to meet with the owners and take a reduction when prices were low.[46]

Ritter saw, as well, the extravagance of those who made their fortunes in Park City. Kearns built the Alta Club in Salt Lake City for his millionaire friends, as well as the Kearns mansion on "millionaire's row" on South Temple Street in Salt Lake City, now the governor's mansion. The Kearns family, including Jenny Judge Kearns, helped finance the Cathedral of the Madeleine and established Kearns St. Anne's Orphanage.[47] Mrs. Mary Judge, widow of John Judge, built the Judge Building in Salt Lake City and Judge Memorial Hospital for old and sick miners, now Judge Memorial High School. Newhouse built the Newhouse Building, Boston Building, Salt Lake Stock Exchange, Commercial Club Building, and Hotel Newhouse. Hotel Semloh (*Holmes* spelled backward), Bransford Apartments, and "Amelia's Palace," the mansion built by Brigham Young for one of his favored wives, were built or purchased by the "silver queen." The Brooks-Arcade Building, Thompson Building, Murdock Building, Summit Building, New Grand Hotel, Moxum Hotel, Hotel Little, Westminster College, and Ferry Hall were all built, purchased, or established with fortunes taken out of the Park City mines.[48]

Ritter surely saw the contrast between the lives of the ordinary people in Park City and those who rose to fame and fortune on the backs of workingmen. His decisions during his judicial career that most often drew criticism from authority figures were usually associated with empathy for the lot of the less fortunate. Ritter was surely struck by the inequity of such wealth being acquired at the expense and hardship of his father, himself, and the other miners. His father was an ordinary laborer in the mines who lacked the means to support his son and gave him up to Willis and Mary Adams as foster parents, then died of silicosis.[49]

In the process of working in and experiencing the hardship of life in a mining community, Willis came to the realization that he was not cut out for that sort of physical labor.[50] Events beyond his control would shortly take him out of that community, eventually leading to law school.

While Ritter was away to law school, Willis and Mary Adams moved to a cobblestone Spanish bungalow in Sugarhouse, on the edge of Fairmont Park in Salt Lake City. Willis Adams died in 1932, of uremia poisoning, after Ritter had returned from law school and his initial employment as a lawyer. Ritter begged Aunt Mary to call a doctor, but because of Mary's religious beliefs, "that woman let that man lie there and die and wouldn't call for help for him." Willis Ritter cared for him during Willis Adams's last illness, washing the sheets and doing whatever he could for him.[51] It was a terrible way to die, and Willis believed Mary's beliefs contributed to Adams's death and had nightmares about it.

3

FRIENDS

In these vernal seasons of the year; When the air is calm and pleasant, It were an injury...against Nature not to go out and see her riches, and partake in Her rejoicing With Heaven and earth.

—JOHN MILTON

On October 7, 1918, Willis W. Ritter was inducted into the United States Army, at Lehi, Utah. He served as a private in the Student Army Training Corps at Fort Douglas, taking training at the School of Engineering of the University of Utah, contiguous to the fort. His supervisor in the student military group was a Latin and Greek instructor, secretary-registrar of the university, and a major in the Utah National Guard named Elbert D. Thomas.[1] Thomas was to be the first in a long series of significant friendships, and most important to his eventual judicial career.

Despite the precautions taken by Dr. LeCompte in Park City, Willis contracted influenza-pneumonia on Thanksgiving Day 1918. Because of fears over contagion, and according to the practice of the day, Willis was wheeled out on the porch, in the cold of winter, to protect others judged to have a better chance of recovery. There was little else that could be done for him. Willis nevertheless did recover, following the usual three-day course of the flu, and they eventually moved him back in. He was quickly discharged, apparently for medical reasons, on December 31, 1918.[2]

Induction into the army and into the university environment took him out of the mining community and launched him into a course of higher education. Willis attended Valparaiso University School of Law in Indiana in 1920-1921 and the University of Utah in 1921-1922.[3] At the University of Utah, Willis studied at the law school as an undergraduate. In those days, the law school was essentially an undergraduate department, not far removed from an advanced high school, with but one full-time teacher, Dean William H. Leary. Classes, conducted by judges and lawyers acting as part-time instructors, were held off-campus at courts, public buildings, and private offices. The law school, such as it was, was not yet accredited. Many members of the bar therefore took their legal training at eastern institutions, of which Harvard, Columbia, and Chicago were considered in the "first class."[4]

Meanwhile, subsequent to leading Ritter's Student Army Training Corps, Ritter's drill instructor and newfound friend Thomas earned a Ph.D. in political science at the University of California and became a professor of political science at the University of Utah in 1924.

Leary allowed Ritter to attend classes but told him he would never get a law degree without first getting an undergraduate degree. After a year Leary was sufficiently impressed with Ritter's ability to suggest that the University of Chicago might admit him to law school as an undergraduate. Ritter went to Chicago in a Model T Ford with a cousin who was in school there and thirty-five dollars in his pocket. The dean of the University of Chicago Law School told Ritter that if he could get straight As, he could earn a law degree. He attended the University of Chicago Law School as an undergraduate from October 2, 1922, to June 10, 1924, while holding down three jobs: stoking furnaces, selling suits and overcoats at Hohfels Haberdashery and Men's Clothing Store at Clark and Randolph, and waiting tables in Mrs. Brandenburger's Campus Restaurant.[5] Ritter met the dean's challenge, receiving an LL.B. degree and graduating cum laude. He was admitted to the Bar of Illinois on October 16, 1924.

After his admission to the Illinois Bar, Ritter was an associate in the Chicago firm of Morris, Kixmiller, and Baar, 11 South La Salle Street, with branch offices in New York City. He was assigned, almost immediately, to open another branch office of the firm at 718 Union Trust Building in Washington, D.C. The only representation of the firm in Washington, D.C., prior to that time was through a local attorney who was paid a yearly retainer to handle the firm's business. The plan was to send Leo H. Hoffman, a partner in Morris, Kixmiller, and Baar, to establish an active office. Ritter wrote to his uncle Willis and aunt Mary, expressing his belief that "a real good thing might develop for me right here should I care to encourage it a little, which I'm going to do."[6]

Washington, D.C., seemed smaller than Salt Lake City, as Ritter remembered it. He was impressed, however, with being "in the heart of things" and with all of the government departments and appellate courts, which had previously been "mythical things [with] regard to which a person felt considerable awe. Here they are just workaday things functioning along just as everything else in the world goes."[7]

The young Willis W. Ritter quickly formed an opinion that "they are a lazy lot here in Washington, as a rule," and that "working for the government spoils a person for worthwhile service for the wheels go whether he produces anything or not." He learned lessons, nevertheless, that would become important to him lifelong. Notably, just as his own developing career was advanced by his contact with Leary, and was soon to be further advanced by his friendship with Thomas, he learned that "life is made up of contacts, for the only way things are accomplished in Washington is through the good offices of someone in authority."

Ritter's letter home to his foster parents, the Adamses, affords a glimpse into his philosophy and plans for getting ahead in life and the legal profession. Because of the living expense he found in Washington, Ritter concluded that "lesser income and recognition in a smaller place seems more desirable." He surmised, "I think life is such a gamble that the real success is in 'hitting the ball' and being an opportunist who can fearlessly grab hold of things as they arise and tear into them. A fellow who carefully plots out the big things to do will probably scare himself to death doing it. The fellow who can fall into them easily when they come along gets carried away upward before he has a chance to mess things up with his impotent planning."[8]

He continued working out of the Morris, Kixmiller, and Baar firm's Washington office, later moved to the American Security Building, 815 Fifteenth Street, Room 410.[9] He acquired a reputation as being capable, conscientious, conservative, of good moral character, and the brightest of the young associates in the firm.[10] Within a year he had authored, jointly with George M. Morris and Fred Pearce of Morris, Kixmiller, and Baar, a text titled *Practice and Procedure before the United States Board of Tax Appeals,* published in Chicago in 1925.[11] He also prepared a five hundred-page manuscript on evidence that was never published.[12] He was admitted to practice before the United States Board of Tax Appeals and to the District of Columbia Bar on May 10, 1926.

Ritter thus quickly established himself in the legal community as an expert on practice before the Board of Tax Appeals. In 1926 he published an article in the *National Income Tax Magazine* on the obscure subject of the jurisdiction of the Board of Tax Appeals to consider tax liability, in a hearing on an appeal from a notice of deficiency, for years other than those for which an appeal was taken. The question, which may seem abstruse to some, was important because the adjustment of liability for the tax years appealed could be affected by taxes paid in other years, both before and after the years in question, or could require adjustment of tax liabilities, before or after the years in question. Ritter's "careful legal analysis" and "creative thinking" was lauded as "unusual" by the publishers of the *National Income Tax Magazine.*[13]

Professional interests did not prevent Willis's finding time to strike up a special friendship with a woman named Frankie. They went out on the town with Fred Pearce and Pearce's eventual wife. The relationship was shortly interrupted, however, when Frankie left the District of Columbia in July 1926, returning to her home at Crescent Park in Houlton, Maine, where her father conducted an orchestra.[14] She wrote fondly of their romance conducted in District of Columbia coffeehouses until Ritter also left Washington, in August 1926, after receiving a letter from Dean Leary and George Thomas, president of the University of Utah, offering him a job teaching law.

Willis returned to Park City and lived for a short time with Min, who was back in Park City after a divorce. He purchased a pale-blue Buick convertible coupe with a rumble seat and exhibited the vanity common to small-town youth recently risen from poverty. Willis made sure everyone saw him when he drove into town in his flashy roadster.[15]

As Willis W. Ritter was pursuing his legal education at University of Chicago Law School, and beginning a legal career in Washington, D.C., the mysterious workings of fate had put a young woman named Ireta Olson on a course that would soon merge with his own. Ireta was born into the Mormon Church, in Provo, Utah County, in 1903 to Edwin O. and Dora L. Olson, who lived at 340 East 200 North. She had an older sister, Maurine, and another younger by fourteen years, Ida. Her father operated a photography business on Academy Street, under the name Olson and Hafen. "Rita," as she was known, was learning a love of nature during long hikes in the mountains east of Provo with her father. She prayed daily and declared her belief in Mormonism with all her heart and soul, but when mature she chose, without compromise, to practice no organized religion. Rita felt closer to her creator in the mountains, the forests, and by the streams than in any man-made shrine.[16] At an early age, Rita became very independent, adventurous, and self-assured. At age sixteen she journeyed to Canada, whereas few of her friends had ventured outside of Utah County.

The first in the chain of events bringing Rita into Ritter's life eventuated in 1921, when Edwin O. Olson's brother died, leaving a bungalow in Long Beach, California. Olson left his photography business in the care of two Mormon missionaries from Salt Lake City who were his former employees; purchased for seven hundred dollars a second-hand, nine-passenger Nash touring car with running boards, two jump seats in the back, and isinglass curtains to be snapped on in case of rain; and with his family went to Long Beach. Running-board guards were acquired, and the family loaded their personal possessions on the sides of the vehicle, like the "Oakies" of John Steinbeck's "Dust Bowl," though that was still in the future.

With no driver training and a half hour of experience at the wheel, Rita piloted her parents and two sisters from Provo to Long Beach, California. She was the only member of the family who could drive, and she just barely, so she never took the car out of second gear and never went more than fifteen miles per hour, all the way to Long Beach.[17] Her confidence was fueled by resolve to see what lay ahead in California, beyond the provincial confines of Provo.

There were no road maps in those days, and the vehicle was so overladen that the passengers had to get out while Rita coaxed it up the hills. They stayed with relatives in Spanish Fork, Utah, the first night, but after that they slept under the stars between infrequent gas pumps. They had car troubles in Panguitch, Utah, and had to wait while spare parts arrived by train. Repairs were paid for with bottled fruit.[18] After they finally arrived in California, the Olsons lived in Rita's late uncle's house for about a year, but Edwin Olson was unable to find work in Long Beach.

The second step in the tangled workings of fate setting Rita on a course with Ritter occurred when Edwin Olson went to Berkeley seeking work, where he found employment as a custodian for the YMCA. In Berkeley Rita became acquainted with Adolph LaDru Jensen, a fellow Mormon from Sanpete County, Utah, and former professor of history and political science at Brigham Young University (BYU). Jensen was pursuing graduate studies in law at the University of California at Berkeley.

Three years later Rita drove the Olson family safely back to Provo. The roads were improved, or perhaps being a more experienced driver made them seem so.[19] Rita attended BYU for a time, while Ritter was being initiated into the practice of law with Morris, Kixmiller, and Baar. She became a friend of Helen and Don Lloyd, lifelong friends and business associates of Ritter, and of Algie Ballif, head of the Physical Education Department. Algie was married to George S. Ballif, a lawyer prominent in the political affairs of Utah County who also became a colleague and friend to Ritter, beginning about 1932.[20]

Rita was an attractive young woman, voted the most beautiful on the

BYU campus, and very popular. "Ireta attracted boys like flies," Ida recalled. "In our basement were stacks of candy boxes that reached higher than my head, boxes from gifts given to her by boys."[21] One of the boys apparently attracted to Rita was the brother of her girlfriend at BYU, the daughter of prominent Provo lawyer A. H. Christensen. The young swain's name was A. Sherman Christensen. Rita and Sherman never had a big romance, but Christensen was to become a lightning rod in the tenure of Ritter as a judge.

In 1926 the University of Utah College of Law was still unaccredited. It had modified its admission standards to require two years of prelegal study at the university level, instituted a three-year course for graduation, and acquired a library marginally adequate for accreditation. Still lacking, however, were the two full-time law professors, in addition to Dean Leary, necessary to becoming accredited. Leary "noticed Ritter having an excellent mind that year he was here" and recruited him to help fill that deficiency. "I knew he had made an excellent record at Chicago, a cum laude man at Chicago. Well, when I was looking around for somebody to put in as a full time teacher, knowing his record there and here, I thought he would be about as good a man as we could get."[22]

Adolph LaDru Jensen, in the meantime, had earned his J.D. from Boalt Hall School of Law at Berkeley. Leary recruited Jensen to be the second full-time professor required to satisfy accreditation standards. He would be known professionally and academically as "Dr." A. LaDru Jensen.

And so it happened, in the fall of 1926, that Ritter and Dr. A. LaDru Jensen were simultaneously employed as full-time professors of law.[23] With a full-time faculty of three, the school was finally accredited. The employment of Dr. Jensen to be a fellow law professor with Ritter proved to be the final step in the course of fate merging the lives of Willis W. Ritter and Ireta Olson.

Ritter moved to the cobblestone Spanish bungalow of Willis and Mary Adams, at 2269 McClelland Street, on the edge of Fairmont Park in Sugarhouse. Before long, he was invited to a big dinner. Because Ritter was new to the community, without a special girlfriend other than Frankie in faraway Crescent Park, Dr. A. LaDru Jensen arranged for Ireta Olson, the young woman he had met while attending school in Berkeley, to attend the dinner with Ritter.[24]

Rita was living in Salt Lake City with her sisters, Maurine and Ida, behind the home of an artist, Lee Green Richards, at 125 South 200 East, and working as a billing clerk in the office at Auerbach's department store located at 300 South and State Streets in Salt Lake City, after abandoning her education at BYU.[25] The upper part of a carriage house behind Richards's home and studio had been remodeled into two apartments, known as "Walker's Rooms."

Willis thus met Ireta Olson for the first time the evening of the dinner party, and a lifelong romance was launched in the process. But the nascent romance was not without obstacles to overcome. Love letters from Frankie were arriving at 2269 McClelland Street pledging "*all* (yes every bit, there isn't any more) of my love and trust." Frankie proclaimed Ritter "my law professor!" and was "look[ing] forward to seeing you at Xmas." She detected, however, that Willis's letters arriving at Crescent Park in response seemed "distant" and inquired, "Who is your new thrill?" The romance soon expired after her caution that "unless *that* feeling is mutual please don't feel obligated to accept" her invitation to Houlton, Maine.[26]

Another obstacle was Aunt Mary, ever possessive of her foster son, who refused to let Willis bring Rita to the Adamses' home to meet her. There was also resistance from Rita's sister Maurine, who tried to caution against Willis, asserting that he was headstrong and reckless.[27] Maurine also knew that Rita, despite her independence, had led a very sheltered life and may have been a poor match for a personality as strong as Ritter's—Rita was even naive, in some respects, and believed a woman could get pregnant from kissing a man.

Willis nevertheless courted Rita in his Buick convertible with the rumble seat. They courted in common with Joe Jones and Marjorie Allen, Rita's cousin and daughter of her aunt Ida, the widow of Dr. S. H. Allen.[28] Willis and Rita finally married on August 22, 1928, at the home of Aunt Ida at 206 East Eighth Avenue. The setting, on the corner of A Street, was a beautiful one for a wedding. Perched high on the rim of City Creek Canyon, overlooking Salt Lake City and the state capitol, and what became a memorial park known as Memory Grove, Aunt Ida's home was a prairie-style bungalow built by Dr. Allen in 1909, posh for the day, and remains a very nice home still. The wedding was performed by Levi Edgar Young, a history professor at the University of Utah, grandson of Brigham Young, and himself a high-ranking member of the Mormon first council of the seventies. Rita was twenty-five and Willis twenty-nine.

When first married, Willis and Rita lived in a third-floor apartment in the back of the Roosevelt Apartments at 256 East Broadway. In 1930 they moved to the Madsonia Apartments, a complex of ground-level residential suites at 651 East 100 South. While living there their first child, Willis William "Bill" Ritter Jr., was born.

In 1932 Willis and Rita purchased a fashionable two-story brick home at 27 University Street, on the corner of Butler Avenue.[29] It was a mere block from the University of Utah and became the domicile of the Ritter family. It was large enough for three more children, and had four spare bedrooms upstairs, together with a sleeping porch. They made the upstairs rooms available for Rita's sister Ida to stay while she attended the University of Utah, together with her mother, Dora, by then widowed, and other sister, Maurine. They converted one of the bedrooms into a living room, giving them a more or less private apartment.

It was Depression times in 1933 when Ida, her mother, and her sister moved in. Times were hard, and Ida may never have been able to attend the university without the generosity of Ritter. Ida recalled that when Rita, and her older sister, Maurine, attended BYU, they were not serious about the practical aspects of education, including the need to matriculate. They "fiddled around and did what they wanted, taking painting classes and literature, but neither graduated. When I came along my parents saw the mistake and were bound and determined I would get through." Willis introduced Ida to the librarian and got her a job at twenty-five cents an hour.[30]

Willis and Rita had three more children while they lived on University Street—Nancy, Mary (Puddy), and John—and Willis was proud and affectionate of them all. When Rita wanted the children to help with the dishes, Willis would say, "Let them play. They have childhood only a little while." But he always made sure Rita had help, by employing unwed mothers and Japanese immigrants to work in the home.[31]

Rita's independence and love of nature and the out-of-doors continued during their marriage. She and Willis took short trips with Helen and Don Lloyd to Canyonlands, Navajo country, Uinta Basin, and other nearby attractions. At first, they traveled by automobile and Willis insisted on staying in the best motels, but after a while Rita revealed that she would rather go by horseback and camp out.

Rita and the daughter of Ogden, Utah, publisher Abe Glassman, Gene Hatch, went camping and hiking into the Henry Mountains. They also went to the heights of the Kaiparowitz Plateau, a region little visited and perhaps less touched by human beings than anywhere else in the lower forty-eight states. Charles Wilkinson, in his work on the Colorado Plateau, called it a place where "you have to scour the topographic maps, plan your trip with care (being sure to hit the springs), and stick to your plan.... You can get lost, snakebit, or otherwise injured. There's no one to call."[32] They went on horseback and on foot over trails often too narrow for horses, reputed to be the first women to do so alone.

In the early 1970s Rita went on a six-week jeep trip through the Baja. She was a rock hound and in her sixties would go, alone, into the Arizona desert. The family worried, but Rita paid them no heed. Ritter would say to his children: "There has never been a woman who could match your mother." When Ritter was appointed United States District Judge, some saw him as going overboard in favor of environmental issues and attributed it to Rita's influence.[33]

The perspective of life learned from his uncle and foster father, Willis Adams, perhaps magnified by the influence of Rita, gave Ritter a keen sense of cultural and artistic values. In the early 1930s he went with Don Lloyd on a project, for the Department of Commerce, researching the commercial potential of Navajo art, which aroused his interest in Native American artifacts.[34] Knowledge of Ritter's interest led Hugh Bryan, a neighbor in the Federal Heights area near the university, to approach Ritter about a collection of Navajo weavings. Bryan had grown up in the Four Corners area of the Navajo reservation, and a number of the items were collected during the 1930s by members of his family. "Well, the Interior Department made it possible for Bryan to take a trip to Iran and he decided he'd like to take his family with him, but he didn't have the money," Ritter recalled. "So he came over to the house one day and asked if I wanted to buy his collection; I took the textiles and his basket collection, too. It became the nucleus of my collection. It's a treasure, all of it, a trove of western Indian cultural history."[35]

Ritter added to the collection. Traders learned of his interest, and by the 1940s began to make the Ritter home a regular stop. In the winter they had little to do on the reservation, so they would pile the blankets and rugs into their trucks and wagons and come knocking on Ritter's door. It was a tribulation, Nancy recalled, growing up as a child in a home "filled with rugs."

> Dad would tell them to bring the blankets in and spread them out. There were blankets, rugs and saddle blankets on the living room floor, in the dining room, on the hall floor—everywhere! And we weren't allowed to step on them, we had about three inches of space between rugs and Dad used to warn us: "Watch out, those are treasures."

> In those days, I used to hate Indian blankets. Then, after a few days would pass, the traders would come back and the bargaining would start. It was a ritual.[36]

The collection eventually included a fine example of "second-phase" Indian chief's blanket, which Ritter described as "a precious thing made before 1850 of native wool dyed with indigo." There was also an Indian woman's dress, black and red with indigo design and a tasseled edge, and a half Beyeta Indian woman's dress, which Ritter claimed Navajo women made from recarded wool from red uniforms of Spanish soldiers who had been killed. Beyeta dresses were woven in two halves and stitched at the sides. The mate to Ritter's half-dress was in a collection in Florida. There was a striped "chief's" blanket from 1890 and double saddle blankets hand-spun in complicated twill weaves dating from the 1920s and '30s.[37] Willis's collection of Indian blankets and weavings was his pride and joy. Chinese porcelain, ivory and jade, and several art collections were also displayed at the Ritter home, notably the oil paintings, drawings, and water colors of Willis Adams.

Those were heady days at the University of Utah. The university community was alive with what was happening in the country, with interesting people who had achieved prominence in thinking about social problems. George Thomas, a recognized scholar in the field of economics, had been president of the university since April 5, 1922. Risen from adversity in Cache County, Utah, he graduated from Harvard in 1896, attended the University of Berlin, and received a Ph.D. in 1903 from Halle, Germany. He had administrative experience in the public schools and with the Federal Land Bank at Berkeley, California.[38]

President Thomas was interested in building a strong university, put money into acquiring books, and wanted to get distinguished people on the faculty with varied backgrounds and training. He thought Leary was building a sound law school and that Ritter was part of it. Even though himself a Mormon, he found the university too much in-grown with Mormon influence and avoided adding to that situation. When he found that the Mormon Church had someone attached to the university, he asked, "Why is he here? He has no business here," and saw that he was removed.[39] It was his practice to alternate appointment of Mormons and non-Mormons to important positions. He was thus pleased to have Leary, a Catholic, as dean of the law school and enthusiastic about bringing Ritter, who had a Catholic background, to the campus.

Willis Ritter was young, attractive, highly intelligent, and interested in the social conditions of the community. He quickly became affiliated with a small liberal wing, including President Thomas and Myrtle Austin, who came to the University of Utah in 1926, about the same time Ritter came to the College of Law, and became dean of women in the early 1930s. Through Myrtle, Willis and Rita became close friends with Sydney Angleman, dean of the English Department and Myrtle's best friend in the department. Sidney and Mildred Angleman were great socializers, and their friends immediately met one another. Willis Ritter's circle of liberal friends thus grew and included his friend and former instructor in the Army Training Corps Elbert Thomas and Leo Marshall, dean of the Medical School. They all got to know one another very well.[40]

Willis and Rita were very active in the university social life. They hosted frequent dinners with their intellectual friends at their home on University Street, which were formal affairs, always with white linen tablecloths and napkins—Willis was always insistent on white tablecloths and napkins, even in later life. The discussions were often heated—never dull—with Ritter displaying his uncommon passion for the common man, ruthless condemnation of hypocrisy, delight in "twisting the nose of Dame Orthodoxy," and attitude about the cosmetic effect of institutional religion in solving basic problems. His inherent, classical appreciation of beauty, nature, and the arts helped open what Blake called "the doors of perception." His was a determined stand that we should spend more time in reforming our environment and less in reforming people. Conversations were heavily laced with liberal philosophy. Emotions were often stirred and voices raised, but always there was a happy ending, with Rita performing as the gentle, gracious host.[41]

Willis was the caricature of a college professor: standing five foot eight and weighing 140 pounds, he had a full head of dark, wavy hair over a broad forehead. Well groomed, he had an artistic look about him, wearing a pince-nez, exuding class, like his uncle Willis Adams or a tiny Brandeis. With his keen intelligence and sharp wit, he was a gracious, popular member of the university community and an entertaining host.

Ritter's circle of progressive-minded friends was not confined to the university faculty. In addition to Don Lloyd, executive director of Associated Food Stores, an association of independent grocers, there was Morris Rosenblatt, a successful and prominent industrialist with an interest in social and political affairs, the nearest neighbor to the Ritter family's home on University Street, at 1355 Butler Avenue, contiguous to the Ritters' on the east. Rita's best friend was an actress and University of Utah professor of dramatics, Lila Eccles Brimhall, who was married to Dean Brimhall, an outdoors man and self-educated expert on Indian rock art.

Dean Brimhall, who had earned a Ph.D. in psychology at Columbia University, was the son of former Brigham Young University president George H. Brimhall and uncle to Fawn Brodie, controversial biographer of Joseph Smith, and had himself been a member of the BYU faculty, then became interested in aviation. Together with Robert Hinckley he developed the Ogden airport and Utah Pacific Airways. Hinckley was born in Fillmore, Utah, in 1891, and served on a Mormon mission to Germany with Brimhall. Hinckley established an automobile dealership in Sanpete County in 1915, and in 1927 moved on to the Ogden area, where he established a Dodge dealership with the help of Brimhall. Afterward, they expanded into airplanes, arms, and broadcasting.[42]

Brimhall and Hinckley were affiliated with a group of liberal-thinking businessmen in the Ogden area, which included Ogden Standard-Examiner publisher Abe Glassman and his news reporter Darrell Greenwell and Marriner Eccles, a banker later to become chairman of the Federal Reserve Board. Organized at first under the name "Friedenkers," to signify their open discussions, they dropped the name after town folk began referring to them as "free-drinkers."[43] They all became members of Ritter's expanding circle of liberal friends.

Already a law professor, Ritter continued to enlarge his education. He attended the University of Washington in the summer of 1936 to study geology. Still without an undergraduate degree, he finally earned an A.B. degree from the University of Utah in 1937, where he was Phi Kappa Phi and Phi Beta Kappa. He attended Harvard Law School in 1938 and 1939 under a Langdell Fellowship and was awarded an S.J.D. from Harvard Law School in 1940. While at Harvard, Ritter was asked to teach classes for professors who were ill or otherwise unavailable, sometimes for months at a time.[44]

Ritter was admitted to the Utah State Bar on August 11, 1927. Thereafter, he acted as counsel for the University of Utah.[45] He also acted as counsel for many in his expanding circle of liberal friends, including Morris Rosenblatt, Abe Glassman, and Robert Hinckley, particularly with respect to tax and estate matters, which were his academic specialty.

At the College of Law, Ritter taught a tough course. He was "a big little man" who "teaches more in an hour than other professors do in a week." He could expound on the law, on the rules of property law, for example, and talk about the evolution of the law from feudal days in a way that made sense. He used the jury system to explain that the law is constantly evolving, not rigid, as advocates of strict construction maintained. "The genesis of our jury is found in the inquest of the Norman Kings," he explained, but by the 1600s "the notion was growing that in order to find a verdict there ought to be some evidence to go on." Then, "the proposition that the evidence must be sufficient to fairly and reasonably warrant the finding" developed, "and that is the present state of the law."[46]

He was "popular" and "highly respected." A group of students, including his future critic John S. Boyden, petitioned the law school in 1929 to include in the curriculum "a course in Trial Practice as taught by Professor Ritter during the Summer School of 1928," for it "would be a very great advantage to us just before entering into the practice of law," and "we would derive [practical benefit] from such a course" if conducted by Ritter.[47]

His was a liberal view of the law. "The theory of our common law system invites changes.... The logical process of applying a principle to new cases can be made a rigid one. It can be so inflexibly applied as to leave no room for change. It has been so applied. But the whole life and vigor of the common law has been found in regarding those principles as sufficiently flexible to adjust to new conditions and demands." Legal scholars, and judges, must adjust the law to those changed conditions. "But above all we need *men,* strong men of enlightened judgment, well informed, widely and carefully trained who know the law and have the courage to enforce it. The common law is the precision instrument. It won't perform the operation—a skilled and nicely balanced human organism alone can do the job."[48]

Thus, the story of our development—our essential history—is mirrored in the controversies before the Supreme Court, Ritter explained. "Things are not what they used to be," he declared, and as "Mark Twain adds, 'what's more, they never were.'"[49] By contrast, "the so-called conservative or reactionaries have favored last century *laissez fair* economic doctrines." He made examples of opinions of the United States Supreme Court by Utah's justice, George Sutherland. "They have favored an economic individualism which brooks no governmental restraint on private enterprise."

But under the theory of the law Ritter espoused, the so-called liberal justices on the Supreme Court, "Holmes, Brandeis, and their colleagues believe in the theory of letting legislatures make social and economic experiments." Evolution of the law regulating hours of labor was used to give meaning to those distinctions. He explained that in 1906 the Supreme Court, in the case *Lochner v. New York,* ruled bad "a statute that forbade employees in bakeries working more than 10 hours per day." Holmes dissented. But "in 1917 only four of the justices who had participated in the Lochner Case remained on the bench and three of those had dissented" when another case involving a statute regulating hours of work went to the Court. "The earlier decision in the Lochner case was overruled," and as per his concept of the law as responding to the societal needs, "the fight for the states' power to regulate hours of labor had been won." He reasoned, "The law... must not get so far behind that it retards our progress. It must not get so far behind that it does not serve the moral, social, economic and industrial needs of our times."[50]

In contrast with Ritter's manner when he became a judge, students at the time considered him shy and introverted. He had little patience with those who were not prepared, and had a way of making them do more than they thought they were able. But he would "wipe the floor" with those who were barely getting by. He didn't waste time in class, exhibiting an impatience that would be the focus of much criticism when he became a judge; if he did not get an adequate response from his students after going through a number of cards with their names on them, one indicating that they were prepared, he would just fold up his notes and leave, even if he had only been there ten or fifteen minutes. His standard quip in those situations was, "Have you ever considered enrolling in engineering school? They work with their hands there."[51]

But he also had a compassionate side. When A. Wally Sandack was in his last year of law school, he had surgery for appendicitis. He was in the hospital for a week, and in those days convalescence was extensive. Sandack missed much of the last academic quarter, including several weeks of Ritter's wills and trusts courses. Sandack visited Ritter in his office after the operation, as soon as he could, and announced that, because he believed he could not pass the final exams after missing so much of the courses, he intended to abandon law school and go back to Illinois, "where [my] people came from." Ritter took down his bound volume of notes from his courses at Chicago and Harvard, all neatly typed. "Here, take this Mr. Sandack,"

Ritter said. "Study them and I'm sure you'll get enough out of them to pass the course."[52]

Here was the human side of Willis W. Ritter. Contrary to his reputation in later years, Nancy described him during this period as "caring." He would bring students home with him, those who were not making it in particular, sit with them and counsel them. It was his way to show kindness and good deeds privately. His toughness was the public side of him, and the side that provoked controversy.[53]

On a Sunday morning in February 1932, Willis received a telephone call at home from Dean Leary telling him that university president George Thomas wanted to see him in his office in a half hour. When he arrived, Ritter was informed that Thomas had deposited $52,012.06 of university funds, a large sum in those days, at Deseret Savings Bank. The bank was among the many that failed during the epidemic of bank closures during the economic crises of the period. The deposit was in a general account, as a reserve of sorts for unforseen contingencies, but the university was threatened with the loss of the entire amount and Thomas with violation of law for mishandling university funds.[54]

Ritter put his expert knowledge of trust law to good advantage. He convinced the banking commissioners that Thomas's general account was a trust account, reasoning that as president of the university, Thomas was in effect trustee for the university. The object of Ritter's resourceful theory was to establish that the university had a preferred claim to the remaining funds of the bank and was able to recover all but $723.39 of the deposit.[55]

The Board of Regents approved $300 for "a large amount of very excellent work on the Deseret Savings Bank matter." Ritter submitted a bill for his services in the amount of $1,700, stating that it was "proper, after mature consideration." The matter was referred to Leary and regent Robinson, who concluded that $800 would be "fair compensation." Ritter agreed, then compromised for the total sum of $650.[56] Ritter continued to represent the university, principally regarding bonded indebtedness for buildings and equipment, through April 1942.

While engaged full-time as a law professor, other opportunities to engage in the practice of law outside the university also presented themselves from time to time. He did tax planning for Bradshaw Chevrolet of Cedar City, Utah, formed by Stanley Bradshaw in 1920 and reorganized by

Ritter in 1937 as a partnership including Bradshaw's wife, Christy, and their children.[57]

Ritter's salary as a professor of law was supplemented with professional fees for services, and he acquired practical experience in the law. One such engagement, which was to have an effect on Ritter for a lifetime, particularly economically, occurred when C. R. Jones employed Ritter in 1937 to complete a mortgage foreclosure action pending in Sevier County, Utah. Jones operated American Keene Cement and Plaster Company, a cement plant in Sigurd, Utah. The United States Gypsum Company acquired land adjacent to the gypsum property operated by Jones and American Keene Cement in the mid-1930s and began casting an acquisitive eye on the neighboring deposits, then initiated a suit to foreclose on a deed issued by a predecessor corporation to one of American Keene's former officers. The foreclosure had overtones of conspiracy described by Ritter: "They hired Henry Moyle," a prominent Utah lawyer, fellow professor of law with Ritter, on a part-time basis, and future counselor to future Mormon Church president David O. McKay, who "found out that Ted Jones and American Keene held a mortgage through a fellow in Pittsburgh, his name was Golden . . . and Henry went back to Pittsburgh and inspired that fellow to file a mortgage foreclosure suit down in Richfield to squeeze out Jones and American Keene and this was the first serious business I did for them."[58]

The foreclosure action had already been tried, by Harvey H. Cluff of Provo, Utah, representing Jones, and was awaiting decision. Cluff, former attorney general of Utah, could not conclude the case. "Well, anyway he tried it and he had a heart attack at the end of the trial," Ritter explained. "He came up here and went to bed." Ritter had represented American Keene in a collection matter or two, "so Jones came around and asked me if I'd take on where he left off and I said I will if you will take me over to him and have him agree to it. I don't want to steal his business while he is in bed with a heart attack and that was done and I took on the after trial motions and one thing and another."[59]

"Henry removed it to the federal court" for trial of the remaining issues. "We tried that lawsuit before [Judge Tilman] Johnson and I won it."[60] Johnson was renowned for turning his head to the side, as if he was not listening, and pretending to stick a pencil in his ear. "Along late in the day one afternoon, Johnson wound that pencil up in his ear and he said, 'Mr. Moyle, I don't see how you are going to recover in this lawsuit.' Well, that was how I got into the [American Gypsum Trust]," which was to become the principal source of Ritter's fortune for the balance of his life.[61]

The product of small-town Park City, and former laborer and mucker from his days working underground in the mines, had thus become an established player in the intellectual society of Utah. His friends who would stand with him, and he with them, and whose support and loyalty would be critical in the controversy ahead were thus established. Meanwhile, laissez-faire ideologues, both in Salt Lake City and the Republic of Mexico, were aligning themselves with centers of religious and political control in Utah and would challenge the philosophy of Ritter and his progressive-minded friends. The conflict that would result would become pivotal to his venture into politics, as it developed during the decade of the 1930s, and to his eventual nomination to the federal judiciary. The outfall from that conflict would consume his career.

4

RIVALS

The first requirement of a sound body of law is that it should correspond with the actual feelings and demands of the community, whether right or wrong.

—Oliver Wendell Holmes Jr.

Law is experience developed by reason and applied continually to further experience.

—Roscoe Pound

With their progressive attitude toward use of the law and government to improve social institutions, Willis W. Ritter and his expanding circle of liberal friends found themselves, inevitably, in conflict with the predominantly conservative political climate in Utah, having its roots in the history of the Mormon Church.

Early Mormons voted as a bloc and blatantly negotiated for the balance of power their vote represented. Their practice in doing so contributed to their persecution in Missouri and Illinois.[1] After their exodus to Utah, they conducted a virtual theocracy, with Brigham Young as their chief minister. Territorial governors appointed by the federal government were largely figureheads. The "manifesto" of 1890 by the fourth president of the Mormon Church, Wilford Woodruff, discontinued the practice of plural marriage and paved the way for Utah's admission to the Union on January 2, 1896. It also marked a period when, at least officially, Mormon Church leaders remained aloof from partisan politics.[2]

Joseph F. Smith, the sixth president of the Mormon Church, deviated from nonpartisanship and championed the Republican Party. In 1902 Smith supported Mormon apostle Reed Smoot in his election to the United States Senate as a Republican. Smoot retained his ecclesiastical office, even while serving in Washington, D.C.

Smith's successor, Heber J. Grant, was nominally a Democrat at the beginning of his ministry.[3] Most church leaders were increasingly conservative, however, and probusiness in their outlook and tended toward Republican candidates, whether members of the church or not. Disinclined to control the political activities of the church's members, Grant preoccupied himself with his ministry and moral or public issues of overriding concern. The issue of repeal of Prohibition, which was prominent in 1932, made it difficult for Grant to remain out of active politics or to continue his passive support for Democrats. Grant opposed repeal, privately, while trying to maintain a public stance of neutrality.

That, essentially, was the status of church-state relations in Utah when Ritter began getting interested in politics. While at law school in Chicago and practicing in Washington, D.C., with Morris, Kixmiller, and Baar, Ritter was conservative and essentially apolitical. After becoming a professor of law, and becoming exposed to the progressive social thinking of his university and community friends, Ritter became involved in liberal politics.

He became interested, first of all, in the Republicans. Calvin Behle, one of Ritter's students, a little older and a Republican, invited him to the Salt Lake County Republican Convention. He found a cold and closed atmosphere there, where everyone appeared to be at least seventy years of age, and no one spoke to him or seemed to care whether he stayed. "I've had it with the Republicans," Ritter said. Behle suggested that they go to a "hole in the wall" where they could contemplate their experience over a meat pie and glass of beer.[4]

After his disappointment at the Republican convention, a group at the University of Utah was getting organized to promote a candidate to run against Reed Smoot, who by then had been a Utah senator for thirty years. Elbert Thomas, Ritter's friend, teaching colleague, and drill instructor in the 1918 Student Army Training Corps, was their candidate.

The grandson of a pioneer Mormon stonecutter, Michael Stockdale Sr., and the son of R. K. Thomas, a leading Salt Lake City merchant and Mormon, Thomas's childhood was spent in the Thomas family home at 137 North West Temple, in the shadow of the Mormon temple.[5] He had been a Mormon missionary and mission president to Japan. Thomas was a devout Mormon, but of a different stripe than Smoot; he was receptive to the progressive thinking that put him well within the liberal philosophy Ritter had adopted and the Democrats were about to espouse.

Willis went to the 1932 Democratic State Convention being held at the Orpheum Theater in Ogden to help promote Thomas and found the people friendly and the atmosphere charged with the programs Franklin Delano Roosevelt proposed to bring the country out of the Great Depression.[6] Twenty-five-year-old Warwick C. "Rick" Lamoreaux, a political tyro and himself interested in the nomination of Thomas, was also at the convention. Lamoreaux was without credentials, not being a delegate, but, by his description, was "good at sneaking in." William H. King, U.S. senator from Utah since 1916, a self-styled "constitutional Democrat" and outspoken opponent of Roosevelt and the New Deal, was presiding.[7] Lamoreaux had not heard of Roosevelt, but King's strident opposition seemed without reason and convinced him: "I'm voting for Franklin Roosevelt," he said to himself.

Thomas's name was placed in nomination, but there was no second. Lamoreaux mumbled, four or five times, as he sat at the back of the hall: "Isn't anyone going to second Dr. Thomas's nomination? It's a shame to put up a good man and let him die." "Why don't you?" someone asked. "I will," Lamoreaux replied. But he needed someone with credentials to get him to the front of the convention and to the floor. "Will you please come with me?" he asked the delegate who made the suggestion.

Lamoreaux was led around through the back of the theater. When he got to the front of the convention, he was told that in fact there were several people to second the nomination of Thomas, but King had refused to recognize them. "Sic'um," a lawyer standing nearby said, and young Rick Lamoreaux took the floor and seconded the nomination of Elbert Thomas.[8] After Lamoreaux broke King's attempted freeze-out, Ritter also seconded Thomas's nomination, and in the process became a New Deal Democrat.

But John M. Wallace, a non-Mormon, charming and highly popular, meant to have the nomination for himself, and by most estimates had a good chance of getting it. Chairman of the board of the Walker Brothers, Bankers, in Salt Lake City, Wallace was son-in-law of the late Matthew Henry Walker, one of the four Walker brothers who founded the bank with profits from mining ventures and trade with Colonel Patrick Connor's California Volunteers stationed at Fort Douglas.[9]

Wallace appeared the favorite, but stumbled over the issue of Prohibition. Wallace was against repeal and wouldn't budge, but a majority of the delegates, like Roosevelt, opposed Prohibition, and for that reason the convention turned against Wallace, leaving the field open.

The leading contender to Wallace for the Senate nomination was not Thomas, however, but Dan Shields, former Utah attorney general. Shields was also from Park City, where he had been a classmate of Ritter's mother, May. It became widely known among Democratic Party leadership that a deal was struck between Shields and Thomas that the convention would choose Thomas and that he would nominate Shields as United States Attorney for the District of Utah and for United States District Judge for the District of Utah upon the retirement of Tillman Johnson, who was then seventy-four years of age.[10] Pursuant to the deal with Shields, the convention settled on Thomas as their nominee. After the convention in Ogden, and Thomas's nomination, young Rick Lamoreaux met Dan Shields one day in the entry of the Judge Building in Salt Lake City. "You don't know it," Shields informed Lamoreaux, "but you deprived me of the nomination when you seconded Thomas."[11]

Once Thomas was nominated, Morris Rosenblatt, Ritter's next-door neighbor on Butler Avenue, together with a small group including Ritter, Leo Marshall, and Delbert Draper, became a tight committee that plotted, planned, and executed the election campaign of Elbert Thomas.

If the issue of Prohibition had not been challenge enough to the stance of neutrality espoused by Heber J. Grant, president of the Mormon Church, the influence of Joshua Reuben Clark Jr., an influential and well-connected Mormon who served the Republican administrations of Calvin Coolidge and Herbert Hoover in the State Department, as undersecretary of state and U.S. ambassador to Mexico, would do so. He had coveted election as U.S. senator from Utah for himself in 1922 and campaigned unsuccessfully for nomination to that office in 1928. Clark's return in 1933 was preceded by Thomas's campaign against Smoot for election to the Senate.

Previously, Clark also espoused noninvolvement in politics by church officials, so much so that it was his opinion that partisanship by the church or its officials was "un-American." He drafted a resolution in 1923, never presented to the Mormon membership at General Conference, declaring that high church officials not "participate in any political discussions or activities of any nature whatsoever, nor seek to exercise either directly or indirectly or publicly or privately any influence or control in political matters" or "accept any office or employment of profit or trust" under federal, state, or local government.[12]

Clark, while still stationed in Mexico City with the consular service, was already designated to become a counselor to Grant. Just before Christmas in 1931 he received a letter from Grant advising that, after "prayerful consideration," "our minds revert to you as the man whom the Lord desires to fill this vacancy" as second counselor. Clark accepted, contingent upon completion of his service, with the caveat that "if you do not care to postpone filling the vacancy" by waiting for him, "I hope you will feel entirely free to act."[13]

Previously, Clark was not shy about giving unsolicited advice to the president of the church, and now he was emboldened to do so by the letter.[14] He changed his position on noninvolvement of the church in face of the Thomas-Smoot election campaign, actively advocating Smoot's reelection, and placed Grant in a contradictory position. Being of advanced years and in poor health, the church president may have lacked acuity or energy to resist Clark's influence. Grant published a statement, inspired by Clark; "I am a staunch supporter of the Senator [Smoot] and President Hoover and intend to vote for them," then published a clarification the day before the election, apparently on the advice of Heber Grant Ivins, Grant's first counselor and an ardent Democrat. The statement of support he had just issued for Smoot and Hoover, or by "any other officers of the Church, is his personal preference and is not intended to influence members of the Church," the clarification read.[15]

Thus, through the 1932 election, the church maintained at least the appearance of noninterference in politics, against the pressures of Clark, and did so largely as a result of the influence of Ivins. Ivins always maintained a policy of church nonintervention in politics, even through his advocacy of Thomas in the 1932 election and consequent opposition to Smoot. He became the "conscience" of the Mormon Church in that regard, by virtue of being de facto chief administrator of the church during extended periods of Grant's illness.[16]

It turned out that Smoot, despite his standing as a Mormon apostle, and despite his open advocacy by Clark and virtual advocacy by Grant, was vulnerable. In that year of poverty, unemployment, and related miseries, Smoot's incumbency associated him, in the minds of many voters, with those in government who were seen as the source of the problems. The day after publication of Grant's "clarification," Smoot was voted out of office and Thomas elected.

Once elected, Thomas and members of Ritter's circle of liberal friends became important players in the administration of Franklin Delano Roosevelt. Thomas denounced opponents of the New Deal for catering to special interests, usually large corporations. He quickly became a spokesman for the New Deal on foreign affairs, warning that promotion of private agendas and hegemony amounted to "rivalries for national gain," which Thomas considered the ultimate cause of World War I and predicted would be the cause of wars in the future.[17] He coauthored the "Connally Resolution" for international collaboration for world peace, represented the United States at the Interparliamentary Union in Budapest in 1936 and Paris in 1937, and chaired the Senate Military Affairs Committee. He authored or supported the New Deal farm programs, federal aid to education, and legislation on work hours and a minimum wage, social security, public health, and child care. After World War II he wrote the educational features of the "GI Bill of Rights," including its provisions for hospitals, nurses, and loans.[18]

The New Deal, and officials in Utah who came to positions of influence under Roosevelt, was critically important to salvaging the Utah economy. When the worst drought in Utah history occurred in 1933, and continued in 1934, with precipitation 50 percent of normal and average temperatures four degrees above normal, agriculture and livestock on which Utah depended were threatened. Great Salt Lake was two and one-half miles within its borders and Bear Lake fourteen feet shallower than normal. Ritter's friend and fellow Thomas supporter Robert Hinckley, head of Utah's chapter of the Federal Emergency Relief Association (FERA), contacted Harry Hopkins, president of the national FERA, who secured Roosevelt's agreement to grant six hundred thousand dollars to help establish a water-resource board. Hinckley convinced Hopkins that the money would save the state three million dollars in crops and pull ten thousand families off the relief rolls.[19]

In the process of nominating Thomas and working for his election, Ritter's friendship with Dean R. Brimhall became closer. Brimhall became involved with the New Deal early in Roosevelt's first term as Utah planning director of FERA. In 1935 he became director of the Utah State Planning Board that developed policies for the extensive federal work programs in the state. Later that year he accepted a position as assistant administrator of labor management with the Works Progress Administration (WPA) under Harry Hopkins. In 1944 he was an assistant to Hinckley, who had become assistant secretary of commerce for air in Washington, D.C., and Brimhall served as director of research for the Civil Aeronautics Administration, where he developed a stall-warning system for military and commercial aircraft. He was executive secretary of the Psychological Corporation of New York, coeditor of *American Men of Science,* and a member of the board of trustees of the Utah Historical Society. All the while, Brimhall maintained an active and lively interest in Utah politics.[20]

Marriner S. Eccles, president of First Security Corporation, one of the first multibank holding companies in the land, expressed the view in meetings of the Friedenkers in Ogden that "the only way we could get out of the depression was through government action in placing purchasing power in the hands of people who were in need of it." In February 1933 he was invited by fellow Friedenker Hinckley to a luncheon speech by Stuart Chase, but Chase was delayed by a snowstorm and Eccles was asked to explain his own views, impromptu. Chase arrived as Eccles was speaking. Impressed by what he heard, Chase arranged for Eccles to meet and explain his views to Paul H. Douglas of the University of Chicago, soon to become U.S. senator from Illinois, who directed him to New York City and Rex Tugwell of Columbia College, one of FDR's "brain trusters." Through Tugwell, Eccles was sent to Washington, D.C., and introduced to Henry Wallace, Harry Hopkins, and Jerome Frank, to whom he explained his ideas on the need for a compensatory fiscal and monetary policy. "They needed arguments on how a planned policy of adequate deficit financing could serve the humanitarian objective with which they were most directly concerned," Eccles recalled, "and second, how the increased production and employment that the policy would create was the only way a depression could be ended and a budget balanced." Eccles helped draft the Federal Housing Act of 1933 and the 1933 act creating the Federal Deposit Insurance Corporation.

In June 1934 Henry Morgenthau invited Eccles to a White House conference. During its course, Morgenthau leaned over to Eccles and told him he was being considered for the then vacant post of governor of the Federal Reserve Board. At a subsequent White House conference in September, Roosevelt confirmed, directly, that Eccles would be so nominated.

On November 4, 1934, Eccles presented FDR with a memorandum that led to the Emergency Banking Act. That month Eccles was nominated to head the Federal Reserve System, and his appointment was ratified in April 1935.[21] Eccles was the principal sponsor of the Banking Act of 1935, which restructured the Federal Reserve System into its present form. He was appointed chairman of the board of governors of the newly organized system and served for seventeen years. He was one of the architects of the World Bank and the International Monetary Fund in 1946.[22]

The return of Clark to become a member of the leadership council of the Mormon Church, simplified by the landslide for Franklin Delano Roosevelt that coincided with the election of Thomas in 1932, would eventually bring the church into open partisanship on behalf of the Republicans and into conflict with Ritter.

Ivins died in 1934, removing the most effective restraint on partisan church activity. Constant pressures on Clark, who had been confirmed in 1933 as second counselor to the Mormon president, to return to politics, both elective and appointive, weakened whatever reservations he had remaining about church involvement in politics. In 1934 a campaign was mounted by influential Republicans, including Harry Chandler, owner of the *Los Angeles Times,* to get Clark to accept nomination to the United States Senate. Grant initially opposed the idea, citing possible charges of church influence, then finally agreed, but Clark declined at the last minute. In 1936 Clark met with an emissary of Alfred Landon, eventual Republican nominee for president, who solicited Clark to become delegate at large from Utah to the Republican National Convention and assist in drafting the 1936 Republican platform and offered to appoint him secretary of state if Landon was elected. Grant encouraged Clark to join Landon's campaign, and announced from the first presidency's office: "Governor Alf M. Landon of Kansas will make a great president." Believing he "would harden this situation and solidify opposition rather than gain votes," Clark declined requests of the Republican National Committee that he give twelve speeches for Landon in Utah, but campaigned for Landon in Idaho, California, Arizona, Texas, and Colorado. Thus, by the next presidential election Clark, and under his influence the Mormon Church, had embarked in partisan politics, and did so on behalf of Republicans. Grant came out publicly in an unsigned editorial in the *Deseret News* in 1936 stating, crudely, that the choice between Landon and Roosevelt was a choice between the Constitution and communism. Despite the editorial, and Clark's campaigning, the state went overwhelmingly for Roosevelt.[23]

If Ritter's loyalty to Elbert Thomas had not been enough to ignite his enthusiasm for party politics, Franklin Delano Roosevelt's wit, charm, and obvious intellect finished the job of making an unrepentant Democrat out of him. Those factors influenced Ritter as much, or more, than the New Deal philosophy, but thereafter FDR had Ritter's unreserved admiration and endorsement, as few men were given. It was almost as if FDR were Ritter's philosophical father.

In 1931 Ritter was part of a slate of University of Utah professors who presented a series of lectures at the Hotel Utah called Our Changing Social World. Lecture 8 presented by Ritter on February 11, 1932, was titled "Law and Social Progress," and expanded on the liberal view of the law he had been presenting in his law school lectures. "Law does change," Ritter opined, "sometimes for the worse, but in the main for the better. It is much more closely related to our social, economic and political thinking than we are in the habit of believing. It is not only shaped by us but it shapes us. We are what we are, and we do very much because of law. On the other hand, law conforms to community standards. It is what we make it. Much in it that is subject to criticism is merely a reflection of the law ideals of you and me and the community at large." Such notions would be heresy to the "strict constructionist" advocates then, as well as those of the twenty-first century. Ritter explained, as if in anticipation of them, that his was not a view that admitted of judges "making the law." "Disregard of legal principle and precedent is worse than rigidity," he warned. "It is chaos. Both stability and susceptibility to change are needed."[24]

In 1933 Ritter presented another series of lectures at the Hotel Utah on contemporary political trends, in which he extended his liberal view of the law to the realm of politics. One lecture was titled "The American Constitution and Political Change." In 1936 he presented a series of fifteen lectures on similar subjects to a University of Utah Division of Continuing Education class. The lectures were to become controversial when Ritter was appointed to the bench, including for his quotations of the liberal views of Justice Oliver Wendell Holmes ("There is nothing I more deprecate than the use of the Fourteenth Amendment beyond the absolute compulsion of its words to prevent the making of social experiments that an important part of the community desires") and Justice Charles Evans Hughes ("A fundamental principle of our constitutional system" is that "government may be responsive to the will of the people"). The lectures exposed his liberal philosophy, setting him apart from the conservative stance of Clark and Grant. His conclusion was that "they [conservatives] join with the American Liberty League, to urge preservation of the Constitution against the liberal extension of the Roosevelt regime." He ridiculed the conservative stance. "Absent a precedent, you were told to go to the legislature, or perhaps to a warmer place." But "Dean Pound's 'sociological jurisprudence' reintroduced ethics and social cause and effect into the law," and Pound's was the correct view, according to Ritter. "His work marks a revolt against case law positivism."[25]

By 1936 Ritter had established himself as an expert on politics and government. His lectures provide insight into his thinking that would continue the rest of his life. He emphasized, as he had done in his law school lectures, the maxim of Justice Holmes that "if there is any principle of the constitution that more imperatively calls for attachment than any other it is the principle of free thought—not free thought for those who agree with us but freedom for the thought that we hate." He explained, "We must square current necessity with the Constitution, and we do, and have done, since the beginning of this nation. There are terms in the Constitution which are absolute, but there are other terms, and they are by far the more important, which are flexible, which are relative, and with respect to those terms, the Judges of the Supreme Court tell us what they mean. It is a live, vital instrument," he continued, reciting Holmes on the common law, "flexible and adaptable enough to change and accommodate itself through the conduct of the judges of the Supreme Court of the United States to our changing needs and conditions."[26]

Freedom of speech and expression was illustrated by a landmark decision of the Supreme Court challenging the California red-flag law, which prohibited communist symbols. "A little girl whose folks were Communists went to a Communist picnic and was seen waving a red flag. Some overzealous peace officer arrested her and she was convicted." "Justice Hughes said this" in reversing the conviction, Ritter proclaimed: "The maintenance of an opportunity of present political discussion [is necessary] to the end that the government must be responsible to the wishes of the people, and that changes may be brought about by lawful means as essential to the security of the public and as a fundamental principle of our constitutional principles!" According to Ritter, "I know of no more significant thing that this court has said. 'An opportunity of present political discussion to the end that the government must be responsible to the wishes of the people,' so I say to you, the proper subject for discussion is not 'Can We Square Current Necessity with the Constitution' but rather, 'We Must.'"[27]

Applying those legal precepts to politics, he declared that Roosevelt's New Deal was a continuation of Jefferson's Republican Party, which changed its name to the Democratic Party in 1828. The modern Republican Party, on the other hand, was a continuation of Hamilton's Federalist Party. Jefferson's party was representative of a republic of farmers of colonial times, or an economic group composed of "plain people." Hamilton's party was composed of the holders of personal property, the "fancy people," the "wise, the good and the rich." Ritter jested, "God made many more plain people than fancy people."

The Hamiltonian/Republican attitude toward business was laissez-faire, or liberal construction of the Constitution so as "not to interfere with my business." But Republicans opposed liberal extension of the Constitution by the Roosevelt administration. They "favor federal authority against states rights," Ritter proclaimed, "but not when President Roosevelt is exercising it." In his view, Republicans and their appointees, in the era before Roosevelt, "zealously fought to keep the under-dog under" and were "inflexible in defense of *laissez faire* doctrines of the last century. [Their] answer to economic unrest is *laissez faire*! But lazy fairies did not do the job! The result is the New Deal."[28]

He recognized, however, that because each state has sovereignty, and considering the size of the territory of the United States, American political life is sectional. "If one party [were] extinguished there is no shade of opinion which would not be represented in the other."[29]

The central idea of the New Deal, to Ritter, was that the person is more important in a civilization than property, that government itself must and should be used to make freedom the expanding force it can and should be when the individual has the opportunity to develop his own soul. He recognized it as a trend toward greater emphasis upon the dignity of the individual, which some called a trend to the Left.[30]

By March 1937 Ritter was of the opinion that the laissez-faire element of the Supreme Court, led by Justices George Sutherland, Pierce Butler, Willis Van Devanter, and James C. McReynolds, and its opposition to New Deal programs, was antithetical to his liberal view of the law. "Their philosophy of governmental non-interference with private enterprise has been too long read into our constitutional system. If our constitutions do not permit regulation of private initiative for the general good, they are not likely to endure very much longer.... The whole legal profession is too darn conservative and one suspects has been too long in the employ of the 'interests!'" He therefore "resigned from the American Bar Association and Dean Leary is threatening to do so," because "we both feel that the Association is composed of die-hard railroad and corporation lawyers."[31]

The response of Clark and under his influence Grant to the New Deal was intensified, bringing them into greater conflict with Ritter, and furnished a textbook example of the laissez-faire doctrines his lectures alluded to. Grant finally became alienated from the Democratic Party by the welfare programs Hinckley, Brimhall, and Eccles promoted, Ritter advocated, and the New Deal initiated to bring the country out of the Great Depression, for Grant thought they contributed to the curse of idleness and threatened old-time virtues. As early as 1933, Grant and Clark undertook to devise a positive response to the welfare programs of the New Deal. Its model was an initiative in Salt Lake City's Pioneer Stake, where unemployment was more than 50 percent. The Mormons bought a farm and put their unemployed to work in exchange for food. Then they branched out into operating a bishop's warehouse and cannery. Inspired by their efforts, Clark undertook a campaign to convince the church bureaucracy to launch its own relief program.[32]

Clark fretted over the fact that Utah was one of the largest recipients of federal welfare funds. Finally, after three years of internal debate, the church announced that it was establishing a welfare program. Production assignments were given to the 117 ecclesiastical divisions known as stakes in existence in 1936, and at October Conference of that year Grant reported, with pride and satisfaction, what had been accomplished. "Our primary purpose was to set up ... a system under which the curse of idleness would be done away with, the evils of a dole abolished," Grant declared, in obvious criticism of the New Deal. "Independence, industry, thrift and self respect [will] be once more established amongst our people. The aim of the Church is to help the people to help themselves. Work is to be re-enthroned as the ruling principle of the lives of our church membership.... I do not ask any man or child in this Church ... to work any more hours than I do," Grant proclaimed. "I do not think work ever hurts anybody."[33]

Clark claimed that the program would remove eighty-eight thousand Mormons from the relief roles and make them self-sufficient. Popular wisdom was that the Church Welfare Plan was a "deep-laid political scheme" by Grant and Clark to undermine the New Deal. Utah remained a leading recipient of federal aid, nevertheless, and continued to be dependent on government programs for employment.[34] The "lazy fairies," as Ritter had observed in his 1936 lectures, failed once more to do the chore.

To the disappointment of Clark and Grant, Thomas was reelected in 1938, over their continued opposition and that of the Mormon Church to New Deal policies. He defeated Franklin S. Harris, president of Brigham Young University and a former professor of agronomy at Utah State Agricultural College in Logan.[35] Harris was a member of the General Board of the Young Men's Mutual Improvement Association of the Mormon Church and campaigned on his ecclesiastical callings. Thomas, always loath to attack an opponent personally, acknowledged Harris as a "great educator" who "made a great race." But, Thomas claimed, Harris had been selected by a group of men in the church office building in Salt Lake City, and "the great rank and file of Republicans did not go along."[36]

Thomas was an unusual, gifted person. Thomas Jefferson was his idol. Pratt Kesler, whose best friend was the brother of Paul Badger, Thomas's administrative assistant, visited Thomas in his Washington office. Kesler reported that Thomas put his feet up on the desk, rolled his eyes back, and said—seriously—that he believed he was Thomas Jefferson reincarnate.[37]

Thomas's strength in a campaign was his dignified presence and high-flown public speeches about peace, prosperity, and the dream of a world community. Like the "heavy" in a good cop–bad cop team, Ritter's job was to plot the battle, position the traps, and deliver a grittier message to party leaders and rank-and-file Democrats about bread, butter, jobs, and patronage—subjects he had learned well as a child in Park City and with his liberal friends at the University of Utah—and probably about the dangers of church control.

Ritter became a consistent advocate of the New Deal philosophy and played an indispensable role in Thomas's campaigns. Ritter played a prominent role as well in the elections of New Deal advocates Abe Murdock to the United States Senate and Walter K. Granger to Congress, both in 1940.

Academically, Ritter's star continued to rise. In November 1940 University of Utah president George Thomas announced that he would retire. Two hundred and ninety names of possible replacements were received during early 1941, and by the middle of July a committee of the board of regents presented a list of seventy-seven for consideration by the board. Ritter's rise in the academic world was confirmed by the fact that he was one of them, having been recommended for the position in a letter dated August 11, 1941, by the Harvard Law School. The letter said that Ritter "appeared to have the qualities that would secure for him a place of leadership in the University world." Harvard professor W. Barton Leach was "convinced of his sound judgment and scholarship and capacity for dealing with people smoothly and efficiently." He was "one of the two outstanding graduate students" at Harvard during his time there.[38]

William Kixmiller and Arnold Baar recommended him "most enthusiastically." When he worked for their firm, he "quickly showed his extraordinary legal talent and also his ability to work with other people." He was "well qualified, with a great sense of integrity and unusual balance."[39]

A faculty committee report of September 17, 1941, on inside candidates listed Ritter as one of five suggested for the position. He was regarded as of "high character," a "good speaker and appears well before the public," and was "tolerant toward all political, educational, business and religious organizations and able to resist pressure groups with firmness and justice." Criticism of him was that he lacked administrative experience. He was one of three inside candidates recommended.[40]

At its October 11, 1941, meeting the board proceeded to vote on the candidates. Nine names were placed on the ballot, then reduced to three, then to two, after which there was a tie vote for two successive ballots. At that point a new name, that of Dr. LeRoy E. Cowles, not previously mentioned, was elected after a recess of only five minutes. Because he was within four years of normal retirement age, President Cowles was considered to be an interim appointment.[41]

Cowles had been appointed dean of the School of Education a matter of weeks before his election as university president. He was born in Chester, Weber County, on April 13, 1880. Educated in the public schools, he received a Ph.B. at the University of Chicago in 1910 and an A.M. from the same institution in 1913. He served as principal of Carbon County High School for one year in 1913-1914, then as assistant professor of education and then professor at the University of Utah, during which time he earned a Ph.D. from the University of California in 1926. He was dean of the Lower Division of the Department of Educational Administration until being made dean of the School of Education immediately before being elected president.

By the early 1940s, the last remaining influence from Ritter's family beginnings in Park City was taken from him. After Willis Adams's death, Mary Adams lived alone in the bungalow at the edge of Fairmont Park. Willis was devoted to her, taking a hot meal to her every day for seven or eight years until she died in March 1945.[42] Ritter's mother had left him when he was seventeen, taking his sister and two brothers with her. His father gave him up to Willis and Mary Adams shortly after and died in 1925. Willis Adams died in 1932, and now Mary, his foster mother, was gone. Family underpinnings, support, and stability for the tests of character that lay ahead were surely diminished in the process. He was left with the newfound friends and associates of his professional life to defend against the assault on his character that would shortly be mounted by his political and religious rivals.

But the warfare Ritter was conducting with Clark, Grant, and the conservative Republican establishment was about to be snuffed out—replaced by real and deadly warfare. The consequences, for Willis W. Ritter, would be the issues of character that would dog him for the rest of his life.

5

ASPIRATION

> The heroic hours of life do not announce their presence by drum and trumpet, challenging us to be true to ourselves by appeals to the martial spirit that keeps the blood at heat. Some little, unassuming, unobtrusive choice presents itself before us slyly and craftily, glib and insinuating, in the modest garb of innocence.... Then it is that you will be summoned to show the courage of adventurous youth.
>
> —Benjamin N. Cardozo

Captain Mervyn Sharp Bennion's torso was ripped by a bomb as he stood on the bridge, in command of the battleship *West Virginia.* Seaman Dory Miller, a cook on *West Virginia,* braved the inferno created by burning oil from *Arizona,* sinking adjacent to *West Virginia,* risking his life to carry Bennion from his command station, over protests that he must do what he could to save the men and the ship and resist attack.

Bennion originated on a remote cattle ranch along Vernon Creek in Tooele County, Utah. He did not stay long on the ranch, appointed to the United States Naval Academy in 1906. He married Annie Louise Clark, a farm girl originating in Grantsville, Utah, a few leagues beyond the lower end of Vernon Creek. Bennion met and wooed Annie at her father's home on Sixteenth Street, Washington, D.C., rather than on the farm, while he was assigned to the Bureau of Ordnance. Annie's father had become an important official in the Office of the Attorney General, then an international lawyer in New York City, assistant secretary of state, and ambassador to Mexico.[1] After that, he became a prominent leader of the Mormon Church. Captain Bennion was the son-in-law of the arch political rival of Willis W. Ritter, J. Reuben Clark Jr.

The chaotic scene that morning of December 7, 1941, was at Pearl Harbor, Oahu Island, Territory of Hawaii. Bennion had been given command of *West Virginia,* on June 21, 1941. He was helpless, however, to save his ship and his men from the torpedoes launched by a sneak minisubmarine or from the swarm of Japanese bombers that attacked, without warning, out of the clouds. Captain Bennion was mortally wounded and awarded the Congressional Medal of Honor, posthumously, for his valor, Miller the Navy Cross, for he was African American, and blacks were not awarded the Medal of Honor in those days.[2]

The attack on Pearl Harbor thrust the United States into World War II. Large numbers of students were diverted to the war effort and professional personnel and resources of higher education converted to the national defense. The immediate consequence, for Willis W. Ritter, was a forced truce in the political warfare he had engaged in with Clark and a rather abrupt end to his teaching career, at least as a full-time professor of law.

Not long after Pearl Harbor John A. Carroll, of Colorado, came to Utah, recruiting the best men he could find to staff the Office of Price Administration, which had been formed by the federal government to control and prevent wartime inflation. Carroll, who had been given the job of organizing the legal staff of the OPA for the states of Colorado, Wyoming, Montana, Idaho, Utah, and New Mexico, asked the University of Utah and the Utah State Bar for the names of outstanding lawyers who could be recruited to staff the important wartime program. On the recommendation of Dean William F. Leary, Carroll recruited Ritter.[3]

Ritter was reluctant at first, but after a great deal of persuasion finally agreed to go with the OPA for a period of six months, then remained with the agency much longer. On July 25, 1942, Ritter was appointed OPA area rent director in Salt Lake City. State administrator for Utah was H. Grant Ivins, son of the late Mormon leader Anthony W. Ivins. Rents were fixed under legislation enacted by Congress, but Ritter's attitude, and the policy of the Utah office, was that the owners of apartments would have a fair opportunity to establish rents that were in effect on the date of the act creating OPA, thereby protecting them from an unreasonably low rental that might bankrupt them.

The owners of rental properties in Utah were generally pleased with Ritter's appointment at first, but within two months there was a division of local enforcement from executive functions. On September 16, 1942, Ritter was transferred to Denver, Colorado, as regional rent executive, where he lived at the Denver Athletic Club. He no longer established policy and was required to implement instructions from Washington. The strategy, directed from above, required him to drive rents down to the lowest possible level.[4] As a consequence, relations between Ritter and the Utah rental property owners, and with Ivins, became unsatisfactory. His attitude appeared to have become arbitrary, and it was, because of the policy imposed on him. His arbitrariness may have been the beginning of a similar attitude for which he was criticized after becoming a judge.

A considerable part of Ritter's work at the OPA involved recruiting employees. He acquired a reputation for accurately sizing people up quickly, a trait that would later distinguish him as a judge and at the same time provoke controversy. Ritter was absent from his desk in Denver a great deal of the time. His duties required him to visit cities in six different states covered by the regional office. During his trips to Albuquerque, a friendship evolved with a female employee named Phyllis Katz, the secretary to George C. Taylor, the OPA administrator and rent executive in the Albuquerque office. "She was a great reader and they would talk about different things, lots of such conversations about books." Ritter was "sociably inclined," always taking people with him to lunch and dinner, and Katz was often in the crowd. "Phyllis had rather poor health," Taylor recalled, "and they were concerned about taking care of her." Ritter, with his expertise in trusts and estate planning, suggested means to do so, and the Katz family wanted to do what he said.[5]

Ritter had a reputation for having a quick, brilliant legal mind, as one who handled matters assigned him ably and with dispatch. His background as a tax attorney, and earlier experience before the Board of Tax Appeals in Washington, D.C., gave him considerable experience in administrative law; he was considered a good lawyer, and his opinions and judgment were solicited and relied upon in legal problems that arose at the OPA. He also had the ability, when concentrating, to ignore extraneous things not pertaining to the matter at issue, which made him appear to some as aloof and arrogant. Others found him uncompromising or tactless. All in all, he was not a smooth administrator.

Because it was necessary for Ritter to enforce rules and regulations established by his superiors and see that their orders were obeyed, many resented his authority and considered him autocratic. His personal traits of quickness, concentration, and ability to size up a person magnified that impression. Clerical employees who worked with Ritter had varying impressions of him, some finding him brusque, dogmatic, and dictatorial, while others saw him as able, efficient, and commanding of respect. Unanimous, however, was their opinion that he was temperate, loyal, and of good moral character.

Friction between Ritter and the owners of rental units in Utah eventually erupted on March 10, 1943, when the OPA promulgated what was known as "Regulation IX." Intended to protect the large influx of tenants in areas surrounding defense-related facilities, it provided that if a tenant had continuously occupied a motor court for sixty days or more, the landlord was obligated to fix a monthly rental rate. The Utah Motor Court Association opposed the regulation, reasoning that they should be subject to the same regulations as hotels and that motor-court owners in the Ogden area were discriminated against because of the large number of defense-related facilities in the vicinity.

A meeting with the motor-court owners was arranged in Salt Lake City, with Glen D. Reese and Grant Ivins in attendance. Ritter explained the regulations and that it was his duty to enforce them. Dean Daynes, president of the Utah Motor Court Association, was vigorous in his opposition. There were "hot words on both sides." The Utah group declared that it would not comply with the regulation, that it was a deliberate attempt to ruin their business, and Daynes walked out of the meeting.[6]

Rep. Howard W. Smith (D-VA) held hearings in Washington, D.C. Ritter testified before the Smith committee on May 20, 1943, and denied being the "father" of the regulation. The regulation was "hatched" in Washington, Ritter declared, but he admitted that the Denver office of the OPA had a hand in putting the heat on the motor courts. The motor courts themselves had changed the nature of their business from a daily to a monthly basis, Ritter explained, and had served some tenants for as long as ten months but were still charging on a daily basis. The industry's recourse was to "show cause" to Reese why the regulation should not be enforced. "The situation in Utah as regards those motor courts is so unique," Smith declared, "and the practices of OPA rent control officials so arbitrary [that] we must have an explanation."

The press reported that committee chairman Smith dismissed Ritter, declaring his testimony evasive. "We are going to get to the bottom of that Utah situation," Smith concluded. "If governmental practices are being invoked which will drive a legitimate industry into bankruptcy, we will try to find some way of changing all that."[7]

Paul Porter, deputy administrator in charge of rent in Washington, D.C., evidently disagreed with the press accounts and wrote an open letter to Ritter, published in the *Salt Lake Tribune* on June 16, 1943, thanking him for a "forceful and lucid explanation before that committee of certain of the problems which face us in the Rocky Mountain region." Claims in the press were refuted by Porter.

> I think it is quite unfair to the committee as well as yourself to say you were dismissed with "open expressions of disgust." ... [T]he decision to call on this office for explanation was announced at the hearings before you took the stand and not afterward.... Our efforts to control rents, which constitute the largest single item in the cost of living have so far been successful largely due to patriotic efforts of men such as yourself in whose selection patriotism and ability have been the sole test.[8]

Congressman Smith apparently agreed with Porter's account, and differed with that of the press. When questioned about it by the FBI, he was able to recall nothing irregular about Ritter's testimony.[9]

In January 1944 Ritter went to John A. Carroll, who had recruited him to the OPA, and announced that he intended to resign. The strife generated by the Smith committee hearings and implicit in administering wartime price controls might have been reason enough to leave, but Ritter had a special reason. He confided in Carroll that he was leaving to reestablish himself in Salt Lake City, revive and enlarge his law practice, make some money, and otherwise place himself in the best possible position to secure an appointment as United States District Judge for the District of Utah, which had been promised him by his friend Senator Elbert D. Thomas.[10]

Ritter's resignation as OPA regional rent executive was on January 20, and his service was terminated February 8, 1944. When he took the job he said he would stay only six months. Not until a year and a half later could he bring himself to believe the program could continue without his personal skills, which by then he was well aware of. He returned to Salt Lake City and his family, which continued residing in the house on University Street.[11]

As Ritter was confiding in Carroll, and returning to Utah, word had been circulating in Utah legal and political circles that eighty-six-year-old United States District Court judge Tillman D. Johnson was ready to retire. He was a lifelong Democrat who came from Tennessee in his early years to practice law in Ogden. President Woodrow Wilson appointed Johnson United States District Judge for the District of Utah in 1915.

Lawyers and politicians had been anticipating Judge Johnson's retirement for years. He could have retired in 1928, at age seventy, and lived comfortably on his pension. He boasted over the next sixteen years that he had saved the government many thousands of dollars by not retiring, for otherwise the government would have had to pay him and his replacement simultaneously.

The matter of Judge Johnson's replacement was of considerable importance, for appointments to the United States District Court are among the prized plums of politics. Federal judges at the district level have great influence. They are few in number, compared with state judges, and although their decisions are subject to review and correction on appeal, few of them are challenged, and the presumption in favor of regularity of the trial court decision results in far fewer of them being reversed. The doctrine of federal supremacy adds to the importance of decisions by federal judges, and, in 1944, the trend commencing with the New Deal era to usurp the minutia of commercial and social intercourse with federal laws and regulations, which tended to dilute the majesty of federal decisions, was still in its early stages. All of those factors were magnified in one-judge districts like the District of Utah, where judicial authority was vested in a single person.

Darrell Greenwell, the newspaper man from Ogden having associations with prominent Democrats of the 1930s and '40s dating from his days as a Friedenker, reported that Abe Murdock, the junior U.S. senator from Utah, had approached Thomas about the judgeship sometime in early 1943: "I sounded out Abe Murdock on the Judge situation in Utah. It seems evident to me that he would like to be U.S. Judge but he told me that Thomas is pledged to Dan B. Shields for the job. Abe seemingly is quite provoked about Elbert's attitude."[12]

Shields was an eminent, successful Salt Lake City lawyer and a prominent Democrat. It was widely known in Democratic Party circles that Thomas was committed to Shields as a result of their exchange of political favors in 1932, when Shields agreed to withdraw from seeking the Senate nomination and leave the field to Thomas. Thomas kept the first part of their bargain and nominated Shields as United States Attorney for the District of Utah, which office he had held for more than a decade, but before Judge Johnson gave up, implicating the second part of the bargain, Shields gave out—in the sense that he reached an age beyond which he could reasonably expect to be named by Thomas to the judgeship. Johnson had frustrated their deal by living longer than either of them anticipated and refusing to retire.[13] Thus, if Thomas's commitment to Shields was still in effect at the end of 1943, it was of little concern and soon to expire. Unknown to the community at the time, Thomas had promised Ritter the position, in lieu of Shields. Therefore, Ritter had good reason to expect to be Judge Johnson's replacement.

Ritter reported to the University of Utah Board of Regents on March 10, 1944. True to the information he had given Carroll, he confirmed that he had resigned from government service to engage in private practice and requested that he be allowed to continue on leave as a professor of law without pay. The request was approved, subject to recall if his services were needed for teaching.[14]

He established an office in the Walker Bank Building, in the heart of the business district of Salt Lake City. Stationery was printed: "Willis W. Ritter, Attorney at Law and Tax Counselor." La Rue Burke was employed as his secretary.

Ritter's demonstrated, widely acknowledged, extraordinary talent—his fine scholastic record at the University of Chicago and Harvard, twenty years as a respected law professor and part-time practitioner, and expert knowledge of tax, property, and trust law—would be qualifications he could offer in support of his candidacy. He knew, however, that within hours of public announcement of his nomination, there would be those who would say, whatever his accomplishments and no matter how distinguished, that he had never been a significant practitioner of the law. A man can't run a courtroom, they would say, if he's never spent years fighting it out in one.

He had practiced law, of course. He had practiced with Morris, Kixmiller, and Baar, and carried on a private practice, to a limited extent, during all his years as a teacher. His work at the OPA was also in the capacity of a lawyer. Ritter knew, however, that Morris, Kixmiller, and Baar was too far in the past and too early in his career to prove his ability as a practitioner, and his work while engaged as a professor would be dismissed as mere dabbling. His employment at the OPA was administrative and did not require him to go to court. But when his name was announced to fill a judicial vacancy, if he were visibly engaged as a working lawyer serving a substantial clientele, that should provide strong evidence of his ability to conduct a traditional practice that would be clear and immediate and should surely allay questions about his professional credentials.

He quickly readjusted to life on University Street with his wife and four children. The home was filled with books, which the children were encouraged to read, and a piano each of them learned to play. "Always ask why," Willis instructed, and he echoed Roosevelt's precept that "the only thing to fear is fear itself." Dinner, always served meticulously on white linen, was a time when the family shared their feelings, thoughts, and experiences.

On Sundays they often drove to Park City and visited Aunt Min or other friends of Willis. Ritter explained how the canyons were formed, why the rock formations were of different colors, and the causes of erosion and earthquakes. Rita, the naturalist, joined in the discussions and urged Ritter to talk about growing up in Park City, about going into the mines riding a bucket tramway, about life at the hot pots and childhood fantasies, like planting a nickel to see if it would grow a money tree. Many weekends they went on hikes, picnicked in the mountains, or went horseback riding.

The Ritters were an affectionate, caring family. If Rita had anxiety, any at all, concerning Ritter's year and a half spent with the OPA, she never let on to anyone outside of the family. She did suggest to Nancy that they should go to Albuquerque and confront Phyllis Katz,[15] however, and the following typewritten lover's note of June 25, 1947, delivered to his law office, may have signaled some apprehension:

It only takes a little wound
To bleed a dream to death,
And loveliness may die, deprived
Of but a single breath.

No less may love, that joyful tree
Which bears divinest fruit,
Be toppled by a single fear
Gnawing at the root.[16]

Summer vacations were also educational experiences. There were visits to state parks, old mining towns, places of historical interest, and Indian reservations. The children invited their friends to go with them, but many of them couldn't because their Mormon parents considered it a sin not to rest on Sundays. Some even objected that the Ritters drank Coca-Cola. Many of their friends couldn't go to the Ritter house to play because Ritter was Catholic. Rita, of course, was Mormon, as were Ritter's paternal grandparents, the Chamberlains, and the children were all baptized into the Mormon Church but were largely nonpracticing. Rumors were circulated about them, and one neighbor wouldn't speak to them because they were not active Mormons. Ritter's attitude was that children should make those decisions for themselves, when old enough to do so.[17] Others' viewpoints seemed so complicated, restrictive, and full of fear, compared with the Ritters' respect for nature, individual rights, interest in people, and appreciation for life. The family had a talk about it and decided to go on with their lives. They felt sad for those who did not share their love for life, but wished them well.[18]

Christmas was special. They would get a tree—Willis's favorite was a blue spruce. They would decorate, then make taffy. Willis seemed to have the recipe in his head, no doubt from when he was left in charge of the children in Park City, and they would pull the candy until it was almost white. Willis remembered that from his childhood, too. Willis was a "hugger," and both he and Rita were sympathetic, giving, and caring.

Bill and Nancy were the eldest, separated by two years. Five years separated Nancy from Mary (Puddy) and two between Puddy and John. Nancy married at seventeen, and Bill went away to school at Stanford when Puddy and John were still children. There was thus a demarcation between the two older children and the two younger ones. They were in some respects like two families.[19]

Ritter's return was not with a vague plan and the mere hope that he could corral enough new business to add to his former clients to make it succeed. He had an agreement in hand that almost, by itself, constituted a law practice. His next-door neighbor on Butler Avenue, Morris Rosenblatt, and Morris's brother Joe, had been his clients from time to time during his years as a professor and had asked him to come back to Salt Lake City and attend to their personal affairs, their tax problems in particular.[20] The Rosenblatt family and their enterprises would be Ritter's principal clientele. Morris and Willis shared an enthusiasm for and commitment to the New Deal philosophy and FDR. They were friends of Elbert Thomas and had worked closely with him on each of his election campaigns.

The Rosenblatts had been engaged in steel fabrication for many years. Their companies, which included Eimco Corporation, Structural Steel and Forge Company, and American Foundry Plant and Machine Company, employed six hundred and manufactured steel and iron castings, fabricated buildings, and bridges. The hardware requirements of the war had made their business into an enterprise equal in size to any comparable in the United States, including U.S. Steel. They supplied the government, among other items, with mine-loading machines used for excavations in Malta and bomb-proofing material that went to London and other Allied target areas.[21]

The Rosenblatts had promised Ritter an annual retainer of $9,000. In 1944 that sum was more than a comfortable income. It was much more than his 1941-1942 law school salary of $3,885, and nearly double his annual OPA salary of $4,600.[22] He was, indeed, going to make some money and clearly liked the idea. But money was not the important thing to Willis W. Ritter. If it were, he would never have wanted the judgeship, nor would he have stayed in teaching for almost twenty years. Those occupations may bring satisfaction, and prestige, but they don't bring riches. This is not to say that he disdained money, for he enjoyed the things that money brought him. Pursuit of money did not rule Willis W. Ritter, however. The pursuit of a judicial appointment was the important thing.

Retaining him was not a matter of friendship or politics, for the Rosenblatts valued his counsel and advice. "His work was very satisfactory," Joe Rosenblatt affirmed. "He was entirely reliable. He knew the tax code." Ritter was only one of several attorneys employed by the Rosenblatts, but he was the sole attorney who handled their tax and estate matters.[23]

Ritter would not be a "kept" lawyer for the Rosenblatts, however. Abe Glassman, his Friedenker friend and occasional client from pre-OPA days, also had need of his services. A major part of the Glassman business was the *Ogden Standard-Examiner,* a newspaper and related publishing business that had prospered during the war, due in part to the population increase that had resulted from military-related facilities in and around Ogden. George Hatch, who married Glassman's daughter and Rita's friend and fellow outdoor enthusiast, Gene, had broadened the family interests into broadcasting and also needed Ritter's services.

The Rosenblatt and Glassman enterprises accounted for a large portion of Ritter's business, at least initially, but it was not long before other friends and former clients engaged him. The Stanley Bradshaw interests in Cedar City, which had expanded to include Bradshaw Home and Auto Supply, Bradshaw Finance Company, and Arrowhead Gas and Oil, in addition to Bradshaw Chevrolet, were reestablished as his clients and reorganized by Ritter as a corporation in 1948 as part of a continuing tax plan. Don Lloyd was manager of Utah Retail Grocers, whose articles of incorporation were written by Ritter in 1940. The association had grown into Associated Food Stores, many of the members of which used the articles composed by Ritter. He continued to do such legal work as Lloyd and his associated businesses required, and together with Rita attended conferences, seminars, and other conclaves with Lloyd and his wife, Helen, on the West Coast and in Chicago, New Orleans, Washington, D.C., and Honolulu.[24]

Ritter's reputation quickly grew. He became counsel to real estate promoters in the Ogden area, including the Washington Terrace residential project. Arthur Wooley, an Ogden trial lawyer with an extensive practice, observed that after Ritter came to town, he took the "cream" of the Ogden business. "I just know from the fact that I didn't get it that he got quite a lot," Wooley declared. Particularly with respect to trust matters, income tax matters, and winding up people's troubles generally, "I know my expectations were not always realized that they were going to hire me."[25] Wooley thus paid sideways tribute to Ritter's success as a lawyer and ability to bring in clients who gave him a lot of work and paid him well for his services.

Among the friends and former clients resuming their relationship with Ritter was C. R. "Ted" Jones and American Keene Cement and Plaster Company. American Keene's plaster and cement mill at Sigurd, for which Ritter won the foreclosure suit in 1939, had not been a very successful operation through the Depression. Jones got sick, decided he wanted to get out, and talked to Sid Eliason, the western sales manager of United States Gypsum Company, about buying it. Then Jones died without any sale being negotiated, Ritter explained.

> We went through a lot of estate problems [resulting in Ritter becoming a principal]. This is how I got my interest [in the company]. I acquired stock for my fees and very early turned that stock, all of it as it came along, over to a trustee, a family trust. My wife's been a trustee, has been since around '37 for herself and my four kids.... I have acted as a trustee simply to represent my family there and primarily because I had grown up with this thing."[26]

After Eliason turned Jones down on the proposed sale, he decided, in 1946, to lease the American Keene claims and negotiated an agreement to that effect, drafted by Ritter, on behalf of United States Gypsum Company. When the negotiations started, and they could see that they would no longer be carrying on gypsum operations, the American Keene shareholders abandoned the corporation and exchanged their stock for shares in the property. They established the American Gypsum Trust, composed of the Ritter family and approximately fifty or sixty persons in Sevier County, Utah. "United States Gypsum Company owned some gypsum claims here at Sigurd," Ritter explained. "They adjoined the American Gypsum Trust claims on the west... so United States Gypsum people were well acquainted with the gypsum deposits down in this area."[27]

Ritter said of his meeting with Eliason, "When he came in, he was interested in acquiring some kind of an ownership in our claims. They wanted to put a plant in down here at Sigurd and they wanted to make some deal with us and so we had some negotiations about that."[28] The plant was a success, eventually dominating the market west of the Rocky Mountains for wallboard, which was replacing plaster in building construction.[29] Ritter gradually acquired the interest of the small owners in Sevier County and transferred them to his family trust. The plant and properties of the American Gypsum Trust were eventually acquired by the Georgia-Pacific Corporation, subject to a fifty-year lease with royalties on production, also negotiated by Ritter.[30]

In the courtroom, Ritter marked himself as an "ardent protagonist" and "an extremely strong advocate" who "sees things his way and drives by every means possible to that end." That trait was described by Quentin Cannon, who knew Ritter at the OPA where Cannon was an investigator. Cannon was an assistant district enforcement attorney for the OPA after Ritter had returned to private practice in Salt Lake City and was assigned to prosecute Salt Lake City car dealer Ivy Walton for excessive prices under the Emergency Price Control Act. The car dealer was a friend and roommate of Ritter from his days at the University of Chicago, and Ritter agreed to represent him.[31] Perhaps thinking his association with Walton and his former position with the OPA would raise questions, Ritter associated another Salt Lake City lawyer, Ed Jensen, to present the evidence for the defense. Jensen angered Cannon by calling the OPA investigators "stool pigeons" and "under cover men." Cannon thought those accusations unfounded and offensive, for Ritter knew, Cannon said, that OPA investigators were required to disclose their identities and had no power to arrest anyone. Ritter himself presented the closing argument to the jury, echoing Jensen's accusation.

After the jury retired to deliberate, Ritter followed Cannon into the cloakroom. "In his scornful manner...he berated me, used profane language, charged me with persecuting honest businessmen and stated that he was surprised that I would bring such a case, and that no jury would ever convict on evidence such as I had presented." Further offensive was Ritter's assertion, according to Cannon, that he would write to Senator Thomas and tell him of Cannon's action and "get [me] canned."[32] Cannon felt vindicated when the jury found Walton guilty on all counts.

When Ritter decided to leave the OPA, he couldn't know how much time he would have to bolster his credentials and add to his bank account—maybe weeks and perhaps months. Custom, however, and practicality in ensuring continuity in the operation of the courts gave him reason to expect that Judge Johnson would give notice for a substantial period before stepping down—perhaps even years. Whether the interim period was long or short, though, his downtown office, his substantial clientele, and the reputation he was building as one primarily occupied with the practice of law would diminish, at the very least, any claim that his only credentials were academic.

The rumors of Judge Johnson's imminent retirement, which had brought Ritter back to Salt Lake City, were uncertain, at best. Ritter therefore had to occupy himself with other pursuits, while he waited for Johnson's decision. Meanwhile, Arthur Vivian Watkins, Ritter's virtual neighbor from his childhood days in Midway, was emerging as a player on the Utah political scene. Watkins was about to become a threat to Ritter's aspirations, or attempt to be one.

6

DEFERRAL

> Competition has many times caused distress and failure; for competition does not think or feel; still, thus far, we have found nothing to take the place of competition excepting monopoly, which is but a modern form of slavery. Unrestricted business tends toward monopoly. It gives an advantage to the strong, the clever, the selfish and unscrupulous. It is the rule of the jungle. The problem in business, and in life, has always been to preserve freedom without monopoly.... We have solved it as we do most questions by taking both courses at the same time.
>
> —Clarence Darrow

Ensuring that both Elbert Thomas and Franklin Delano Roosevelt remained in office had become most important to Willis W. Ritter's aspirations. Both must face reelection in 1944, and Roosevelt, whose health, persistently raising questions, was already subject to public outcry against seeking an unprecedented fourth term. Should Thomas lose or the Republicans defeat President Roosevelt, as they and their prospective nominee, Thomas E. Dewey, were getting ready to mount an all-out campaign to do, Thomas's promise would amount to nothing. Ritter therefore occupied himself with helping with the reelection of both of them, and adding to his own political credentials as well.

He got in touch with his old friends and political compatriots. He was voting-district chairman and a member of the Democratic Party Committee in the elections following his return. In 1946 he was made chairman of the Democratic State Convention.[1] He may have served in those capacities because of a taste for politics, developed during his campaigns on behalf of Thomas, but he was surely aware that in the political climate of the day, party officials would be consulted on any appointive office. Active involvement in the affairs of the Democratic Party would be qualifications he could point to when the time came for judicial appointment.

Senator Thomas announced publicly in April 1944 that he would seek a third term. In May the delegates to the Utah Democratic Convention nominated Thomas to be the party's senatorial candidate by acclamation. They further showed their regard for him by mandating that the state's ten votes be cast for Thomas as vice-presidential candidate in July at the impending National Democratic Party Convention. President Roosevelt fared a little less well, with a scattering of nay votes heard among the near-unanimous yeas when his name was called.[2]

Ritter's return to Utah occurred just in time for him to get involved in Thomas's reelection campaign. The small group that had planned and executed the two previous Thomas campaigns—Morris Rosenblatt, Leo Marshall, Delbert Draper, and Ritter—came together once again. The Ritter home was designated the mailing bureau, and his office was the campaign headquarters. He was, even more than in previous campaigns, the central, moving force in the reelection effort.

The outlook for Thomas's reelection was favorable. Twelve years as senator had made him well known in his own right, and as an ally and supporter of FDR and his policies, especially those calculated to bring the country out of the Great Depression and those that mobilized and prepared the nation to fight the largest war in history. Thomas could, and did, point to his record in Congress and claim responsibility for much progressive legislation "which curtails dangerous Wall Street speculations; which guarantees the safety of our bank deposits; that gives labor its constitutional right to organize, and bargain collectively; that gives us electrification on the farms; that builds the dams; repletes our ruined forests; conserves the soil; helps poor but deserving students to finish their college training... removes the curse of insecurity, gives us unemployment insurance and old age pensions."[3]

To assume that Ritter's motive in working for Thomas's reelection was purely self-serving would be to ignore the fierce loyalty and persistence of which he was capable. It would also ignore his political views and the fondness and regard he felt for his long-time mentor, friend, colleague, and political compatriot. He also loved to get into a good political fight, especially with the Utah Republican establishment.

Whether the public's perception, linking Thomas to Roosevelt, would help or hurt was an open question. Most incumbent Democrats running for national office were linked in the public mind with Roosevelt, but for Thomas that perception was so entrenched that his reelection would depend as much on how the Utah voters felt about Roosevelt as how they felt about Thomas. Thomas came into office with Roosevelt and throughout his twelve years in Congress had been a vigorous and outspoken advocate of New Deal policies.

The most immediate, pressing domestic, national, and international issues came together under one heading—the war— winning it and winning it soon, and getting back to normal domestic life. But more attention and debate centered on Roosevelt's frail physical condition and concern that he was not strong enough to endure another term, particularly the strain of presiding over the war. Roosevelt had already shattered precedent, however, by running for and being elected to a third term. At the same time, the idea was difficult to swallow, including to some Democrats, that any president would run for, much less serve, an unprecedented fourth term.

As it happened, the Allies had made important, though costly, advances in 1944, including victory in the European theater. News articles about reconversion were a sign that the war was going well. "Output Controls Wait Slash after Nazi Fall," read the headline of a report that the War Production Board was making plans to end most of the wartime controls that had been created to minimize inflation and the manufacture of civilian goods, some of which Ritter had administered. "The fewer the restrictions the quicker will be reconversion and re-employment," said a spokesman for that agency.

Questions about Roosevelt were secondary to the pervasive reality of the war—loss of loved ones, upheaval in domestic life, and the lingering possibility of defeat in the Pacific theater. Reelection of Roosevelt could be a sign that the public was not displeased with the administration's handling of the war. Such reports may have helped the incumbent administration, and Thomas, as did perhaps a fear of changing leadership while the war continued.

The Republicans assembled in Chicago the last week in June 1944 and formally nominated Thomas E. Dewey. He accepted the nomination, blasting the "tired old men" of Roosevelt's administration, thereby setting the tone of the campaign to follow. The war was declared "outside the realm of partisan politics," but Dewey declared the New Deal had grown "old and tired and quarrelsome." Then he charged, quoting a *New York Times* columnist, that FDR instructed Democratic Party chairman Robert Hannegan to "clear everything with Sidney." Sidney Hillman was a Lithuanian-born Jew, leader of the Congress of Industrial Organizations (CIO), and former Socialist who had kind words for the Russian people, allies of the United States in the war. As the campaign progressed, Dewey lumped Hillman with Earl Browder, chairman of the Communist Political Association, and called them "the Hillman-Browder axis."[4]

When the Democratic National Convention convened in July, expectation of Ritter and Utah Democrats that Thomas might attain the vice-presidential nomination was real and greater than with ordinary favorite-son nominations. In that era, when vice-presidential candidates were selected by delegates rather than by the person heading the ticket, in actual contests usually influenced and sometimes controlled by power brokers, there was reason for Ritter's confidence that a favorite-son candidate might succeed. Henry A. Wallace, the incumbent vice president, was favored by labor and other liberal elements of the party, but linked with the Communists and opposed by southerners and conservatives, whereas James F. "Jimmy" Byrnes of South Carolina, favored by southerners and conservatives, was looked upon as a segregationist and opposed by liberals and labor. The situation was ripe for a dark horse.

Thomas's impressive legislative record, important committee assignments, seniority in the Senate, and monthly Japanese-language broadcasts at the behest of the U.S. government had all marked him as an important man in Washington. The *New York World Telegram* had published an article the previous year stating that Jack Bell, an Associated Press political writer, had called Thomas a "dark horse" candidate for the vice-presidential nomination.[5] Bell cited Thomas's expert knowledge of Japan and the overriding significance of the war in the coming election as reasons for believing that he was a serious candidate.

Thomas was not, himself, a delegate to the national convention. It was the custom of the time for major office holders to automatically be delegates, but Thomas had declined because he would be on the road from Washington to Salt Lake City to attend the annual state holiday on July 24 commemorating the arrival of the Mormon pioneers. Neither was Ritter a delegate, but he went to the convention anyway, and Rita went with him. He went as a spokesman, of sorts, for Thomas, but may also have gone for the fun of it. Besides the parties (not of the political variety), the convention was a lively one.

An old-fashioned party row, with President Roosevelt and a host of vice-presidential hopefuls at the center of it, engulfed the first wartime political convention in eighty years in tumultuous discord Wednesday. The storm broke while delegates crammed Chicago's big brick stadium to hear Governor Robert Kerr of Oklahoma, the keynoter, start a whooping, stampeding, parading demonstration by declaring the war was being won by some "tired old men," including the sixty-two-year-old President Roosevelt. It reached its intensity after the chief executive, wielding remote-control influence on the convention, purportedly communicated to national chairman Hannegan that after Vice President Wallace, he favored Senator Harry Truman of Missouri or Supreme Court justice William O. Douglas for a running mate.[6] A "surprise" candidate had appeared, and it was not Elbert D. Thomas. As a result of President Roosevelt's very specific statement of preference, little room was left for favorite sons.

On Thursday, the day following the president's statement, Ritter sent Thomas a telegram describing the situation and asking suggestions for organizing a "Thomas for Vice President" campaign. Receiving no response, presumably because Thomas was still on the road to Utah, Ritter told reporters that Abe Murdock, Utah's junior senator and head of the Utah delegation, would place Thomas's name in nomination as planned.

Senator Harry S. Truman, the surprise candidate that had appeared, was lightly regarded in the Senate but had won stature and respect for his investigation, largely one-man, of corruption in wartime defense industries. Some may have thought that the president's statement would cause such upheaval among supporters of favorite sons that only a dark horse could get enough votes to win. Ritter appears to have been among those of that view. He said that he believed scattered support for Thomas existed in other delegations and that Utah would solicit that support as soon as Thomas gave the word. Members of the Utah delegation, loyal as they were to Thomas, were nevertheless saying privately that because of the president's statement, they hoped he would withdraw and do so soon.[7]

On Friday, July 21, 1944, President Roosevelt accepted the party's nomination to run for a fourth term and predicted that the world would be at peace within four years.[8] On Saturday, Murdock placed Thomas's name before the convention, citing his eminence in the Senate as a ranking member of the Military Affairs Committee, chairman of the Education and Labor Committee, and the experience and knowledge he had gained during his twelve years in Washington. He referred to him as an FDR Democrat, a scholar, author, and liberal humanitarian who had demonstrated courage and persistence in the fight against labor espionage (that is, through the Taft-Hartley bill).

Under the prevailing-unit rule, the Utah delegation's votes went to Thomas on the first ballot. Truman won nomination on the second ballot. Utah was the last state to give its votes to Truman. Utah's votes went to Murdock's favorite, Wallace, on the second ballot, then were changed to Truman.

Meanwhile, Ritter was confronted with ever more powerful adversaries at home. J. Reuben Clark Jr., who had already abandoned the policy of noninterference in politics by the Mormon Church on the death of Anthony W. Ivins in 1934, was freed of the former first counselor's restraining influence. He responded by launching an all-out campaign against the New Deal.[9] In 1940 Clark gave vent to the church's thinly disguised, if at all, support for Republicans. The church-owned *Deseret News* published an unsigned "Church and State" editorial, composed by Clark, declaring—contrary to his 1923 statement of noninvolvement by church officials—that "church leaders had the civil right to speak out on political issues," and the next day the *News* published an editorial of Clark titled "The Third Term Principle," asserting the "Constitutional danger" of electing a president to more than two terms. The rise of Clark, which was complete by 1944, marked a period of active, open support by the church for Republican candidates in opposition to policies of the New Deal and presented a formidable challenge for Ritter in the 1944 election.[10]

In February 1944 Ritter's friend Dean Brimhall, who was then in Washington, D.C., discovered a speech by Clark praising the United Nations Relief Administration and, in what he perceived as a "slip of the tongue," admitting that women of the Mormon Church Relief Society were "sometimes asked to help political candidates." That statement was to foretell the increased church involvement that was to be employed against both Thomas and Roosevelt, and in favor of their opponents, in the coming campaign. "Although you have lived in Utah these many years, I doubt very much whether you have heard such procedure admitted by a high Church authority," Brimhall remarked. He sent excerpts of the speech to John Fitzpatrick, publisher of the *Salt Lake Tribune,* and on June 30, 1944, enclosed excerpts from the same speech, including the relief-society item, in a letter to Ritter.[11] Brimhall then came to Utah in July to help in the Thomas campaign.

Ritter therefore found himself ever more in conflict with church influence in political affairs on behalf of Republican candidates, by Clark and other church officials with similar lack of constraint. Anti-Roosevelt and anti–New Deal since 1932, the church, and Clark in particular, appeared to have become less discreet about the constitutional separation of church and state. Ritter thus found "Rube" Clark an increasingly more influential adversary in the campaign to reelect Elbert D. Thomas, particularly after Thomas's opponent was nominated.[12]

Clark was no new adversary. He had opposed Thomas's initial election in 1932 and his reelection in 1938. His emergence as de facto leader of the

Mormon Church and its emissary to the Republican Party, and his connections with Thomas's opponent in the 1944 election, made his open use of his ecclesiastical calling for political purposes more of a challenge and all the more inappropriate.

The Republicans nominated Dr. Adam S. Bennion to be Thomas's opponent. Born at Taylorsville in 1886, and fatherless at an early age, Bennion worked on the family farm as a youth. He graduated from the University of Utah, became an English teacher at L.D.S. High School, principal of Granite High School, English professor at the University of Utah in 1917, and superintendent of education for the Mormon Church in 1919. After earning a Ph.D. in education at the University of California in 1923, and more than ten years of teaching, he became personnel director for Utah Power and Light Company in 1928. Levi Edgar Young, the Mormon "general authority" who performed the marriage ceremony for Willis and Rita, proclaimed Bennion "one of the most eloquent speakers in his [Mormon] church."[13]

Bennion was the cousin to Clark's daughter, Annie, by virtue of her marriage to the late hero of Pearl Harbor Captain Mervyn Sharp Bennion. Captain Bennion's appointment to Annapolis came through Senator Reed Smoot, and his marriage to Annie was at Clark's swank home at 21 West Twenty-third Street in New York City.[14] Clark, already an outspoken opponent of Thomas dating from his long and deep relationship with Smoot prior to 1932, intensified his opposition to Thomas in response to his familial connection with the Bennion kin.

If there is any constant in American politics, the practice of demonizing the opposition is nearly predictable. "Soft on crime," "right to life," and "moral majority" are slogans familiar to any observer of the American scene, used by actual conservatives and, as the twentieth-century wore on and the twenty-first arrived, by their "neo-con" decision makers to assign onus to their ideological counterparts, usually Democrats. Communism was the "bogeyman" of the Republicans in the 1944 election. As September 1944 wore on, Dewey addressed claims of Roosevelt's "indispensability," linking it to the bugaboo of communism, claiming: "He's indispensable to Sidney Hillman and the Political Action Committee, he's indispensable to Earl Browder, the ex-convict and pardoned communist leader."[15]

Whether because of a commitment to "take the high ground," by not criticizing the conduct of the war, or for lack of substance, Dewey continued in that vein for the duration of the campaign:

> Confronted with such a dearth of winning issues, Dewey fell back in the homestretch on the bogey of Communism. In a speech in Charleston, West Virginia, on October 7, he said that Washington now owned or operated a fifth of the nation's industrial plant, and accused Roosevelt of developing "little by little... our own corporate state." He reminded his audience that Earl Browder, just one week before, had endorsed the President in Madison Square Garden. Sidney Hillman became more than ever a lightning rod for criticism.... In the last week... [Dewey] painted a picture of Hillman "stalking the country squeezing dollars for the Fourth Term Campaign" from individual union members... and bluntly charged Roosevelt with pardoning Browder in time to organize support for the President's reelection.[16]

Dewey and other prominent Republicans accused the Democrats of "selling out" to radical elements, personified by Earl Browder and Sidney Hillman. The rise of J. Reuben Clark, Jr., intensified that rhetoric in Utah.[17]

Bennion picked up on the theme of Dewey and the national Republican Party and extended the anticommunist theme further by charging that "these leftists" wanted Thomas returned to the Senate. Bennion called Thomas a "rubber stamp" and said the voters had a choice between "New Dealers who would socialize us and Americans who would preserve our constitutional safeguards of liberty." Bennion charged, "Senator Thomas is either a communist or is a fellow traveler, or at least he is a henchman of Sidney Hillman," because "he has contributed articles to a magazine called 'The New Masses,'" favoring leftist causes.[18]

"Major problems" outlined by Bennion were all built on the communist bogeyman theme. He reasoned that his own election would be "the restoration to individuals [of] control of their lives, reestablishment of the Governmental balances which safeguard the republic; recognition of the mutuality of interests of labor and management under an American system of free, competitive enterprise; protection of management against the tyranny of racketeers, and freeing [of] farmers from regimentation."[19]

Ritter and the small group of confederates who planned and executed Thomas's campaigns countered that "Governor Dewey and Dr. Bennion are 'malefactors of great wealth,'" the "robber barons of our day and time." They were "controlled by the Republican old-guard," which led the fight to defeat the League of Nations in 1920—"the 'little group of wilful men,' as Woodrow Wilson called them." Ritter tied them into his 1936 lectures on politics and American government. "The issue in this election is an old one.

The objective of Jeffersonian Democracy from the beginning has been the welfare of the masses, who have always been its supporters in face of bitter and consistent opposition of wealth and the favored classes. The Republicans have supported Hamiltonian Republicanism from its origin to date."[20]

Ritter discovered a news item about a meeting of Utah mayors in Vernal that he thought confirmed his view. At the meeting, Bennion said he could "speak freely now that he had resigned as assistant to the President of Utah Power and Light Co." "Power trust Charlie McCarthy," Ritter crowed. What an "astounding admission! That he doesn't belong to the power trust anymore."

Thereafter, the "power trust" became a prominent theme of Thomas's campaign. "Dr. Bennion...used his abilities in a cause which his utility employers call 'the American way of life,'" Ritter wrote in a campaign flyer titled "The Power Trust Record of Dr. Adam S. Bennion." "For 16 years he has preached that cause...waving the flag of 'free enterprise' like a child in a parade."[21]

The power trust was not "free enterprise," Ritter rejoined. "It is amazing that the men who cry loudest these days for free enterprise are men associated with monopolies. The railroad magnate, the public utility executive, and their candidates for office make more noise about 'free enterprise' than anybody else. Now isn't that striking. Monopolists are not in favor of free enterprise. They are in favor of monopolies, and monopoly is the exact opposite of free enterprise."[22]

Ritter gave other speeches on behalf of Thomas, sometimes as his stand-in, broadcast on radio, in which he charged that Bennion, like Dewey, failed to take a meaningful stand and painted him as another laissez-faire warrior. "He will oppose everything that interferes with the special privileges of his associates and himself," and "in the event of Adam Bennion's election, he would represent the Chamber of Commerce, the corporations owned by out-of-state interests, the equivalent in this state of wealth, big business and old guard republicanism in the nation."[23]

Thomas was "incorruptible," by contrast, according to Ritter. That was proved by the fact that the Public Utility Holding Company Act of President Roosevelt passed by only one vote—that of Thomas. Thomas voted yea, while pressures were being applied by representatives of Utah Power and Light Company and the Electric Bond and Share Company, its owner. Thomas graphically demonstrated that he would not yield to intimidation by having their representatives seated in the gallery to witness his vote against them.[24]

> No campaign in recent years has sunk to such low levels as has the campaign of the opposition to Senator Thomas. They have no program. The candidate has gone up and down this state throwing out vague and windy generalities. His speeches are full of such empty generalities as, "America, the Land of Opportunity," "Work is the real magic of discovery," "Free Enterprise," "Youth of today have all of the potentialities of the youth of yesterday," "The American Way of Life." Mr. Bennion... said, "The future lies before us." Now isn't that profound! These quotations are a measure of the depth of candidate Bennion's thinking. If he had a program, he would state it. But he has none![25]

For fifteen years Adam S. Bennion had been a utility company executive, Ritter explained in his speeches to the voters, during which time no dividends were paid to stockholders. "But dividends were paid to the holding company in New York. He must have known what shenanigans they were up to. If he did know it, he should have resigned. If he did not know it, he is not smart enough to be a United States Senator."[26]

The Mormon Church itself, ever on the lookout for ways to weaken the New Deal in Utah, added its imprimatur to the Clark-Bennion rhetoric by publishing another *Deseret News* article against Utah's pro–New Deal governor, Herbert B. Maw. Claims that Maw's Republican opponent, J. Bracken Lee, a non-Mormon, ran a wide-open town as mayor of Price were discounted. Apostle Ezra Taft Benson said that he preferred "a non-Mormon with high principles to a Jack Mormon."[27]

As Thomas's campaign manager, Ritter was concerned that such misuse of the Mormon Church's powerful influence over politics might turn its members away from Thomas. Mormons were, nevertheless, overwhelmingly supporters of Roosevelt and the New Deal, so much so that church president Heber J. Grant complained that the saints "almost worship him."[28]

In October Thomas and Bennion appeared together in a debate in which Thomas said that the election amounted to a choice between tested programs and people and "the unknown." Bennion countered by repeating the anticommunist theme employed by Dewey and saying that "the indispensable-man philosophy," again expanding on Dewey's attack on Roosevelt, "is a step toward totalitarianism... a sign of decay."[29] Thomas's and Bennion's arguments echoed those made by the Roosevelt and Dewey supporters in the presidential election. That made the connection between Bennion's argument and the church position all the more obvious, as well as that Clark and the church were actively advocating the election of Bennion and the defeat of Thomas.

Thomas may have had little concern over the church's anti-Thomas, anti-Roosevelt, anti–New Deal attitude or Bennion attempting to link himself to it. Thomas had managed to win decisively in the previous two elections. His political views in opposition to those of the leaders of the church and his record as a U.S. senator were well known. Bennion was a member of the General Board of the Mormon Sunday School and of the Mormon Church Board of Education, which most Mormons would recognize as elevated positions within the church hierarchy, and he campaigned on his church credentials. But Thomas was a Mormon too, and indisputably a devout one.

Popular wisdom aside, born of Ritter's conflict with Clark and the church hierarchy, Ritter was not anti-Mormon. He had strong Mormon ties of his own. His grandmother Emma Chamberlain was a Mormon convert and pioneer settler of Charleston. Rita and the children were baptized Mormons. Those who worked closely with him when he became a judge observed him as being very fair in any case that had anything to do with the church. He went so far as to encourage his court reporter, Lucille Hallam, to take a leave of absence to go on a Mormon Church mission to Denmark.[30]

"You asked me... to explain why the Mormons take their politics so seriously," Ritter wrote to his friend and political soul mate since 1931, Dean Brimhall, in September 1944. Brimhall had questioned him concerning Clark's speeches about church welfare programs and the number of offices in the state capitol designated "business regulation." "I'll reply by asking you why so many of the Mormons are apparently going to vote for Adam Bennion this year. I am almost losing my faith in the people's intelligence."[31]

Voter surveys in October and early November 1944 indicated a general Democratic advantage, but not a large one. Ritter was not satisfied with winning by a little, however. He always set his sights on winning by a lot, and said as much to Brimhall:

> This is not only a good time to win an election for Tomie, but as I view it, this is the time to bury the myth that Adam Bennion is a great man. I should like to see such an avalanche of votes in opposition to him this time that not again in a generation would the cause of liberal government in this State be in jeopardy. To paraphrase the language of a man for

> whom I have little respect, let's assure liberal government to Utah "in our time." Adam is talking about a "crusade." My guess is that he's having a lot of difficulty thinking up things to talk about in his crusade. So far, all he has been able to talk about is glittering generalities like "the American Way of Life" and "Free Enterprise."
>
> You ought to be out here Dean. It is a good scrap, and it's one in which the issues are viewed clearly, though I hope the campaign soon will begin to throw the kind of stuff at Adam that he has coming to him.[32]

On Sunday, November 5, 1944, the *Salt Lake Tribune* editorialized against Roosevelt and in favor of Dewey. The *Tribune* had never supported FDR for election as president or vice president back to 1920, the editorial stated, and it criticized his supporters and administration for "riding a willing horse to his collapse." Bennion was quoted in the same edition, making the communist smear explicit by stating that "the election Tuesday is no ordinary election" but "a decision between new dealers who would socialize us and Americans who would preserve our constitutional safeguards of liberty," repeating again his claims throughout the campaign that Thomas was "a rubber stamp of the New Deal, one whom the leftists, including Sidney Hillman's PAC, wants returned to Washington."[33]

On Wednesday, November 8, 1944, Thomas was declared the winner in the Senate race. Nationally, Roosevelt was also the winner, but in Utah, other races, including for president, were yet too close to call. Utah was the last state to give its votes to Roosevelt. Ritter wrote to Brimhall, exuberant over the results. "It was a lot of fun.... Tomie defeated [Reed] Smoot by 30,000 votes (1932), Frank Harris by 21,000 votes (1938) and now polished off Adam Bennion with around 50,000 votes. I should think they would begin to see the writing on the wall pretty soon. Next time we can pull it off by acclamation, excluding [Rube] Clark and one or two of his satellites."[34]

Ritter's exuberance in victory came as much from the image of the vanquished lying beaten and bloodied on the battlefield as from the confirmation it gave him of the promised judgeship. The election was a vindication of Thomas's Senate record and of Democratic ideology. Thomas, in contrast, "viewed the campaign as a teaching process" and "disclaimed the tactics of those who... abandoned scientific objectivity."[35] Questions of whether Ritter abandoned scientific objectivity aside, he operated, at least partly, at a much more visceral level than did his friend and provided that essential element to the Thomas campaigns that Thomas was not capable of.

The 1944 election gave Ritter reason to believe, no doubt, that Thomas's promise of the judgeship was a good one. The two officials most important to the promise had been swept back into office. Exuberance aside, the 1944 election established a trend that was to bode ill for Thomas, and also for Ritter. The anticommunist rhetoric that had characterized the campaign would be used again against Thomas. Moreover, the 1944 election marked a disturbing political trend. Roosevelt had carried Utah, unexpectedly, by 31,999 votes in 1932 and increased that majority to 85,691 in 1936, but his majority shrunk to 61,126 in 1940 and narrowed further in 1944.[36] Republicans were resurgent in Utah, and elsewhere across the nation. Their tactics were established, and the communist bogeyman would soon be unloosed again, with Willis W. Ritter its prey.

7

VACILLATION

A university is a place from which men start for the Eternal City. In the university are pictured the ideals which abide in the City of God.

—Oliver Wendell Holmes Jr.

Throngs grieved for their fallen national leader at every whistle stop from Warm Springs, Georgia, to Washington, D.C., as the railroad car, veiled in black, passed by. The flag-draped coffin, carried by a caisson to the Capitol, might well carry the undoing of Willis W. Ritter's ambition as well.

The April following the 1944 election, President Franklin Delano Roosevelt died. Great numbers of the public mourned openly. Many who professed hatred for him, his politics, and his programs felt bewildered by his sudden absence. For some—maybe for Ritter—it was like losing one's father. FDR had been, in an indirect way, Ritter's political alter ego. Ritter gave his unreserved admiration and endorsement to few men—FDR was one of them.

Ritter also mourned, but for him the loss was more ominous. Back in Salt Lake City for well over a year, in prospect now was the upset of his carefully laid plans to secure the judgeship. The 1944 election seemed to have reinforced his claim, at least if Tillman Johnson retired and Senator Elbert D. Thomas kept his promise, but now the loss of FDR threatened his aspirations.

The Constitution provides that U.S. judges shall be appointed by the president, with the "advice and consent" of the Senate.[1] The political situation in 1945 was described by the cliché "To the victor belong the spoils." The reality of those two propositions, in combination, was that appointment of judges was the prerogative of the senior senator of the state involved, provided she or he was of the same political party as the president, and provided the nominee could pass the test of being qualified, by legal ability and temperament, to win the consent of the full Senate.

Thomas remained the senior senator from Utah, and would have the prerogative of nominating any federal judge to serve in Utah until his term expired in 1950, provided a Democrat remained in the White House.[2] But the new president, Harry S. Truman, was lightly regarded and unpopular with the voters. Judge Tillman Johnson still had not retired, and if he stayed on much longer and Truman was defeated in 1948, as appeared likely, Ritter's aspirations would be finished. Moreover, even if Johnson's retirement was imminent, a new president must now act on any nomination, and it was yet to be seen if Thomas would have the same influence with Truman that he had enjoyed with Roosevelt. Also, it may be unlikely, by the time a nomination could be made, that it could be confirmed before 1948. The promised judgeship had thus become doubtful for assorted reasons.

The end of the war in Europe came barely a month later. In August the Japanese surrendered. After nearly four years of incipient doom the world seemed about to realize a renaissance of harmony and well-being, and the concerns of everyday life were temporarily subdued. It was time to get on with life, for everyone, and Ritter must get on with his. The wait had become uncertain, and the judgeship no longer something his future should depend on. Ritter's attention, and his ambitions, reverted to his earlier interests.

Dr. LeRoy E. Cowles resigned as president of the University of Utah in June 1945, and Ritter was among the field of prospects named for his possible replacement. He would have been interested in the job at any time—his bid for the position in 1941 attests to that. Becoming a candidate nevertheless confirms his restlessness and the uncertainty created by the death of FDR.

On August 3, 1945, a faculty committee recommended four inside candidates, including Ritter and his friend Dean Sydney W. Angleman.[3] The decision would be made by the board of regents, who were appointees of the governor, with the consent of Utah's senate, mostly conservative, prominent business and professional men, and devout members of the conservative Mormon establishment. They and Ritter might as well have lived at opposite ends of the globe for all they had in common.

At a meeting of the board of regents on August 10, 1945, Sterling W. Sill, a prominent Mormon who would become one of the church's general authorities as a member of its first council of the seventies in 1954, moved for the appointment of Dr. A. Ray Olpin, effective July 1, 1946.

It was then suggested that absent members of the board be advised that the vote would likely take place that day. Dean William H. Leary was chairman of a faculty committee to cooperate in finding qualified candidates. When Leary and Dean Angleman learned of Sill's precipitous move to hasten and ensure Olpin's appointment, they advised that it was a mistake to proceed with the election on that day. Leary protested that the inquiries of his committee should be completed before a vote was taken. Further, he did not think the faculty "would favor this action at this time." The board proceeded to prepare a ballot, nevertheless, "should voting for a president take place later." Angleman's name, along with Olpin and seven others, not including Ritter, were placed on the ballot. The board reconvened at seven thirty that evening, and Olpin was unanimously elected.[4]

Olpin was Mormon, born in Pleasant Grove, Utah, on June 1, 1898. A graduate of Brigham Young University, he was on the technical staff of Bell Telephone Company from 1925 to 1933, during which time he completed work at Columbia University for a Ph.D. in physical science. For six years following 1933 he was director of research at Kendall Mills in North Carolina. Following that he went to Ohio State University as director of its Research Foundation and professor of industrial research.[5]

Utah and its flagship university were not yet ready for a nonmember of its religious majority in administrative leadership. Ritter saw, and was surely affected by, what he perceived as religious bias in reverse, by an abusive exercise of power by a conservative establishment with a Mormon stamp. Utah would not rise above those strictures during the balance of the twentieth century.

As Ritter's bid for advancement in academe was being thwarted, Joseph Rosenblatt noticed what, from his point of view, was a disturbing change.

> The Willis I knew from the time he first came with us until after his OPA job—he was not the same Willis. The total care of detail, our reliance on him to think creatively, constructively in problems we had in a growing manufacturing business—his capacity was not up to what it could be, what we had relied on. He was different with the years that had gone by. I remember saying to my brother that our relationship with Willis as our tax attorney was no longer the type of highly satisfactory, reliable work we'd become used to. I felt that the reason was that his interests had turned elsewhere. The high level diminished. I recall being very sad about it because his involvement with the OPA and people there left me confronted with a Willis I wasn't comfortable with.[6]

The change was evident when Ritter went to Washington, D.C., in 1945 on radio-station business involving the Abe Glassman family and Robert Hinckley. Hinckley had continued holding several high posts in the

Roosevelt administration, including board member of the Civil Aeronautics Administration and assistant secretary of commerce, and he was one of the founders and the vice president in charge of American Broadcasting Corporation's (ABC) Washington office. Hinckley reserved a room for Ritter at the Mayflower Hotel. The room was not needed, however, for Ritter left Washington the same day he arrived. Hinckley wrote to Glassman and Glassman's son-in-law, George Hatch: "I will never be able to understand why people come so far and work so hard to get here and leave before they have accomplished what they came to do."[7] The incident may have been a mere misunderstanding. It plainly was an example of the change Rosenblatt, and now Hinckley, saw coming over Ritter, possibly the result of his frustrated ambitions.

Ritter's anxiety was further evident after he went to the annual reception of the new president of the University of Utah on New Year's Day 1946. A few days later he wrote to Dean Brimhall, asking that he "write me the interesting things that are going on around Washington. I hear nothing at all out here. Thomas's office rarely sends on any information, and I have a notion that they know nothing about what is going on." The hint of annoyance or perception that Thomas had turned his back on him was allayed in November, when he and Rita, Leo and Lucille Marshall, and Morris and Molly Rosenblatt jointly threw a grand party for five hundred guests at the Hotel Utah. Edna Harker, Thomas's wife, had died April 29, 1942, and the party was in celebration of Thomas's marriage to his secretary, Ethel Evans.[8]

The elections of 1946 spelled more trouble for Ritter's judicial ambitions. By then Willis's virtual neighbor from his childhood in Midway and his soon-to-be nemesis, Arthur V. Watkins, was becoming a force on the political scene. That would bode ill for Ritter's plans, already placed in jeopardy by the death of FDR, and for the prospect of Truman surviving the presidential election in 1948.

Watkins interrupted his education at Brigham Young Academy to serve a mission for the Mormon Church in its Eastern States Mission, where he encountered the sometimes bitter misunderstanding that results from trying to influence the religious beliefs of others. Watkins stayed in the East long enough to obtain a legal education at New York University and Columbia, then returned to Utah, where he was appointed district judge in the state's Fourth Judicial District, including Provo and portions of Utah extending east to Vernal, where the Watkins family had located after leaving Heber Valley. Watkins was defeated for reelection as judge in the

Roosevelt landslide of 1932, and then defeated as a candidate for United States Congress in 1936. He returned to the practice of law and eventually settled in Orem, in Utah County, where he became a law partner in nearby Provo with A. H. Christensen and counsel for the organization of local water users' associations and water districts under the Provo River Reclamation Project. Watkins was also president of the Sharon Stake of the Mormon Church, an ecclesiastical administration over local congregations called wards, and published a weekly newspaper called the *Voice of Sharon* (the plain bordering Utah Lake, named after the plain in Israel bordering the Mediterranean).

Watkins offered himself as a candidate to challenge for the United States Senate seat held by one-term senator Abe Murdock in 1946, although "the idea of winning seemed utterly impossible." Ritter had assisted in Murdock's election six years earlier. Murdock quickly established himself as one of the leading progressives in the United States Senate, and thus appeared to be a strong candidate for a second term.

The popularity of the New Deal, and the prominence of Murdock, made it difficult for Republicans in Utah to even field a candidate to oppose him. Utah Republican Party leaders told the Republican National Senatorial Campaign Committee that Watkins did not have a chance and not to send him any money. So Watkins ran on his own, with eight thousand dollars, mostly out of his own pocket. He received a paltry three hundred dollars contributed by constituents and a modest contribution from Senator John Townsend (R-DE).[9]

The 1946 election proved to be an extension of the Republican Party's postwar anticommunist campaign against Democrats, begun with the campaign of Thomas E. Dewey in 1944, that lured many conservatives and jingoists to the Republican camp. The bogeyman tactic had already been used by Adam Bennion against Elbert Thomas in the 1944 election campaign, and the same slurs would now be used against Murdock. As the election approached, J. Edgar Hoover told an American Legion convention in San Francisco that there were as many as one hundred thousand communists running loose in America, and that they included sympathizers "ready to do the party's work" identified as "so-called progressive[s] and liberal allies."[10]

The Republicans contrived a spurious claim that Roosevelt tried to appease Joseph Stalin at the Yalta Conference in 1945 by handing over eastern Europe, though the fact was that Stalin was already in firm control, he refused to withdraw his troops, and the United States was left with no realistic option. Through the summer and fall of 1946, the Republicans expanded on the "selling out to radical elements" theme used by Bennion in his campaign against Thomas and accused Murdock and the Democrats of being "red fascists" and of being guilty of the "Three Cs: Confusion, Corruption and Communism."[11]

Stalin fueled the Republican smear by asking the American voters to support candidates backed by the CIO Political Action Committee.[12] In Utah that included Murdock and Elbert Thomas, though the latter was not a candidate in the 1946 election, both of whom had a strong identity as supporters of labor. It also included Ritter through his campaigning for Thomas and Murdock. Continuing its opposition to Democrats, church-owned radio station KSL, a CBS media giant, and others in the Salt Lake City market boycotted Thomas's speeches. "Every station on this network has accepted your broadcast excepting Salt Lake City," a telegram to Thomas advised. "Gee! What a backhanded swat I got," Thomas complained in a letter to Ritter.[13]

The Democratic Party was accused of "leading the country toward Communism" and of "permitting men with communistic ideas to dictate Administration policy." The issue of anticommunism struck a nerve in the American postwar electorate. It was estimated that 23 percent of FDR's supporters turned Republican in 1946, and the communist scare was an important factor.[14] Watkins joined in the red-baiting during his campaign to defeat Murdock.

Watkins surprised everyone, himself included, by winning. He was swept along in the political upheaval of 1946, with the help of the Mormon Church, J. Reuben Clark Jr., their minions—and the communist scare. The minority party generally gains congressional seats in midterm elections, but even in light of that phenomenon in political history the 1946 election, sweeping the Republican Party into control, was a shock. The Republicans won twelve of the sixteen seats up for reelection in the Senate, Watkins winning one of them, and gained fifty-five seats in the House.

Walter K. Granger, a farmer and former mayor of Cedar City who had served in the Utah House of Representatives and been its Speaker in 1935 and was then elected to Congress in 1940 where he had served three terms representing Utah's First District, barely survived the 1946 upheaval. Ritter had been involved in the campaigns of Granger and became engaged in helping secure his slim victory.[15] When the vote tally was complete, Granger was declared the winner over Republican challenger David J. Wilson by 104 votes, out of nearly 90,000 votes cast. Wilson contested the election, alleging numerous irregularities in voting and the counting of ballots. It was claimed that there had been voting by nonresidents and that government employees in Davis and Weber Counties were improperly registered and influenced to vote for the Democrat. Granger responded to Wilson's challenge by pointing out that his allegations were vague, conclusory, and unsupported by any facts, and defended the challenge on the basis that they did not conform to the act of Congress defining grounds for election contests.[16]

Clinton D. Vernon, Utah chairman of the Democratic Party from 1946 to 1948, was in charge of the defense of Wilson's election contest. Stuart P. Dobbs of Ogden and Ritter were employed to represent Granger and assist Vernon. They took extensive depositions in Weber, Davis, and Carbon Counties and presented the matter to Congress. Willis and Rita traveled to Washington, D.C., by train with the other members of the legal team, where Ritter appeared before the Committee on House Administration of the United States House of Representatives on April 6 and 7, 1948, in support of Granger. The contest of the election by Wilson was dismissed as lacking in merit.[17]

The political upheaval of the 1946 election appeared to make Ritter more certain that he wanted to make his big mark in the world at the university. Leary, whose efforts to stall the hasty election of Olpin had failed two years earlier, was sixty-four years of age and ready to retire after service as dean of the College of Law since 1915. Ritter's feelings that the conservative Mormon establishment was depriving him of advancement, and his continued belief that his prospects for the judgeship were diminished, if not ended, are all reflected in a letter from his friend Dean Brimhall prior to the 1946 elections:

> What have you decided about the deanship at the University? Maybe your liberal history has kept them from offering it to you. It would be a very difficult thing for me to decide how to advise you. Much could depend on the role that the University is going to play in the State under the new President; certainly you will have much better administration but the University may need one or two people to lead the fight for liberalism and God knows, there are few of them in the University at the present time.[18]

Ritter positioned himself to secure the deanship by becoming employed again as a professor of law in 1946, on a part-time basis. Leary retired in

1948, but agreed to continue as acting dean until a successor was appointed. Whether by choice or the decision of those having control over the issue, or because of his perceptions of a bias by the conservative Mormon establishment, the deanship also came to nothing. His perception of bias may have been increased when Spencer L. Kimball, a distinguished scholar but also the son of Mormon apostle Spencer W. Kimball, was eventually appointed dean.[19]

But for Ritter, the unsettled political landscape as calendar year 1947 arrived had an even more ominous meaning. The election of Watkins and a Republican majority in the Senate was a further threat to Ritter's judicial aspirations, for any judicial nomination must be with the consent of the Senate. Watkins's views must therefore be considered, even if he could not himself make the nomination. Thomas remained the senior senator, but President Harry S. Truman was very much in danger of being retired by the voters in 1948. A defeat of Truman, which seemed probable after the Republican sweep in 1946, would prevent Ritter's judicial appointment. Without Truman, Thomas's promise, already rendered doubtful, would be as valueless as an unsigned IOU.

In addition to the problem of the Democrats having lost control of the Senate, President Truman suffered from inexperience and bad advice during the first two years of his administration, which, together with the hardships of reconversion from a wartime economy, caused his popularity rating to crash from 87 percent when he took office to an anemic 32 percent on the eve of the 1946 elections.[20] It was generally assumed that Truman would be turned out of office in 1948.

Still, Thomas remained prominent, at least with the core support of the Democratic Party. A new movement to nominate him for vice president began in November 1947. The "little committee" of Morris Rosenblatt, Leo Marshall, Delbert Draper, and Ritter met and invited Clint Vernon, state chairman of the party, to join them. They considered it "fairly certain" that another favorite-son movement might succeed because of "support stem[ming] from labor and zionist movements." True to their prediction, the State Central Committee adopted such a resolution.[21]

Evidence that Ritter recognized his diminished prospects for judicial appointment, and had perhaps abandoned that ambition altogether, was provided when he became a candidate himself for the Democratic nomination for Utah's Second District congressional seat in 1948. His public explanation was that he was induced to run by friends, fifty of whom signed a petition asking him to do so. He responded to their petition, saying:

> As you well know, your group meetings were held without my knowledge and you circulated the petitions, as you said to me, "whether you like it or not." ... Although I have not sought political office I would be less than frank if I did not assure you that I am impressed by the action of the influential and representative people who in signing the petitions ... have encouraged my candidacy. My decision to accept is prompted by two considerations ... the challenge of the fateful issues confronting this country and the world today, and the duty of a citizen to make whatever contributions he may to their solutions.[22]

His response may have been genuine, but the uncertainties created by the 1946 election and the dim prospects for Truman's reelection had everything to do with convincing Ritter that he should look elsewhere for challenges. Seeking election to Congress was inconsistent with continued belief that judicial appointment was forthcoming in the near future.

Elective office was not to be the answer to his evident frustration, however. He came in third in a field of four at a nominating convention on July 30, 1948. Ray Leavitt, chairman of the Utah Road Commission, and Salt Lake City judge Reva Beck Bosone were nominated, with Bosone winning in a primary and defeating the Republican incumbent, William A. Dawson, in the general election. Ritter's late entry into the contest and the "potency of the State Road Commission" accounted for Ritter's defeat, according to the *Salt Lake Tribune.*[23]

Meanwhile, there were events going on in Washington, D.C., during 1946-1948, unbeknownst to Ritter and virtually everyone else, that would reverse the dismal outlook for Democrats, and revive Ritter's aspiration to the judgeship.

Truman, with the help of Clark Clifford and a group of prominent Democrats known as the Wardman Park Group, so named because they held weekly meetings at Washington's Wardman Park Hotel to discuss Democratic Party strategy, was engaged in an analysis of the 1946 election and saw a more positive message in it. The group saw the 1946 debacle as a combination of factors, many the product of a volatile postwar economy. Price controls during reconversion, which Ritter had responsibility for administering during wartime, hurt farmers; they also kept wages low, resulting in hundreds of strikes during 1946. Government policies seen as antilabor, such as drafting of strikers and federal seizure of several industries, made Truman unpopular with Democratic core constituencies.[24]

The African American minority, essential to the Democratic coalition, was alienated by Truman's apparent duplicity over continuation of the Fair Employment Practices Commission (FEPC). Roosevelt had established the FEPC to end racial discrimination in wartime industries, but it was scheduled to expire in 1946, and although Truman called for a permanent FEPC, he appeared to undercut its authority when he issued an executive order eliminating its "cease and desist" authority and outright duplicitous when he cut its funding. The result was that the members of the FEPC resigned, and many African American voters in northern urban districts either sat out the 1946 election or voted Republican. The firing of Henry Wallace as secretary of commerce in September 1946 angered many liberals, resulting in their lackluster turnout in November. Many conservatives, meanwhile, who saw Wallace as too far to the Left, were scared into voting Republican.[25]

Truman was convinced by his advisers that these were the lessons of the 1946 election, rather than a swing by the voters to the Right. On November 9, 1946, four days after the election, he removed all controls on wages and prices by executive order. The OPA was dissolved in the first months of 1947. A hard line was adopted against communism, culminating in the policy of containment, the Truman Doctrine and the Marshall Plan. His advisers persuaded him that a liberal swing—a reaffirmation of the New Deal—would bring voters back to the party in 1948.

The Republicans, in the meantime, were misreading the upheaval of 1946 as a rejection of the New Deal and a mandate for return to probusiness, antiprogressive, laissez-faire policies of pre-Depression days. The Eightieth Congress drove labor back into the Democratic fold by enacting the Taft-Hartley Act, eliminating the union shop. Republican leadership convinced African Americans there was no home for them in the party of Lincoln by declaring that they would not enact an FEPC bill because Republican industrial supporters in New England and the Midwest were opposed to ending racial discrimination in employment. The Republican-controlled Congress was content to do nothing, its representatives assuming that they would gain control of both branches of government in 1948.[26] The essential members of the New Deal coalition became convinced that their interests were best served by working for the election of a Democratic administration, even if Truman was unpopular. Truman shored up the coalition by paying better attention to both labor and civil rights.

Strom Thurman and Henry Wallace, meanwhile, unwittingly transformed the Democratic Party into a more centrist alliance that could appeal to moderate swing voters of diverse stripes. Thurman made the Democratic Party alliance more hospitable to African Americans and their sympathizers by bolting and taking the right-wing, southern segregationists with him in his Dixiecrat third-party bid for the presidency. Wallace mounted his own third-party bid, taking the ultra-Left communists and their sympathizers with him. Truman and the Democratic Party were left with the centrist, moderate swing voters.

When the 1948 campaign got under way, Truman made good use of his advantages and of the Republican failings. The Republicans renominated Thomas E. Dewey, who ran a bland, uninspired campaign. Confident of victory, he confronted no issues, answered no questions, and avoided making promises that would have to be kept after the election. Truman therefore made the "do-nothing" Eightieth Congress the issue. In the closing weeks of the campaign Truman boarded a train and took his appeal to Midwest farmers in a "whistle stop" marathon that most observers credit with winning enough farmers, urban workers, and minorities in Ohio, Wisconsin, Iowa, Illinois, and Missouri to swing the election in his favor.[27]

Ritter rode with the president on his campaign train from Denver to Salt Lake City. Truman's upset victory in 1948 was the most stunning in the history of presidential politics. Ritter's plans for the judicial appointment were suddenly revived. He was pleased, of course, but his postelection letter to Brimhall reveals more joy from Dewey's defeat than enthusiasm for Truman:

> Dear Dean:
>
> I have been too damn busy to spit. However, I was just as exuberant as were you about the results of the election. Never have I seen such a fall being taken out of the "fat cats." [Columnist] David Lawrence just can't get away from attempting every morning to explain away the Democratic victory.
>
> There is one disquieting suggestion which I am getting through my *Prentice-Hall Lawyer's Weekly Report.* They say that Truman thinks he won the election single handed and that labor or the liberals are not going to be received by Truman with nearly the same gratitude as we have expected. The suggestion is that Truman is going to move much less far to the liberal side than is desirable. Of course, you and I never did like Truman's attitude and on the basis of your own analyses tending to show

> that the leopard doesn't change its spots, I don't know why anybody would expect Truman to be too consistently liberal.
>
> We had a very pleasant dinner with Lila at the Town Club the other evening and I am hoping that we will see you out here during the holidays.
>
> All in all it was a wonderful election result in view of the alternative of having Tom Dewey President of the United States. I think I liked as much as anything what Alice Roosevelt Longworth said of him, "You can't raise a souffle twice."[28]

The election gave Ritter a lift such as he hadn't had since Thomas and Roosevelt won in 1944—in the first attempt at raising the "Dewey souffle." Thomas's IOU was suddenly valuable again. A Democrat was now secure in the White House for another term, available to act on a nomination by Thomas. If only Tillman Johnson would resign. Ritter was at the prime age, at forty-nine, to become a federal judge—even a bit on the youthful side.

He resumed pursuit of his carefully laid plan to secure appointment to the bench. Whether by dint of circumstances or by force of his own calculations, it was becoming clear that Willis W. Ritter was not to spend the balance of his working years practicing law or teaching.

At the same time, Thomas's attitude toward Ritter became increasingly disturbing. Thomas spent a lot of time in Utah prior to the general election, speaking for Truman and other party candidates. He saw Ritter hardly at all. Ritter put the blame on himself in a letter to Thomas in early December: "Wish we could see you more often and I have regretted greatly that I got ill while you were out during the campaign and as a result saw so little of you." Ritter's letter has the ring of irony, as if he were saying, "I'm sorry for my reluctance to arise from my sickbed and chase you down so we could have a visit." Thomas returned the courtesy, answering Ritter and saying that their sparse contact was due to his demanding speaking schedule.[29] Thomas's apology may have been genuine and his excuse valid, but there may have been another explanation.

Even as he agonized over Thomas apparently distancing himself, the word had spread fast and far that Tillman Johnson, who by then was within a month of ninety-one, had decided to step down. Judge Johnson had been traveling through Oklahoma City and visited the United States District Court of Judge Alfred P. Murrah. Murrah interrupted court, introduced Judge Johnson, and explained his long and distinguished history. It was rumored that, in the process, Johnson more or less blurted out that he had had enough and announced his retirement.[30]

Credibility of the incident may be measured by the packet of letters that arrived in Thomas's office beginning in mid-December. Thomas had left Washington in mid-November, traveled by automobile to California, and did not return to the nation's capital until shortly before Christmas. In his absence, stacks of letters arrived at his Washington office about whom the new judge should be. Interested persons wrote to register their opinions almost simultaneously, endorsing and condemning various of the most likely prospective candidates to take Judge Johnson's place. Some included brief sermons reminding Thomas that the position was an important one and that he had a moral obligation to appoint the best available person, in each case claiming to know who that person was. Thomas did not see those letters until his return, but he was informed of them by his office, and they probably were the reason for him distancing himself from Ritter, or appearing to do so, while he gave appropriate consideration to the choice it was now his to make. In any event, it marked the revival of Ritter's aspirations to the judgeship and the beginning of the end of his long wait.

There was one final matter that was to threaten Ritter's prospects for the judicial appointment—gossip about womanizing that would give rise to persistent rumors hanging like a cloud over his entire career and create marital difficulties with Rita as well, resulting in their eventual separation in 1958 though never eventuating in their divorce.

The rumors began during Ritter's OPA days. They were related to his apparent habit of spending an inordinate amount of time in Albuquerque, New Mexico. His trips to Albuquerque usually took two or three weeks. Those who replaced him when he left the OPA found that they could handle the same meetings in one week, and there was talk in the Albuquerque office of "wild goings-on" there and in Juárez, Mexico, that may have explained the inordinate time spent. Stories were also circulated by Ritter opponents, with some basis in fact, about a possible liaison with a woman in Albuquerque.

There were similar rumors, almost immediately, concerning La Rue Burke, who had been hired by Ritter on his return to Salt Lake City, continued as his secretary through 1949 when he was nominated to the bench, and went with him as his secretary when he became United States District Judge for the District of Utah. She was a striking young woman but was fired when she came to work wearing an engagement ring, giving rise to speculation that she was also Ritter's girlfriend and that he was too jealous to allow her to stay. Nancy, who knew La Rue and liked her, believed that her father may have fired her out of paternalism, because the young man had proposed marriage without checking with him first.[31]

Allegations of infidelity and sexual impropriety, which had their root in his tenure at the OPA and would be exploited by his opponents throughout his judicial career, may be traced to this period in Ritter's life. In his early days, Ritter saw much of the seamy side of life while growing up in Park City, with the ever present whorehouse of a mining community located across the street from the Ritter home and a pharmacy with a self-service back room where men could pick for themselves among vials of medicine for the treatment of venereal disease. At the same time, paradoxically, there seemed to be considerable naïveté where women were concerned. He knew nothing about menstruation until Ireta's first period after they were married; he was aghast and shunned her for a time, refusing to believe that it was common to all women.[32]

By contrast, there were persistent rumors of crass worldliness. Throughout, or at least in the wake of, the allegations, Ritter himself added to the rumors and speculation by boasting, from time to time, of his sexual prowess. He dismissed his critics, for example, in a statement to Salt Lake City attorney Clair Senior with a claim that he knew better than they what his penis was for and put it to its intended use.

In addition to La Rue Burke, suspicions and accusations of impropriety implicated other employees after Ritter was appointed judge. La Rue Burke was replaced, initially, by Ruth Bailey, an employee in the Office of the Clerk of Court. Bailey did not feel comfortable with Ritter, however, and was succeeded by Catherine Jensen, who remained his secretary for the major part of his judicial tenure. There was never any suggestion of impropriety between them. In the twilight of his tenure, after Catherine Jensen left to have surgery for cancer, Vicki Jolley, also employed by the clerk of court, acted as his secretary. Vicki was very smart and described by fellow employees as manipulative. There were rumors that she was Ritter's girlfriend. Ritter's behavior toward Vicki, detailed hereafter, gave credence to the rumors. Along the way there was Mary Kelly, whom Ritter met at Sam Weller's bookstore on a Valentine's Day. Mary "was wonderful to him," according to Nancy. Ritter confided in Nancy that Mary, who was divorced and had children, wanted the security of marriage, but Ritter would not and could not marry her, for he and Rita had never divorced. Nancy went with Mary on a long automobile trip to Milwaukee, at Ritter's request, taking a load of personal belongings to a son who lived in the area, and in the process they became very fond of one another. Mary subsequently married, moved to Houston, and was diagnosed with cancer a short time later. Nancy went to Houston and cared for Mary until she died. Stricken, Ritter went to Idaho to be alone, then never said anything to anyone about it.[33] The life, story, and times of Willis W. Ritter would be embroiled with these women for the balance of his life.

8

RESOLUTION

A man cannot be too careful in the choice of his enemies.

—Oscar Wilde

In late January 1949, Willis W. Ritter received a note from Fisher Harris, mentioned by some as a possible candidate to replace Judge Tillman Johnson. "This is probably unnecessary," Harris confided. "However, I hope YOU get it, and it is only in the highly improbable event that some obstacle intervenes that I have any interest whatever. You are my first choice—which reminds me of Macaulay's comment on Boswell's work... 'Eclipse is first, and the second nowhere.'"[1]

It was the beginning of the period of controversy at the end of the long wait. Within weeks after Ritter's election-toasting letter to Dean Brimhall, the rumors that Johnson had decided to retire had apparently reached every interested person in Utah, and the scramble for appointment as his successor was on.

Harris was right. Ritter was determined to "eclipse" the race for United States District Judge for the District of Utah. His first step was to register an endorsement for himself by passing that of Harris on to Senator Elbert Thomas. "In view of a suggestion that Fisher Harris's name had been thrown into the judgeship situation, I think you may be interested in the enclosed note he wrote to me."[2]

Most of the letters to Thomas's office came from lawyers. Some were from Democratic Party regulars. A few came from Thomas's relatives and friends. There were letters from Mormon Church leaders, including one from its president, George Albert Smith. Thomas answered them all in much the same way—thanking them for their advice, asserting his impartiality, and, in some instances, claiming to have but a small part in selecting Judge Johnson's successor. "When we are informed, my first task will be to consult among the three of us here [the Senator and the other two Democrats in the Congressional delegation, Arthur Watkins pointedly excluded] and then we will get in touch with the State Chairman, State Vice Chairman and the National Committeeman and Committeewoman. As you know I have always been a stickler for party regularity."[3]

According to a literal reading of the Constitution, nominations of persons to become United States District Judge are the president's prerogative.[4] Presidents customarily rely on the advice of people who have knowledge of the most qualified persons in the state where the vacancy exists, however, and the time had not yet arrived when senators not of the president's party, nominating commissions, or bar commissions controlled or had any significant influence over the process. The political reality, at least in 1949, was that the president could not ignore the preference of the senior senator of the state involved, if he was of the same political party as the president, for if he were to invoke "privilege" on the floor of the Senate, his fellow senators would show him courtesy and the nomination would be blocked.

Ritter's nomination was a textbook example of the process. Truman and the senior senator from Utah were of the same party. Senator Elbert D. Thomas was in his third term and enjoyed a splendid reputation among his colleagues.[5] Barely having passed his fiftieth birthday, and with outstanding intellectual and professional credentials, Ritter appeared to be a prime candidate, assuming that he had Thomas's endorsement.

Touching on the changed circumstance of President Truman having succeeded Roosevelt, and not certain of how appointments would be completed under the new administration, Thomas explained that "in the one or two jobs that the Civil Service has left us to give advice on, with appointive powers in the hands of the President, there has been a tendency lately for the White House to act without consultation. If that is done, of course, there is nothing that we can do."[6]

Ritter wrote Thomas in December too, several times. The first was shortly after Thomas had left Washington and before most people had heard about Judge Johnson's announcement of his intention to retire. He wrote on behalf of some of Utah's labor leaders to suggest that a representative of labor be placed on Thomas's staff "who could act as a liaison between yourself and all of the liberal elements here." Ritter thought the idea "an excellent one,"[7] but the senator disagreed, with some impatience and at length. His response provides a glimpse into Thomas's attitude toward the kind of solicitations he was then being subjected to on the judgeship:

> We have access to all of the labor leaders and their representatives are not backward in calling on us. There is no vacancy on my staff....

> I know the spirit of the suggestion made but the spirit would be one that would soon be misinterpreted by the…press and nothing could do any of these humanitarian causes more harm than to have the public told that we here were agents of some special group or activity. This is most difficult to explain to anyone's friend because on all sides of our political life are the various lobbies of various kinds and many well-wishers' well-wishing has an objective behind it. Then, too, there is the law itself which makes all persons with axes to grind register.
>
> One of our greatest difficulties is to live down a dubbing—friend of labor, friend to the school teacher, friend to the military. I have had them all in my day and I know. But so far I haven't been accused of being a special advocate for any interest, excepting the Government's and the People's.[8]

After thirty years of association with Thomas and being at his side through three senatorial campaigns, Ritter was used to the senator's tendency to pontification and his sensitivity to anything that might bring criticism. The whole labor question seemed unimportant, anyway, by the time he got Thomas's return letter in late December, but Ritter was dismayed by the first curt paragraph about the judgeship: "Clint [Vernon] was in yesterday and we had a talk about things. I explained to him what you already know, that no signal had come from either the White House or the Justice Department so there is nothing we could do. I would like to have the vita though just on general principles."[9] "Just on general principles"—that was an odd thing to say. Just what did it mean? Thomas appeared to be suffering, too, and may not have been altogether happy about appointing Ritter. At least his letter gave that impression.

Ritter was annoyed. His résumé had been on file with Thomas for years. Was it just something to have around, in case Thomas should consider him for the appointment? Not only had Ritter's long-standing friend misplaced the first vita, but he seemed to have forgotten about it entirely, a slip that might have been overlooked if everything else seemed normal. Ritter was puzzled when Thomas seemed to make so little effort to see him during his time in the state during the last election campaign. Whether intentionally or not, Thomas seemed to be distancing himself from Ritter. Willis sensed it and was deeply hurt—in a personal way, rather than out of fear of not getting the judicial appointment. He hardly knew what to make of the senator's formal manner toward him and was miffed about the sudden offishness toward Utah's labor representatives. He failed to see, in both instances, that it was Thomas's way of dealing with solicitations for political patronage.

Putting his annoyance aside, Ritter sent Thomas another copy of his résumé, with a note explaining that "in the month of May, 1945, I submitted to your office a dossier containing information about myself in connection with the Federal Judgeship." He reminded the senator that "attached thereto were numerous letters from prominent persons, copies of which I shall again be glad to supply you if the file is not available there," chiding him over their apparent loss. Ritter's note then made pointed reference to his feeling about Thomas's sudden formality: "If there is any additional information which you will need I should appreciate an opportunity to hand it to you."[10]

The issue became intensified as the new year began. On January 10, 1949, George Hatch, president of the Intermountain Network of radio stations, wrote on Ritter's behalf to Robert Hinckley, then with the American Broadcasting Company in New York. "The Federal Judgeship is really getting hot," Hatch advised.

> Judge Johnson has authorized Calvin Rawlings, as National Committeeman, to inform the Attorney General and the President, on his current trip East, that he is preparing to resign as soon as a successor can be appointed.... I will appreciate anything you can do and any suggestions you may make on behalf of Willis. I know that Thomas would also like a letter from Ma[r]riner Eccles [of the Federal Reserve, then its Vice-chairman], if he is inclined to favor Willis's candidacy.[11]

Though he said nothing directly to Thomas, Ritter did confide in some close friends his sense that Thomas had become cool and formal with him. Clint Vernon was one of them, and, whether at Ritter's behest or not, Vernon broached the subject with Thomas. Willis also talked with Morris Rosenblatt about it and showed him Thomas's letter saying "there is nothing we could do" and that he would like to have the vita "just on general principles." Rosenblatt wrote to Thomas:

> Dear Tomie:
>
> ... Willis showed me a letter from you today which gave me great concern. As you know, Willis has his heart set on the Federal Judgeship and I know of no one who is better qualified to do the job. I can well understand that it is tactful to give the general impression that all candidates

will be given thotful [*sic*] consideration by you but I do not think it is your intention to convey to Willis the impression that he is in the same category as other prospects. I told Willis that I felt sure you would be for him first, last and always and not only because of his outstanding qualifications but because of our years of intimate friendship and his endless hours of hard work during your last campaign....

I feel certain that the patronage here involved should be and can be controlled by the Senior Senator and even though Party unity and obligations are important they cannot equal the more personal responsibility. I know that my approach in this matter may seem presumptuous but I do feel this is not a time for equivocation. If it is not your intention to support and fight for Willis's appointment I think he should be so advised immediately so that he does not get himself all set for it, solicit outside endorsements, and find in the end that he is to be disappointed.

I cannot, by any stretch of the imagination, believe that anyone, whether in our little group or outside, is better qualified or more deserving. Further I firmly believe that a strong recommendation from you will definitely make the vote of the other six members of your delegation unanimous.[12] If I have spoken out of turn in this matter please forget it but at any rate please let Willis understand just what your position is going to be.[13]

Abe Glassman wrote to Thomas in a similar vein about two weeks later:

It has come to my attention that Tillman Johnson will soon resign.... I have talked with Willis about this, and he seems to be keenly interested in securing the appointment. I know that your contacts and friendship with Willis are of the highest....

I also understand that Willis has been ordered by his medical advisors to reduce strenuous activities. Judges seem to live long lives. This appointment might mean that we keep for a few extra years that rare specimen of "Homo Sapiens" a true friend.

Of course there will be a lot of pressure brought in favor of other candidates some of whom have worked very hard for you and the Party, but all of whom worked for themselves first and you afterwards....

From the first inception of the idea that you would make fine Senatorial timber, Willis has been the "Keeper of the Fires." Down the years his untiring, unselfish energies have gone to you and the Party.

> This is a helluva way for a Republican to be writing, but as a not too unfriendly observer sitting on the sidelines, it seems that Willis has first choice on both you and the Party.[14]

Scolding from close friends, especially from Morris Rosenblatt, was disagreeable and added to an already wearing task. The responsibility of eliminating everyone who was qualified and wanted the job, and that included the most eminent and qualified lawyers in the state of Utah, most of whom had contributed to Thomas's political success, placed Thomas in the familiar position of creating ninety-nine enemies and one ingrate every time he handed out an appointment. That dilemma, familiar to most politicians, explains neither his distant attitude toward Ritter nor his attempts to disclaim personal prerogative in the selection of a new judge. Those were the pitfalls of his job. He knew it, his constituents knew it, and he had survived that kind of storm in the past. His attitude toward Ritter, so obvious that two of his good and trusted friends felt called upon to harangue him about it, must be attributed to something other than a desire to present an image of impartiality.

Thomas appears to have been torn by two separate conflicts. First, he had given his promise to Ritter but for some reason seems to have come to regret it. Something about Ritter had come to his attention that caused Thomas to doubt his suitability for the position. Thomas did hear from Quentin Cannon, who had worked with Ritter at the OPA, implicitly charging that "some [namely, Ritter] would be horrible judges," and indicating that others had advised Thomas of Cannon's friction with Ritter while prosecuting for the OPA.[15] It thus appears that Thomas had heard from other detractors of Ritter, possibly from critics in Denver.

Thomas may have feared that appointing Ritter would be so unpopular that it would affect his own career and reputation. He may have sensed the same apparent change Joseph Rosenblatt had observed in Ritter during the years since his return from the OPA. There may have been something Thomas perceived in the change that he did not approve of. He may also have heard grumbling from Joe Rosenblatt that differed from his brother's letter of endorsement. Then again, it may have just been his way of dealing with solicitations, whether from Ritter or from others.

A more plausible explanation, albeit related to the others, was that someone else had come along, someone who could be appointed without any adverse consequences. Such a person had in fact interposed himself: John S. Boyden. Thomas was under considerable pressure, inspired by Boyden himself, to appoint Boyden, and may have found that alternative much more comfortable. Unbeknownst to Ritter, Boyden had vigorously solicited the appointment, by devious means, maliciously planting seeds of doubt concerning Ritter. That factor at least contributed, no doubt, to Thomas's change in attitude.

Boyden received the largest number of endorsements in Thomas's mail. Quentin Cannon's letter critical of Ritter recommended Boyden. Thomas had also been pressured for months by officials of the Mormon Church, at the behest of Boyden. They contended that, with Shields out of the way, "now is the time" for one of their own and presented Boyden as their choice.[16]

Before responding to any of the letters of endorsement, Thomas wrote to Boyden asking him to submit a résumé.[17] Boyden's professional credentials were well suited for the position. He had worked in the United States Department of Justice for thirteen years, and his résumé named FBI director J. Edgar Hoover as a reference. He had been an assistant United States Attorney for the District of Utah and carried on a private practice, both of which required his frequent appearance in the United States District Court for the District of Utah and the Court of Appeals for the Tenth Circuit in Denver. He was also a prominent Mormon and an active and popular Democrat who had very nearly defeated Utah's incumbent Democratic governor, Herbert B. Maw, in the 1948 primary election.

Boyden and Thomas were connected through their respective families. Thomas's brother, Kendall, had a stepdaughter, Frances, who was married to John Boyden's brother, William Everett Boyden. Kendall lived in the San Francisco area but wanted to return to Salt Lake City. He needed a job to make the move possible and had been waiting for years for Judge Johnson to step down, allowing his brother, the senator, to appoint a new judge who, in turn, might find a job he would consider of suitable dignity.

Kendall cared little about who the appointee might be. His letter to Thomas at a time when the selection process was at its inception nevertheless provides an interestingly accurate view of the ambitions of Kendall, the dilemma facing Thomas, the pressures being intensified in favor of Boyden including solicitations by Boyden himself, and the opposition being mounted to Ritter:

> I presume there is a new flury [*sic*] concerning the judgeship in Salt Lake as Tillman Johnson is reported ill and about ready to withdraw, according to talk. No doubt you have seen Boyden again.... If it breaks quick I think John Boyden would be a popular choice, aside from commitments and seekers. No one seems to have anything to say about Ritter and I am wondering if he is too good to be noticed or just... unpopular. I suppose Dan Shields is about... to [retire]—certainly well-to-do—and I am wondering if he would still be seeking? You did not answer my last note re above but presume there was nothing to say until the thing popped—I suppose many of the matters are expressed in Chiyo's words: "I've heard about that for the last 12 years," etc.[18]
>
> Well, certainly the breaks have come full and complete and I would be happy if they could extend to a real spot for me.
>
> You [Democrats] are all back with power that few had the courage to anticipate and I wish with all my heart we could raise our sights on "limitations" and really draw one. People do things for the man in the saddle—if he isn't downright impossible the clock goes around just the same. A good spot would lift and no one would be surprised if I draw the best....At any rate it seems certain we must leave the Bay Area. Marie fights too hard to feel herself here and no bunk. Certainly she is anything but the type to enjoy poor health. I don't know about any rehash of the Boyden situation. They are both great boys and would do anything for anybody on all sides of the families. As you view the new program let me hear.[19]

Thomas made no exception for his brother and refused to be drawn into a discussion about his promise to Ritter, or the solicitations in favor of Boyden, other than to say that he would "move in the regular way" and attempt to unite the state's congressional delegation and party officials in a decision.

The United States Attorney for the District of Utah, Scott Matheson Sr., father of future governor of Utah Scott M. Matheson, wrote to Thomas extolling Boyden's experience with federal procedure. He "is in a position, as no other man in Utah, to step upon the bench and carry on immediately with confidence and without loss of time in which to learn," Matheson said. He spoke with equal directness about misgivings over political appointments, apparently intending subtle criticism of Ritter: "I also know that no man other than you possesses the practical power to determine who shall be appointed.... A lesser appointment could only mean nearsighted political strategy and a relegation of the interests of the people to a lesser position than they deserve."[20] Even if Matheson did not know that Thomas had specifically committed himself to the appointment of Ritter, he knew, as most lawyers and politicians knew, that Ritter was a likely appointee because of his academic and intellectual abilities and, most important, his long-standing friendship and association with Thomas.

Mrs. Adele A. Matheson also wrote to Thomas, without the knowledge of her husband, and dissented from his recommendation of Boyden. He would also be a political choice, she warned, and urged that "the best qualified man be given the upmost [*sic*] consideration." Like everyone else, she knew who that man was. "This man is my own husband, Scott M. Matheson," who is "most eminently qualified, both by long experience and extreme brilliance of intellect."[21]

Scott Matheson's assessment that "only [Thomas] possesses the practical power" to make the appointment was correct. Truman had, in accordance with the political reality of the day, consulted with Thomas, whose views would control the "advice and consent" of the Senate.

Other candidates for the judgeship were named in George Hatch's letter to Robert Hinckley:

> As you know, Abe Murdock has been to the White House, and Calvin Rawlings is making his pitch on his current trip. It is my understanding he is seeking the position personally, and then if his position as National Committeeman bars that he will try to get it for Pete [Parnell] Black. If Black's position as County Chairman keeps him out of the running, then they are going after [Brigham H. "Bob"] Roberts for the job.
>
> I am satisfied that Thomas and Granger will go all-out for Ritter, but I do know that they would appreciate letters sustaining them in this matter, as the party pressures are great for a multitude of candidates. Judge [then Congresswoman Reva Beck] Bosone would like it for herself, as would [state party chairman] Grant McFarlane... and, of course [former governor Herbert B.] Maw is available and eager.[22]

Among the more than half-dozen candidates Hatch alluded to, all were prominently mentioned, but they were really only names on a list as far as their chances of being appointed were concerned. Roberts, district attorney for Salt Lake County, was frequently mentioned in Thomas's mail, along with Murdock. Utah Supreme Court justice Roger I. McDonough, Bosone, Maw, Black, and Rawlings were also included in most of the lists circulated among interested observers. Any of them would have been considered a respectable choice, but Thomas's private commitment to Ritter and his regard for and family connections with Boyden essentially narrowed his choice to the two of them.

Ever the master manipulator,[23] Boyden publicly posed as a supporter of Ritter, but behind the scenes he conspired to torpedo Ritter's chances and secure the appointment for himself. Whether he structured and solicited the letter from United States Attorney Matheson may be open to doubt, but it is clear that he did so with others. He importuned attorney general Tom Clark, somehow managed for Frances to intercede with Thomas *repeatedly* on his behalf, and made promises to Kendall Thomas, and to Frances, to induce them to bring pressure in his support, as a letter to Thomas from Frances reveals:

> Uncle Tommy,
>
> I'm writing in regard to John and the Federal Judgeship *again.* I know John would make an excellent Judge.... (emphasis added.)
>
> Perhaps John has written you that he saw Mr. [Tom] Clark, the Attorney-General, while he was in Washington, and that Mr. Clark told him that if you would heartily endorse John, he was all set for the position. This would be wonderful for a lot of reasons, besides the fact that a better Judge could not be found.
>
> ...If he should receive this appointment, the folks would have the opportunity to move back to Salt Lake which they really must do. Mother's health has never been good in the Bay Area, and the doctor says that Kenie [Kendall] should not be in that damp climate either, with only his one kidney.
>
> Of course, Kenie can't come home unless it is to something dignified, because he is a very sensitive fellow, as you no doubt know....
>
> I feel that since the election, you're more than ever one of the top guiding powers of our nation. If there is any definite reason why you cannot support John, I would surely appreciate knowing something about it. We know that there are several other people after the appointment, but no one, I am sure, who is more capable than John, or who is a better friend of yours.[24]

Pressures on Thomas mounted. He had made a promise to Ritter but may have had a change of heart. At the very least, he was being told by friends and family, at Boyden's behest, that Ritter was not of the temperament he once believed. Already looking for a way out, pressure from those who wanted Boyden, and from Boyden himself and his high-placed friends, magnified the dilemma.

Fortunately for Ritter, Judge Johnson did not formally announce his retirement until June 1949. In the intervening months, Thomas resolved his doubts and overcame his misgivings. He got in touch with Calvin Rawlings, Democratic National Committeeman since 1948, and asked him for help. Rawlings told him there was talk going around that Ritter was arrogant, dictatorial, and autocratic and that he was in favor of Bob Roberts. Thomas told Rawlings that he had an obligation to Ritter and that he was going to fulfill that obligation. Rawlings had a talk with Ritter, telling him he was worried about his temperament, that he should get an outstanding lawyer involved in federal practice to advise him, but that he would go along with supporting him because Thomas had insisted.[25]

Thomas acted in the public interest, as he saw it and as he said he must do when Ritter approached him on the labor question, and disregarded all of his self-serving advisers. He came through, on June 3, 1949, and announced to the press that he had recommended Willis W. Ritter to President Truman as Tillman D. Johnson's replacement.[26] Thomas also said in his announcement that he had consulted Harvard's celebrated liberal professor of law, Thomas E. Powell, about Ritter. Powell, who had recommended Ritter in 1941 for the University of Utah presidency, said that, in his judgment, Ritter's personal and intellectual qualities were perhaps even more relevant to a federal judgeship.

Ritter's nomination was an issue on which the *Salt Lake Tribune* and Abe Glassman's media interests found common cause and acted in concert. George Hatch, Glassman's son-in-law and manager of radio station KALL, wired Thomas the day of the announcement that he "had good reaction from our news broadcast and Fitzgerald [publisher of the *Tribune*] reports all comments to papers favorable. *Ogden Standard-Examiner* and *Tribune* will both carry approving Sunday editorials welcoming recommendation as merit appointment."

"Our Senator chose wisely and well from a strong field," the *Examiner* said in its promised editorial, adding that Ritter had a "profound knowledge of the laws" and a "rich background of experience of men and affairs." The *Tribune* editorialized that "although confronted with the difficult responsibility of indicating preference among distinguished jurists and attorneys [Thomas] made a choice which...was wise and commendable," touched on Ritter's major achievements, scholastic and professional, and that he was a private in the army in World War I and might have been a major in World War II had he chosen to accept appointment. Much was made of his native-son status, his parents' western origins, and the humble circumstances of his upbringing in Park City.[27] Reference to his rags-to-riches ascent made an appealing sketch of a man whose personal history was in the best tradition of the American ideal that anyone can become president—or, in this case, federal judge.

A few days after announcing Ritter as his nominee, Thomas responded to the criticism he had been receiving concerning Ritter, with respect to lack of temperament in particular, by sending Ritter an excerpt from an opinion he wrote in 1933 regarding a judicial impeachment proceeding before the Senate. The essence of Thomas's message was that the nature of the federal judiciary, the high degree of autonomy the office bestows on those who hold it, and the difficulty of removing a federal judge from office—those aspects of a federal judgeship that are unique among all official government positions—dictate that federal judges must possess a finer character and display more circumspect conduct than any other group of public officials. But lest Ritter miss it, he added in a postscript, "I am sure I need not say more now but to express the hope and the prayer that your tenure will reflect at all times the ideals of our Constitution and the ideals of the people of our State."[28]

Ritter felt so good that he took Rita and the four children—Bill and Nancy were well-nigh adults by then—on a vacation to Colorado. He went to attend the Tenth Circuit Judicial Conference in Denver. On the way there, and on their return, they traveled through Rocky Mountain National Park. "With such beautiful country around us here I marvel at myself for doing any work during the summer months," he said in a letter to Dean Brimhall. "One of these days I am going to get smart and enjoy my family more."[29] A fine feeling it was, too, to be at the conference among the federal judges and eminent lawyers. He had been to these conferences before, but this time it was different. Everyone called him "Judge," and roundly congratulated him, and of course the Utah lawyers, even those who lobbied for the appointment of Boyden, wanted him to know that they had been "pulling for him all the way."

The fact was that he was not yet confirmed. In fact, President Truman had not yet officially nominated him, but that seemed an insignificant detail. The delay seemed inordinate, and Ritter, Thomas, and state party leaders became impatient and a little nervous. On August 2, 1949, Hinckley, who maintained an active role in Utah politics, inquired about the status of the nomination. The answer he received was that the Justice Department investigation of Ritter was not yet complete. "Informed everyone that continued delay is embarrassing to Ritter, to Thomas, to the state and national Democratic organizations. Believe some of the people talked to are doing all possible to expedite the matter," Hinckley said in a telegram. He sent another wire on August 8, 1949, saying: "Everything seems to be in order. Nomination should go up this week."[30]

When two more weeks passed without action by the White House, Thomas went to attorney general Tom Clark to ask for help. Thomas was told that the FBI had submitted its report, that it was being processed "in routine fashion," and that the length of time being taken was "nothing unusual." At the time, Clark was about to be sworn in as United States Supreme Court justice, and J. Howard McGrath had been appointed to succeed him. It might be some time, Clark told Thomas, before the new attorney general got around to "taking up the Ritter case."

Justice completed its part of the process three days later, earlier than Clark had predicted. Thomas requested that Democratic National Committeeman Calvin Rawlings, who was en route to Washington, inform the president on the subject. Before he could do so, President Truman put his signature on the nomination on August 25, 1949.[31] Thomas was present at the signing and sent word to Ritter and KSL, the LDS Church-owned radio station.

"Truman Names Ritter Federal Judge," read the caption on a *Salt Lake Tribune* editorial the next morning.[32] Another editorial appeared the next day, together with a story headlined "Willis W. Ritter Named to Utah Federal Bench." The editorial indicated that confirmation was ensured, the hearings only a formality, and that the appointment would most certainly meet with general approval in the state and throughout the intermountain region.

Ritter, in the meantime, acted on Thomas's message about circumspection by answering a letter he had received from Dean Brimhall sending a packet of information concerning hidden tax benefits to the Mormon Church. The *Deseret News* had published an editorial, which Brimhall believed was authored by J. Reuben Clark Jr., contending that taxpayer support of activities "the people should do for themselves" by the WPA, the agency Brimhall was associated with, "resulted in demoralization of the recipients and finally of the state."

"It seems clear that Mr. Clark forgot or ignored the taxpayer support the Mormon Church gets in operating its publications and I should enjoy reminding him of it," Brimhall declared, listing taxpayer-paid services to church property for fire and police protection, paving of sidewalks and streets, street lighting and maintenance, garbage removal, and a "healthy subsidy" to "the 'army' of 5,000 or more missionaries" in the form of reduced fares on railroads. Someone should look into it, Brimhall suggested, but concluded: "It seems unrealistic to me to ask you to get involved in this matter just now."[33]

Ritter agreed. "The church is so vulnerable and someone should show them up," Ritter observed. "Every time Rube Clark shoots off in this fashion somebody ought to jump right straight back at him. They get away with murder anyway and if enough of us worked them over in the vigorous way in which we ought they might become better Indians."[34] But he felt he should not, at that time, while the appointment was pending, involve himself in the question.

As he basked in the attention bestowed upon him at the judicial conference, marveled at the beauties of the Rocky Mountains, and pondered the implications of Thomas's advice, the storm that was to surround his confirmation was brewing.

Brewing as well were two of the pivotal events that would evoke controversy for Ritter. In San Diego, two young sailors named Verne Alfred Braasch and Melvin LeRoy Sullivan were being mustered out of the United States Navy. With time on their hands, they drifted to Utah, where they ran out of money for beer, cigarettes, and other needs and robbed a service station in Parowan. While that was going on, in the Four Corners area of southeastern Utah, just off the Navajo Reservation, a cattle rancher named W. R. Young, together with fellow livestock men in San Juan County, and the range manager of the United States Bureau of Land Management (BLM) for District 6 in Utah were holding meetings and devising a strategy for getting horses and burros off the range that were grazing there without a permit. The animals belonged to Bill Hatahley, Hosteen Tse-kesi, and a half-dozen other families.[35] None of them had permission to graze on the federal range, but they were Navajo who had grazed their animals on the range for generations, long before the non-Indian ranchers arrived or the BLM was even created. They believed they had a right to go on the range, as they had always done. The Indians therefore ignored the range manager and the rancher's demands, and trouble quickly followed.

9

SUSPENSION

I don't say embrace trouble. That's as bad as treating it as an enemy. But I do say meet it as a friend, for you'll see a lot of it and had better be on speaking terms with it.

—Oliver Wendell Holmes Jr.

Willis W. Ritter found himself in Washington, D.C., on September 29, 1949. But for that fateful day in 1932, when he drove to Ogden to help his friend and teaching colleague Elbert D. Thomas wrest the Democratic Party nomination for U.S. senator from John Wallace, he probably wouldn't be there. Those political events in 1932 had changed the future course of Ritter's life and eventually brought him to Washington as nominee for United States District Judge for the District of Utah.

He didn't mind. He was pleased to go. He liked Washington, D.C., knew some people there, and he knew the town. Though born, bred, and trained in relatively remote, largely rural Utah, he had been to Washington first in 1924 as a young law school graduate and employee of Morris, Kixmiller, and Baar[1] and more recently on behalf of Abe Glassman, George Hatch, and his other tax-media clients.

Washington politics was another matter. His wartime stint at the OPA required Ritter's presence in the nation's capital a time or two, including for the Smith Committee hearings. He had developed an appetite for Utah elective politics, and appeared in Washington for hearings on the Granger election contest, but he might as well have been in another country, for all the experience he had with the Washington-style intrigues.

The important matter bringing Ritter to Washington on this day was another hearing, to be held at Room 424, United States Senate Office Building, at 10:00 AM on September 29, 1949, convened by a subcommittee of the Senate Judiciary Committee. The senators would scour the details of his history, to determine of what matter he was, and recommend if the Senate should approve or reject his nomination. Disposition would ride largely on their impression of him.

Better that those passing judgment should see him in person. Seeing a person can make a difference in what you think of him, as opposed to merely hearing or reading about him. And if a man's appearance complements his good credentials—and Ritter's did—he'd do well to meet his critics in person.

Willis Ritter was fifty when Senator Thomas recommended his nomination. His stout but fit-looking five-foot eight-inch frame; confident bearing; high, broad forehead; and direct gaze suggested the energetic, acute, and professionally successful man that he was. He was obviously no country lawyer, even if he did come from the rough mining culture of the West.

The judgeship was all but his. He had only to gain the approval of the United States Senate, a process that was normally little more than a formality in the 1940s. The Senate usually took the position that unless a senator from the nominee's state declared himself dead-set against the nominee, or the candidate was otherwise shown to be a scoundrel or a fool, it would go along with the president.

Before the body of the Senate would speak, however, the Senate Judiciary Committee must review Ritter's credentials as well as a Justice Department summary of his past life and an FBI report, considered strictly confidential. "No one is allowed to see the FBI files, not even senators, except under very special circumstances." The practice was for an officer of the Department of Justice to call on the chairman of the Senate Judiciary Committee with the FBI files, give an oral résumé of anything in them that might be considered derogatory, and answer any questions the chairman may have. The chairman, and sometimes another member of the subcommittee, might be permitted to look at the reports, but only in the presence of the officer. The report was not left with the chairman or any other member. "As a practical matter, therefore, the members of the Judiciary Committee only know what the Department of Justice or the Chairman of the Committee wishes to tell them."[2]

Prior to the hearing on September 29, 1949, the FBI investigation and its report to the chairman of the subcommittee had been completed. Months had been spent investigating Ritter. Agents had interviewed scores of people in every state where Ritter had lived, worked, or gone to school and had examined the records concerning him. Report on the investigation had been given to the chairman, according to protocol, and the chairman read excerpts from the report at a meeting of the Judiciary Committee on September 3, 1949, which the junior senator from Utah, Arthur V. Watkins, had been invited to attend, even though he was not a member. Nothing had been reported by FBI to the chairman that reflected adversely on Ritter's qualifications for judicial appointment. Watkins claimed to have heard something in what was read that raised questions. But he never identified what those questions were, if they were in the report itself or only suggested in his mind, or presented any facts supporting his claim.

The committee would also consider testimony—written and oral—from any citizen who wished to say something about the nominee. A summation of the committee's findings would then go to the full Senate for a vote.

Thomas had told Ritter that he might have to go to Washington to meet with the Judiciary Committee once Truman sent it the nomination. The committee had made it a practice in recent times to ask the nominees to meet with it in person. That proved to be the case with Ritter. The committee asked him to appear before it near the end of August, then postponed the appearance at the request of Watkins, who indicated he wanted to be present at the hearing but would be in Utah, talking to people back home about the nomination, at the time originally scheduled.

Ritter had no doubt that Watkins's delay was calculated, at the least, to prevent a smooth confirmation process. Watkins and his fellow Utah Republicans wanted the appointment for one of their own but knew it was out of the question with a Democrat in the White House and a Democrat of considerable standing as senior senator from Utah. Watkins and the Utah Republicans could delay, and they might plant doubt at home, but they did not have the votes to stop Ritter. He was confident of that.

Senator Warren G. Magnuson, Democrat from Washington, was the chairman of the subcommittee Ritter was in Washington to appear before. Democrat Bert M. Miller from Idaho and Republican William Langer from North Dakota were the other members. Ritter, Thomas, and several witnesses were there, along with committee staff members, including counsel J. G. Sourwine. Sourwine probably knew more about what was going on than anyone, for it was his responsibility to sort out the affidavits, reports, letters, and telegrams about Ritter and talk with people at the FBI and the Justice Department or anyone else who wanted to register an official statement about the appointment.

Despite having requested a postponement of the hearing so that he could attend, Watkins was not present. Magnuson, who presided, invited Thomas to speak first, which he did in his florid style. Recommending Ritter for the judgeship was "one of the happiest acts I have ever done here in Washington," Thomas said. "Dr. Ritter, as a student and as a trained lawyer, and from his military and administrative experience, and as an instructor of youth, fits in very well to that ideal scheme which we work out for the American who is able to do the most for his country." Not one letter opposing Ritter's nomination "that I know of" had been received, Thomas declared. Desiring to appear entirely objective, Thomas then recalled the letters touting others, John S. Boyden in particular. "Before [Ritter] was named, of course, there were many candidates, and each person stood on his own merit, and some persons sent letters like they always send against a given person, instead of entirely for them." He finally added, apparently seeking a more positive stance, that none of the Democrats in Utah's congressional delegation had opposed or criticized the nomination.

A telegram from H. Austin Hauxhurst, vice chairman of the Special Committee on the Judiciary of the American Bar Association (ABA), was read into the record. The ABA "begs to inform you that it does not oppose the nomination of Willis W. Ritter as district judge for the district of Utah," the letter read.[3]

But opposition, both veiled and direct, was about to be presented. Magnuson read from two previous communications from Watkins, one dated September 20, 1949, addressed to Senator Harley M. Kilgore as acting chairman of the committee, the other dated October 5, 1949, addressed to Magnuson. The letter to Kilgore reaffirmed that "I am not making any personal objection" and confessed that "I am not acquainted with Mr. Ritter and only know him by reports made to me by people who are interested in securing his confirmation and those who are opposed."[4] Thus, the only basis for opposition by Watkins, other than pure politics, was letters of others, which were made a part of the record.

One of the two people who objected to Ritter's appointment, according to Watkins, was Knox Patterson, a Democrat "of the Jack Garner–Pat McCarran type," as he described himself, a Salt Lake City lawyer, former state legislator, and former assistant attorney general of the State of Utah. Patterson had already written two letters to the committee. "You replied that if I had any specific information showing that [Ritter] was not fit to be a Federal judge" or "any leads with respect to specific information" the Committee would consider them, Patterson's second letter stated. Patterson had no information, or leads, and alluded only to gossip. He confessed that "there is no pretense that I have exact knowledge of matters stated herein, but I am sure they are not just common rumors, and that they do have sufficient foundation in fact to justify a thorough investigation." Patterson asserted his "belief [that Grant Ivins] would testify to the arbitrary actions of Ritter while he was rent director of Utah" and that "T. Quentin

Cannon...would probably testify if called as to the unfair manner in which Ritter managed this office." True to his disclaimer of "exact knowledge," Patterson stated nothing specific—only unsubstantiated rumors—and "definite evidences that Ritter does not believe in the Constitution of the United States; that he believes it is outmoded and obstructs social progress."[5]

Ritter already knew that the Judiciary Committee had a negative letter from Knox Patterson in hand—saying essentially that Ritter was a political subversive. He may also have been aware that his former colleague, Ivins, had written to the Committee saying that Ritter was temperamental and otherwise unsuited to be a judge. Ritter was concerned that the senators might not see through such actions by his detractors. He was concerned further that delay to investigate such blind alleys would be to dawdle through never-ending mazes, while the District of Utah was buried under an increasing backlog of cases.

Ritter also knew that the junior senator from Utah, Watkins, had a knack for obstruction. He had probably heard that Watkins had written twice to Judiciary Committee chairman Patrick McCarran, who would have passed that information down through the grapevine of the Democratic Party, where it would have become known to Ritter, to express concerns about Ritter's character and requested that he postpone a decision on the nomination to hold additional hearings.

Watkins had, in fact, returned to Washington. Senator Miller had seen him in the hallway as he walked to the hearing. Later in the morning Watkins informed the subcommittee that he would not attend and preferred to stand on the letter dated September 20, 1949, that he had written to Senator Kilgore. Magnuson, addressing Ritter as "Judge," asked if he was familiar with Watkins's letter. Ritter said he was not. Magnuson read portions of the letter aloud when Thomas finished his statement, at the request of Miller:

> I suggest that a hearing be held on this nomination to permit residents of the State of Utah to state their objections to the confirmation....
>
> ...A number of reputable Utah citizens have told me they desired to present matters to the Judiciary Committee of the Senate, which they felt should be considered by the committee before it makes up its mind whether or not to recommend the approval of Mr. Ritter. In their behalf, I am urging that these witnesses either be subpoenaed to come to Washington or that arrangements be made to take their testimony at Salt Lake City. I understand that one of them, Mr. Knox Patterson, has already

> communicated with your committee. Another, Mr. H. Grant Ivins, of Salt Lake City, a former associate of Mr. Ritter in the Rent Control Administration for Utah, also desired to be heard. There are still others who are willing to testify if given the opportunity.[6]

The tone of Watkins's letter was calculated to appear neutral; he was just a dutiful public official doing his job. The hearing he requested was to provide a forum to *oppose* the nomination, however, without himself submitting a blue slip of opposition. Thus, Watkins in effect was *challenging* the subcommittee to solicit testimony adverse to Ritter. If the challenge was ignored, the subcommittee might at least appear negligent and at the worst prejudiced in Ritter's favor. For Watkins, early in his first term and lacking the stature to get into a battle with his fellow senators, that may have been a clever strategy.

Watkins's letter proclaimed, "I don't believe that it is the duty of any one Senator to fight the confirmation of appointees to Federal posts"—which is to say that he did oppose the nomination. The letter's request that the witnesses he named be "subpoenaed" is also curious, for presumably anyone with knowledge about the candidate's shortcomings, and who believed that they made him unsuited for judicial office, would come forward on his or her own, or at least on a mere request by Watkins to do so.

The Patterson and Watkins letters, whether by coincidence or design, meshed nicely with one another. Patterson stated nothing of substance, but he did raise the inference that Ritter did not believe in the Constitution and named persons who could be the object of the subpoenas Watkins had in mind. Watkins's letter suggested a hearing to which they could be subpoenaed.

Ritter was by nature an impatient man who liked to control whatever situation he found himself in. One quickly sensed that Ritter was not accustomed to sitting on the sidelines. The delays while waiting for the retirement of Judge Tillman Johnson had already put him under a heavy strain, and further delay would oppress him still more. And it was not just the delay that was troublesome. There was the possibility that the senators would not see through the lies and the rat's nest that might materialize if they decided to investigate.

Ritter did not like people opposing his nomination but thought to himself that that miserable little bit of sniping wouldn't make a pissant's worth of difference. The nation was experiencing jitters about communism, and espionage, during the period when it was struggling to get on a sound postwar economic course. Watkins had been swept into office in the 1946 election when the Republicans fashioned the political tactic of red-baiting, and he would now make capital of that strategy to oppose Ritter's nomination, or try to do so.

As for Watkins jumping in and changing the hearing, well, that was just typical of him and those Utah Republicans—getting in a few last licks, even though they knew it wouldn't do them a bit of good. Democrats were in a period of decline, however, and several of Truman's appointees had been embarrassed in the confirmation process. Neither Senator McCarran nor Senator Magnuson was going to be slipshod in the process of trying to get confirmation for a Truman appointee to the federal bench. They would go the extra mile, to avoid making any errors, and give Watkins an opportunity to make his case against appointment to a post as pivotal as that of federal district court judge for Utah.

Magnuson asked Ritter, "[Do you have] anything personal that you would like to add to what has been said by our colleague about you?" Ritter replied, "Nothing at all, Mr. Chairman. I am here at your disposal. If you have anything that I can help you with, I will be delighted to speak about it."[7]

With the reading of Patterson's and Watkins's letters, the essentials of the case that would be made against Ritter's appointment, other than a matter of sex that would come up later, became part of the public record. The charges were that he did not believe in the Constitution, that he had shown himself to be arbitrary in nature, that he had discriminated against landlords while at the OPA, that he was "far to the left" in his politics, and that his background and experience in the law were inadequate to qualify him to preside over a United States District Court. "I might say, Mr. Chairman, and I am not concerned with these personal accusations," Senator Miller said, after hearing Patterson's allegations, "I think they are inconsequential, save and except the accusation that Mr. Ritter does not believe in our Federal Constitution. That is pretty positive and probably such a matter as would warrant some little investigation."[8]

Thomas assured the subcommittee that the allegation was the most preposterous of all, for lawyers and anyone who had ever been in the military, as Ritter had been, were required to swear allegiance to the Constitution. "Have you made lectures or speeches... which could give rise to that sort of an accusation?" Magnuson asked Ritter. Yes, Ritter explained, he had delivered a series of lectures some years back through the University of Utah

Extension Division about the Supreme Court and some of its decisions. "At that time, the court was divided, with Holmes and Brandeis and Harlan Stone and after awhile Cardozo on one side and Butler and Van Devanter and McReynolds and our own Justice Sutherland from Utah on the other side—and I think what Mr. Patterson is talking about is that series of lectures."[9]

Patterson made clear that he referred to that 1936 series of Extension Division lectures, precisely, in a letter published in the *Salt Lake Tribune* dated October 1, 1949. "I made no specific charges of disloyalty" by Ritter, Patterson declared, but that "series of public lectures…clearly justified said statement."[10] Ritter said he would try to find copies of the lectures for the Committee. Magnuson asked if anyone had objected at the time to what he said. No one had, Ritter said, not the public, the press, or university officials.

Then Magnuson asked Ritter if Patterson had reason to fear reprisals. "Well, my dear sir, if a fellow is going to hold grudges, he ought not to aspire to that bench," Ritter replied.[11]

Magnuson summarized:

> What we are dealing with here is communications and expressions of opinion from residents of Utah and we have in the file, and that is all we have in the file; one man who says he was tyrannical and dealt in the OPA matters in a wrong way and we have maybe two or three hundred testimonials, affidavits, unsolicited from other prominent citizens, granting that they both are, from the State of Utah, who say just the opposite and who say that his integrity is of the highest, his ability is of the highest, and that he is more than qualified to be a judge.[12]

"The man ought to be given permission to establish that fact, if he can," Miller said of Patterson's charges, "not that he could do it, but I would be very happy to listen to him if he has anything in connection with it." Magnuson indicated, "We do have funds, but very limited funds," then put the matter in perspective: "The hearings on Judge Ritter were delayed at the request of Senator Watkins, who made a trip to the State and…has nothing further to present.…[N]o other witnesses have seen fit to show up.…But to send a man out to Utah to investigate the matter, I do not think would serve a great deal, or any purpose whatsoever, because all he would do would be to find out the facts that could be said here anyway, unless we could go ourselves."[13]

"It is very seldom that you do not get a letter from somebody about a man," Thomas explained. "I know that people say the sort of things which Mr. Patterson has said here: 'this man is no American,' or 'he does not stand by the Constitution,' and so on."[14]

"The charge that he does not believe in the Constitution is ridiculous," Senator Langer, the Republican from South Dakota observed. "They have a bar association out there. If he was not fit, they would have representatives here, I am sure." Then Langer questioned Ritter about his experience as a practicing attorney, and whether he had ever represented Utah's copper-mining interests. "I have always been on the other side of the copper interests," Ritter replied. He said he had tried three or four cases having to do with mortgage foreclosures, a complicated defense of foreign corporations, and some condemnation cases. "I have never had any criminal practice. Mr. Patterson suggests in his letter it is generally known in Utah that I don't have any practice. It is immodest for me to say anything about that. It is going to be a financial sacrifice for me to take the federal judgeship as a matter of dollars and cents.... I make no apologies for the practice I have. If you make any inquiries out there you would find that out."[15]

Magnuson then asked if any other witnesses wanted to appear, and Representative Walter K. Granger, Congressman from Utah's First District, offered a statement in support of Ritter. The Utah State Bar was "almost unanimous" in support of Ritter, Granger declared. The committee in fact did have on file letters of endorsement signed by all commissioners of the Utah State Bar and the Utah County Bar.[16] "The greatest complaint I could have against him is that he does represent the clientele of the upper crust," Granger continued. "I thought he was to the left," said Langer. "Everybody is to the left" of Patterson, Granger replied, "and if Mr. Ritter does not believe in the Constitution, neither do I, and I have represented my people and they know exactly where I stand on these matters for the last five terms in the Congress of the United States." Granger then explained that he had served in the Utah legislature with Patterson, and that he was a great liberal then, but "got off the reservation... so far off that anything that he might say... I would give very little weight to." Granger asserted, "If he had any information," Patterson should present it, "instead of quoting Grant Ivins, [who] is a good friend of mine and you could not drag Ivins before this committee to testify against Ritter."[17]

True to Granger's prediction, the *Tribune* quoted Ivins as saying, "I have not seen Knox Patterson in 20 years, and I have never discussed the

Ritter case with him." Cannon was also quoted as saying he has "never had any occasion to question [Ritter's] loyalty to the United States, its Constitution or its laws, rules or regulations. It was a surprise to me that the question of his loyalty was ever raised."[18]

Reed Smith, one of Ritter's former students, testified that he considered him one of the best professors at the school and never heard him say anything that suggested he was opposed to the Constitution. Thomas added that he had been Ritter's teacher in American Government and would have known if Ritter did not believe in the Constitution.

The charge of "disloyalty," the whipping boy of choice of Republicans during the era, had nevertheless been unleashed, but Watkins would not acknowledge authorship of the attack on Ritter's character. Despite his rather obvious tactics of delay, and the inferences he had raised, Watkins continued the pretense that he was not opposed to Ritter's appointment—only insisting that interested persons from his state who *might* be opposed be given an opportunity to testify.

Salt Lake Tribune articles, including those quoting Patterson and Cannon, countered the suggestion that Ritter was subversive in his political views.[19] The charge had been made public, however, and its mere suggestion was damaging all by itself.

There is no indication that a copy of Ritter's 1936 lectures was ever made a part of the record, but when examined they contain nothing more controversial than that the "sparsely settled rural country" of the days when the Constitution was adopted was "distinguished from our modern day industrial empire." His "Lecture II, Democracy—Has It a Future?" may have been the source of Patterson's charge of not believing in the Constitution. In it Ritter explained that "the founders desired to avoid consequences of the failure of popular rule," referring to the French Revolution and the execution of Louis XVI. Ritter alluded to Chrétien-Guillaume Malesherbes, "a great French lawyer" who defended Louis XVI and followed him to the scaffold, after which Ritter declared that the fathers of the Constitution "knew the dangers of popular rule" and "set out upon the most important deliberate attempt ever made by men to render popular rule safe." They did so, according to Ritter, by means of "a political miracle, namely, a self-checking government." He then concluded that "today, in this country, liberty is still steering the perilous course" and, with what may have been misinterpreted as an expression of belief that the Constitution is outmoded, that despite the difficulty of amendment, "our institutions have changed greatly."[20]

Magnuson then declared adjournment of the open hearing. The subcommittee went into executive session.[21] It was there resolved that Watkins's request that Grant Ivins and T. Quentin Cannon be called to testify be presented to the full committee for its consideration the following Monday, together with the nomination.

On September 29, 1949, the *Salt Lake Tribune* reported, erroneously, that "Ritter Wins Okay of Senate Committee." The headline in the evening paper, the *Deseret News,* stated "S.L. Attorney Clears Up Ritter Muddle," in reference to the inferences raised before the subcommittee. Another headline in the *Salt Lake Tribune* on September 30, 1949, proclaimed "Ritter Passes U.S. Senate Loyalty Test." It was incorrect either that the subcommittee had approved the nomination, that the muddle soon to follow had been cleared up, or that Ritter had passed a "loyalty test." The articles correctly reported that the subcommittee had discussed a letter from Knox Patterson suggesting "definite evidence that Ritter does not believe in the Constitution."

When the full Judiciary Committee convened the following Monday, it was resolved to refer the nomination of Willis W. Ritter back to the subcommittee for consideration of the request by Watkins for the taking of additional testimony.

The stage was thus set for a contest over Ritter's qualifications. His opponents were beginning to assemble. The defining event in the life and times of Willis W. Ritter, with Arthur V. Watkins his protagonist in chief, was soon to begin.

10

SMEAR

Treating your adversary with respect is giving him an advantage to which he is not entitled.

—Samuel Johnson

While Willis W. Ritter was enjoying the splendors of nature at the Rocky Mountain National Park and his praise at the judicial conference by judges and lawyers alike in the weeks following announcement of his nomination, there were those who were not yet resigned to his confirmation being a matter of course.

The president of the Mormon Church, George Albert Smith, had been among those who wrote to Thomas favoring the candidacy of John S. Boyden. He wrote to Thomas again, this time urging the withdrawal of the Ritter nomination. A letter from the leader of the Mormon Church was troubling. To one of Thomas's indoctrination and discipline, a letter from the church president and prophet was right next to one from Joseph Smith, or perhaps God himself, tearing at his impartiality. The first letter was at the behest of Boyden. Whether Boyden instigated the second letter is obscure. Meanwhile, others were getting organized to oppose the nomination. They were about to get more aggressive.

Ritter's virtual neighbor from his childhood days at Midway Arthur Watkins had been planning a strategy to block the Ritter nomination with a Washington, D.C., lawyer named Ernest Wilkinson. Wilkinson had been familiar with Ritter and his reputation for at least twenty years, through their mutual friends Louis Crandall, Paul Ray, Henry Moyle, and Elbert Thomas, and had direct dealings with him over a period of more than four years, asking for and receiving advice from Ritter on employment of personnel to do legal research. Ritter was considered by Wilkinson to be "honest in making that appraisal." Ritter had responded to Wilkinson with a brutal candor that confirmed his honesty and directness.[1]

Wilkinson originated in Utah, had strong Mormon ties, and would become president of Brigham Young University in 1951. He and Watkins held at least a dozen meetings, at Watkins's Washington office, starting in early 1949.[2] Knowing that they could not challenge Ritter on his academic and professional qualifications, they resolved that they must develop evidence that he lacked the character and integrity expected of a federal judge.

Watkins and Wilkinson were, in some respects, improbable confederates and conspirators. Wilkinson, fifty years of age, was a small man, with straight dark hair; a strong, Dick Tracy–like jaw; and a bulldog personality to go with it. Watkins was meek and mild, tall and angular, with a full head of white hair. Old enough to be Wilkinson's father, Watkins actually appeared ancient enough to be Wilkinson's grandfather. Wilkinson went to Washington in 1923 as a supporter of Democratic Senator William H. King but parted with the Democrats with the coming of the New Deal. What they had in common was Mormonism and the Republican philosophy, together with a desire to defeat the Ritter nomination. Wilkinson was cocounsel with John S. Boyden in the presentation of Indian claims and sometimes shown as his professional partner on their stationery and at their respective offices.[3] Wilkinson wanted the judgeship for Boyden; Watkins had no desire for Boyden, who was a prominent Democrat, but was aware that Boyden was favored by Mormon Church leaders and was willing to accept him as a compromise for that reason. Wilkinson was given the task of developing evidence concerning Ritter's character and temperament that could be used to defeat the nomination.

Critical to the innuendos Watkins and now Wilkinson were about to raise was the report to the Justice Department by the FBI, routinely prepared for every nominee. Federal judges are fundamentally expected to be of unassailable integrity. The FBI investigation is calculated to demonstrate if they are so qualified. If there had been evidence of disloyalty, or any other matter that disqualified the nominee, it was expected to have been revealed in the FBI report.

Watkins had attended a meeting of the full Judiciary Committee on September 3, 1949, at which it was reported that there was nothing reflecting adversely on Ritter, and an excerpt was read from the FBI report. Afterward, he wrote his letter of September 20, 1949, to Senator Kilgore stating, "I am not making any personal objection" and "only know [Ritter] by reports made to me" by others. On Monday, October 3, 1949, Watkins attended another meeting of the Judiciary Committee, this one closed, where it was decided to return the nomination to the subcommittee.[4] The FBI investigation and the Knox Patterson letter suggesting that Quentin Cannon and Grant Ivins might give testimony against the nomination were discussed again. Watkins did not hold a position that entitled him to see the report, but nothing prohibited him from raising questions about it or the chairman from disclosing what was in it.

The "un-American" and "communist" charges quickly proved "ridiculous," as Republican senator William Langer had predicted at the September 29 meeting. The FBI reports indicate that Ritter allegedly made the statement to his law school class that there was "nothing wrong with the Communist Party"—plainly repeating the Knox Patterson letter. They also state that he "associated with Communists." The basis for the latter claim was that "he was a protege of [Senator] Thomas" who "associated with numerous communists" and "was connected with Edward I. Aronow, the attorney for Earl Browder in 1942," who "substantially aided in the campaign of 1944 for the re-election of Senator Thomas." Because Ritter was in communication with Aronow, being manager of Thomas's campaign, the reports drew the illogical and untenable conclusion that he was also "associated" with communists. Evidently unaware of the long, friendly, and professional association of Thomas and Ritter with one another, and of Thomas's high regard for Ritter, the FBI agent who wrote the reports concluded that the Aronow connection was the reason Thomas "nominated Ritter to be Federal District Judge for the District of Utah." In short, the claim was that because Ritter was a friend and confidant of Thomas, and both he and Thomas were in contact with labor leaders and their attorneys, and because Republicans of the era had painted Thomas and other New Deal lights as communists or sympathizers, Ritter must also be a communist.[5] No one, including Republican colleagues of Watkins such as Langer, would give credence to such a claim, considering the high regard in which Thomas was held.

When the subcommittee reconvened, the underpinning for the FBI reports, the Patterson letter, vanished when the letter of Patterson to the *Salt Lake Tribune* asserting "I made no specific charges of disloyalty against Mr. Ritter" was read into the record. Congressman Walter K. Granger, who was at the continued hearing, took exception to what Patterson said in his original letter, and declared that Patterson had, in substance or effect, charged disloyalty, for "if a man is going out preaching that he does not believe in the Constitution, I would consider that a very dangerous thing, to say the least, and it may border on being disloyal because that is the charter of our liberty. [Patterson] said in no uncertain terms that Mr. Ritter did not believe in the Constitution." Subcommittee chairman Warren Magnuson advised, "Now he has apparently changed his mind." "Evidently so," Granger agreed.[6]

After the October 3, 1949, meeting Watkins said that he found the FBI report, which he did not object to after the September 3, 1949, meeting, "surprising" and raising questions as to Ritter's "integrity" and "morality." Apparently, his surprise related to references to Ritter having been absent from his desk at the OPA in Denver for what some considered an inordinate amount of time during trips to Albuquerque. A subsequent letter by Watkins outlining his objections to the Ritter nomination expanded on that portion of the FBI report, inferring that it confirmed the gossip that Ritter had carried on a relationship, of an undefined nature, with a female employee of the OPA in its Albuquerque office. The allegation of a "love affair," even if that could be considered grounds of disqualification for public office, nevertheless stood without any support, so Watkins requested that the committee subpoena, among others, "Phyllis Katz, a former employee of the OPA at Albuquerque, New Mexico." Watkins also intimated, without proof, that Ritter "submitted false or fraudulent travel vouchers" while at the OPA and "various charges respecting his private conduct and personal life."[7] Watkins was thus left with an attack based almost entirely on the matter of sex.

Senator Thomas contacted the Justice Department to determine if there was information in the FBI report supporting the charges being made by Watkins. Peyton Ford, assistant to the attorney general, advised Thomas by letter dated October 19, 1949, that reports of Justice Department investigations "are, by their very nature, strictly confidential" and "not permitted to be reviewed by anyone outside of the Department of Justice. Occasionally this rule has been relaxed in favor of members of the United States Senate Committee on the Judiciary as a matter of courtesy. This privilege, however, is not extended to anyone other than a member of the Judiciary Committee," which did not include either Watkins or Thomas. But Ford reassured Thomas that "after having carefully read the report we were unable to find any real evidence of anything to impugn his integrity, ability, character, loyalty or judicial temperament."[8] The full FBI report was obtained by coauthor Patricia Cowley, pursuant to the Freedom of Information Act, and has been examined. Based upon interviews with persons who observed the two of them, the report indicated nothing irregular in Ritter's conduct toward Phyllis Katz.

Though liberally expurgated, the report contains nothing else that could be considered derogatory and generally describes Ritter to be brilliant, loyal, and of good moral character, though headstrong and, by some witnesses' accounts, "dictatorial" during his OPA tenure. Considered in context, those conclusions appear sufficient to negate the possibility of any salacious or derogatory material concerning Katz in the expurgated material.

Moreover, content of the expurgated material itself is easily determined. Because of the practice of FBI agents beginning their reports with a summary of prior information in the file, and because Ritter was under constant investigation over the decades that followed, reference to the summary in subsequent reports, including in particular an FBI memorandum to Director J. Edgar Hoover dated June 18, 1952, reveals, with rather obvious embellishment, that "our [prior] investigation disclosed that Ritter... had a 'love affair' with a young woman when he was an attorney [with the OPA]." The source of that information and witnesses supporting it are not stated. The name, or names, of the agents authoring the reports was also expurgated, but it became widely known that the special agent reporting those rumors was Delmar "Swede" Larson, who had Utah ties, surely including Watkins and Wilkinson, and later became sheriff for Salt Lake County after his service with the FBI was terminated.[9]

Watkins wrote a third letter to the chairman of the Judiciary Committee on October 5, 1949, still professing that he "was not making a personal objection" but stating, in contradiction of the statement of Ford and his own letter to Senator Langer acknowledging that he had no information and unsupported by anything factual in the FBI report, that "while at that meeting, an excerpt was read by a member of the committee from a report that was in the possession of the committee.... The full report is not available to me. I understood from reference to it in the committee that it comprises more than 30 pages." Watkins requested, with innuendos that could not be ignored, that "H. Grant Ivins... and Quentin Cannon of [Salt Lake City] be subpoenaed to attend the hearing next Monday or at such other time as will be convenient to the committee and these gentlemen."[10] Watkins appears to have put his own gloss on whatever he heard repeated from the report. The smear had been unleashed, nevertheless, and was quickly repeated and magnified in the press.

The gossip about an illicit romance with a woman in Albuquerque being collected for Watkins by Wilkinson was then passed to Jack Anderson, an investigative reporter for columnist Drew Pearson and an active Mormon.

After Anderson met with Wilkinson and Watkins, Pearson published the gossip as fact and claimed that salacious testimony was forthcoming.[11]

Commentator Fulton Lewis Jr. stated in an October 8, 1949, newscast that Ritter was totally unfit and should never have been nominated. "The appointment is unnecessary and unfortunate," Lewis said, quoting Utah's controversial governor, J. Bracken Lee, that "there are many fine Democrats in the State of Utah with the necessary qualifications to make excellent judges." Lewis asked, "Is this the type of appointment that should be railroaded? With the charges and criticism that have been made would it not be better to hold the appointment over until next year so a thorough investigation can be made?"[12]

The "revelations" in the FBI report were thus leaked to Lewis and Pearson by someone, and that someone must of necessity be Senator Arthur V. Watkins himself, or someone connected with him or in his office.

Before reconvening on the return of the nomination from the Judiciary Committee, the subcommittee contacted the witnesses Watkins indicated should testify and invited them to do so at continued hearings on Monday, October 10, 1949. The hearings were then postponed further, until Tuesday, October 11, 1949, because of the death of Senator Miller. When the subcommittee reconvened at 4:30 in the afternoon, again in Room 424 of the Senate Office Building, Senators Magnuson, Langer, Thomas, and Watkins were present, together with Senator Estes Kefauver (D-TN), who had been assigned to fill Miller's vacancy, and staff counsel Sourwine.

The two additional witnesses Watkins wanted subpoenaed then proved illusional. Cannon responded to the wire inviting him to make a statement, if he had any information, saying, "I do not desire to testify." Ivins was sent the same wire, and responded with a special-delivery letter to Magnuson repeating his claim that Ritter was "arbitrary, tyrannical, arrogant, and abusive" while at the OPA. He stated no facts and asserted that "correspondence in the files of OPA would substantiate these accusations."[13]

In apparent response to Ivins's charges, Representative John A. Carroll (D-CO), who had been the regional attorney for the OPA and Ritter's superior, was at the reconvened hearing and testified concerning his experience with Ritter. "It was one of the most important wartime programs of a civilian nature," Carroll explained, "and we wanted to get the outstanding men," one of whom was Ritter. "I had not known Willis Ritter theretofore, and nobody had recommended him to me outside of Utah, and I found him to be a very outstanding man. He was at all times absolutely fair—a man of great integrity and in my opinion outstanding from the standpoint of learning. And I think he would be a credit to the Federal judicial system. I should like to give my wholehearted endorsement."

"Mr. Ivins has written a letter to this committee," Magnuson informed Carroll, "and it is on the stationery of the Salt Lake Horse Show Association, of which he is the secretary," reciting its substance. Magnuson inquired if Carroll had "anything to say to that." "I think, gentlemen, you would have to understand the climate at that time," Carroll explained. "Grant Ivins... opinions must be colored by the pressure of landlords; and, of course, Willis Ritter's duty was to enforce the regulations, and he did have to fight landlords; there is no question about that and he fought them." Contrary to Ivins's assertion that inquiry at the OPA would substantiate his pronouncement of Ritter as "tyrannical," Carroll testified that "we found him to be a very kindly man, a very sympathetic man."[14]

Langer now appeared to join cause with his Republican colleague Watkins. Langer inquired if Carroll had heard or was aware of "common knowledge" that Ritter had submitted false or fraudulent travel vouchers and that the practice became known in the OPA's Denver Office as "pulling a Ritter." Carroll stated, "It was never brought to my attention; and therefore I would say it was not true, Senator."[15]

Langer then asked, "Did you ever hear that he was intoxicated?" Carroll replied, "I have never heard that and as a matter of fact I would say, Senator, if he was a candidate or applicant for the Federal bench in Denver, I would be testifying as favorably and as vigorously as I hope to do today. I have the very highest respect for his character and his integrity and moral conduct."[16]

Watkins spoke up, asking if the chairman intended to put the Ivins letter in the record. "They will all be in the file," an evidently annoyed Magnuson said. Watkins persisted, making clear that he wanted to make the record public. "I have a reason why I want that in the [public] record," because "I asked for an investigation largely made on the statement given by Mr. Ivins." Watkins did not elaborate on his "reason," but a public record is necessary only if it is intended to be available to the news media or seen by others.

Magnuson read a long list of testimonials and endorsements of Ritter and the one from Ivins in opposition but not questioning his ability or loyalty. "We will be glad to put it in the record," Magnuson reluctantly agreed. The Ivins letter quickly found its way into the campaign being waged in the press.

Among the endorsements Magnuson referred to was a letter of J. Lambert Gibson, who responded to Patterson's claims that Ritter lacked practical experience. Gibson had been chairman of the Utah State Tax Commission for six years and stated that to his knowledge "derived from appearances of Ritter" before the commission, Ritter "has a large practice involving tax, estate and trust matters" representing steel companies, radio stations, newspapers, drugstores, and other interests. "My opinion," Gibson concluded, is that "Ritter's is one of the better practices in the State of Utah and in relation to tax matters, the best practice in the State of Utah."[17]

Congressman Granger was recalled and objected that "allegations... about his not believing in the Constitution, about his being subject to drink... anything of that nature, or accusations made of that kind, is a lie and there is nothing to it." Magnuson asserted, "I will say, Congressman, that there is nothing before the committee in the way of evidence from anybody in Utah to that effect at all." Granger explained, "I know on the radio last night Fulton Lewis was given some information by somebody that there was going to be a spicy hearing today and that the moral character of this man was going to be advertised to the world. Now, somebody did that." That "somebody" was not identified, but George Hatch, presumably privy to what was going on in the media, was of the opinion that Watkins's "office gave Drew Pearson and Fulton Lewis, Jr., statements with clear libel."[18]

Watkins, perhaps in the face of the mounting evidence that he or someone connected with his office was releasing derogatory information to the press, was constrained to affirm that "if you asked me what the general reputation of the nominee was in Utah, I would say that all I had heard was good."[19] He continued to maintain, despite having acknowledged that he had no such information, that Ritter was unqualified and stubbornly pressed his demand that confirmation be delayed and hearings held in Salt Lake City.

Magnuson continued with his questioning of Granger:

> Congressman, the only letter here which we have is from Mr. Ivins, of Salt Lake, on Salt Lake Horse Show stationery and I quote him as follows: "I am astonished at the statement of Congressman Walter Granger... that members of the legal profession in Utah favor the appointment of Mr. Ritter. I have talked to many prominent lawyers about this matter, and I have yet to find one who does not say that such an appointment would be little short of a calamity. Everyone, however, has added that he

> would not say a word against the appointment, adding that having done so, he would never dare appear in Federal court before Mr. Ritter." Do you think that Mr. Ivins should be astonished by your statement?

"In view of the fact that you have the endorsement of him by the Salt Lake County Bar Association and the Weber County Bar, it would rather refute what he said," Granger responded. "I know Grant Ivins," Granger continued, "and I was in a lot of those controversies that they had in OPA. I cussed Willis Ritter and Grant Ivins, too, with the best kind of swearing language that I could use during OPA days.... It was a difficult time. In its very nature it is a position that is arbitrary."[20]

Langer, apparently probing a foundation for the unsavory and salacious items Watkins and Lewis had promised, asked if Granger had heard of Ritter "being associated with a girl named Phyllis Kay," apparently intending reference to Phyllis Katz, or of Ritter being intoxicated "where people had to wait three or four hours to do business with him." Granger had never heard of Ritter being "associated with any girl except his own people," and if testimony to that effect were produced, he would be "very, very much surprised."

Reva Beck Bosone, Democrat congresswoman from Utah's Second District and former judge at four different levels of the Utah judiciary who had bested Ritter in the 1948 nominating convention for the seat she now held, testified that she knew most of the lawyers in Utah and had known Ritter for twenty-two years. The many lawyers who had testified and written letters supporting Ritter are "some of the West's best" who "would have the nerve not to send a letter of recommendation if that is [not] the way they felt about it." Bosone declared, "I heard that the reputation of Willis Ritter was being questioned. To me that is ridiculous."[21]

Parnell Black and Calvin Rawlings then testified in support of Ritter's nomination. "Do you know of a young lady by the name of Phyllis Kay?" Langer inquired of Black, apparently still meaning Katz. "Did you ever hear about any voucher for a trip to Albuquerque that was turned down by the OPA?" "Never until this day," Black replied, "I heard the statement made today in this hearing for the first time."[22]

"Mr. Chairman," Watkins then said, "I would like to make a statement while we are in public session." When advised by Magnuson that he could do so in executive session, Watkins insisted, "I would rather make my statement in public, Sir," and he was allowed to do so. Watkins's prepared statement indicated that "while at that meeting [of the full Judiciary Committee on September 3] an excerpt was read... from a report [that] raised serious questions as to the integrity and morality of the nominee." Magnuson explained again that there was one lone "opinion from... one man who says he was tyrannical and dealt in the OPA matters in a wrong way."[23]

"Wait a minute," Langer objected. "There is something the chairman has forgotten, statements that were made at the table when Senator Watkins was present." "I have not forgotten," Magnuson replied. "However, it is my opinion that there are certain matters that we should go into in executive session."[24]

"I have called your attention to something that is definite and I have asked for witnesses to be subpoenaed," Watkins persisted. His proposed witnesses had already denied having any testimony to give, yet he was still pressing to make Patterson's unsubstantiated charges part of the public record and for there to be continued hearings in Salt Lake City. "It may be that the committee will decide to go into this matter further, or it may be that they will not. I do not know."[25] Watkins said that he was through, and Magnuson invited Thomas to speak.

Now that the proposed judicial appointment had come to all-out political warfare, the reversal of Thomas's and Ritter's roles proved somewhat wanting. Thomas's dignified, high-flown style was ill-suited to resisting the attacks by Ritter's critics. Ritter, now the candidate, was disabled from plotting the strategy, setting the traps, and doing the gritty work. "I, of course, have not seen the FBI reports, and, as the chairman of the committee announced, it was contrary to the rules of the committee to make them public," Thomas explained. Someone, of course, had made them public, or at least given the media their interpretation of what they contained. "I called the Justice Department several times. Each time they said there was nothing in the report that would in any way interfere with our recommendations." Thomas pointed out, "The only person who is writing about Mr. Ritter and protesting his appointment is H. Grant Ivins. Grant Ivins has said nothing about the character of Willis Ritter, nothing about his habits that in any way reflect on him... except the fact that he as an administrator disagreed heartily with Dr. Ritter." Thomas then referred to the "radio broadcast of last night" that "'very, very interesting things' would be foretold today," but "I want to emphasize... that those things have not been foretold."

"If anything has been disclosed," Magnuson cautioned, "someone has violated the rules of the committee on this matter because the session was executive and I, out of courtesy to both you gentlemen, asked you to sit in on that executive hearing. I may say that I shall ask you again."

On October 13, 1949, Magnuson said the subcommittee voted approval. The acting committee chairman planned to call the full committee together at 4:00 o'clock, but Langer blocked Judiciary Committee action by objecting to a meeting while the Senate was in session considering the displaced persons' bill.[26]

"There is no point in blaming it on Watkins—blame it on ourselves for ever letting a Republican come back here; for any Republican would have acted in much the same manner," Robert Hinckley wrote to George Hatch. "Sorry to tell you [a] colleague has deemed it necessary to inject partisan opposition [to] this appointment and am afraid [it] has now become a party issue," Thomas wired future governor Calvin Rampton. "Appears Comm[ittee] may decide on a strictly party line basis." The vote would be close, Thomas indicated, for the eight-to-five majority of Democrats was reduced by Senator McCarran being in Europe and the death of Senator Miller, and two other members of the majority were "Dixiecrats" who may see the nomination as another opportunity to embarrass the administration.[27]

By insisting that his statement at the reconvened hearing be made public, Watkins's "surprise" at the content of the FBI report quickly became a part of the media campaign against Ritter. On Friday, October 14, 1949, syndicated columnist Drew Pearson reported the rumors passed to his investigator, Jack Anderson. Pearson claimed that the FBI report, which was not to have been released, showed that, back in OPA days, Ritter had a clandestine "romance." Ritter allegedly made some phone calls, at government expense, to a girlfriend in Albuquerque and took a trip to see her at government expense. Ritter never should have done this, Pearson opined, but "still, if all the private calls—air junkets made at government expense—were held against government officials, a lot of admirals, generals and even the Secretary of Defense would be out of their jobs today."[28]

In a handwritten note to Hinckley dated Saturday, October 15, 1949, Hatch reported: "Now that [the] Magnuson sub-committee has approved Ritter, the whole issue would seem to depend on the action of the full judiciary committee. Thomas advises Kilgore is going to try to get a meeting Monday." According to Hatch, "The doubtful democrats are [Herbert R.] O'Connor of Maryland and [James O.] Eastland of Mississippi." McCarran's secretary said O'Connor wanted to help Thomas on this nomination and had promised to telephone McCarran in Italy and have him send a wire favoring speedy action and approval. Abe Murdock contacted Langer, asking for his support as a personal favor, but Langer reported he was under heavy Republican pressure.

"Many Republicans here are shocked by Watkins personal mudslinging," Hatch's personal note continued. "Lou Callister, Dick Hoggan, Ren Mabey and other top Republican attorneys have advised Watkins [and the] judiciary committee they feel Republican tactics [are] disgraceful and asked immediate confirmation of Ritter. Dean Leary, several Utah Supreme Court justices, all district court judges have wired approval." The entire executive committee of the Salt Lake County Bar Association did so as well.[29]

On October 19, 1949, Magnuson informed President Truman that circumstances prevented Senate action on confirmation of Ritter before the close of the session and urged a recess appointment.

The United States Court calendar was very crowded. In a wire from V. P. Ahlstrom, clerk of the court, the Judiciary Committee received the following information:

> There are pending 47 motions to be argued in civil cases and 54 jury and non-jury cases at issue, plus a number of criminal cases. The retiring judge is limited in assignment to criminal emergency cases which he handles only when the defendant desires to enter a plea of guilty. All cases involving a plea of not-guilty have been continued for trial, pending appointment of a permanent judge. Early in the next session, we believe the Committee on the Judiciary will act on Mr. Ritter's nomination. In the meantime the judicial process will be unduly hampered and delayed unless you find it possible to act on the recommendation we have made.[30]

Thomas said that he was "hopeful" a recess appointment would be made but would not press the president to make it.[31]

Watkins's relentless campaign to undermine the Ritter nomination, which he still had not declared himself to be opposed to, then turned to blocking the recess appointment. On Thursday, October 20, 1949, Watkins said he was undecided whether to write the president arguing against the recess appointment and replied "no comment" when questioned whether he would oppose the appointment, but on Friday, October 21, the president received a letter from Watkins urging Truman to hold up any recess appointment of Willis Ritter as federal judge until Watkins could discuss the matter with opponents. His reasoning was that a recess appointment was unnecessary, for recess appointments extend only until Congress reconvenes and would be for only a few months. It would therefore not be of great importance, and the backlog in the District of Utah could be handled by temporary assignments of other judges. "I am not opposed to the Ritter appointment personally," Watkins said.

"Here is some more of Watkins's business," Hinckley wrote to Hatch. "It is high time someone was building a fire under him and also under the alleged Democrat, Grant Ivins. Hasn't Ivins been the recipient of party favor?"[32]

Magnuson delivered a letter to President Truman, responding to Watkins, advising that the subcommittee had considered the nomination carefully and at length and recommended it favorably. A request for further consideration was granted to hear two opposition witnesses, but one declined to appear and the other submitted a letter opposing the nomination on grounds related to the nominee's administration of the OPA Rent Regulation Office. Based upon the impressive testimony in support of the nomination, including scores of telegrams, letters, and affidavits from bar organizations, leading attorneys, and prominent citizens, Magnuson recommended that Truman appoint Ritter promptly. Truman did so, on October 21, 1949, appointing Ritter on a recess basis, subject to further consideration when Congress reconvened on January 3, 1950.[33]

The *Salt Lake Tribune* editorialized on October 23, 1949, under the headline "The President Has Named a Native Son as Judge," that "the recess appointment of Willis W. Ritter as federal judge for the Utah district... will give general satisfaction." The editorial continued, "It is almost impossible to name any person for a high position in this era of controversy, competition and condemnation," and "The President was recently quoted by the press as saying that it had become difficult to find qualified and eminent people to consider acceptance of responsible positions because of a growing custom of making accusations that are equally injurious, whether true or false. This procedure, a bloodless variety of the Soviet purge, has a tendency to create a similar reluctance to serve the public."

The *Salt Lake Tribune* of October 25, 1949, reported that Ritter was sworn in, under a recess appointment, without formal ceremony. When Clerk of Court Ahlstrom began laying files down in front of them, Judge Tillman Johnson, who attended the proceeding, said "show them to Judge Ritter. I've already seen them."[34]

Ritter's decorum appeared to disprove his critics when he assumed the bench. He displayed mild temperament when he ordered three men accused of car theft held for further investigation and placed an alleged perpetrator of mail fraud on probation.[35] With his unique ability to get to the heart of an issue—he could recognize faster than almost anyone where the substance of an issue lay—he quickly disposed of the backlog of cases awaiting him when he assumed the bench.

Hinckley was nevertheless concerned about what Watkins might do when Ritter's nomination came up again. "Everything possible must be done out there and at this time to offset Thomas's lethargy and lack of willingness to really move in and slug it out, both before the committee and possibly on the floor of the Senate," he counseled Hatch.[36]

The campaign to attack Ritter's character and reputation, and thereby defeat the nomination, that Senator Arthur V. Watkins had been hinting at and had been discussing with Ernest Wilkinson was set to begin. Watkins already knew of the Knox Patterson letter, suggesting that Quentin Cannon and Grant Ivins might give testimony critical of Ritter, for it was a part of the FBI report discussed during the meetings of the Judiciary Committee in September and October 1949. He, no doubt, gave that information to Wilkinson.

After his meetings with Watkins, Wilkinson went to Utah in early 1950 and contacted the possible witnesses named in the Patterson letter. He went first to Cannon. Wilkinson told Cannon he had come from a meeting of the American Bar Association, asked if Cannon knew anything about Ritter's "un-American activities," and asked about other things Cannon had never heard before, "all of it derogatory."[37] Cannon had no such information, but told Wilkinson to see Ivins.

Wilkinson went to the home of Ivins, where he again represented that he had just come from a meeting of the American Bar Association and said he was a member of the ABA Committee on Judicial Appointments. Wilkinson said he was interested in blocking the Ritter nomination. Ivins told Wilkinson he assumed that the Ritter appointment would be a matter of course. Wilkinson said that there was still time to block it, that Senator Thomas's wife was interested in another man, and that man's name was John S. Boyden.[38]

Wilkinson then admitted that he was actually investigating for Senator Watkins. Ivins gave Wilkinson the names of former personnel of the OPA in Denver to contact. After being contacted by Wilkinson, Ivins wrote another, even stronger letter to his friend Senator Thomas, urging him to withdraw the Ritter nomination. He told Thomas that the nomination would not be in the interest of the State of Utah or the Democratic Party and would injure the reputation of the senator.[39]

When questions about Wilkinson's actions arose, Watkins stated, "Ernest Wilkinson has never been employed by me at any time." His choice of words was careful, however, and did not deny their numerous meetings or that even if Wilkinson was not his "employee," they were working with one another. Neither did he disclose that, on the very day Watkins made the statement, Wilkinson was appearing at the annual meeting of the United States Chamber of Commerce in Washington, D.C., "pinch hitting for Sen. Watkins" in support of a bill related to reclamation projects. Moreover, Watkins maintained, "I don't think Mr. Wilkinson ever told" Ivins that he "represent[ed] the Judicial Section of the ABA," thus denying the plausibility offered to Cannon and Ivins for Wilkinson's investigation and confirming, implicitly, his connection with Watkins.[40]

Nevertheless, the stage was now set. The battle was about to be joined. Watkins and Wilkinson were poised to get more intense—and dirty.

11

WATKINS' FOLLY

The greater the truth, the greater the libel.

—A LEGAL MAXIM

The cascading fresh waters flowing from the snowpack high in the Wasatch Mountains overlooking Salt Lake Valley were interrupted, eons ago, by a huge sand and gravel bar deposited by ancient Lake Bonneville at the mouth of Big Cottonwood Canyon. That act of nature, forcing these waters to flow north for a stretch along the base of Mount Olympus before continuing their westerly course to the Jordan River, created a lush garden spot for many of the most private and expensive estates in Salt Lake Valley.

Into that posh idyllic setting, a group of Navajo Indians entered, as the decade of the 1950s began. They were from Montezuma Creek, in the Four Corners region of San Juan County, Utah. They arrived in the back of a truck driven by Ira Hatch, the trader at the Hatch Trading Post, under the leadership of one of their head men, Hosteen Tse-kesi. The Indians went to Wander Lane, where a lawyer, Milt Oman, lived. They knew and trusted Oman, for he had herded sheep with his father in the expanse of public lands between Price and Green River. The Indians camped at the Oman ranch when they rode their horses, their sole means of transportation, from Montezuma Creek to Salt Lake City.

Oman rounded up tents and allowed the Indians to camp in an orchard on his land at Wander Lane. He warned the Indians that they must conduct themselves better than the white man. They did. Every morning at daybreak they went up on Mount Olympus to commune with their gods, and when they left Wander Lane was as unspoiled as when they arrived. Between their prayer sessions, they were paraded into the courtroom of Willis W. Ritter, where the United States, through its Bureau of Land Management, had filed suit to enjoin Tse-kesi and his fellows from grazing livestock on public lands north of the San Juan River in Utah. Byron Mock, who was regional director of the BLM for a region that included Colorado and Utah, with offices adjoining Ritter's court in Salt Lake City, claimed that Ritter participated in the Indian's communion on Mount Olympus.[1] The Tse-kesi group counterclaimed for money damages, complaining that the United States had interfered with their ancestral home and grazing rights. Tse-kesi and his fellows engaged Knox Patterson to represent them at first, rather than Milt Oman. Later, Oman succeeded Patterson as their counselor.

Ritter had been serving as United States District Judge for the District of Utah, under recess appointment, for little more than eight months when the dispute between the United States and the Tse-kesi bunch came before him on July 12, 1950. Proceedings on his permanent appointment were still pending. He approached the Tse-kesi case with classic judicial restraint. "It was the obligation of the Department of Interior and the Commissioner of Indian Affairs to find Tse-kesi and the Navajo a place to live and confine them there," Ritter wrote. He believed that the United States should exhaust that remedy before asking for injunctive relief. He therefore denied the complaint of the United States. He also dismissed the counterclaim of the Navajo, directing both sides to resolve the problem with the secretary of the interior.[2]

Ritter disposed of all other accumulated matters pending when he took over from Tillman Johnson, including motions in civil disputes, preliminary proceedings in criminal matters, and cases awaiting trial, and did so with similar fairness and dispatch. He worked long hours, handling two, three, and sometimes more jury trials in a single day, often having several juries deliberating simultaneously.

"I have seen more books on Judge Ritter's desk in the short time that he has been the District Judge than I saw in all the time Judge Johnson sat on the bench," Dan B. Shields reported. Shields had formerly been attorney general for the State of Utah, after that United States Attorney for the District of Utah for sixteen years, and, but for age, would himself have been the appointee. Ritter is "an indefatigable worker," who is "patient and painstaking," Shields observed, noting that he was "thoroughly convinced that [Judge Ritter] is bound by the law" and that "no case is cited to him by an energetic attorney" that he does not read. Ritter "has a very human understanding of what the ordinary man will do under ordinary circumstances," said Shields, touching upon a singular quality that would characterize Ritter's judicial tenure. "I have talked with many of the men who have appeared before Judge Ritter since his appointment, and I think without exception they are all pleased with the way he handles himself and the way his court is conducted."[3] One of the persons Shields referred to was Knox

Patterson, Tse-kesi's attorney and Ritter's former critic, whose letter Senator Arthur V. Watkins had used to influence the Judiciary Committee to continue hearings on the appointment.

While Ritter was clearing up Judge Johnson's calendar, Watkins was making preparations to mount a vigorous campaign of opposition to his permanent appointment. A recess appointment extends only while the Senate is in recess. Thus on January 5, 1950, President Truman renominated Ritter, then already serving as a judge, and after the Eighty-second Congress convened, Senator Pat McCarran, chairman of the Senate Judiciary Committee, requested that Watkins give his opinion and any information he may have concerning Ritter's permanent appointment.[4]

Watkins responded to McCarran on January 19, 1950, again stating that "I have no personal objection to Mr. Ritter as a judge" and that "he is [not] personally obnoxious to me."[5] "Personally obnoxious to me" was the accepted manifestation of privilege by a senator from the state affected by the nomination, usually honored by fellow senators, even if it came from a junior senator of the minority party. The two letters Watkins had written, to Senator Kilgore on September 20, 1949, and Senator Magnuson on October 5, 1949, were attached, together with the letter of H. Grant Ivins, who had already declined to appear and give testimony against Ritter. Watkins's letter furnished no information, of any description, but indicated that his negative view on the Ritter nomination was unchanged.

Utah's junior senator launched a clever stratagem of deception to manipulate the Senate Judiciary Committee into a position of opposition to Ritter's confirmation. His letter stated that he had neither the time nor the facilities to investigate matters he claimed to be inferred by the three attachments but "that it is the duty of the Senate Judiciary Committee to make that investigation." Watkins listed fifteen people he wanted called as witnesses when the hearing reconvened, including Phyllis Katz and others in Albuquerque. Despite his demand that hearings be held in Salt Lake City, so that witnesses from Utah could testify against Ritter, only five of his proposed witnesses were from Utah, and they included Ivins and Quentin Cannon, who had also indicated he had no testimony to give. Despite the fact that Watkins had Ernest Wilkinson "beating the bushes" for someone who would testify against Ritter, they were the only persons who had stated negative opinions. Yet Watkins continued to maintain that he had no personal objection and that Ritter was not personally obnoxious to him.[6]

In seeming contradiction of his "no personal objection" stance, Watkins issued a statement, published in the *Deseret News* on January 20, 1950, that during the congressional recess he had talked with people in Utah who "are certain [Ritter] does not qualify from any standpoint to be a Federal District Judge." The statements were by "people who cannot be ignored," Watkins said, and he called for an investigation. It was followed up with a radio broadcast on February 3, 1950, in which Watkins stated the basis for his questioning Ritter's qualifications: "Mr. Ivins wrote a very strong indictment of Mr. Ritter and filed it with the Committee. Those charges, if proved true, would in my judgment be sufficient to sustain the Senate in refusing to go along with the President on this appointment. In addition to that I was before the Judiciary Committee when one of the Senators read from a [FBI] report . . . which raised serious questions as to the integrity and morality of Mr. Ritter."[7]

Throughout January 1950, despite Watkins's demand for hearings in Salt Lake City, there was tacit understanding that further hearings would be held in executive session, in Washington. On February 9, 1950, Watkins repeated his claim of additional witnesses who should be contacted in a telephone conversation with McCarran. In a letter of February 10, 1950, McCarran asked Watkins to send the names of his additional witnesses. Watkins furnished no names in addition to those he had furnished on January 19, but reaffirmed his expectation that OPA records would contain evidence of Ritter's unfitness. Watkins demanded that committee staff investigate the allegation of Ivins. "I hope the committee is having a trained investigator examine these files to discover if there is such evidence," Watkins's letter read. "In the event the committee needs assistance in this matter, I shall be glad to designate a member of my staff to aid in the investigation."[8]

Watkins then embarked on a bid to make trouble for the nomination by laying a procedural snare for Judiciary Committee chairman McCarran. In a letter of March 13, 1950, Watkins acknowledged that his request for an investigation was granted but asserted that McCarran had agreed that Watkins had the "right to use the evidence produced on the floor of the Senate in the event I do not agree with the findings of the committee." He then stated, "I find that it is traditional that Senators other than members of the committee making an investigation are permitted to interrogate witnesses," and "[I] request that I have that privilege when the hearings are held."[9]

McCarran responded angrily to Watkins's bid to manipulate an exception to the traditional rules of Senate procedure.

> I believe you are in error in stating you discussed with me the question of using, on the floor of the Senate, the record of hearings held before the committee in closed executive session. I do not recall discussing this point with you. You speak of this as a "right" which is "traditional." On the contrary, the precedents appear to support the view that hearings held in closed executive session may not be made public, nor discussed in the Senate in open session. Proceedings before the Committee are proceedings of the Senate.... [A]ny Senator not a member of the Committee who is by courtesy granted the right to be present is equally bound [to keep executive proceedings confidential].

After the request for continued hearings was granted, Calvin Rawlings arranged, through John Fitzpatrick, editor of the *Salt Lake Tribune,* for a meeting with McCarran in Las Vegas, Nevada, on St. Patrick's Day 1950. Rawlings told McCarran he was worried about the pending appointment being dragged out so long, but McCarran assured Rawlings there was plenty of time and "we'll get him appointed."[10]

McCarran informed Watkins on March 30, 1950, that "with regard to evidence allegedly contained in the files and records of the Rent Control Division of the OPA, a subpoena duces tecum will be issued if you will... 'specify, with as much precision as is fair and feasible, the particular documents desired.'"[11] McCarran then told Watkins that he had already breached the rules of the Senate by making his letter to McCarran public, for he had released it, or allowed its release, to muckraking columnists Fulton Lewis Jr. and Drew Pearson.

By April 11, 1950, McCarran had yielded to Watkins's demands and changed the forum, ordering on that date that hearings be public and held in Salt Lake City and Denver because of Watkins's claim that he intended to call a large number of witnesses. Watkins telephoned McCarran's office and asked a staff member, Elizabeth Heckman, not to subpoena his proposed witnesses to Washington. McCarran was presiding over a meeting of the Judiciary Committee, but Heckman handed him a note relating the conversation.[12] But by April 15, 1950, Watkins had not responded to McCarran's letters of April 11 and 13 requesting names of witnesses, so McCarran indicated that subpoenas for the witnesses Watkins had identified in his letter of January 19, 1950, would be issued, unless he requested otherwise by April 18. McCarran's letter continued:

> As you know, you have not furnished the committee with the street addresses of all the witnesses named in your letter of January 19; and unless you can furnish us with the addresses, we shall have to do the best we can. Let me re-emphasize that the committee is perfectly willing to issue subpoenas duces tecum for any books, papers or documents, which you desire to have brought in, if you will just describe them with any reasonable particularity, and let me know where they are and in whose custody.[13]

Finally, McCarran granted Watkins's request that he be "granted the privilege not only of appearing in opposition to the nomination, but also of being present at all hearings and interrogating witnesses." The condition of making that exception to normal Senate procedure was that the nominee, and his counsel, had the same privilege. Watkins was so advised.

By stubborn persistence, Watkins had secured both public hearings and their removal to Salt Lake City and Denver and a right to participate in questioning witnesses. After the hearings were scheduled, the issue came up again of what the committee should investigate. Watkins still had identified nothing in particular. Watkins continued to try to manipulate the committee into securing documents to support his charges, rather than furnishing them as requested.

Watkins may not have intended to play "dog in the manger" on the issue, but McCarran clearly believed that he had. Watkins did not conform to McCarran's instruction that he must be informed of desired witnesses and documents by April 18, but on April 20 McCarran received a request from Watkins for the subpoena of twenty witnesses. McCarran advised Watkins that his witnesses had been subpoenaed and that "you will be given the privilege of presenting your witnesses in such order as you may determine, and you will have the right to question or cross-examine any witnesses who appear." On April 21, 1950, McCarran wrote to Watkins again, referring to a request through Senator William E. Jenner (D-IN) that "a member of the professional staff of the Committee on the Judiciary be assigned to assist you in connection with the coming hearings." Furthermore, "Upon mature reflection, I have some doubt about my authority to grant this request," McCarran said, "but I told Senator Jenner last night that I would do it, and so I have done it. This morning I assigned Mr. J. Carlisle Ruddy, senior member of the professional staff of the committee, to assist you as you may request, in connection with the Ritter hearings."[14]

Watkins responded by renewing his bid to paint the committee into a corner. In a lengthy letter dated April 24, 1950, "with all the emphasis at my command," he denied that he was "'opposing' the nomination of Judge Ritter": "The witnesses I have suggested be called are not my witnesses, but the witnesses of the committee. As an aid to the committee, I have suggested their names." Ignoring that McCarran had assigned a senior staff member to assist him, Watkins asserted (failing to advise of the investigation being conducted on his behalf by Wilkinson) that "I have had neither the time, the staff, nor the money to investigate these matters…nor the means to make an investigation of the records of the OPA.… [I]t should be clear to the Committee that I am not in a position to get these files opened up for my investigation—only the Committee has that power."[15] On May 1, 1950, Watkins was once more requested to advise if he wanted witnesses subpoenaed for the Salt Lake City hearings.

For his part, Senator Elbert Thomas furnished the names and addresses of ninety-two prominent Utah lawyers and acquaintances of Ritter he wanted to testify in Salt Lake City who had "been carefully selected and the testimony which they will offer is not intended to be cumulative, but rather, in sum, to traverse and effectively refute every charge or intimation of a charge which has been made against Judge Ritter" by Watkins.[16]

As the May 1, 1950, date for the hearings in Salt Lake City approached, Wilkinson reported to Watkins that he had finally developed what he hoped would be evidence to be used against Ritter. The case of a medical doctor from Price, Utah, charged with tax fraud amounting to hundreds of thousands of dollars came up among those in the backlog Ritter inherited from Judge Johnson. The doctor engaged Wilkinson's sometimes partner John S. Boyden to enter a plea of nolo contendere, which is a fancy legal term for "no contest," in lieu of trial. On April 7, 1950, Ritter refused to accept the plea. He explained to Boyden and Assistant United States Attorney Bryant Croft, in chambers on April 21, 1950, that he wanted no inference that he had agreed to any leniency (which remained Ritter's policy throughout his judicial tenure). Ritter then refused Boyden's request for a continuance of the trial, scheduled for the following Saturday, and directed Boyden to have the doctor in court the following day to enter a "not guilty" plea. Boyden wanted to enter a plea that day, for the doctor was in town, but because he had several juries out and only a five-minute recess in which to talk with Boyden, Ritter refused.[17]

Boyden considered Ritter's treatment of him "cold." It had been common practice while Boyden served as Assistant United States Attorney for him or other lawyers to merely walk down the hall and make informal arrangements with Judge Johnson for the entry of a plea or other procedural matters. Ritter's insistence on formality, especially considering their past association with one another, suggested to Boyden that he somehow knew, perhaps from Senator Thomas, of Boyden's clandestine campaign of opposition to his confirmation through the Mormon Church and the Thomas family.[18] The doctor saw a different message in the incident, concluded that Boyden did not have the influence with the court he had bargained for, discharged Boyden, and replaced him with Delbert Draper, Ritter's longtime friend and political ally. Draper, new on the case and needing time to prepare, secured the continuance on an application made when Ritter was not under pressure with multiple jury trials, which magnified Boyden's paranoia.

Boyden, a prominent Democrat, was not in communication with Watkins but brought it to the attention of his partner from Washington, Ernest Wilkinson. Wilkinson presented the incident to Watkins as proof that Ritter lacked judicial temperament.

The continued hearings on the nomination of Willis W. Ritter convened in Salt Lake City on May 1, 1950, at 9:30 in the morning, in the Grand Jury Room, United States Post Office and Federal Building, with McCarran presiding. Senators Garrett Lee Withers (D-KY) and William Langer (R-ND) were present, together with J. G. Sourwine, counsel to the committee, and J. Carlisle Ruddy, who had been assigned to assist Watkins. Maurice Covert and Mike Horan, special assistants to the U.S. attorney general; Watkins; Ritter; and Rawlings, counsel for Ritter, were also there.[19] Rawlings presented the case for confirmation.

Letters received by the committee were inserted into the record, including one from Howard F. Burns, chairman of the Standing Committee on the Judiciary of the American Bar Association, dated February 7, 1950, stating that "the Association does not recommend the confirmation of Mr. Ritter to be United States District Judge."[20] Burns's letter did not indicate what had changed since the previous August, when the letter of Austin Hauxhurst indicated the ABA did not oppose the nomination.

The ABA committee contacted the two delegates from Utah in January 1950, both of whom were unqualified in their endorsement of Ritter. That was proved in testimony at the hearing by the state delegate to the ABA, Sam Thurman, who "unhesitatingly recommend[ed]" him and introduced into the record his letter to Milton J. Keegan, representative to the ABA for the Tenth Circuit, affirming that "never once have I heard anything derogatory about his reputation or character," that he was "eminently qualified," and that "if a vote were taken among the lawyers of the state, Mr. Ritter would receive the endorsement of not less than eighty percent of those participating." Thurman further testified that he had talked to the other delegate, Lee Cummings, who was in agreement. Keegan had no other information. He was to have passed on the recommendation of Thurman and Cummings.[21]

So what had changed? Was it possible that Ernest Wilkinson really had been influencing the ABA process, as he claimed to Cannon and Ivins? Under the practice of the time, investigations were not conducted by the ABA Committee on Judicial Appointments directly. The practice was to have an investigation conducted by a lawyer from the home district of the nominee, and although Wilkinson was a lawyer practicing in Washington, D.C., rather than Utah, he was also a native Utahn with strong ties to the state, through both the Mormon Church and John Boyden. His claim to have been investigating for the ABA, though later denied, may have indicated that he was passing his negative gossip to the committee unofficially.

Ritter was disappointed by the ABA letter but not dismayed. He knew that the ABA, which began an effort to inject itself into the judicial selection process when the Republicans won control of the Senate in 1946, was viewed as a Republican-oriented organization. President Truman, whose appointment it was to make, was hostile to the ABA, and although McCarran continued the practice initiated by the Republicans of requesting an ABA opinion, he was "firmly resolved that the bar associations shall not choose the judiciary of the country."[22] The ABA letter might therefore be just another negative opinion Watkins and Wilkinson had engineered and not fatal to Ritter's confirmation.

Rawlings introduced into the record forty-three additional letters of endorsement from present and former law professors, judges, prominent Utah lawyers, officers of the bar association, civic and business leaders, and personal acquaintances of Ritter, indicating that he was highly qualified, by legal ability and temperament. Many described Ritter as the best appointee that could be found. In addition, there was a letter from Peyton Ford, of the United States Department of Justice, asserting that "after having carefully read the [FBI] report we were unable to find any real evidence of anything to impugn his integrity, ability, character, loyalty or judicial temperament."[23]

Significantly, the letters introduced by Rawlings included one from Knox Patterson, whose allegations that Ritter displayed a lack of judicial temperament and did not believe in the Constitution were supposedly the origin of Watkins's objections:

> Subsequent to the writing of the aforesaid letter, I made it my business to ascertain the extent of truthfulness of rumors which I had heard or suspicions which I had. Also subsequent to such letter I have observed Judge Ritter in court. You will recall that my chief objection to the Judge was my belief that he was wholly lacking in experience to handle the job. Now having observed him in court and listened to his analysis of law problems, I am rather favorably impressed with the clarity of the analysis which he makes of these problems.[24]

Patterson affirmed, after conferring with lawyers who went to school with Ritter "who would not mislead me," that "there is nothing about him from which it may be inferred that he has any left-wing propensities or that he has any sentiment adverse to our Constitution" and concluded, "I would cast a vote confirming his appointment" and "write this letter to the end that I do not mislead you and that I do not do an injury to the Judge."[25]

There were also some crank, or sour-grapes, letters, such as one from Salt Lake attorney Lewis S. Livingston, asserting that the attack on Ritter was "the pure result of jealousy on the part of certain lawyers and firms in this state who would seek to place on the bench a judge of their own choice. It is a well known fact in this city that the firm of [name censored by the Committee] (better known as the 3 little pigs) were disappointed in the appointment because a judge of their own liking would give them greater personal gain." But "the three little pigs" was the firm of Rawlings, Wallace, and Black, so dubbed by wags of the Utah State Bar because their connections with the New Deal enabled them to "sup at the public trough" more than their critics thought fair, with matters like personal injury suits under the Federal Employees Liability Act or the Railway Labor Act. But Calvin W. Rawlings was Ritter's attorney in the hearings, Parnell Black was present as a principal witness in Ritter's favor, and they had testified on behalf of their firm in his support in the Washington hearings.[26] So much for the "well-known facts" in Salt Lake City!

Rawlings then asked to "have from the Senator [Watkins] what his specifications of incompetency and immorality are and the names of every person in the State that he says would give testimony against Mr. Ritter." Watkins did not furnish any names, and did not specify any incompetency or immorality, but objected, instead, to Ritter and Rawlings even being present. "Ordinarily in Senate Committees neither the person we are talking about hiring or confirming his employment is permitted to be present, nor to have his attorney here.... I did not make any charges against the nominee myself. I only repeated what some others had said certain testimony will show.... I have been forced to do some things I would not do and I have done them under protest." McCarran demanded, "What are they, please?"—stripping away Watkins's pretense of impartiality—"the things you are doing under protest." Watkins replied, "I am being put in a position of calling my own witnesses." McCarran retorted, "I told you that you might call your witnesses in the order you might see fit. If you don't want that, all well and good." The ever pusillanimous Watkins rejoined, "I asked that they be subpoenaed and heard," still taking the position that it was the committee's responsibility to prove his charges against Ritter. "Wait just a moment," McCarran shot back. "I gave you the privilege of naming your witnesses in order. If you don't, the Chairman will." Watkins replied, "I will leave it to the Chairman then, sir."[27]

Dr. Leo Marshall, dean of the University of Utah College of Medicine, read letters of recommendation of Ritter from James M. Landis, dean of the Harvard Law School: "I think everyone here was extraordinarily impressed with him. He has intellectual capacity. Certainly to those of us who know him he was an outstanding graduate at Harvard University." From Harvard's celebrated professor of constitutional law, Thomas Reed Powell: "Mr. Ritter has both firmness and a gift of conciliation. He is independent but cooperative. His personality and character command confidence on all sides. He will be effective by his full command of facts and by his judgment and persuasiveness in presenting them." And from Harvard's professor of the law of property, Barton Leach: "I was particularly impressed with two of Mr. Ritter's qualities—his sound feet-on-the-ground judgment and a capacity for getting on with people. Of course I do not need to say anything about his intellectual qualities. You in Utah must be closely familiar with them. I will say that Mr. Ritter was one of the two outstanding graduate students at Harvard Law School during the period he spent with us."[28]

Watkins called Ivins, the only other detractor, who had declined to testify in Washington. Watkins had persisted in his demand that continued hearings be held in Salt Lake City so that he could get the Ivins testimony.

Ivins operated a poultry hatchery in American Fork, Utah. He testified that he was regional administrator of the OPA for Utah while Ritter was the state director of rent, and later regional rent director, both of them working under Clem Collins, regional director of the OPA.[29] "The Utah office was bitterly opposed by the Apartment House Association here," Ivins testified. "The Apartment House Association attacked rent regulation and even attacked Mr. Ritter personally and that created a very tense situation.... [W]e sat and listened to some very bitter attacks on the OPA regulations," Ivins continued, "in a sense I didn't blame them either, nor in a sense Mr. Ritter." The Apartment House Association was "always against the regulations of the OPA," Ivins acknowledged. After Ritter became regional rent director he said, "They are a bunch of violators and they are trying to evade the regulations." That attitude, according to Ivins, was rigid and arbitrary and disqualified Ritter to be a judge.

A dialogue between Ivins and Committee Chairman McCarran followed:

"I want to ask you if you carried out any of the regulations with any fixed purposes, with any precision in the performance of your duties?" McCarran inquired.

"In every way, sir," Ivins agreed.

"You operated with fixed decisions?"

"Yes sir."

"You made up in your mind what was right?"

"Yes sir."

"You stood by that?"

"Yes sir."

"Then would you call that arbitrary?" McCarran queried, making his point.

"You know all of us are considered arbitrary when we make up our mind," Ivins agreed. "I have been told my father was stubborn and my grandfather was stubborn and I am equally stubborn."

"So any man might be considered arbitrary when he arrives at an opinion that becomes fixed that he must carry out, is that correct?" McCarran pressed him further.

"I agree with you, Senator."

"The nominee really put up the battle for the people who were renting those places against the landlords," Senator Langer interjected, "trying to get them their rent as cheaply as he could?"

"I think he did," Ivins agreed, "and we all did."

"Well, you don't condemn a man for that, do you?"

"No, I only condemn him for the methods he used."[30]

It was becoming clear that the character, role, and motives of the several figures in Watkins's campaign of opposition were diverse. Ivins's charges that Ritter was arbitrary, tyrannical, and abusive were the observations of a man of integrity and courage who saw tendencies that he found objectionable hinted at during his tenure at the OPA. Patterson's charges that Ritter had a dangerous leaning toward communism and away from constitutional principles had the ring of fanaticism, and also being a man of integrity he retracted his comments after seeing Ritter on the bench. Watkins's tactics, however, were those of a spoiler and a coward who avoids specificity or accountability and, like Iago in *Othello,* works on innuendo.

Watkins then called John S. Boyden. Boyden evaded the question of whether Ritter and Boyden were the two main candidates and whether he wanted the judgeship for himself. He refused to acknowledge, with candor, his desire for the office, but agreed that "the papers said so." Boyden testified: "I had been very friendly with Judge Ritter since school days and he had invited me to his house to eat and we had associated with him considerably during college days, not so much of late. In politics he supported me for Governor and I supported him in his run for Congress." Boyden defended Ritter, or appeared to do so, to Sourwine: "I think he is honest and fearless." He continued: "The only question I would have in any way is on judicial temperament." Then Boyden went into detail about Ritter's refusal to give him a continuance in the tax case and his client discharging him and hiring Delbert Draper. It proved Ritter lacked temperament, Boyden insisted. "I have never felt that he had any disloyalty for the country in any way, or [that] any of his personal traits would embarrass the court."[31] Boyden finally agreed that the nomination really was between himself and Ritter.

On cross-examination, Rawlings exposed Boyden's affiliation with Ernest Wilkinson since 1946. Boyden agreed that "he tried to assist me in many particulars...when the hearings with Mr. Ritter came about" and "he was here during [Mormon Church] Conference time, about the time that this happened [and] we had a special meeting."[32]

After Watkins declined to have Knox Patterson testify, possibly because he had observed Ritter's conduct of his court and concluded that his former opinion that he was unqualified was incorrect, Rawlings called another long procession of lawyers, judges, college professors, businessmen, associates of Ritter during OPA days, neighbors, and community leaders, all of whom affirmed his professional competence and moral character. McCarran, seeing that the hearings would be overwhelmed by the number of witnesses Rawlings had yet to call, suggested that Rawlings merely give the names of his additional witnesses and state that their testimony would be the same.

Among the final witnesses was Dean William H. Leary, who testified again that he knew Ritter "intimately," that he had to check in with him every day, and that he was not arrogant and dictatorial. "He expresses himself forcibly and I think on some of these political issues has aroused some antagonism amongst people in the opposite Party, but I have always gotten along with him. Now insofar as you people know who have handled any group of school teachers or actresses, or anybody of that sort, you have always got little troubles with them," but that he had not "had any more trouble with him...and not half as much as I have had with a lot of others. For instance, there was a charge here about his drinking. I don't know of any more abstemious fellow than Ritter is." Leary added that "he wasn't the type of fellow that would be going out and having a good time. As a matter of fact, if there is any defect in his character I would think that is what it is. He don't play, don't know how to relax. He don't play golf, he don't play cards, he don't belong to any clubs. I think—well, he would be a better man if he did some of those things."[33]

Among the letters Rawlings introduced was one from Robert L. Cranmer, a Republican commissioner of Salt Lake County, indicating that "not all Republicans are in accord with Senator Arthur V. Watkins. I feel that his actions are untimely, ill-advised, and unwarranted" and that "no dissatisfaction [with Ritter's appointment] has occurred among the Republican County Officials." Darrell Greenwell, the political writer from Ogden, confirmed Cranmer's opinion and reported that Republicans in Utah did not support Watkins's opposition. Judge J. A. Howell said he did not like Watkins's repeated assaults on "Will" Ritter and that some Republicans had tried to call Watkins off. Howell said Watkins seemed determined to raise as much trouble as possible, and Abe Glassman thought the only guy who could call Watkins off "is J. Reuben [Clark Jr.] and he won't."[34]

When the hearings reconvened in Denver on May 5, 1950, Ritter responded to charges that he did not believe in the Constitution:

> Now what I said [in the series of lectures on the Constitution] you gentlemen can read if you will get Holmes on the Common Law, which was published in 1883, and read page one of it. There is a quotation there in

> those speeches [of Oliver Wendell Holmes Jr., Benjamin Nathan Cardozo, and Louis Brandeis] that the Constitution of the United States was so wisely drawn that it is adaptable to the changing social and economic needs of the nation, and that is what I said and what I believe. I will say that again and I will say it now.[35]
>
> Now, for anybody to get up and make a Tom Fool statement that I don't believe in the Constitution is just silly and doesn't deserve any answer.[36]

Ritter was correct. But his 1936 lectures reveal comments on the California "red-flag" law, and the Supreme Court ruling that a child could not be arrested for merely waving a red flag at a picnic attended by her parents, which may have been fodder for Watkins's accusations. Defense and justification of the waving of a red flag by civil libertarians had become "red meat" to the anticommunist cold warriors attacking Ritter and about to launch their crusade under Senator Eugene McCarthy.

Ritter also answered to Watkins, directly, on his charge that he was anti-Mormon:

> As you know, Senator, I have relatives in my background who lived over in Charleston, in Heber Valley, who were Mormon pioneers. Now, I'm not Mormon. I don't belong to any church. It just happens so because I was not brought up that way.... Yes, [I was baptized in the Catholic Church] when I was 3 years old, and as far as the Catholic Church is concerned it ended there. My mother was a Catholic; my father came from a Mormon family. My father's mother and grandmother were Mormon converts...and for anybody to charge me with having that kind of bias—my wife comes from a Latter Day Saint family. I don't know what difference this makes.[37]

To the charge that he was "vindictive" toward Watkins or Ivins, Ritter answered Watkins directly: "No, I never mentioned Grant Ivins and you," but "Fulton Lewis, Jr., has put out 8 or 10 broadcasts on me. I don't know what you know about them [but] I think a fellow who is so irresponsible as that ought to be brought to task for it. I'm not vindictive....I think the fellow who carries that in his soul hurts himself more than he does anybody else."[38]

Drew Pearson got information from an executive session of the committee, Ritter observed, in which "we three [Ritter, Watkins, and his administrative assistant, Dick Cardall]" were present, and "I had a strong suspicion that that was emanating from Mr. Cardall...or somebody in your office, because of the connection."[39] Watkins denied—again—the obvious inference that no other source was possible but his own office.

Watkins then intensified his attack and made clear that it had been stripped of any basis other than sex. Ritter protested that any suggestion of impropriety or personal misconduct of "that girl" just wasn't so, and that "whatever you might believe about me you couldn't believe about her."[40] He acknowledged only that he sent Phyllis Katz flowers once when she was sick.

George C. Taylor, who had been OPA administrator and rent executive in Albuquerque, testified that Katz was his secretary, the best and most competent, and that she was very vivacious and had become good friends with Ritter. "Well, her most conspicuous feature was a very noticeable Hebrew nose which was a very sore point to her," Taylor said, describing her to Sourwine. "She always said if she got the price, she'd have it amputated. She could put on makeup and really look quite attractive, but without her makeup I had occasion to see her several times when she was sick in bed, and she's nobody's beauty under those conditions, no sir. Rather tall, maybe 5'6". Guys would say, 'you're so skinny people will think you're starving to death.'"[41]

Staff attorney Maurice Covert then had Taylor testify that the association was not confined to the office. "I think that's true," Taylor replied. "I was at her house to dinner. Her parents were there. My recollection is that it was a Sunday luncheon." Ritter "had been there once that I didn't see him, because the old man said, 'that guy sat up and we chewed the fat until it was time for me to go to work at 3:00 in the morning.'"

"Was it current there in the office force that there was an affair going on between Judge Ritter and this girl?" Covert asked, exploring the gossip collected by Wilkinson and alleged by Watkins. "The rumor came to my mind largely from another source," Taylor replied. "I got concerned and made a little investigation....It was just a villainous rumor....I was convinced there was not anything to it."[42]

Joseph W. Penfold, formerly assistant regional rent executive for the OPA, testified that nothing in Ritter's conduct was other than routine. Asked whether Ritter had taken extraordinarily long trips to Albuquerque, he said he had not heard those rumors.[43]

"Ever talk marriage to her?" Watkins asked, confronting Ritter directly. "I told her as I have everybody else in my life that there would never be any divorce in my family."

"Have you been down to California to visit her?" Watkins pressed. "I think on one occasion.... My whole family and I went down there to buy [a] car and on that occasion I saw her for about a couple of hours at lunch time."[44]

Watkins inferred, finally, that Ritter's marriage had been ruined, or was about to be ruined, over Katz. Ritter admitted that Rita had heard the rumors generated by Watkins's accusations at the hearings in Washington, D.C., that he "came home and talked to my wife about that," and that she had seen a lawyer once. The lawyer—Lynn Richards, the Mormon bishop in the university neighborhood—discussed with Ritter that Rita "was a little unhappy." Both of them went to Richards's Salt Lake City office. "They came at different times. He seemed to be very willing to make amends. I didn't hear any more from them about it."[45]

Watkins: "Did [Rita] go to California to see the girl... beg her to lay off you?" "No, no," Ritter protested.

After Watkins's relentless suggestion of improper sex, commencing with the Washington hearings, Ritter was no longer able to restrain himself:

> Now I'm going to say it. Next time you are in our state, Senator, I want you to come up to my home and I want you to meet my wife and I want you to meet my family. There isn't anything I would do to hurt that family and hurt my wife. Now, we're all the victims of a pretty bad smear in this. That little family of mine has been hurt in this. But in a way that has drawn us closer together instead of pulling us apart. There is nothing going to happen on that at all.[46]

At that point, the hearings ended. On June 4, 1950, McCarran requested that the Justice Department question Katz, who was at a sanitarium near Los Angeles. A week later, Senator Langer, the Republican on the subcommittee, stated that he was satisfied by the Justice Department report. McCarran said, "There was nothing in it." Langer signed the unanimous report recommending Ritter.[47]

As the June 29, 1950, date arrived for the full body of the United States Senate to vote, finally indicating if it would advise and consent to the nomination of Willis W. Ritter to be United States District Judge for the District of Utah, Watkins appeared to be prepared to assert that Ritter was personally obnoxious to him. That would doom the nomination under the protocol of the Senate. His intention was suggested by his statement of opposition on June 20, 1950, when the Judiciary Committee voted approval, five to three, "despite opposition of Senator Arthur V. Watkins."[48] The negative testimony he had produced was scanty, to the point of being nonexistent, but his relentless charges of impropriety and use of the news media to impugn Ritter's morality and integrity demonstrated that he was prepared to make the "personally obnoxious" claim.

Watkins was the only senator to speak in opposition to the nomination. He read his own letters to the committee and quoted at length from the letter of Ivins, interpolated with comments about Ivins's friendship with Thomas and his credibility, charging that Ritter was not qualified to be a judge, and that the records of the OPA contained documentary evidence that would substantiate his charges. There was no mention that the hearings produced no such evidence or that Ivins's opinion had been shaken during his testimony and that OPA officials in Denver had refuted the charge. Watkins also alluded to the letters of Quentin Cannon and Knox Patterson, but did not read from them or explain that both had recanted.

Watkins's statement, after its emphasis on one lone letter of dissent, repeated his insistence that it was the duty of committee staff to investigate Ivins's allegations, rather than merely afford him an opportunity to present evidence. A "professional staff of investigators should be used to obtain proper information for committees on any appointments that might be questioned," Watkins suggested.[49] Ignored, it seems, was that the FBI discharged that responsibility, exactly, and the Justice Department found nothing suggesting that Ritter was not qualified. Ignored, as well, was that Watkins had the assistance of a senior committee staff attorney, in addition to Ernest Wilkinson and Richard Cardall, but none of them had produced any evidence.

Watkins offered nothing, of any description, concerning Ritter's temperament or professional qualifications. He used the opportunity to make a public record of the alleged affair with Phyllis Katz:

> Statements were made that during the time when Judge Ritter was rent director...he met a young lady in the employ of the [Albuquerque] rent director, Mr. Taylor; that on several occasions she drove him to the area rent director's home, some 7 to 10 miles out in the country to attend

> dinners and parties at the area rent director's home; that a more than ordinary friendship developed between them; that he sent her flowers and other gifts; that he was her escort to at least one dance; that he had been to her home rather frequently, had met her parents, and had continued whatever friendship existed.

Watkins thus distorted the testimony of Taylor, and did so again by suggesting that he had warned Katz not to engage in conduct that would bring criticism on the rent administration. "This gossiping had apparently reached the State of Utah and the ears of Mr. Ritter's wife even before the President had sent the name of nominee to the Senate for confirmation," Watkins contended.

When the moment arrived for Watkins to assert his "personally obnoxious" objection, he failed to do so. He finally admitted, instead, that "in all fairness...not enough evidence to convince anyone of an offense was brought to my attention." Senator Robert Taft (R-OH), fearful Watkins was about to embarrass the Senate, had telephoned J. Reuben Clark Jr. and told him to have Watkins back off. Watkins stated, in the end, that Ritter was not personally obnoxious to him.[50] If Clark made such a request, it cannot be confirmed, but it is ironic that Ritter's nemesis during the election campaigns he managed on behalf of Thomas appears to have become savior to his nomination.

Watkins read the letter of the ABA committee on the judiciary, indicating that it "does not recommend the confirmation of Mr. Ritter," but admitted "that the members of the Bar Commission of the State of Utah...personally endorsed Mr. Ritter, as have the many members of bar associations of Weber County, Utah County, Salt Lake County, and other sections of the state." Only two senators indicated that they would vote against confirmation, and the nomination was confirmed without a roll call.[51]

As calendar year 1950 progressed, the seeds of controversy that would swirl about Willis W. Ritter were sprouting. While events leading up to the Ritter hearings ground on, the fate of the two drifters mustered out of the navy, Verne Alfred Braasch and Melvin LeRoy Sullivan, had escalated to a catastrophe.

After wandering around California, Braasch and Sullivan arrived in Cedar City, Utah, during the deer-hunting season. They took a room, paid a week's rent in advance, and before the week was up they moved on to Beaver, a town about fifty miles to the north.

On October 22, 1949, after an afternoon and evening of drinking, Braasch and Sullivan decided to rob someone and steal a car. Around midnight they went to a gas station where Howard Manzione, twenty years old, newly married, father of an infant, prominent member of the basketball team at the local college, and member of the dominant Mormon religion, was on duty. They chatted with Manzione, left a few minutes later when a friend of his came in, then returned a few hours later. They shot Manzione from behind, apparently without conversation, hitting him in the back and arm, panicked when he fell to the floor, shot him again in the head, and fled, taking neither money nor the car.[52] Manzione died three hours later in a Cedar City hospital.

The two young men, twenty-one and nineteen years of age, caught a west-bound bus, were arrested in Las Vegas, and were returned to Parowan where they were convicted of first-degree murder after confessing. Their court-appointed counsel questioned the manner in which the confessions were obtained, but Judge J. Allen Crockett ruled them admissible. The jury made no recommendation of leniency. Given a choice between a firing squad and hanging, they chose the firing squad.

The dispute between Bill Hatahley and Hosteen Tse-kesi and the livestock men in San Juan County had also escalated. The BLM grazing supervisor and the secretary of the interior did not find Tse-kesi and his fellows a place to graze their animals, as Ritter advised was their obligation.

The Tse-kesi group lived along Montezuma Creek, outside of the Navajo Reservation. They and their progenitors before them had lived and grazed their livestock on the land since before non-Indians settled in the area and pointed to the Treaty of Guadalupe-Hidalgo with Mexico in 1848 obligating the United States to respect the rights of Indians occupying the lands.[53]

The BLM range managers insisted that Tse-kesi and the others must keep their animals on the reservation, that the Navajo had agreed in a treaty with the United States to do so in 1868, and that the treaty eliminated the rights of the Tse-kesi bunch under the Treaty of Guadalupe-Hidalgo.

But Tse-kesi claimed that the 1868 treaty had no application to them.[54] He agreed that they were Navajo, but pointed to the well-known historical facts that there was no Navajo Tribe until Kit Carson rounded up the Navajo and confined them at Bosque Redondo in 1863-1866, where they acquired a tribal cohesiveness. Prior to then, they were scattered, isolated bands having no tribal structure or leadership. The families of Tse-kesi and his group were never rounded up by Kit Carson, never went to Bosque Redondo, and never became a part of the Navajo Tribe that originated there.[55] Congress recognized that to be so when it adopted the act of 1933 adding the Aneth Extension in Utah, north of the San Juan River, to the Navajo Reservation in recognition of the scattered bands of Navajo who had fled north and located there.[56] Tse-kesi and his fellows continued to live outside of the reservation and outside of the Aneth Extension, as they always had, and claimed that they had a right to continue to do. Furthermore, the 1933 act was not a treaty. It did not, and could not, extinguish rights under the Treaty of Guadalupe-Hidalgo, and the Tse-kesi group had never agreed to stay within the lands set aside in the 1933 act for the Navajo.

12

TOMIE'S AUTUMN

It is a fair summary of history to say that the safeguards of liberty have frequently been forged in controversies involving not very nice people.

—Felix Frankfurter

North of the Craters of the Moon in southern Idaho, the Lost River disappears in a barren expanse of lava. More than a hundred miles away, these clear, cool waters burst forth beneath the basalt capping the cliffs of the Snake River's Hagerman Valley near Wendell, Idaho, about twenty-five miles northwest of Twin Falls. Before the Thousand Springs Power plant harnessed the never-ending flow in 1912, they were literally a thousand springs, gushing forth like Niagara.[1] Over eons, sediment washed from these countless springs formed a peninsula several miles in length, creating a haven for diverse domestic animals and wildlife. Sand Spring Creek aggregated the one thundering spring and several smaller ones that remained with the flow issuing from the power plant into a stream going in both directions along the course of the Snake River when it reached the peninsula, forming an estuary approximately one thousand feet in length before its confluence with the river. The peninsula was thus separated from the mainland into a sort of island.

Late in the nineteenth century the area was homesteaded by Polina Lewis. The peninsula, or island, was patented to Lewis in 1896, then lost in 1918 by mortgage foreclosure to Lee Charles Miller of Miller and Viele, a farm-loan mortgage company headquartered in Salt Lake City. Miller turned the Thousand Springs farm over to his wife, the former Minnie W. Viele, daughter of Abram Viele, his financier and partner. Minnie introduced imported purebred Hampshire sheep and Guernsey cattle in 1919, and conducted a model livestock operation. Lee Charles Miller died at the Thousand Springs farm on April 23, 1930, and title then vested in Minnie on August 4, 1930. Willis and Ireta Ritter were friends of Minnie Miller dating from their academic life, when Miller and Walter Granger were trustees of Utah State University. She invited the Ritters to the farm many times.

While the Ritters, Rita in particular, were captivated by the natural wonders of the Thousand Springs farm, the campaign against Ritter's appointment played out, and he was administered the oath of office as United States District Judge for the District of Utah on August 1, 1950. The Honorable Orie L. Phillips, chief judge of the United States Circuit Court of Appeals for the Tenth Circuit, traveled from Denver to swear him in.

Afterward, there was a ceremonial dinner at the Hotel Utah. Arthur A. Allen, president of the Salt Lake County Bar Association, was master of ceremonies. Judge Tillman D. Johnson, ninety-two years of age, attended and recalled that at his swearing-in some thirty odd years before, the U.S. marshal "carried me to one of the merchants...and he fitted me out...with tails, with a plug hat, with a broad-bosomed shirt, and he brought me in...and put me up as an exhibit."

Most of the lawyers in attendance had been Ritter's students. Allen recalled that Ritter had taught a course called Future Interests, considered by some to be abstruse, or worse. The grading system was even more mysterious, according to Allen, "and among the legends that had grown up about the course was one that even the most deserving students there had never come away with a grade better than a D," but one who had compiled an excellent record "in a burst of intellectual brilliance...had been accorded the satisfaction of receiving a C." Ritter responded, "You have seen exhibited here tonight one of the reasons that a fellow should not undertake teaching, at least not teaching law, for it will be held against him all the rest of his life."[2]

When Ritter assumed the bench, the District of Utah did not have a probation office. Judge Johnson never utilized probation officers, relying instead on reports from priests, bankers, and others who had his confidence concerning those convicted of crimes in his court. Having long been eager to find employment of suitable dignity for his brother, R. Kendall Thomas, Senator Elbert Thomas saw the prospects for creation of an office of probation as an opportunity to fulfill his long-standing promise and requested that Ritter appoint Kendall as chief of a newly established office of probation.

Ritter believed that Kendall was not qualified. Although he could be, and frequently was, generous and kind to those he found in unfortunate circumstances, Ritter also had little patience with and could be brutal to those he considered incompetent. On that basis he tried to avoid appointing Kendall, but Thomas insisted. Ritter finally relented and made the appointment, but belittled Kendall in public until he would actually break down and cry. Frances had obviously been correct in her assessment of him as being proud and sensitive.[3] He was a hard and difficult taskmaster, just as he had demanded high performance as a law professor. Opinions of him as an administrator were mixed, but generally favorable, at least during the early years of his judicial tenure.

Ruth Bailey went to work for Ritter in 1951, at first as his secretary after La Rue Burke. Her husband had died, and she had suffered a nervous breakdown. Ritter "was very kind to me," she recalled, and if she experienced a nervous relapse, which occurred five times, she would go to the hospital for two or three weeks, but he would always let her come back, arranging things so they were easy for her. "It was exciting," Ruth remembered. "He was a brilliant man, he really was," and "you didn't get bored." But Ruth wasn't comfortable around Judge Ritter and didn't think he was comfortable with her. She requested a transfer to the clerk's office and was replaced as secretary by Catherine Jensen, who served in that capacity for the bulk of Ritter's judicial tenure, from 1957 until 1975.

Jensen was perfect for Ritter. A former resident of Park City, like Ritter, she had been secretary to James Ivers Jr., president of the Silver King Mining Company. Jack Gallivan at the *Salt Lake Tribune* was married to Ivers's daughter, recognized Catherine as an excellent person, and when he learned that Ritter was looking for a secretary persuaded her to apply for the job. Catherine explained to Ritter that she had two young boys living at home. "I'll work with you," Ritter said, and arranged a flexible work schedule that allowed her to be at home when necessary.[4] She became Ritter's conscience, in many respects, until she was forced to resign in 1975 for health reasons. She became a buffer between the attorneys who appeared before Ritter and the most difficult aspects of his personality and judicial style. Lawyers could go to her and explain the nature of their problem; she would make an appointment for them with the judge and pave the way so that his impatience with those not having his mental acuity would be avoided.

When Ruth Bailey returned to the clerk's office, she found that life was difficult there because of Ritter's practice of not having regular rule days, making it necessary for the clerks to get notices out in short time or call attorneys when Ritter abruptly canceled them. "You can love him and hate him at the same time," she explained.[5]

As the election of Senator Thomas to what would have been his fourth term approached, in November 1950, J. Reuben Clark Jr. and other Republican partisans in the Mormon Church were looking for a candidate to run against him. Intelligence agents of Clarence Palmer, president of the CIO in Utah, reported that "the church crowd would like to run Wallace Bennett against Thomas but the Church is inclined to think [his] NAM [National Association of Manufacturers] association is not good."[6] They overcame their objections, however, and nominated Bennett, a Salt Lake City paint manufacturer and automobile dealer.

"McCarthyism" was to be the model for the campaign that would be waged against Thomas. Senator Joseph McCarthy (R-WI) launched his attack on alleged communists in high places, now stigmatized by his name, in Wheeling, West Virginia, on February 9, 1950. McCarthy claimed that the Department of State was a haven for 205 members of the Communist Party. The next day, McCarthy appeared in Denver, where the 205 "Communists" had become 205 "bad security risks," and the following day in Salt Lake City they had changed to "57 card-carrying Communists." "McCarthyism" was on the rise, with particular application in Utah.[7] The campaign, when it got under way, was described by professor of political science Frank H. Jonas as nasty, the worst in American history.

The Republican National Committee designated Thomas one of its "prime targets" for defeat in the campaign.[8] The Utah Anti-Communistic League, operating out of the apartment of Marilyn R. Allen, following the McCarthy incrimination, painted Thomas as a communist sympathizer.

The same strategy had been employed against Ritter during his confirmation hearings in 1949-1950, led by Senator Arthur V. Watkins. The "un-American" smear during the confirmation process can be seen as a prologue to McCarthyism and proved to be but a "warm-up" or "preliminary event" to the tactics Watkins would wage against Thomas. Preliminary to the campaign, Jonas reports that Watkins prepared a full-page newspaper advertisement containing charges that Thomas associated with communist-front organizations. A sheet, captioned "Senator Elbert Thomas presides at Communist meeting," was composed featuring photographs allegedly showing Thomas presiding along with Paul Robeson at a *New Masses* awards dinner of the Communist Party.[9] In fact, Thomas did not preside at the meeting, although he had been invited to do so, and neither he nor Robeson attended. The circular had the effect, nevertheless, of declaring Thomas a socialist and, by association, a communist or communist sympathizer. Republican Party officials had enough conscience to object to release of the phony advertisement and refused to publish it, forcing Watkins to finance and distribute it himself. Allen produced a pamphlet of her own, titled

"Let's 'Can' Senator Thomas," republishing copies of the invitation to the *New Masses* dinner, with Thomas and Robeson listed, falsely, as "Co-Chairmen of the Dinner Committee."

Walter Quigley, a political operative and self-styled "dynamiter" from Minnesota, whose specialty was distortion of the truth by innuendo, was then engaged to discredit Thomas. Quigley met with Watkins; members of Watkins's staff, including his administrative assistant, Richard Cardall; Pratt Kesler, Utah state chairman of the Republican Party; and Bennett. They planned a "vigorous" campaign, as Kesler euphemistically described it. "Our program was to attack him...and put him on the defensive to begin with and to keep him there at all times, which we were able to do."[10]

Because Thomas always championed world order, humanitarian causes, and labor—publicly and in print—Quigley seized upon an innocuous publication by Thomas in 1944 titled *The Four Fears,* designed to assist in creating friendly relations with Russia when it was a wartime ally by advising people not to fear.[11] Quigley misstated its purpose and used it to play the politics of fear over the bogeyman of the era, communism, and paint Thomas as a communist sympathizer.

Late in the campaign, Quigley unloaded what Jonas characterized as his "dynamite." He published a four-page smear sheet in the form of a newspaper called the *United States Senate News,* ordered by Kesler, graphically amplifying the charges that Thomas was communistically inclined, or a sympathizer and "fellow traveler."[12] It charged that Thomas advocated socialization of America, wrote books praising the communists, and sponsored rallies to honor the Communist Party and the Soviet Union. Bennett campaigned on it. Watkins reappeared from time to time and provided members of his staff, including Cardall, to edit and prepare final delivery of the *United States Senate News.*

Quigley republished the charges originated by Watkins and the fictitious photographs previously published by Watkins and Allen. Bennett publicly claimed to be embarrassed by the excesses, but did not hesitate to charge that Thomas promised "free medicine," larger assistance checks, bigger farm subsidies, and better pay, which in the climate of the times was equivalent to repeating the "fellow traveler" charges.[13]

The Mormon Church's opposition, both overt and covert, to New Deal policies, and to Thomas as a leading New Deal light, became more open. Church leaders expressed favor for Bennett's career as NAM president. Speeches at April and October church conferences and quotation of Bennett's speeches in church classes were interpreted as favoring him politically. An unofficial group called the Salt Lake County L.D.S. Law Observance and Enforcement Committee, consisting of representatives from the twenty-six Mormon stakes in Salt Lake County, released a list of endorsed candidates, from which Thomas's name was pointedly scratched.

The American Medical Association weighed in on the campaign against Thomas, opposing the "National Health Insurance and Public Health Act" sponsored by Thomas in 1949 and labeling it "socialized medicine" and a step toward communism. The Farm Bureau also lined up against Thomas, charging that his support for labor made him subservient to "union bosses." Finally, on November 3, 1950, immediately before the opening of the polls, the church-owned *Deseret News* published a picture of David O. McKay, counselor to the church president, greeting Allan Kline, president of the American Farm Bureau Federation. Kline had been sent to Utah by the Republicans, and publication of the photograph conveyed the unmistakable message that the Mormon Church approved of Kline, the Farm Bureau, and Republicans.

Throughout it all, Thomas remained dignified and reserved. He declined to respond, categorically, to the political assassination directed at him. "Thomas's basic motives were to serve his God, his country, and his fellow-man," according to Jonas. "He was a pragmatist at times, an idealist at other times. . . . a Democrat in the tradition of Thomas Jefferson and Woodrow Wilson . . . who placed a concern for others around them above . . . self-advancement."[14]

Thomas proved in need, desperately so, of the trench warfare waged on his behalf in earlier campaigns by Ritter. But Willis, now a federal judge, was prohibited from taking part in political activity. He helped in ways that he could, editing outlines of Thomas's speeches, but was unable to help his longtime friend directly.[15] George Hatch joined Thomas's close circle of advisers, but his skills were in advertising, and neither he nor the members of Thomas's professional staff had the temperament to cope with the muck that infiltrated the Republican campaign.

"I was running interference at every intersection and crossroads in the state, accusing Senator Thomas of being 'putty in the hands of the pinks,'" Rue L. Clegg, Bennett's rival in the Republican primary recalled. "Mr. Bennett was bringing up the rear with his sermons on faith, hope and charity, but at the same time silently acquiescing in all that was being said about Senator Thomas. And what is more, he remained silent during the balance of the campaign while much more vicious and unfair statements were being circulated about his opponent.... I regret very much the part I played in it... because of the misconceptions that developed in the public mind." According to Jonas, "The 'misconceptions' added up to the murder of a reputation—they killed Senator Elbert D. Thomas politically."[16]

Thomas was defeated in November 1950. The president of the Salt Lake County Medical Association wrote to Bennett after the election, claiming they had elected him and "would forever stand by their program to keep our county from going socialist." "It is at least nice to know who licked us," Thomas declared in a postelection letter to Ritter. He wrote to Ritter again on December 29, 1950, while cleaning out his Washington office. "Here's a photostatic copy I think you ought to salt down," he suggested to his old friend. "This is the bill that gave Ernest Wilkinson the start in his big case. How anyone can do the things he has done is more than I can understand," Thomas continued. "At the very time he made himself interested in your case I had actually recommended [Wilkinson] to the President of the United States for a member of the Circuit Court of Appeals.... I think you ought to just keep this in your files."[17] Enclosed was a copy of a page from the *Congressional Record,* containing a 1938 amendment to the jurisdiction of the United States Court of Claims over Indian claims, which was the basis for all of the Indian claims that had been prosecuted by Wilkinson.[18]

After his defeat, Thomas was appointed governor of the mandate islands, the former Japanese-controlled Caroline, Mariana, and Marshall Islands, governed by the United States under United Nations mandate following World War II. He was given access to a yacht and the best house on the islands. On August 15, 1951, Thomas wrote to Ritter, affirming, "I appointed or rather recommended" you because you were "the best man the state had to offer for the judgeship despite what [Wilkinson] a fellow for whom we both had done so much told the Saints in a quarterly conference in Rich Stake. I'm afraid their hate is not waning," Thomas continued. "Once that starts it grows."[19]

On January 2, 1953, Thomas announced his intention to resign his position in the islands but died before he could do so, on February 11, 1953.[20] The cause of death, in medical terms, was an embolism. To Ritter, that meant, and he remained convinced, that Thomas died of a broken heart.

Bennett rewarded Kesler by securing his appointment as Assistant United States Attorney by the newly elected Eisenhower administration and then his promotion to head the office as United States Attorney for the

District of Utah. Ritter, still incensed by the ploy against Thomas, was forthright with him in their private conversations. "You killed my best friend," Ritter accused Kesler. "I mean Senator Thomas," making clear that he was referring to the 1950 campaign.[21] Thereafter, Ritter heaped unmerciful abuse on Kesler. At one point, he even ordered Kesler not to come in his court.

Not many years after he was confirmed to the bench, Ritter returned to Germany, where his paternal progenitors originated. After confirming that it had been approved with Richard Straus, acting public affairs adviser to the State Department, he accepted the invitation dated November 23, 1953, of Walter Hallstein of the German Federal Government to participate in a four-week study tour on legal affairs under the "American Exchange Programme."[22] Together with two lawyers from the United States, he attended a reception in Bonn and was given briefings on legal problems and procedure of the country, including comparative law briefings, by the minister of justice. After five days in Bonn, he was taken on a tour of the Ruhr Valley to Monchau and Achen, then to Karlsruhe, where he attended Sitzungs of Bundesverfassungsgericht (the Supreme Court) and was hosted at a formal luncheon by the mayor and justices. Then he was taken to Munich, Munster, and the Hall of Westphalia, where the treaty of that name was signed three hundred years earlier, and to Dortmund, Hamburg and finally Berlin. He was hosted by local dignitaries at every stop and by the U.S. consul general. Along the way, he found time to attend Faschings, visit Berchtesgarten, and drink German beer at the Hofbrauhaus.[23]

It was not long before the strengths and weaknesses of Ritter's character at issue during the confirmation process were displayed. Rick Lamoreaux appeared in his court with a case in which Ritter's capacity to be vengeful over his grudges was given vent. By then, Lamoreaux, the young political tyro who had helped secure the nomination of Thomas in 1932, had graduated from Harvard Law School in 1938 and was practicing law in Salt Lake City. Together with future North Dakota senator Quentin Burdick, he brought suit on behalf of the National Farmers Union Service Corporation against the Utah State Farm Bureau Federation, claiming that the Farm Bureau had libeled the Farmers Union by calling it "Communist dominated." The Farm Bureau had circulated a letter claiming that Congressman Walter K. Granger "has exhibited his evident animosity toward farm organizations (except the Communist dominated Farmers Union)" during the same 1950 campaign in which the Farm Bureau helped to paint Thomas a communist.

Ritter said, "Rick, but for you, I wouldn't be sitting here."[24] The case then became a vehicle for Ritter to express his feelings about the "communist" and "fellow traveler" charges that had been leveled against himself in the 1949-1950 confirmation hearings and vent his anger over the tactics used to destroy the reputation of Elbert Thomas in the 1950 campaign. Ritter had represented Granger in his 1946 election contest, but Granger was not a party to the suit, so Ritter did not have to disqualify himself. Moreover, the question was adjudicated in a jury trial in which Ritter's biases were not an issue.

Ritter ruled "as a matter of law that the words 'Communist dominated' were libelous per se," leaving to the jury the clear-cut issue whether the libelous statement was true or false. "The label of 'Communist' today, in these times in which we live, in the minds of the average and respectable persons," Ritter instructed the jury, "places plaintiffs beyond the pale of respectability and makes them a symbol of public hatred, ridicule or contempt" and "to designate plaintiffs herein as 'Communist dominated' is to cripple the functioning and damage the reputation of those organizations in the communities in which they do business."[25]

The jury found for the Farmers Union and awarded it twenty-five thousand dollars. It also condemned, at least by implication, the dirt that had been thrown at both Ritter and Thomas by Watkins, Bennett, and Kesler, with the help of Wilkinson, Cardall, FBI special agent Swede Larson, and FBI director J. Edgar Hoover. The Farm Bureau appealed, but Ritter's decision was affirmed.

Ritter's capacity for the brilliance displayed in his 1926 article on the jurisdiction of the United States Board of Tax Appeals was displayed early in a defining case also filed by Lamoreaux, who was employed by Aboitiz and Company, Inc., a banking corporation in the Philippine Islands, to collect on some promissory notes. The notes were executed by Albert E. Price, an American bank examiner who lived in Salt Lake City. Ritter took what appeared on the surface to be a routine commercial transaction and made it into an epic cause of international proportions.

Price had been in Manila on business of the U.S. government at the time of the Japanese invasion of the Philippines and was imprisoned, first at Baldwin House with members of the diplomatic corps and then at the notorious Santo Thomas prison after the diplomats were repatriated. He avoided starvation by bribing his Japanese guards for food. The bribes, in military pass money known as "Mickey Mouse" money, was secured in a complex scheme with a woman prisoner who had been employed in the high commissioner's office and a Chinese intermediary with access to the prison, in exchange for promissory notes to Aboitiz payable in U.S. dollars. All the while, Price was accruing a healthy unpaid salary, for he was still an employee of the United States. Furnishing the money put Aboitiz at great risk, for trafficking in money between civilians outside and internees inside prison camps was forbidden by the Japanese under penalty of death.

Price was eventually rescued, Ritter wrote, when a tank with a white star marking and 75-mm gun crashed through the gate of the Santo Thomas prison on February 3, 1945, troops of the United States Army's First Cavalry following behind. He returned to Salt Lake City, emaciated and nearly starved to death, but safe. Eventually recovered, he was paid his large accumulated salary.

When Lamoreaux tried to collect on the notes given to save his life, Price refused to pay. He did not receive real money, Price explained, but only "Mickey Mouse" Japanese pass money. If the Japanese proscription against traffic in money was valid, the notes were illegal and void, Price asserted in answer to Lamoreaux's complaint; even if the notes were valid, the war crimes tribunals at Nuremberg and Tokyo had declared the whole Japanese enterprise criminal, and its "Mickey Mouse" money was therefore illegal consideration. "He claims the acts of the Japanese army of invasion and occupation either were legal or they were not," Ritter summed up the implications of Price's defense. "Either way, he says, [he] is entitled to win."[26]

"The conclusion is inescapable that Price was the beneficiary of most courageous, generous and unselfish assistance," Ritter explained in a brilliant twenty-five-page opinion. "It would not be honest to let him keep the money. One's mind rebels against such unjust enrichment. Happily, no authority has been referred to which requires that result."[27] Ritter reasoned that "there are but two questions for determination" as he searched for a way to avoid the dishonest result Price proposed. "First, shall a United States Court recognize as a valid medium of exchange the Japanese army pass-money received for the notes in question? Second, shall a United States Court, long after the war is won, recognize as valid the Japanese army edict forbidding traffic, under penalty of death, in that money between internees and their friends outside the war prison camp?"

Ritter analyzed contract and commercial law, municipal law, constitutional law, international law including The Hague Convention, military law, the law of belligerent occupation, conflict of laws, and fiscal, monetary, and economic policies. He invoked obscure legal opinions from the Philippines, England, Belgium, Holland, and Germany; analogous circumstances in the Civil War and the American Revolution; and treatises, contemporary and ancient, on laws of warfare and related arcane subjects. He struck a balance between "laws necessary to the existence of organized society" and laws "injurious to the public interest," which "destroy the safeguards of the social fabric" or are a "treasonable conspiracy against its existence."[28]

"The acts of the belligerent occupant are valid which benefit and protect the inhabitants," Ritter wrote, answering the first question. "And, so too are his acts which provide against the unnecessarily severe derangement of the ordinary pursuits and business of society." The "Mickey Mouse money" was therefore a legal medium of exchange. "On the other hand," his opinion continued, answering the second question with the distinction necessary to avoid excusing Price of liability, "those acts of the belligerent occupant are not valid which are directed by the enemy against this nation or its citizens, are obnoxious to our ideas, and are intended primarily to aid his efforts to put us down. The acts of the occupant must not offend *odre public.*"[29] The proscription against trafficking in "Mickey Mouse money" was not legal. Price must pay.

After his *Aboitiz* decision, Ritter saw Lamoreaux on the street. "You damn fool, you had a jewel and didn't recognize it. I did your work for you. I spent months in research because it merited it. I had to go to the treatises, protocol—you'll never know the research I did for this case. It was a cause célèbre and you didn't recognize it." Lamoreaux agreed and praised Ritter's opinion "as a masterpiece without the aid of counsel."[30]

On February 21, 1952, the case of Verne Alfred Braasch and Melvin LeRoy Sullivan, the two murderers of Howard Manzione, by then sentenced to die before a firing squad, found its way before Ritter. An odyssey that was to dominate the early years of his judicial career, and bring ignominy upon him, thus began.

Shortly after they were sentenced, Sullivan's mother came to Utah to ask Governor J. Bracken Lee's help in seeing that her son got vigorous representation in an appeal. On Lee's recommendation, the courts appointed Ritter's former law school student A. Wally Sandack, by then a practicing Salt Lake City attorney, to represent Sullivan. Sandack filed a petition for a writ of habeas corpus with Ritter—the legal device, dating from the days of the British common law, to require public authorities to show the basis, or lawfulness, of a person being detained. Sandack's claim was that the confessions obtained by the police in October 1949 were in violation of Sullivan's right to counsel secured by the Sixth Amendment to the Constitution.

When Braasch and Sullivan wound up in Las Vegas, Nevada police did not yet know of the Manzione murder. They found the two young men among a collection of suspects rounded up by the Las Vegas police in connection with an unrelated California robbery. Neither had graduated from high school, and both had grown up in unstable family circumstances. Neither had ever been arrested. They were still in custody, in separate cells, when news of the Manzione murder hit Las Vegas. The police decided to question them about that crime too.

Braasch was questioned first. He told them nothing, but they went to Sullivan and told him Braasch had broken down and told the whole story of the murder in Beaver. Sullivan confessed, and after being told that he had, Braasch confessed too. The technique was so old that it probably would not have worked on any but unsophisticated, gullible youths.[31] Braasch resisted when the police brought him a transcript of the confession to sign. He said he did not want to sign it without talking to a lawyer. They refused to get him one. He signed anyway. After being transferred to St. George, both of them confessed again.

At their preliminary hearing in Beaver, before a justice of the peace, they again asked for a lawyer. They were told that a justice of the peace had no authority to appoint counsel. Braasch persisted and was told he could have a lawyer if he could pay for one. Braasch thought it over for a few minutes, then said: "Well, then we might as well get it over with." They were taken to the service station, where they reenacted the crime for the prosecution, surrounded by a threatening crowd of townspeople, many of them carrying guns in preparation for the deer hunt. Sullivan claimed that an officer threatened to shoot him, and the two men slept beneath their bunks in the jail, fearing for their lives.[32]

Several days later, on October 30, 1949, still without counsel, they entered a not-guilty plea before district judge J. Allen Crockett, who neglected to inform them that they had been entitled to counsel under Utah law and waived any errors in prior proceedings by entering pleas, including errors with respect to denial of their request for counsel. At the time of trial two Cedar City lawyers, Patrick H. Fenton and Orville Isom, were appointed to represent them. Fenton, who had been practicing law for only twenty months, wrote to Sullivan's mother, urging her to get an experienced lawyer to represent her son.[33]

The Utah Supreme Court denied the appeal of Braasch and Sullivan of their murder conviction on March 24, 1951. It was agreed that failure to afford them legal counsel during police interrogation or at their preliminary hearing, during both of which Braasch had requested counsel, was a legal and procedural error. "The state ought to provide counsel for any defendant desiring but unable to procure counsel," the Utah court acknowledged. "This should have been made clear to defendants before they decided whether they were ready for that hearing. But under the circumstances of this case such failure did not constitute prejudicial error." We "found no case which holds that a confession is not admissible in evidence merely because the defendant was immature and without the advice of counsel, friends or relatives," the Utah Supreme Court concluded.[34]

Sandack's petition reasoned that the state had given Braasch and Sullivan only a "hokus-pokus" explanation of their constitutional rights and that they could not expect a fair trial anywhere in the state south of Salt Lake City. Utah attorney general Clinton Vernon, Ritter's longtime friend, responded that the two were advised of their constitutional immunities and voluntarily confessed to their crime and agreed to participate in its reenactment.

A legal battle then developed before Ritter over civil rights and the way local law enforcement officers elicited confessions. Braasch and Sullivan deserved another trial, Sandack argued, because their constitutional and legal rights had been repeatedly denied by legal authorities following their arrest.[35] Had they been afforded counsel at each stage of the proceeding, from detention to sentencing, they might have received—likely would have received—prison sentences rather than death sentences.

Ritter granted a forty-five-day postponement of execution and appointed University of Utah College of Law professors Dr. Edgar Bodenheimer and Sanford Kadish amici curiae (friends of the court) to advise on the request for new trial. Bodenheimer was an expert on constitutional law, and Kadish's specialty was criminal law.

Bodenheimer and Kadish reported to Ritter on April 9, 1952. Bodenheimer urged denial of the petition, arguing that Isom and Fenton had competently represented Braasch and Sullivan. Kadish presented another view, reasoning that there had been a denial of the right to counsel at the preliminary hearing and that Braasch and Sullivan had unlawfully incriminated themselves because they were not properly advised of their legal and constitutional rights. Ritter called for legal briefs and indicated that a ruling would be made after "thorough and exhaustive examination."

Ritter's thinking about the issues presented to him by Sandack, and by Kadish and Bodenheimer, appears to have been shaped by an experience related to interrogation by law enforcement officers while conducting an auto-theft trial of five juveniles, seventeen and eighteen years of age, on temporary assignment in Denver in May 1952. Ritter became critical of the manner in which signed statements were obtained from the boys. He was concerned that the statement was in the language of the FBI agent rather than of the accused. When Ritter inquired if the boys objected to anything in their statement, the agent admitted that the boys objected to use of the term *stolen.* During a conference with the attorneys, Ritter discounted the confessions on the basis that the agents were well-educated men who could easily get minors to sign an admission of guilt. "I won't tolerate the admission of statements obtained in such a manner as evidence in my Court," Ritter declared, "unless an oral admission or a signed statement was obtained from a juvenile under the age of twenty-one in the presence of the parents of the juvenile and his attorney." The cases against the juveniles were dismissed, and Ritter made direct reference to the habeas corpus proceedings he had under consideration involving Braasch and Sullivan, where similar tactics were employed. "I mean for counsel to be present at every sta[g]e of the proceedings, and particularly interrogation of him in the jail house while he is in custody," Ritter explained. "There is, in every interrogation by the police officer, some duress. You can't escape—the policeman doesn't need to use a hose on him. There is a psychological duress inherent in every interrogation by a police officer."[36]

After he returned to Salt Lake City, Vernon advised Ritter, on September 25, 1952, that Braasch and Sullivan had not exhausted all state remedies. The petition to Ritter raised nine points not yet presented to the state courts, and Braasch and Sullivan still had a right to petition the United States Supreme Court. Ritter granted the motion of the Utah attorney general to send the case back to the state courts, but retained jurisdiction.

In the Utah Supreme Court, Ritter's ruling was given an icy reception. Crockett, who was now on the state supreme court but did not disqualify himself, even though he had himself denied or implemented the denial of counsel, saw an "inferential threat to the state courts." Judge Henri

Henriod said he "just can't believe that the judge is attempting to caution us how to proceed" and declared that the fact that the United States Supreme Court denied certiorari "in effect affirm[ed] the decision of the state supreme court"[37]—an error so palpable that it would be apparent to anyone familiar with United States Supreme Court practice. The petition for rehearing was denied on February 7, 1953, without opinion, by a minute entry: "Upon consideration of the petition for rehearing heretofore filed herein, and the arguments of counsel thereupon it is ordered that a rehearing be, and it is denied."

The matter was before Ritter again in early 1953, at which time Sandack's petition was granted. Reaction of the man in the street, particularly in southwestern Utah, was near-unanimous disgust. "The town is very disturbed at this latest action," Mrs. Manzione declared to reporters. "We do not fully understand the reason for the delay in executing these two criminals, but we still have faith in our Utah law and courts. We still have confidence...that honest justice will be meted out and we still have faith in God who rules the destinies of men."[38]

The United States Court of Appeals for the Tenth Circuit reversed Ritter and directed that the writ be denied, declaring that "the right guaranteed by the constitutional amendment does not accrue until an indictment is returned or an information or other like charge is lodged against the accused." The United States Supreme Court denied certiorari for the third time on February 28, 1956. When informed of the denial, Sandack said, "Governor Lee appointed me as an officer of the court, to defend these boys without remuneration," and "I have done so to the limits of the law. The issue has never been simply their guilt or innocence. The issue was, is an accused who is unable to provide counsel for himself in a capital criminal case entitled to aid of counsel at every stage of the criminal proceedings. This constitutional question the United States Supreme Court still did not answer in denying their application for the writs."[39]

"The court tak[es] cognizance of criticism leveled at court appointed counsel," Ritter proclaimed, according Sandack well-deserved respect.[40] He told the attorneys that "although serving with no hope of compensation, they acted in the best traditions of American judicial procedure in their protection of civil guarantees and liberties." Elsewhere, Ritter said, "Mr. A. Wally Sandack...undertook the appeal in the state court, right through the conclusion of the federal habeas corpus procedures, which occupied close to six years....Mr. Sandack estimates that this case occupied one solid year of his time [and] at least $25,000.00."[41] Braasch and Sullivan were executed by a firing squad on May 11, 1956.

In the early 1950s, Ritter began discussions with Mrs. Minnie W. Miller, who was then seventy-three years of age, leading to purchase of the Thousand Springs farm.[42] Now known locally as "Ritter's Island," the Thousand Springs farm became important to the life and judicial tenure of Willis W. Ritter. The purchase was, in a sense, an accommodation to a widow and friend. He asked her how much it would cost. "I haven't decided yet," she said, and asked him to go see what John Holt at Walker Bank would lend on the purchase. After much nagging, Ritter did so and was informed that the bank would go seventy-five thousand dollars on the deal. Ritter told Minnie that amount would not possibly cover it, but Minnie knew of Rita's feeling for wildlife and the Ritter family's strong preservationist ethic. "My dear friend," Minnie wrote to Willis on May 12, 1954, "decided to accept your offer of $75,000.00." They agreed to a cash payment of twenty thousand dollars, with the balance to be paid over twenty years. "That's exactly what I want for it," Minnie said, making clear that she wanted Ritter to have it. "This sale is giving me a great deal of happiness. Thousand Springs Farm is almost like a child to me."[43]

Consisting of more than 300 acres, extending three miles along the Snake River, there were actually three farms: the "island," another up the river a short distance called "the Bonnyview," and one on top of the bluffs bordering the river. About 240 acres were under cultivation, which Ritter referred to as "three 80's," excluding unusable areas of the river, bluffs, and Sand Springs Creek. The Bonnyview belonged to Bonnie M. Walson, Mrs. Miller's daughter, and Major Charles M. Walson, executive officer of Walter Reed Hospital in Washington, D.C. Ritter bought all three pieces of property. There were also three small true islands, in the Snake River by a distance of about ten yards, not described in the original patent but important because if owned by someone else, the islands would cut off the frontage on the river.[44]

Joe Jones, who had been a student of Willis in 1928 and courted together with Willis, in the Buick convertible with a rumble seat Willis was driving when he was going with Rita and Jones with Marjorie, went with Ritter to Idaho to help close the deal. Jones completed his legal education at the University of Chicago, where both Ritter and Dean Leary had their legal training. Afterward, he became a senior partner in the Salt Lake City law firm Ray, Rawlins, Jones, and Henderson and examined the title to the Thousand Springs farm for Ritter.

Minnie Miller, no longer living at the farm, had hired a man named Hanson to take care of the place.[45] The morning after Ritter and Jones arrived, Hanson woke Jones at five and had his clothes laid out, breakfast ready, and a boat in the river. They shot ducks until Jones had his limit, then they went to the big spring and caught a limit of fish, and then Hanson took Jones to the Bonnyview where they shot a limit of pheasant.

After Ritter acquired the farm, Jones tried to get Willis to shoot ducks. Jones took him to the north end of the island. Willis shot one duck, laid his gun down, went across the field to the house, and never shot anything again. He never allowed anyone to hunt there except Jones and George Lamb, and had the property posted with a sign: "No hunting, fishing, or trespassing. Violators will be shot. Judge Willis W. Ritter, proprietor."[46] There was a herd of deer on the property, which Willis guarded like children;[47] there were Canada geese, blue herons, quail, snowy white owls, golden eagles, prairie falcons, woodpeckers, and other wildlife.

The Hansons were religious people and did not get along well with Ritter. Oren B. Hutton was superintendent of the power plant, situated on the bluff above the farm, and after about seven years someone recommended Oren to Ritter, who promptly hired him and his wife, LaVerne, to run the place. Both of them were small, Oren about five feet, five inches, and LaVerne five feet, of ruddy complexion with dark eyes. Oren hired schoolboys to mow the lawn, and LaVerne managed the house.

Willis and Rita developed a friendship with Aldrich "Drich" and Diane "Di" Bowler through a classical theater the Bowlers were developing in nearby Buhl. Di Bowler was a rock collector and operated the Snake River Pottery Shop in Bliss. Di and Rita had common interests and became close.[48]

Willis Ritter had a penchant for collecting. He loved old tools, old farm implements, tractors, wagons, and wagon wheels and gathered them at the farm, even managing somehow to obtain one of the wagons Johnston's army used when they entered Salt Lake Valley during the Utah War.

In 1951, a collection of items belonging to FDR and his family was displayed at the Hammer Galleries in New York, some of which was to be auctioned. Ritter's mania for collecting was heightened in this instance by his desire to own something that had belonged to the president, and he made an impromptu trip to New York, where he placed bids on a number of items, including a pair of small silk American flags that had stood on Roosevelt's desk and were marked "For exhibit only." He got the flags and about fourteen other items, including three English porcelain pitchers; a pair of French porcelain footed compotes; a pair of Japanese octagonal covered vases; an eight-fold Chinese porcelain and carved teakwood screen, and several finely bound books, some bearing FDR's signature. From time to time, through the years, Ritter would laugh and say of the Oriental screen that it was proof the Roosevelts had a pirate in the family, for how else could they acquire such a treasure?[49]

A surplus FBI 1959 Ford four-door sedan, with a "souped-up" engine, was purchased at auction for transportation at the farm. A brand for the Thousand Springs was registered with the Idaho state brand inspector, appropriately a *T* over an *S*.[50]

Ritter saw an advertisement for the sale of surplus steel-truss highway bridges—those bridges, not large enough for two-way traffic, that always have a "Narrow Bridge" sign at either end. He purchased one of them from the Good Roads District, in Jerome, Idaho, and hired Bob Taylor, a house mover, to haul it to the farm on a flatbed truck. "I have bought a steel highway bridge 76 feet long to replace the old wooden one which comes across from the power plant," he informed the caretaker at the Island. "All we will have to do is put a cement abutment at both ends and fit the bridge to them." Ritter told the Good Roads District, "My deal with the house mover is that he will move the bridge down to my bridge-head for $250.00." Approaching the steep dugout road going down from the power plant on the bluff overlooking the farm, the driver looked at the sharp turn and said, "No way!" The driver was right. In July 1963, the son of Oval and Jenny Beads, caretakers on the farm at the time, couldn't make the turn with a tractor and a load of hay. The rig fell seventy-five feet, and the boy escaped death only because the load of hay landed first, cushioning the fall.[51]

Ritter gave up the argument over the bridge and told the driver to leave it by the side of the road. It rested for more than ten years at the top of the grade leading down to the power plant, on the eighty acres belonging to Ritter on top of the bluff. Then someone got the bright idea of measuring the bridge and discovered it was too short to replace the rickety wooden bridge spanning the estuary separating "Ritter's Island" from the mainland anyway. "I have no use for the bridge and desire to dispose of it," he finally conceded, and entertained offers to purchase it.[52]

The Thousand Springs farm was to become a place of refuge for Ritter from the controversy that was about to commence, including over matters such as Braasch and Sullivan that would envelop his judicial career. It would also become a refuge for his entire family, and the focus of even more controversy of its own.

13

TRANSFORMATION

> What a judge does with his time while he is not on the bench is of great interest to the public. It is absolutely necessary that the clear light of day should illuminate any off-the-bench activity by a judge—and particularly any money he makes off of it.
>
> —Roger J. Traynor

On November 12, 1952, Willis W. Ritter was holding court—or trying to—when the trouble began. It was the day after Armistice Day, and postal workers were handling a large volume of accumulated mail. "Where the hell is the goddamn Ogden sack?" someone shouted, his voice resonating through a ventilator, right up to where Ritter was seated on the bench. The court was disrupted by the creaking and banging of steel-wheeled mail carts and an old postal freight elevator, located outside the window behind the bench. "It sounded like a bowling alley," Ritter declared, and ordered use of the elevator discontinued at 10:30 AM. But the mail clerks continued operating it.

The courtroom of the United States District Court for the District of Utah, to which Ritter succeeded Tillman Johnson, was not the beautifully furnished, elegant, modern facility it later became. It was situated on the second floor of an old neoclassical building that had been remodeled several times and housed the post office on its main floor. Before the building was modernized in the 1960s, it lacked air-conditioning, and there were ventilators in the back, behind the bench where Ritter presided, which ran down to the basement where postal workers handled mail.

"Marshal, go arrest that man," Ritter directed Deputy Marshal John L. Babcock, who was on duty in his court. Presently, Babcock returned with postman Francis Newman in custody. Newman had just signed for registered mail, which he insisted he could not leave, so the deputy marshal brought Newman, two boxes of registered mail cuffed to him and gun at his side, and seated him in the front row of Ritter's courtroom. One of the boxes dropped on the courtroom floor. Ritter asked who was responsible for that. Newman replied that he was and was held in contempt and fined one hundred dollars.

The noise continued. Each time it did, Ritter directed Babcock to make another arrest. The noise got worse, and appeared to be intentional. Before long there were twenty-three clerks lined up in the front row. Postmaster David R. Trevithick asked if he would also be arrested. Babcock told him that all he had to do was operate the noisy lift. He did, and was arrested. The courtroom will be quiet "if I have to arrest the whole Post Office Department," Ritter said.

Later in the day Ritter dismissed contempt-of-court charges against Trevithick and all of his employees except Newman, whose one hundred–dollar fine was suspended.[1] "Neither Snow nor Rain Can Stay the Postman in His Appointed Rounds," the *New York Times* headline read, "But Federal Judge Willis W. Ritter Not Only Could, but Did."

Calendar year 1953, the third of the Ritter judgeship, saw events that presaged his tough handling of organized crime—as distinguished from juvenile or petty matters (he could be tough and compassionate at the same time)—obstruction of justice, as well as his conflict with the FBI.

While sitting by assignment in the United States District Court for the District of Colorado, he was assigned a criminal prosecution conducted by United States Attorney for the District of Colorado, Charles S. Vigil, of Eugene "Checkers" Smaldone for tax evasion. Ritter took a dim view of tax evaders throughout his judicial tenure, perhaps born of his own practice in Washington, D.C., before the Board of Tax Appeals, but the Smaldone case was particularly scandalous.

Smaldone and his brother, Clyde "Flip-Flop" Smaldone, had been openly contemptuous of the law and law enforcement. They began their career as runners, during Prohibition days of bathtub gin and speakeasies, for the notorious Joe Roma, then moved to higher crime. They controlled north Denver gambling, and Checkers went to the Canon City Penitentiary in the mid-1930s for conspiracy to commit murder of a gambler named Leo Barnes who had tried to make a few dollars for himself, only to have a bomb explode in his car when he pressed the starter. The murder attempt on Barnes failed, but then another gambler named Mike "Fats" Falbo was found dead in a ditch near Welby, and the trussed body of another, Harold "Murph" Cohen, was found in the waters of Blue Lake. They had both tried to run games of their own. The Smaldones were suspects, but escaped justice for the murders when state district judge Joseph E. Cook upheld the

Smaldones' refusal to answer for either crime, on spurious grounds that it might incriminate them.[2]

The tax evasion trial before Ritter began on Tuesday, June 2, 1953. Smaldone's attorneys had moved for a continuance the previous day, citing health reasons, but Ritter denied their motion because it was not supported by a sworn statement of their doctor. Checkers failed to appear, and sensing another display of contempt for law enforcement, Ritter ordered his bond forfeited, consisting of a major portion of north Denver property worth $105,000. "I thought I made it clear Monday I wanted that man here for trial," Ritter snapped when informed that Checkers was in the hospital for observation of his gallbladder. Checkers arrived later in the morning, dressed in a yellow sport shirt and tan sport coat.[3]

Ritter then delayed the trial when Checkers appeared to be in great pain. He was examined by an independent physician appointed by Ritter, and was taken to Mercy Hospital where he was operated on for acute appendicitis. The case eventually resumed on June 21, 1953, but ended in a hung jury.[4]

Ritter set a new trial to begin the afternoon of September 21, 1953. It was delayed again when Vigil summoned witnesses and jurors in the original trial before a grand jury. Juror Effie Alsup testified to a $250 bribe by William Calvarasi and a visit by Jerry Benalo Jr., both confederates of Checkers, promising her a "nice gift." The grand jury indicted Checkers, Calvarasi, Benalo, and Flip Flop, and Ritter ordered their immediate arrest after receiving the grand jury report at 3:50 PM on September 21. Vigil asked for a bond of $50,000; Ritter set it at $100,000. Checkers didn't have that kind of money, and was ordered directly to the county jail. They were all convicted in a jury trial before Ritter on October 29, 1953. The Smaldones, apparently confident their jury-tampering attempts would succeed, and smug in their prominence on the Denver scene, barely presented a defense. Family members present in the courtroom registered disbelief as the jury returned guilty verdicts on all counts. "In the stillness of the night," the two brothers "sat stunned, unbelieving. Their faces bore the blankness of men who cannot realize what they had heard. They milled around the corridors of the Federal Building tight-lipped, angered, muttering futilely, the bootleg-spawned Smaldone dynasty crashing to final disaster." The Smaldones were given consecutive five-year sentences on multiple counts, aggregating sixty years, and returned immediately to the county jail, where they had been held since their arrest.[5]

Ritter received a flood of correspondence from the Denver area. The "notorious Smaldones...apparently have been able to buffalo judges right and left, whether they be federal or state—that is, until you came along," he was praised by the *Denver Post.* "As a result of your judicial courage, Colorado has been free of a cancerous growth that all but strangled law enforcement and moral values in this great state."[6]

Controversy then developed when Ritter complained that President Eisenhower's attorney general, Herbert Brownell, and the FBI had refused to afford Vigil adequate investigative support. "Ritter chastised the justice department from the bench, when he sentenced the Smaldone brothers to 60 year prison terms on jury tampering convictions, for refusing former U.S. Atty. Charles Vigil the full help of the FBI in his preliminary investigation."[7] Vigil and Ritter were forced to conduct the investigation largely on their own. The Senate Judiciary Committee held an investigation in Denver, at which Ritter testified.

Ritter boasted, in his satisfaction over the result, that with his newfound popularity in the Denver area he should run for public office. His satisfaction was short-lived, however, for the United States Court of Appeals for the Tenth Circuit reversed the bond forfeitures on March 16, 1954; set aside the consecutive sentences as excessive on November 16, 1954; and on March 14, 1955, sensing his brusque treatment unjudicial and signaling bias, the United States Supreme Court "reversed and remanded to the District Court for retrial before a different judge."[8]

Ritter had the appearance of a big man, which he was in a way, though not physically. He was five feet, eight inches and, until middle age, never weighed more than 140 pounds. Through midlife he put on pounds, twenty or so, most of which went to paunch and jowl, companions of age, especially for a gourmand such as he. His voice—resonant, deep, mellifluous at times, and fearsome when he chose—was the voice of a big man, an impression magnified by his extraordinary intellect and wit.

As he reached the midpoint of the 1950s and his fifty-fifth year, the most troublesome change in Ritter's personality, certainly to those whose business was conducted before him on a regular basis, which included most of the prominent lawyers of the state of Utah, was the transformation in his judicial demeanor that was taking place as the decade of the 1950s wore on. The incidents with the Smaldones and the postal workers were the most conspicuous indication of his changing temperament. By midpoint in the

'50s, Ritter had become controversial. The shy, introverted manner of his days as a law professor, expressed as thoughtful consideration in his handling of personnel during his earlier years and in his earliest judicial opinions, was gone. Perhaps like many who are naturally shy, he appears to have gone to the other extreme to overcome it. In any event, he became almost unbearable for those required to appear before him.[9]

The churlish side of Willis Ritter's personality did not just discredit him as a judge but also doomed his marriage and was becoming evident by the mid-1950s, and perhaps before. When Puddy married Tom Kramer, Rita planned their wedding reception at the Ritter home on University Street. Willis disapproved and threatened not to show up, despite Rita's pleading that he should at least be there, for his threatened boycott would be hard on his daughter.

On the afternoon of the wedding, on a sweltering July day, Rhoda Ramsay, who lived at 1370 Butler Avenue, across the street from the Ritters, detected a powerful smell of manure. The odor came from 27 University Street. Willis had it delivered on that afternoon. It was in huge mounds all over the yard, making it impossible for anyone to be outside. It was uncomfortable to be in the house because of the heat. Wedding guests were left to choose which discomfort they could best endure.[10]

Rita confided in another neighbor on Butler Avenue, Peggy Swenson, that she "looked the other way" after the allegations of an affair surfaced during the confirmation hearings. She continued to send lovers' notes, like this one with the handwritten comment "Sweet and tender, I think."

> This day is almost done. When night and morning meet it will be only an unalterable memory. So let no unkind word, no careless doubting thought, no guilty secret, no neglected duty, no wisp of jealous fog becloud its passing.
>
> Now, in token of our deep and abiding love, we would lay aside all disturbing thoughts, all misunderstandings, all unworthiness. If things have gone awry, let neither of us lift an accusing finger. Who is to blame is not important; only how we set the situation right. And so, serving and being served, loving and being loved, we shall make a peaceful home, where we and our children shall learn to face life joyfully, triumphantly, so near as God shall give us grace.[11]

But Rita told Swenson that when Willis brought a girlfriend to the farm, she could ignore the issue no longer. Rita went to a motel in Bliss,

Idaho, for a few days, where she consulted her friend Di Bowler and considered her options. Di had "never seen eyes that were sadder than hers."[12]

On her return to Salt Lake City, Rita contacted lawyer Dudley Amos, an associate in the firm Fabian and Clendenin. Amos requested the firm's permission to represent her, but in a partnership meeting it was determined that they could not do so. They should help her find another lawyer, the firm resolved, and the one selected was Calvin Rampton, a prominent, accomplished lawyer and future governor of Utah.

Peter Billings, Ritter's former neighbor on Butler Avenue and then a partner in the firm, knew that Ritter already held Rampton in disfavor. Rampton conceded that to be so, acknowledging that "there was some damage done to our relationship before Ireta consulted me...and there was some built-in hostility," but "it never got to the stage where we wouldn't speak to each other on the street." Therefore, it was reasoned, Rampton would be in no worse shape with Ritter than he already was. Rampton took on the representation, giving rise to the lifelong myth—incorrect, as Billings's ploy in the Dudley Amos incident demonstrates—that Rampton was disliked because he represented Ritter's wife.[13]

Willis and Rita never divorced, but entered into an agreement formalizing their separation as of August 1, 1958. Rita was given the house at 27 University Street to "do with as she will," together with some securities, insurance, and Willis's federal pension. He further agreed to make monthly payments to her and support her for the rest of her life. Willis kept his personal belongings, including his art collection, Indian blankets, and books. The Thousand Springs farm was to remain their common property.[14]

Willis and Rita still continued to bring the family together, usually at the farm, where both of them spent much time. Children and their families gathered there, and for eighteen years all but three of the holidays were spent with all of the family together.

Members of the Ritter family had four houses at the farm: the "block house" on the island, which was Willis's; the "green house" at the Bonnyview, which was Rita's; the "white" and "pink" houses of Nancy and Puddy, respectively, also on the island near the block house.

The block house was built of gray basaltic fieldstone, two story, with a screened front porch facing east, two daybeds on either end, and a couple of canvas chairs and a small table. On the north end was a milk cooler, no longer in use after Minnie Miller's dairy farm ceased, but still fed by cool flowing water from Sand Spring Creek. An oak door, with oval beveled glass, led from the porch into the house. Inside was a living room–dining room and kitchen on the ground floor. Up half a flight of stairs was a glassed-in sitting room, over the milk cooler, used by Ritter as an office. It looked out to the north upon a stand of maples and oaks. Upstairs were four bedrooms and a bath. Outside, there was a manicured lawn with poplars along the edge of Sand Spring Creek flowing from a power plant situated at the top of the basaltic cliffs. Across the stream a large waterfall fed by the big spring was conspicuous, and drizzles from smaller ones.

Rita's green house was a large frame building about a thousand yards upstream to the south, with a hay field and dirt road separating it from the block house. Rita had a comfortable chair at each window, from which she could watch her birds and squirrels. The farm became a laboratory for her to teach children and grandchildren the beauties and wonders of the environment.[15]

Dr. A. LaDru Jensen, Ritter's colleague from the first year of his teaching career and the person who had brought the Ritters together, came to regret having done so. He believed that Rita was treated badly. "He thought that giving her the opportunity of staying at the farm should make up for everything," Jensen lamented. "Of course, it didn't."[16]

The green house, though large, was not nearly as nice as the block house. A single-level rambler more than a hundred years old, it was the site of an old ferry that Morgan E. Payne purchased a half interest in in 1869, later acquiring the remainder, known as the Payne Ferry.[17] About 1904 the original adobe house was replaced with a frame house, formerly used as a stage stop and a fort during troubles with Indians.[18] After periodic remodeling it became Rita's green house. Every bedroom had an outside entrance—which led Willis to wonder if it had at one time been a house of ill-repute.[19] He may not have been worldly wise as he pretended, or others claimed, for the entrance to bedrooms in a whorehouse must be on the inside, so the madam can control access to her bawdy cache.

Dr. Leo Marshall was helping Rita with the repairs that were always necessary on the antiquated structure when her wealthy neighbor, Ethel M. Clare, owner of nearby Sand Springs Ranch, and G. M. Gehrke, her manager, came to call. Gehrke saw Dr. Marshall, standing in the sawdust, and said, "Oh Rita, I'm so glad you've found a handyman to help you out." Clare saw Lucille Marshall and said, "Oh, and he's brought someone else to help you." They never suspected that they were referring to the eminent dean of a leading medical school and his wife.[20]

Nancy's white house and Puddy's pink house stood about fifty yards to the north of the block house. Both were identical, small but attractive frame houses. Another small old frame building was used to house temporary help, and north of the pink house was a large barn, blacksmith shop, and related outbuildings, vestige of Mrs. Miller's livestock operations.

Ritter planted most of the oaks, with the help of a crew of workmen and a backhoe. He was not hesitant to have a tree moved if he didn't like the way it looked, but otherwise he considered neither disease nor any other condition sufficient reason to remove a tree.

At first Oren Hutton, the caretaker, could not understand why Willis and Rita were not together. They were both such nice people, he said. Then he "saw things going on he didn't think were right" when Willis had company at the farm for a party, and he understood.[21]

They were both strong in mind and heart, never petty, and they respected one another. After the separation agreement their relationship was difficult for a short time, but they remained the best of friends. Willis continued to see Rita, even if "on the sly." Dorothy Watkiss, while a guest at the farm, noticed Ritter slipping out late one night and believed it was to visit Rita. Rita confided to Robert Swenson during a visit to the farm that if Willis ever wanted to come back, she would "take him in a minute," even after she found him bringing other women to the farm. He built two and a half miles of dirt road along the river, placed so that no one could see him going to visit her. Elaborate construction was required, dynamiting of a rock wall, and construction of two bridges.[22]

After Willis and Rita separated, their children were involved with their own lives, and routines changed. Willis began going back to Park City periodically, hanging out with Heinie Herndon and other Park City cronies at the Club.[23] He, along with Roger McDonough and Roger Traynor, were products of the community in whom it took justifiable pride. Ritter's visits to the Club often stretched into long hours talking about old times. When Herndon died, Ritter was one of his pallbearers.[24]

Not long after the purchase of the Thousand Springs farm, a controversy developed over the three small islands in the channel of the Snake River, just off the Bonnyview. The islands, consisting of slightly in excess of eleven acres and the Bonnyview, were originally attached to the mainland before they were separated by Sand Springs Creek. The acres were an extension of the Bonnyview, but when the Upper Salmon Falls Dam was built a few miles downstream, it raised the level of the river several inches and created the three islands. They were always used by Minnie Miller as pasture for her Hampshire sheep, which could easily wade to them even after the water rose, and she believed she owned them. But the islands were not included in the original public land survey, because of an apparent mistake of the original surveyor, or in the description of the deed to Ritter from Minnie Miller—unless the west boundary of the deed could be considered as extending to the river, which Ritter contended that it did.

Hy Berkowitz, who owned a neighboring ranch, learned that the three small islands were unsurveyed and began looking into claiming them for his own. That caused the Idaho Fish and Game Department to begin looking at these and other islands in 1955. On March 10, 1955, Idaho served Ritter with a "Notice of Intention to Apply for Survey of an Island as Public Land of the United States."[25] The policy of the Bureau of Land Management was that "when such islands have been erroneously omitted from the original survey they may be later surveyed." It therefore did so, designating them lots 9, 10, and 11.[26] Minnie Miller and a neighbor, H. W. Langton, composed a letter explaining the facts, and that having "a resort built too close to the Bonnyview farm and Thousand Springs farm," which Ritter believed was Fish and Game's plan, "is very distasteful to the present owner," but the controversy continued.[27]

In 1959, Ritter contacted public lands attorney Clair M. Senior. Senior's office was located directly across the street from the United States District Court in Salt Lake City, six floors up in the same building as Lee Charles Miller's mortgage loan office, and had the distinctive appearance and feel of a rural country lawyer. Senior and Senior was a two-man partnership composed of Clair and his brother, Raymond T. Senior. Their suite consisted of a modest three rooms without a formal library. Law books, including obscure opinions of the Department of the Interior and other agencies regulating public lands and natural resources not generally available in most law libraries, were shelved in the attorney's private offices, in hardwood cabinets with drop-front glass doors, like in offices a century earlier. But they were no ordinary small-town lawyers. Clair was the preeminent natural resources lawyer in the state of Utah, if not the United States. When Congress determined to abandon the policy of exclusive use of public resources under the mining laws or the mineral leasing act and institute a policy of multiple use, it engaged Clair M. Senior to compose the new law.

Clair also had a speech impediment, which he played to an advantage by carefully choosing his words, expressing ideas that others might require lengthy discourse to explain so succinctly that listeners were compelled to hang on his every utterance. And he was a draftsman without peer.

"It is evident to me that somebody up in Idaho is being pretty stubborn about this matter," Ritter's letter to Clair Senior advised, "and it just may be the Idaho Fish and Game Commission. If it is, we will have to bring all of our big guns to bear, no doubt." Ritter in fact did direct some "big guns." He enlisted the aid of Idaho's Democratic senator, Frank Church; Utah's Democratic senator, Frank E. Moss; and the other Democratic members of Utah's congressional delegation. Church introduced a private bill, never enacted, authorizing a patent of the disputed islands to Ritter for $1.25 per acre.[28] The Seniors then contacted Assistant Secretary of the Interior John Carver, former administrative assistant to Church and with whom they were well connected.

Carver interceded with the governor of Idaho, Fish and Game officials, and their lawyer, but his efforts backfired. He sensed and reported to the Seniors a "growing sentiment" with the Idaho governor that Ritter was "attempting to use [his] influence...without a legal right" to the land. "'Anti Ritter' sentiment appears to exist among certain neighbors and this sentiment is being communicated back to the Governor through Republican channels.... [I]t is said that the Democrats are getting ready to pull a fast one for one of their own."[29]

The dispute eventually resulted in a lawsuit. United States District Judge Ray McNichols, in Boise, adopted Ritter's theory that the west boundary extended to the river. The BLM and Idaho "are acting unlawfully and unconstitutionally in an attempt to deprive plaintiff of his lands," McNichols concluded, and they "are permanently enjoined." But the United States Court of Appeals for the Ninth Circuit reversed his decision. It was irrelevant that the islands were originally attached to the mainland, the appeals court reasoned, "in face of the uncontroverted evidence that the islands did, in fact, exist at the time of the 1893 survey." The patent, moreover, described a specific number of acres, which established that the meander line of the river was east of the islands on Bonnyview proper, and that the area of the islands was intentionally omitted and reserved for later survey.[30] The State of Idaho was awarded the three islands.

On February 13-16, 1958, Ritter attended the Judicial Conference of the Tenth Circuit Court of Appeals at the Broadmoor Hotel in Colorado Springs. On the evening of February 15, he was observed "table hopping" in the hotel tavern, by approaching the tables of strangers, engaging them in conversation, and purchasing them drinks. Because table hopping is not permitted by the hotel, the bartender declined to serve any more drinks and called Judge Jean S. Breitenstein, who was in charge of the conference, for assistance.[31] Ritter was described by those who witnessed the incident as "affably drunk." He was not loud or belligerent, nor was there any complaint over his conduct.[32]

Breitenstein had a security officer tell Ritter he had a long-distance telephone call, which he thought was from his wife, and lead him out of the tavern. Breitenstein met them in the lobby, and the three of them went to Ritter's room. After Ritter lay back on some pillows and appeared to go to sleep, the security officer unbuttoned Ritter's collar, loosened his tie, removed his shoes, and hid them behind the bathroom door, then posted hotel security officer Joseph Shawback in the corridor to prevent anyone from leaving. It was surely out of the ordinary, and not exemplary of the abstemious fellow Dean Leary had described at the confirmation hearings.

A few months later Ritter attended the Utah State Bar Convention, on May 15, 1958, at the Hotel Utah in Salt Lake City. In the afternoon of that day Ritter was observed in the lobby of the hotel, waving his arms, laughing, and shouting—obviously under the influence. That evening, at a stag social at the Elks Club, Ritter walked up to Richard C. Dibblee, the master of ceremonies, and in the spirit of good fun took the microphone out of his hand and asked "where a fellow could get a drink." Meanwhile, the FBI was reporting that "Ritter has the reputation of drinking heavily" at the University Club.[33]

These events may also have marked the beginning of the change that was coming over him, and would mar his reputation during later years. Unlike his kindly handling of staff during earlier periods, Ritter sometimes became difficult. Bernice Gibson, who went to work for Ritter in 1962 after the changes coming over him in the 1950s had resulted, was unflattering. She found him "vindictive, pompous, capricious [and] a petty alcoholic who abused his power absolutely." Gibson, a gracious, appealing woman, was married to J. Lambert Gibson, the former chairman of the Utah State Tax Commission who testified in Ritter's support at his confirmation hearings.[34] They had been friends of the judge and Rita when he was a law professor, and preferred "to think of him the way he was before he became a Federal Judge."

Neither marital difficulties, disputes at the farm, nor changes in personality diminished Ritter's capacity for brilliant judicial decisions. With the judicial style exhibited during the period of his interim appointment, Ritter expedited resolution of matters on his own docket and quickly became available to help in other districts, sitting by designation, where dockets were congested and not as current as his own. Among the cases that came before him while serving in that capacity were a series arising out of the death of a protégée pianist.

In the early 1930s, Fan "Fannie" Fox, Freddy Auerbach's mother and the daughter of the owner of the Fox chain of department stores, was walking in Greenwich Village. Fannie encountered a boy, ten to thirteen years of age, playing a classical guitar. Astonished at his musical talent, she learned that his name was Billy Kapell. Being a patron of the arts—in 1959 she established the Fan Fox and Leslie R. Samuels Foundation, which donated some thirteen million dollars to the Lincoln Center for the Performing Arts and four million dollars for renovation of the New York State Theater at the Lincoln Center—she sponsored him in the best musical schools in the eastern United States.[35]

On October 29, 1953, Billy Kapell, then thirty-one years old and known to highbrow music patrons as William Kapell, a noted concert pianist, was returning from a concert tour in Australia on a Douglas DC-6 airliner, operated by British Commonwealth Pacific Airlines. The airliner began its approach for landing at San Francisco International Airport at 8:07 AM. Eleven passengers were on board, including Kapell. The San Francisco Bay area was cloud covered, with a ceiling of approximately two thousand feet, necessitating an instrument flight approach. The pilot came in over Half Moon Bay, west of Palo Alto, where he was instructed, three separate times, to maintain an altitude of five hundred feet above the cloud cover and proceed to an instrument landing signal (ILS) at the west end of the San Mateo Bridge, and not to let down beneath the clouds until he crossed the ILS. But at Half Moon Bay he turned, taking a shortcut to San Francisco International Airport other pilots sometimes used, letting down after making the turn. His deliberate shortcut and letdown put him on a collision course with Kings Mountain, where he crashed at two thousand feet at 8:44 AM. All on board, including Kapell, were killed instantly.

Suit was filed in San Francisco in the United States District Court for the Northern District of California for the wrongful death of a fellow passenger with Kapel. Ritter, sitting by designation, was assigned the case and held a trial, and the jury determined that there was no liability. Ritter obviously disagreed and granted the plaintiffs' motion for a new trial. A second jury found for the plaintiff and awarded damages.[36]

Meanwhile, heirs of Kapell had filed their own wrongful death action in the state courts in New York, which the defendants removed to the

United States District Court for the Southern District of New York. It happened that Ritter was then on assignment in the Southern District of New York, and in a turn of events not unusual at the time the case was assigned to him.[37] In a jury trial, the New York City jury, like the first California jury, returned a verdict for the defendants of no liability on all issues. Still convinced that the jury was wrong, Ritter entertained another motion for new trial and moved the proceedings to his court in Salt Lake City.

The Salt Lake City hearings were concerned with two apparently insurmountable obstacles to liability. First, there was the jury determination of no liability. "No one, seriously, could urge that the crew did not receive or understand these three clearances," Ritter declared after examining the undisputed evidence in meticulous detail, and "there could have been no doubt in this pilot's mind as to what he should have done.... The pilot did not maintain five hundred feet above all clouds until he had crossed the ILS outer marker. The pilot did not fly that aircraft to the ILS outer marker at all."[38] The jury verdict was, therefore, not just contrary to the weight of the evidence but also in disregard of uncontroverted evidence—so much so that reasonable minds could not have arrived at the jury verdict.

The second obstacle was more formidable. Even if liability were found, Article 25(1) of the Warsaw Convention of 1929, which was controlling as to liability on international flights, limited damages to $8,291.87 if "the carrier proves" that it had "taken all necessary measures to avoid the damage or that it was impossible" for it to take them.[39] If the conduct of the pilot was within the scope of that language, the heirs of William Kapell would recover nothing other than the paltry sum of $8,291.87.

Overcoming the obstacle of the Warsaw Convention required construction of the French language phrase "dol ou d'une faute qui, d'àpres la loi du tribunal saisi, est consideree comme equivalente au dol," for the exception to the limitation of liability in Article 25(1) was expressed in those terms, in a single copy in French only. That text alone is authentic. Ritter was therefore left to construe the French terms *dol* and *faute equivalente au dol.*[40] The challenge was a formidable one, for the word *dol* and the expression *faute equivalente au dol* have no exact equivalents in the English language.[41] Ritter was up to the task. As Min had explained in their grade school spelling bee, he studied Julius Caesar, and now he studied the subtleties of the French language, and the intricacies of international airline finance.

Lindbergh flew the Atlantic in 1927, and Amelia Earhart did it in 1928. In 1929, when delegates from the nations of Europe interested in promoting air travel convened at Warsaw, it was doubtful if the infant international airlines could survive. Their principal problem was securing capital, which might be impossible if they were faced with potentially enormous liability of a disaster that might sweep away a large capital investment.[42]

The United States was not a party to the Warsaw Conference of 1929 or to the Paris Conference of 1926 that preceded it, but the United States Senate advised adherence on June 15, 1934.[43] Secretary of State Cordell Hull stated the purpose in adhering to the convention in a letter to President Roosevelt: "The principle of limitation of liability would lessen litigation and prove an aid in the development of international air transportation, as such limitation will afford the carrier a more definite and equitable basis on which to obtain insurance rates and eventually reduce the operating expenses of the carrier."

But international air transportation was no longer in its infancy, and to Ritter it seemed "a strange concept that the subsidy should be taken out of the widows and orphans of passengers" in the United States to benefit "the international air giants of today."[44] The limitation on liability was abandoned, moreover, at the Rome Conference in 1929, and The Hague Conference in 1955 replaced Article 25 of the Warsaw Convention with the phrase, in English, "recklessly and with knowledge that damage would probably result," an expression understood in the Anglo-American legal system. The Hague Protocol had not been ratified in the United States at the time of Kapel's fatal crash, however, so Ritter was bound to apply the Warsaw Convention.

The American officials who agreed to adhere to the Warsaw Convention, and the British and Netherlands delegates who negotiated it, all were of the mistaken opinion that *dol* and *faute equivalente au dol* had the same meaning as wilful misconduct.

Ritter therefore instructed the jury on "wilful misconduct" and that the pilot "need not have intended to cause the harm which resulted from that conduct." Ritter continued:

> The intentional omission of some act in a manner from which could be implied reckless disregard of the probable consequences of the omission would also be wilful misconduct. For example, the breach of some safety precaution in a factory might give rise to some minor injury and in some circumstances the jury might think it was not an act of "wilful misconduct," but with aircraft in the carriage of passengers by air, a minor lapse from the accepted standards of safety might be regarded as an act of misconduct.

With those instructions, the jury had found wilful misconduct lacking. A finding by Ritter of "wilful misconduct" was therefore not enough, for Ritter had instructed the jury on that concept, and the jury had determined that wilful misconduct had not been proved. Ritter must therefore examine *dol* and *faute equivalente au dol,* as used in the treaty, in deciding if a new trial was required. He went to Vaclav Mostecky, assistant librarian at Harvard, for research on the meaning of *dol* as used in Article 25.[45]

> The origin of all this language is what Sir Alfred Dennis [the British delegate] said at Warsaw. And, it is important to observe exactly what that was. . . . He suggested that "wilful misconduct" would cover "not only acts committed deliberately, but also acts *d'insoluciance* sans egard aux consequences." This translates into acts of *carelessness* without any regard for consequences. It is quite a leap from "carelessness without any regard for the consequences" to "*recklessly* and with *knowledge* that damage will probably result. All the more so when a judge is talking to a jury."

Thus Ritter acknowledged that the jury verdict was in error because his own jury instructions had not correctly defined the subtle meaning of *dol,* and perhaps could not do so because it could not be translated into English. He ruled that his own jury instructions were inadequate and that the question should never have been given to the jury because they could not be made adequate. "But what have the British and American translators done? They have translated the word 'dol' *alone* as 'wilful misconduct.' And, yet, they have retained the equivalent fault phrase, which now has no meaning whatever. Furthermore, in the equivalent fault phrase they have translated 'faute' (fault) as 'default' and compounded the confusion."[46] The distinction, though subtle, was of controlling importance.

> Article 25(1) does not mean that . . . the pilot had to have a deliberate intention to kill William Kapell, to wreck this aircraft, or to commit suicide. If the pilot is instructed by the tower to stay 500 feet on top of a cloud cover, and he nevertheless descends into the clouds, the requisite intention is present if he intended to violate his instructions and do what he was doing. In order to be "wilful misconduct" he need not have intended to cause the harm which resulted. . . .[47]
>
> That the pilot intentionally did an act can hardly be disputed. He was directed . . . to "maintain at least 500 feet above all clouds." Well, he

> didn't. He left the sunshine and got down into the cloud cover, and, of course, he knew he was in the clouds.
>
> He, also, was directed to fly from the Half Moon Bay fan marker "direct to the San Francisco ILS outer marker." Well, he didn't do that either. In view of the evidence in this case, he must have known that he was not following that clearance.
>
> He, also, was directed...to cross the ILS outer marker "at least 500 on top." There is nothing more clear than that he didn't do that either....
>
> And everyone agrees that it was a violation of his clearance to let down into the clouds without receiving those signals.
>
> He, also, violated safety regulations, in what he did, and, again, he must have known it.[48]

"The case should not have been submitted to the jury in the first place," Ritter reasoned. "We do not have an attack upon the verdict on the ground, merely, that the jury had made a mistake on the evidence. We have an attack upon the verdict on the ground that the trial judge [Ritter himself] made a mistake in leaving it to the jury at all." Chief Judge Sylvester Ryan of the United States District Court for the Southern District of New York was generous in his praise of Ritter's opinion. "It certainly was a monumental task—an opus magnus."[49]

The Court of Appeals for the Second Circuit disagreed and reversed it. "There is no justification for the conclusion that the *only* permissible inference from all the evidence was that the pilot had been guilty of wilful misconduct," the court wrote, sidestepping Ritter's conclusion that *dol ou d'une faute qui, d'apres la loi du tribunal saisi, est consideree comme equivalente au dol* does not translate into "wilful misconduct." The appellate court failed to approve, or even acknowledge, and may have not understood Ritter's careful construction of the French phrase.[50]

The case of Hosteen Sakezzi (his name had by then been Anglicized by whites), Bill Hatahley, and Little Wagon was back before Ritter by midpoint in the 1950s. The BLM range manager did not pursue administrative remedies with the commissioner of Indian Affairs, as directed by Ritter when he dismissed the *Tse-kesi* case on July 12, 1950, nor did he invoke procedures under the Taylor Grazing Act to require Sakezzie, Hatahley, Little Wagon, and their fellows to remove their livestock.[51]

Rather, the range manager had embarked on a campaign, at the request of the non-Indians and under the direction of Chesley P. Seeley, BLM regional chief of grazing, to destroy the Navajo livestock. Seeley brought an action in the state courts of Utah to enjoin the Navajo while the Indians were still being represented by Knox Patterson.[52] The range manager obtained a resolution of the county commissioners of San Juan County on July 1, 1952, declaring the animals "abandoned" under the Utah "abandoned horse statute," even though he knew who the owners were. In a drive that started September 19, 1952, agents of the BLM, assisted by non-Indian livestock operators and the county sheriff, rounded up the Indians' horses and burros.

The Indians brought the matter before Ritter a second time, with Milt Oman as their new lawyer.[53] Ritter went to McElmo Wash, on the Aneth Extension, with a convoy of news reporters following him.[54] Ritter's long green Cadillac got stuck before they got there, but Jack Goodman, correspondent for the *New York Times* and *Time,* gave him a ride the rest of the way in his '49 Plymouth. The Indians cooked up a batch of lamb and fry bread. Everyone had a good time, while Ritter held court under a cottonwood tree, taking evidence on the value of a horse in the Indian way of life for taking a man to sacred ceremonies and the woman to the market.[55]

Ritter heard evidence that an assistant range manager had been watching from a bluff north of Montezuma Creek while Sakezzi released his horses to forage on the open range, then rounded up Sakezzi's horses, a short distance away, along with those of Hatahley, Little Wagon, and five other Navajo families. One hundred fifteen horses and 38 burros were loaded into trucks. There were legs sticking through stakes of the truck, which were cut off when the doors were closed, before shocked men and wailing women. The animals were then driven, through the night, thirty-five miles to Blanding, after which they were trucked to a glue factory in Utah County and slaughtered.

Little Wagon followed his horses to Blanding and attempted to reclaim them. The BLM demanded that he pay $60 a head, which was beyond his means. A few belonging to non-Indian stockmen had been rounded up by mistake. The non-Indians' animals were returned for the nominal sum of $2.50. The Indians could not till their gardens, gather pine nuts, or go to their happy hunting grounds, or even ride to the Oman ranch and camp on their way to Salt Lake City.[56] They were thus reduced to accepting a ride in the back of the Indian trader's truck.

The BLM ignored the Indians' contention that they had been grazing their animals on the open range since before the United States acquired the area from Mexico pursuant to the Treaty of Guadalupe-Hidalgo in 1848, and were protected in their rights to do so by the treaty.[57] The historical accident of the progenitors of Sakezzi and his followers not having been part of the Navajo Tribe when it renounced rights under the Treaty of Guadalupe-Hidalgo formed the basis for a novel legal contest between a handful of destitute Indians and the formidable power of the United States when the case came back before Ritter.

The BLM countered that in 1934 Congress enacted the Taylor Grazing Act, providing for regulation of the use of public lands. The Taylor Grazing Act stipulated that "preference shall be given in the issuance of grazing permits to those within or near a district who are landowners engaged in the livestock business." Rights of the Navajo were not recognized under that provision, either, according to the ranchers and the BLM, for the Taylor Grazing Act applied "only to citizens of the United States or to those who have filed the necessary declarations of intention to become such."[58]

The BLM range manager administered the public lands under the direction of an advisory board, composed of local stockmen who made use of the range. The Advisory Board for District 6 was composed of non-Indian livestock men, many of them newcomers, brought to the area to work on the railroads or in the mines, but who had a background in livestock. There were Greeks, Turks, Armenians, Romanians, Italians, French, and Spanish Basques, who raised sheep and goats in their native lands—men like the Scorup brothers in the Aneth area; the Redds, who came with the Mormon Bluff Mission but migrated to the La Sal Mountains to range cattle; and others with foreign-sounding names like Chournos and Echina—and, of course, Oman himself, whose father migrated from Sanpete County to establish a livestock operation extending almost to the Navajo Reservation. Some were not American citizens.[59] No Indians had been included on the board, although they had been using the range for more than a century—longer than white men had even been in the area or it had been a part of the United States, and they had been recognized as citizens of the United States by an act of Congress in 1925.[60] The Navajos submitted their applications to graze the public lands surrounding their homes, or at least tried to, but they spoke little English, had no written language of their own, and were at a considerable disadvantage. The BLM and the advisory board ignored the Indians' applications.[61]

Ritter found the conduct of the range manager "horrible," "monstrous," "atrocious," "cruel," and a "cold blooded depredation without a sense of decency." The government agents "knew beyond any possible doubt to whom said horses belonged," Ritter concluded, and they "knew these brands to be the brands used by plaintiffs as well as they knew that the horses belonged to plaintiffs" and "were used daily in the performance of the work of their owners."[62] He granted the Indians, jointly, a judgment for $100,000.

The New York newspapers and the international press gave the decision "big play." They wrote that if the federal government, and the congressional Subcommittee on Indian Affairs, which Ritter had directed to find a place for the Navajos when the matter was before him the first time, would not do anything for them, it was a good thing there was a federal judge who would look after the Indians' problems. The chairman of the Senate Subcommittee on Indian Affairs was Arthur V. Watkins, and he was on the telephone to regional director of the BLM Byron Mock immediately, and came to his office in Salt Lake City, urging that Ritter's decision be appealed. Mock's office was on the same floor of the same building as Ritter's court. When he learned of Watkins's presence, Ritter declared: "If that white-sepulchered son-of-a-bitch comes in my court I'll have him in jail for contempt."

The Department of Justice was disinclined to appeal. The Indians needed help, it was reasoned, so why appeal the case? Watkins went to the attorney general, and eventually to President Eisenhower, to get the opinion appealed, critical as it was of his own administration of Indian affairs.[63]

On appeal the judgment was reversed. The court of appeals reasoned that "actual knowledge of the ownership [of the animals] is not material" under the Utah statute. The United States Supreme Court agreed with Ritter, however, holding that the government agents failed to comply with the Federal Range Code. A joint judgment was improper, nevertheless, according to the Supreme Court, and the case was remanded for a determination of the amount of damages to each individual Indian.[64]

When the Indian pony case came back to Ritter for the third time, he determined the value of each horse and burro to be $395. "It is evident that each and all of the plaintiffs sustained mental pain and suffering," Ritter concluded, and "the mental pain and suffering sustained was a thing common to all the plaintiffs. It was a community loss and a community sorrow shared by all." Each plaintiff was awarded $3,500, plus an amount for diminution of their herds of sheep, goats, and cattle when they were without horses to herd them.[65] The total judgment, after Ritter individualized his damage award, as the Supreme Court directed, was $186,017.50, rather than the $100,000 joint judgment originally awarded.

The United States appealed again. On the second appeal, the court of appeals again reversed, believing that Ritter was "incensed and embittered, perhaps understandably so, by the general treatment over a period of years of the... Indians in southeastern Utah by government agents and white ranchers." Ritter's computation of damages was nevertheless "arbitrary, pure speculation, and clearly erroneous," according to the court of appeals, and it wrote that "we are certain that the feeling of the presiding Judge is such that, upon retrial, he cannot give the calm, impartial consideration which is necessary for a fair disposition of this unfortunate matter, and he should step aside."[66]

While the Indian pony case was running its course through the judicial system, and perhaps because of the controversy generated by it, Senator Arthur V. Watkins was mounting a new campaign, this time to diminish the power and influence of Ritter.

After his decision of the Indian pony case, Ritter was in the club car on the railroad between Salt Lake City and Elko, Nevada, with a group friends on St. Patrick's Day, all of them wearing green cowboy hats and green cowboy ties. Being a corpulent German, without a trace of Irish heritage, he looked ridiculous, so much so that an intoxicated woman who appeared to have been drinking all the way from Lincoln, Nebraska, became belligerent. Why was he wearing that hat and tie? she inquired. "Well, we're all going to Elko to celebrate St. Patrick's Day," Ritter explained. "Why would you want to celebrate St. Patrick's day?" she persisted. "He was just a miserable peasant saint. Why celebrate that? This is America. I'm an American!" "Apache or Iroquois?" Ritter shot back, displaying the sensitivity for Native Americans that motivated him in the Indian pony case.[67]

14

A "LITTLE HELPER"

We can forgive a man the defects of his qualities, if only he has the qualities of his defects.

—Oliver Wendell Holmes Jr.

Changes in the Ritter personality gave his pusillanimous opponent, Arthur Watkins, who became senior senator from Utah after the defeat of Elbert Thomas in 1950, pretext (if pretext he needed) for a campaign to weaken Ritter's office. Watkins secured a commitment from the Eisenhower administration and attorney general Herbert Brownell to support a second judge for Utah.[1] Another judge was not needed, for with Ritter's judicial style his calendar was always current, and he had time to fill temporary assignments in other districts as well. Moreover, the population of Utah did not justify appointment of a second judge, but Watkins and critics of Ritter promoted the idea in the belief that another judge would dilute Ritter's power.[2] The appointment was approved, originally on a temporary basis, to become permanent when population increase justified it, and the person Watkins selected was A. Sherman Christensen, appointed by President Eisenhower and confirmed by the Senate on May 8, 1954. Chief Judge Orie L. Phillips traveled to Salt Lake City again, this time to swear in Associate Judge A. Sherman Christensen.[3] Christensen was a lawyer of impeccable credentials and reputation and a skillful judge, but the workload of the District of Utah did not warrant the appointment of a second judge until 1957.[4]

"Congress has sent me a little helper," Ritter declared. There is little doubt that Ritter recognized the appointment as an attempt to dilute his office, or that his independent style was increased by the appointment of a second judge. Moreover, the choice of Christensen ensured both offense and greater independence, for his nemesis, Watkins, had been law partner to Christensen's father and office colleague to Christensen himself prior to Watkins's appointment as a state judge in Utah's Fourth District in 1930.[5]

More than seventeen years of strife were to result from the appointment of a second judge.

Ritter's attitude toward a new judge might have been the same, whoever the appointee, but the two were as unalike as two highly able judges might be. They clashed, initially, over matters of administration. Christensen believed that associate judges in the same court not only should but also were obligated to confer regularly, not less than once a month, and agree on matters affecting both divisions such as employment of clerks, magistrates, and probation officers. They should also agree on facilities, on the adoption of local rules of practice, and on matters such as the wearing of judicial robes and formalities affecting both courts, such as issuance of checks on funds administered by the Clerk of Court, according to Christensen. Most important, Christensen—himself the consummate gentleman, both to Ritter, lawyers and members of the public, at least when not affected by the dispute between them—thought they should be genial with one another.[6]

Ritter's view, particularly with respect to joint meetings, rules, and action, was contrary. Ritter considered the two judges entirely independent of one another, each exercising discrete prerogatives. "Since 1789 our Federal Judicial System has been handled by trial judges who are answerable to no man, and under no control other than that of their own consciences. We must keep it that way," he explained in a letter to Christensen.[7] He never called for joint meetings, for years at a time. "This is a small court," his letter rejecting the adoption of rules stated, and "it is my view that the simplest procedure is generally the best."[8]

The law in 1954 provided that in districts with more than one judge, the senior judge would be "chief judge." No additional powers flowed from being chief judge, but the chief judge had the prerogative and responsibility of administering all officials, clerks, and employees of the court and its functions, including assignment of cases. Ritter discharged the assignment authority, at first, by assigning all cases of any importance to himself, leaving only trivial matters or those that he chose not to handle for the "junior" judge, Christensen. Ritter's way of carrying out his administrative role was to make all decisions himself, allowing his fellow judge no say at all. Nor was he scrupulous about telling his fellow judge what those decisions were. As a result, Christensen found himself in the difficult position of not knowing things he needed to know, such as the adoption of a new policy affecting the district and its clerk's office, conduct of a trial, or, in some instances, even the identity of personnel selected to staff his own court.

Christensen protested, almost from the date of his appointment. He pointed to language in the law that "each *district court* shall appoint" officials such as clerks or magistrates, and compared it with provisions that "*District Judges* may appoint" their respective secretaries, bailiffs, or law clerks, and said the difference in language meant that "appointees for the court...are to be made by the court as such, rather than individual judges." Christensen insisted, therefore, that he should be consulted, and did not "think [the chief judge] has the power to speak for the court without consultation," for such appointments "must be granted with concurrence of a majority of the judges as I understand it." He complained to the Court of Appeals for the Tenth Circuit that "the control Judge Ritter exercises over the appointment of supporting personnel" was "without prior consultation with me" and that "my status has been reduced well below any justifiable minimum for a coordinate branch of the court."[9]

The logic of Christensen's contention faded when he was forced to concede that the chief judge had the authority to make any appointment "in the event the action cannot be agreed upon." Considering the implications of a two-judge court, if they were in agreement there was no need to either meet or consult; and if they were not in agreement, the chief judge had the right to decide, and there was no need to meet or consult. Ritter concluded, therefore, that there was no need to meet or consult and that Christensen was "a deliberate troublemaker," really engaged in a "rule or ruin campaign."[10] In short, Christensen was trying to force decision by himself, and Ritter perceived that he had been put in office to do exactly that.

In 1957 Christensen began a practice of going over the head of Ritter, taking his frustrations over assignment of the better cases to the chief judge to the Judicial Council of the Court of Appeals for the Tenth Circuit. The "Chicago System" of "automatic alternate assignment" should be imposed by written rule of the court of appeals, he urged. Ritter had a "disinclination" to see me, he objected further, because "I usually have some complaint." Therefore, he alleged that a dispute existed between the two judges requiring such an order. The Judicial Council agreed, eventually issuing an order, on January 20, 1958, that cases were to be assigned by a sort of blind drawing, lot or chance, or on an odd-even basis.[11] The order directed the clerk of the court to take fifty to one hundred cards and write "Chief Judge" on half and "Associate Judge" on the other half. The cards were to be shuffled, placed in opaque envelopes, and the file numbers of the next fifty to one hundred cases to be filed written on the envelopes. As each case was filed, the clerk was to take the envelope with the case number on it, open it, and assign the case to the judge whose title appeared on the card. No one was to know the designation appearing on the card until the envelope was opened. The order was amended by the agreement of the two judges regarding northern division cases, and in 1965 by another order from the Judicial Council, but remained essentially the same. Christensen boasted that he had been instrumental in the adoption of the District of Utah's first modern calendar assignment system.

The clash in judicial style between Ritter and Christensen, and the conflict between them that was to follow, erupted on January 17, 1957, when Christensen called the referee in bankruptcy before him. In open court, before lawyers and members of the public, Christensen directed an order of injunction issued by the referee, in a case over which Christensen had supervisory control, "stricken from the files of this court as impertinent, scandalous, sham and improper."

The referee in bankruptcy was seventy-eight-year-old William H. Leary, the former dean of the University of Utah College of Law who had brought Ritter back to Utah and launched his academic and judicial career. Leary had issued an order restraining an insurance company from contesting liability to a bankrupt estate being adjudicated before him, until such time as the bankrupt should receive his discharge. There was already such a contest in progress, initiated before Christensen, and in Christensen's perception Leary's order affected proceedings of his court. "No one would ever suppose that it would be necessary to apply to a master to inhibit the responsible court from proceeding," Christensen scolded the old legal scholar.

Leary responded that the order was directed to the litigants, not to the court. He explained that he had issued such restraint before, and considered that he should do so whenever protection of the estate required. "No reflection could have been intended by the Referee upon the United States District Court of Utah," Leary explained. Leary disagreed with Christensen that the bankruptcy court was merely an extension of the district court, and that Leary was in effect restraining himself, and more important Christensen, from considering claims of the litigant. "That is the Referee's own court when it is sitting in bankruptcy," the former law professor reasoned, "and it takes a pretty low bird to befoul its own nest. I hope I haven't got that low." Christensen asked, "Would that justify a restraining order by a coordinate branch of court against another coordinate branch?" apparently not acknowledging that the restraint was against the litigants, not the court.

"I regard it as intermeddling" and a disregard of "the proper operation of the court on the theory of comity."[12]

When Ritter learned of the incident, the matter of importance to him was that "one of the most beloved and highly revered members of our profession" was not treated respectfully. "Instead, Judge Christensen tried him in open court, the room filled with local and out of state lawyers and onlookers, and abused him unmercifully." The old man died seventy-eight days later, with Ritter at his bedside, still tortured by memories of the hearing, addressing himself to the "judge" in his dying delirium.[13]

Christensen's reproach of the referee in bankruptcy was repeated with personnel in the clerk's office, who became objects of his petulance. No one, including—perhaps especially—Ritter's most ardent critics, could deny that his clerk's office was a model of efficiency. The personnel, with rare exceptions, were efficient and friendly and rendered helpful service to the public and members of the legal community. Nevertheless, controversy over employment of court personnel was renewed in July 1958 when Ritter discharged Elma Foley, Christensen's minute clerk. Foley, formerly chief deputy clerk, began telling other clerks that the role of the chief judge was "insignificant, unimportant and inconsequential as compared to the Associate Judge," and expressed her dislike for both Ritter and Sharon Hatch, her superior as clerk of court. The financial records of the court, which were Foley's responsibility, were not properly maintained, and she began a practice of not being punctual.

Christensen demanded that Hatch not penalize Foley for lack of punctuality, and insisted that when he held court late, "if she is not in the office the next morning on time she does not have to be as far as I am concerned." Hatch considered the morale and discipline of his office threatened, and both he and the chief judge were further embarrassed when Foley failed to report, or correct, an error in which Ritter's friend Clinton Vernon, appointed by Ritter as referee in bankruptcy succeeding Leary, was erroneously listed in court records published in the news media as having been "discharged" in bankruptcy. These and similar matters led to the termination of Foley.[14]

Christensen demanded that Hatch show him the memorandum explaining the reasons for the firing. Hatch said that it was confidential to the chief judge and in his possession. Christensen then demanded access to all of the clerk's office records.[15]

Hatch eventually resigned and was replaced by Wayne Christopherson. On May 8, 1961, Christensen called Christopherson into his chambers, criticized him over appointment of minute clerks to serve in his court, and said that Christopherson "was carrying on the same pattern as his predecessor in being discourteous to him and ignoring his wishes." A "full dress hearing on why he is not consulted more frequently" was threatened, like the one held on Leary.[16]

After Christopherson resigned in 1968, Christensen summoned Andrew John Brennan, who was appointed the new clerk of court, and Deputy Clerk Hana Shirata, minute clerk in Ritter's court, before him on October 7, 1968, and abused, humiliated, and threatened them over his belief that adequate clerical support was not being provided to him.[17]

The difference between Judges Christensen and Ritter, according to Ruth Bailey, was the "choice of being bored to death [by Christensen] or gored to death [by Ritter]," repeating a familiar quip of attorney and bar wag Ray S. McCarty.

Bernice Gibson resigned as Christensen's minute clerk in early 1970. Her difficulties resulted, at least in part, from her belief that Ritter did everything to make things tough for her in an effort to reflect badly on the associate judge. "He would call me into his chambers and try to goad me into making incriminating remarks about the other judge, with his secretary taking notes for the record. When I declined to make such derogatory remarks I became persona non grata with him."

When Gibson resigned, Christiansen summoned Brennan and Deputy Clerk Deanna Scott to his courtroom on February 2, 1970, held a hearing, and issued a formal order titled "In the Matter of Services from the Office of Clerk of This Court Essential for the Performance of Judicial Responsibilities" in which he detailed his expectation of services equal to those afforded the chief judge. He recited his belief that Gibson resigned because Ritter refused her any help from the other eight deputies in the clerk's office, requiring her to handle all of the work associated with cases assigned to Christensen alone.[18] Contempt of court was threatened if Brennan and his deputies did not comply with his demands.

Gibson's recollection differed. She claimed she resigned after Ritter offered her husband the position of U.S. commissioner, which he declined because he believed it was becoming impossible for anyone to work for the chief judge. Then Ritter

> began a systematic campaign to discredit and demean me. After several sessions in the judge's chambers, to which everyone in the Clerk's Office was ordered to attend to watch the abuse and humiliation he laid on me

> because he was angered at my husband's rejection of his job offer, I looked at his fat, red, alcoholic face across his desk and decided the man was unbalanced. I got up while he was still berating me, went back to my office, cleaned out my desk and quit.[19]

At the afternoon session on February 2, 1970, following Christensen's morning tirade over his perception of Gibson resigning over not being afforded suitable help from the clerk's office, and his order threatening contempt, Brennan was present himself, to act as minute clerk. "I appreciate Judge Ritter's suggestion [that] you come over here," Christensen stated, "but I think it should be clear that I will not participate in diverting the Clerk from his supervisory powers in the Clerk's Office." Further, "my direction stands, to provide the most suitable deputy you can."[20]

The next day, when Christensen convened court in Ogden, Brennan was again present, to act as minute clerk. "My directions were to have a deputy clerk available," Christensen pouted. "I talked with Judge Ritter last night after you had given me that order," Brennan explained, "and I was told that the judge was looking forward to in a very short time having another deputy clerk which would be an experienced person, if possible, and that person would be submitted to you for approval...and that in that period of time for me to serve in your court." The judge retorted, "I don't permit anyone to impose their will within my court. Continue in your efforts to find me a suitable courtroom deputy. No one gives me orders in my court." Christensen's law clerk was then sworn as temporary deputy clerk, and Brennan was directed to return to Salt Lake City. "I would join in that suggestion," Ritter scoffed when he learned of Christensen using his law clerk for his minute clerk.[21]

The exchange with Brennan following the resignation of Gibson resulted in a letter to Alfred P. Murrah, chief judge of the United States Court of Appeals for the Tenth Circuit, in which Christensen expressed discontent that it was necessary to "designate my law clerk as my acting courtroom deputy" to "avoid a continuance at great expense and waste of time." He persisted, "I have insisted and shall continue to insist that during all times my court is in session also [*sic*] a deputy from the Clerk's Office acceptable to me be present."[22]

Friction between the two judges became so severe that rumors began circulating that Christensen would retire. He denied them, but acknowledged that he had "seriously considered the necessity of my simply changing my official duty station to Ogden," but "I have ruled that out."[23]

As Brennan had promised, Ritter sent applicants for the position of minute clerk in Christensen's court to the associate judge for him to interview during February 1970. Christensen sent a memo to Ritter on February 25 stating that "the more promising appear to be Mrs. Vicki Jolley and Mrs. Wanda Curry." The next morning, Jolley was at the minute clerk's desk, already assigned by Brennan to Christensen's court.[24]

Vicki was an intelligent, attractive woman, and Christensen was pleased with her employment at first, for he had an eye for a comely woman like anyone else. But the arrangement ended abruptly and unceremoniously, generating more friction, when on April 9 Christensen "ordered" the clerk to "assign another deputy," for "it is now clear that Vicki C. Jolley is unsuited to act as courtroom deputy in my court."

The preceding day, while Vicki was handling exhibits in a complicated fraud trial, Christensen became suspicious that he had been put on. Odell Anderson, Christensen's bailiff, was directed to check the state court records and reported that she "was the Vicki C. Jolley who was the recipient of two automobiles from an embezzler of large sums of money" from the Mormon Church. Christensen, a devout Mormon, was indignant. Vicki was ordered out of his court and sent back to the clerk's office. Another complaint was then made to the Court of Appeals: "It might appeal to a warped sense of humor or other motivations to have assigned to my courtroom in a position of confidence a lady involved in litigation with my church," Christensen complained to the Judicial Council. "Moreover, it was reported that the attorney who represented Mrs. Jolley in the church litigation at the trial level was the same attorney who is now representing Judge Ritter personally in private litigation in the State of Idaho."[25]

Forgotten, or perhaps ignored, was that Christensen himself had recommended employment of Vicki. Ritter finally issued an order dated April 29, 1970, defining the duties of the seven employees of the clerk's office remaining after the resignation of Gibson. Two (Deana Scott and Ruth Uzelac) were assigned to the clerical work of Judge Christensen. Contrary to Christensen's suspicion, only one (Hana Shirata) was assigned to the clerical work of Judge Ritter. The others were assigned other duties in the court, such as processing passport applications, petitions in bankruptcy, jury selection, or financial matters.[26]

The administration controversy escalated over the matter of the District of Utah consisting of two divisions, created in 1897 when Utah senator Frank

J. Cannon, a resident of Ogden, caused legislation to be enacted providing that the District of Utah be composed of a Northern Division, consisting of all of the state north of Salt Lake County, with a court sitting in Ogden, and a Central Division, consisting of the entire balance of the state, with a court in Salt Lake City. There may have been merit in the division in 1897, for Ogden was then a competing commercial center, with the transcontinental railroad passing through, and though Ogden was only thirty-five miles north of Salt Lake City, transportation limitations of the day meant that a trip to Salt Lake City to attend court might require several days. Those justifications had lost validity by mid-twentieth century, however, by which time the two cities had become part of a single metropolitan area. There was no longer any need for the Northern Division.

Ritter and Judge Johnson before him had routinely required that all Northern Division cases be transferred to the Central Division, and they did not hold court in Ogden. Christensen, as was his characteristic bent, took a contrary position. As long as the legislation creating the Northern Division was in effect, he declared, he was obligated to hold court in Ogden. Periodically, Christensen would go to Ogden to adjudicate the small number of cases assigned to him that arose in the Northern Division, taking his court personnel with him, together with representatives of the clerk's and marshal's offices.

Congress authorized construction of a new federal building for Ogden, with a new courtroom. Ritter himself had written the General Services Administration (GSA) on June 10, 1957, stating that he "had decided to request space" in the new building, "as Ogden is the only designated place for holding court in [the Northern] division," even though he did not hold court in Ogden—only Christensen did.[27]

Thereafter, the two judges resolved their differences over the need to hold court in Ogden, more or less, by agreeing to amend the rule on assignment of cases to provide that all Northern Division cases be assigned to Christensen, in exchange for Ritter being assigned all Central Division criminal matters. The truce ended, however, because after the order was entered, Ritter suspected that lawyers were manipulating the system—judge shopping—by getting their civil cases out of his court and into Christensen's through the expedient of designating them, improperly, as arising in the Northern Division. He therefore instructed the clerk of court that he should not assign a case to the Northern Division solely because the attorneys so styled it, if it appeared that in fact it arose in the Central Division. After being so instructed, a case involving Valley Music Hall, located just north of the boundary of Salt Lake County, was filed and, though styled a Northern Division case, properly so, the clerk mistakenly assigned it to the Central Division. Ritter was designated the judge under the random selection system.

Christensen suspected chicanery. He issued an order requiring the "Clerk of Court and any and all deputies" to show cause whether "the records of the Clerk's Office do not reflect the true facts with regard to the filing of the case and the designation by the Plaintiff of the Northern Division."[28]

Ritter considered Christensen's order as additional evidence that he was a malcontent, demonstrating a petty disposition, and for the apparent purpose of venting frustrations directed at the chief judge—dating from the time of his attack on Leary and extending through his pattern of abusing clerk's office personnel. "Any differences you and I may have should not place either the attorneys or the clerks in the middle," Ritter cautioned in a letter to Christensen dated September 30, 1968, "and that is precisely what your Order to Show Cause of September 25th does.... I am told that you ordered the clerk into your chambers and cross-examined him on a tape recorder as to what had transpired in my chambers." Ritter agreed that "I was mistaken," however, and the Valley Music Hall matter was reassigned to Christensen.[29]

Thus, the dispute between the two judges had resolved itself into one of dignity. The issue of dignity was aggravated, as Ritter became notorious for finding ways around the system the Tenth Circuit Judicial Council had ordered for assignment of cases. An unusually large number of important cases, or those involving questions Ritter had an interest in, somehow turned out to be assigned to the chief judge. Vicki Jolley even claimed that she could control assignment to the chief judge, and inferred that she would do so on request.[30]

More friction was generated, resulting in a seventeen-page order issued by Christensen on March 20, 1961, detailing his grievances and concluding that an "order of March 10, 1961, which purported to withdraw [a]... case from my calendar for disposition by the Chief Judge is hereby vacated."[31] Christensen was further galled by the fact that Ritter's courtroom and chambers were large, occupying an entire second-floor wing of the post office and courthouse, while he was cramped into what had formerly been the grand jury room—the same room where the hearings on Ritter's confirmation had been held. Christensen's chambers, moreover, were separated from his courtroom by a public corridor.

The issue of dignity became exacerbated when, in the 1960s, the General Services Administration undertook to build a new federal building at the corner of First South and State Streets in Salt Lake City, and proposed to have modern courts in the new building. Ritter liked the quarters he had and did not want to move, so he advised Senator Frank E. Moss that the appropriation for the new courts should be eliminated.[32]

Elimination of the proposed new, and equal, quarters caused Christensen, in a series of petulant letters to Judge Alfred Murrah, commencing in February 1961, to complain that Ritter had more spacious quarters, while he was confined to less commodious, cramped, inadequate ones, with his secretary and law clerk separated from his courtroom and private chambers. He declared his intention to have new, more suitable quarters built for himself.

"Of course I am glad to agree with your plans to fix up your quarters," Ritter responded graciously, on June 28, 1961, in a letter that must have come as a shock to Christensen, and probably to Murrah as well, considering the turmoil between them that had raged on for more than a decade. "Don't see why we have had all the circumlocution about it. Why don't you just call up GSA and order it done.... It is my view that you should be entitled to have your quarters fixed up any way that you see fit. A United States District Judge should not be required to ask anybody what he may have in the chambers in which he must live and work."[33]

When Christensen's new quarters were finished, occupying the entire second-floor wing opposite to that occupied by Ritter, they featured a courtroom with columns, like those in a Greek temple; royal blue carpets with gold stars, like those President Nixon had in the carpet of the Oval Office; a large stained wooden bench behind which Christensen sat in his judicial robes before the American flag; and a large replica of the great seal of the United States. There were separate desks for his clerk and court reporter, facing one another at opposite sides of the large room, in front of a paneled witness box. A conveyor with an electric motor was installed on the bench, like a child's toy trolley, to transport documents to the judge, as if no one was to ever touch the sanctified hand of the jurist. The entire pretentious arrangement was separated by a red felt rope that had to be let down when the attorneys approached the bench for a conference with the judge.

The first trial to be conducted in it involved Cal Behle as one of the attorneys. When the first such occasion arrived, bailiff Odell Anderson let down the felt rope. Behle stepped to the bench and inquired: "Do we just stand here, or shall we kneel?" The next day, the felt rope had disappeared, but the conveyor trolley and other contrivances remained.

Meanwhile, the new courtroom in Ogden generated more controversy. Ritter telephoned Wilson F. Collier, chief of the Division of Business Administration of the GSA, and "stated that he did not feel, in view of his conviction that new court facilities were not required in Ogden, that he could approve the space requirement," and declined to sign the request forwarded to him by the GSA. He explained that there was no need for a courtroom in Ogden. Collier, under pressure from Christensen, sent the authorization request to Judge Murrah, who again went over the head of Ritter, signing it on December 8, 1961, on the basis that there was a "disagreement between Chief Judge Ritter and Judge Christensen concerning a need for the facilities."[34]

Ritter claimed that public funds were being wasted. He took the matter directly to Attorney General Robert F. Kennedy and President John F. Kennedy. "I feel I ought to advise you of what seems to me to be an unsupportable and unnecessary expenditure of monies for the inclusion of federal court quarters in the new Ogden federal building." Identical letters to the president and attorney general asserted,

> Senator Wallace F. Bennett...and his supporters are attempting to force the inclusion of federal court quarters only 35 miles from the courthouse in Salt Lake City, with the expectation, I suppose, that there will some political gain to him when he comes up for re-election in November....I humbly suggest that the matter be called to the attention of the Bureau of the Budget for investigation, and also the Administration of the General Services Administration, as well as the majority membership of the Congressional Committee involved.[35]

The letters got the attention intended, but not with their intended result. An investigation was conducted. James M. Landis, who had formerly been assistant to the attorney general, discovered that "Judge Ritter himself...is principally responsible for the project he is now opposing," citing his June 10, 1957, letter to the GSA requesting inclusion of the courtroom, and "is mistaken about the interest and activity of Senator Bennett."[36]

Ritter's duplicity had been exposed in the process, and may have magnified Christensen's pettishness. Christensen took his wounded dignity before the Judicial Council in 1962 in a renewal of the controversy over the assignment of cases. The new issue was over naturalization proceedings, which Judge Johnson had directed the clerk not to accept because the state court clerks' offices, which had concurrent responsibility, were more convenient to applicants in a spacious state such as Utah. Ritter decided to follow Judge Johnson's precedent and issued an order directing the clerk not to receive naturalization applications.[37]

The order on assignment of cases provided that the two judges were to have naturalization proceedings in alternate years, 1962 being Christensen's year, and he reasoned that the order of the circuit "had withdrawn any claimed authority...of a Chief Judge to obstruct...the assigned responsibilities.... I do not believe Judge Ritter has the power to dis-affirm jurisdiction on behalf of the Court without consultation with me," Christensen desisted to Judge Murrah. He followed up with a formal order directing that naturalization filings be accepted, and threatened contempt of court if the clerk of court did not comply. Christensen's order presumed to declare that the order of the chief judge is "adjudged to be void and of no effect." Christensen reasoned, "My view is that to eliminate filings entirely is unseemly, and an unwarranted disregard" of federal statutes and jurisdiction. Ritter's order, "if complied with, or even acquiesced in," he threatened, "may involve personal liability of the Clerk" under his own order.[38]

Ritter considered Christensen's reasoning specious, further evidence of his bent on troublemaking, and calculated to seize control for himself. Naturalization applications did not involve a "case or controversy," and therefore there was no issue of jurisdiction. It was merely an administrative matter, and Christensen had agreed that the chief judge was in control of administration of the clerk's office.[39]

The Judicial Council sided with Christensen, nevertheless, and ordered that "the [District of Utah] shall make, file, docket, hear and determine all petitions for naturalization."[40]

Efforts to weaken Ritter's powers by the appointment of Christensen as a second judge not having had their desired effect, they were renewed and given a new thrust in 1957, when Congress adopted judicial tenure legislation limiting a chief judge from serving past the age of seventy.[41] The bill passed the House of Representatives on May 25, 1957. Expectations that it would curb Ritter's powers were, however, to be for naught.

As the conflict between the two judges raged on, unabated, during the decade of the 1960s, Ritter turned seventy in January 1970. Then the associate judge, Christensen, anticipated that he might retire, or at least lose his status as chief judge. The 1957 amendments to the judicial code so provided.

Heinie Herndon, manager of the bar called "the Club" in Park City, Utah. Courtesy Special Collections, J. Willard Marriott Library, University of Utah.

Dean William H. Leary (*left*) and Professor Willis W. Ritter, ca. 1930. Courtesy S. J. Quinney College of Law, University of Utah.

Willis W. Ritter, ca. mid-1950s. Courtesy Special Collections, J. Willard Marriott Library, University of Utah.

Chief Judge Willis W. Ritter (*left*) and Judge A. Sherman Christensen (*seated*). Chief Judge Orie L. Phillips (*right*). Used by permission, Utah State Historical Society.

Thousand Springs farm, Hagerman Valley, Idaho. View from bluff overlooking the ranch. Courtesy Special Collections, J. Willard Marriott Library, University of Utah.

Convicted murderers Verne Alfred Braasch and Melvin LeRoy Sullivan leaving the Salt Lake City court. Used by permission, Utah State Historical Society.

A. Sherman Christensen (*standing, left*), Willis W. Ritter (*seated second from left*), and German visitors. Used by permission, Utah State Historical Society.

George Lamb, owner of Lamb's Restaurant. Used by permission, Utah State Historical Society.

Utah senator Elbert D. Thomas. Used by permission, Utah State Historical Society.

Utah senator Arthur V. Watkins. Used by permission, Utah State Historical Society.

Robert H. Hinckley, assistant secretary of commerce in the Roosevelt administration. Used by permission, Utah State Historical Society.

Dean Brimhall, director of research in the Civil Aeronautics Administration. Used by permission, Utah State Historical Society.

Ernest L. Wilkinson, Washington, D.C., attorney and later president of Brigham Young University. Used by permission, Utah State Historical Society.

J. Reuben Clark Jr., diplomat and LDS Church apostle. Used by permission, Utah State Historical Society.

Marriner S. Eccles, Utah banker and chairman of the Federal Reserve System. Used by permission, Utah State Historical Society.

R. O. Curry (*left*) and John S. Boyden reviewing Indian land transfer. Used by permission, Utah State Historical Society.

A. Wally Sandack, Ritter student and Salt Lake City attorney who was active in the Utah Democratic Party. Courtesy Parker M. Nielsen.

Willis, Mary (Puddy), John, and Ireta Ritter, 1954. Used by permission, Utah State Historical Society.

Willis W. Ritter standing at Guardsman Pass above Park City, Utah. Patricia F. Cowley Collection.

Nancy and Willis Ritter. Patricia F. Cowley Collection.

Unbeknownst to Christensen, or almost anyone else, critics of Ritter in particular, Ritter had already circumvented the judicial tenure amendments. In 1957, when he learned of the bill, Ritter suspected that Senators Watkins and Bennett were behind it and invited Chase A. Clark, Chief United States District Judge for the District of Idaho, and his son-in-law, Senator Frank Church (D-ID), to Hagerman Valley and the Thousand Springs farm. Clark and Ritter were among the handful of judges who would be affected by the bill. With his subtle mind, pontifical style, and commanding voice, Ritter spelled out the picture of what "those guys," the senators, were doing to them with the judicial tenure act. The three of them agreed that they could avoid any problem if the law applied only to districts with three or more judges. Senator Church was given the responsibility to see that the bill was so amended.[42]

The House bill, without the amendment, passed the Senate by a voice vote on July 8, 1957. The following day, Church moved to reconsider, which was agreed without objection. On July 28, 1957, Church called up his motion to reconsider, and Senator James Eastland (D-MS) offered an amendment, apparently as an accommodation to Church, providing that the bill would not be effective with respect to any district having only two judges in active service as long as the judge holding the position of chief judge on the date of the amendment continued to hold the position. The bill, as amended, passed by voice vote. On July 30, 1957, the House concurred in the Senate amendment, and the bill was signed into law, creating the so-called grandfather-clause exception.[43] The amendment had been inserted so deftly that it was perhaps unnoticed. Certainly, Watkins, Bennett, and Christensen did not notice the change, and that its intended effect on Ritter had been removed escaped their attention.

All the while, Ritter was aware that Christensen, "ever since 1958, has been working hard back in Washington with some of the Judicial Committee to get some legislation passed under which he might become Chief Judge of this Court," and that "he is still very active attempting to knock me out of the chief judgeship."[44] Thus, in 1970, when Christensen expected to at long last realize his ambition of displacing the chief judge, which had been the basis of more than a decade of turmoil with court personnel in the middle, he asked for an appointment with Ritter to discuss the matter, which was ignored. He then made his request in writing—also ignored. Christensen again went to Judge Murrah, who wrote a letter to Ritter indicating that Ritter should probably step down; Christensen should become chief judge and should probably move into Ritter's larger, more comfortable chambers.

Ritter responded with calm dispassion. Murrah should refer to Volume 72 of the *United States Statutes at Large,* page 497, Ritter indicated, containing the "grandfather-clause" exception shepherded through Congress by Senator Church that he himself had engineered.[45]

His ambition to displace the chief judge frustrated, and finally so, Christensen was so disheartened by the incident, and the prospect of remaining embroiled "in the long standing administrative difficulties in the District of Utah," that he took "senior judge" status, a form of retirement, moved his court out of the United States Post Office and Courthouse, and took up new chambers in the Federal Building several blocks away. Christensen acknowledged that conflicts with Ritter "finally led to my taking Senior Judge Status in 1971 before ordinarily I would have considered it," effective August 17, 1971.[46]

Sniping at Ritter did not, however, end, at least not immediately. Ritter considered that the retirement of Christensen as an active judge had the effect of rendering the order on the assignment of cases moot, restoring his authority as chief judge to control assignment of cases. On October 4, 1971, he entered an order adopting, verbatim, the rule imposed by the Judicial Council for assignment of future cases, transferring sixty-four of ninety-three cases previously assigned to Christensen to his successor, Aldon J. Anderson, and transferring the balance to himself, subject to a calendar call to determine their further assignment. The action was on the basis that the provision of the Judicial Code that "no retired justice or judge shall perform judicial duties except when designated and assigned"[47] had the effect of leaving Christensen without jurisdiction as of the effective date of his taking senior judge status, except to the extent designated and assigned by the chief judge. He also acted in the belief that an order by the chief judge reestablishing the Judicial Council Order was necessary "to assure continuation of the satisfactory allocation of cases."

By letter to new associate judge Anderson on the same date, Ritter stated his "hope that we will have an opportunity... to confer about these matters. You will notice that the Order sets down... a calendar call to commence October 18 at 10:00 a.m. in my courtroom. I warmly invite you to sit with me and participate in this calendar call." Anderson declined, stating, "I appreciate your invitation [but] if I am correct on the Circuit rule still being in existence then such would be in violation of the Circuit order." Anderson further stated: "In addition the review contemplated on the 18th seems to me may be embarrassing to Christensen. I would be reluctant to have this happen unnecessarily."[48]

On the Thursday before the Monday when the calendar call was scheduled, Christensen held a meeting with the attorneys in some of the cases Ritter had scheduled for reassignment and told them that Ritter's attempt to assign them to himself was invalid. "Somebody ought to take these cases to the Circuit and apply for an extraordinary writ of mandamus," Christensen urged. He urged further that *Albertson's, Inc. v. U&I Sugar Co.,* filed on January 12, 1971, and originally assigned to himself, would be an "excellent" case in which to take Ritter to the circuit. It was therefore no coincidence that such a petition was filed in the *U&I* case on November 11, 1971, just as Christensen had suggested.[49]

Ritter assigned all of the unassigned cases except the *U&I* matter to Christensen at his calendar call and on that basis denied that any dispute existed between the judges of the District of Utah: "Although there may be theoretical questions raised by the Petitioners as to the need for that action under their view of the continuing authority of the Judicial Council Order prescribing same rule [continued in effect by his order of October 4, 1971], there is no dispute among the Judges of the District of Utah nor among the parties respecting the appropriateness of that rule for the assignment of cases."[50]

Ritter's letter to David T. Lewis, who had succeeded Murrah as chief judge, explained that the District of Utah "is one court" being "properly administered in conformity with statute, precedent and practice," and there was no disagreement. Judge Anderson had requested seventy-four cases formerly assigned to Christensen, all of which were assigned to him. Christensen agreed to handle thirty-two of thirty-three remaining cases, and they were assigned to him. Six cases were disposed of, leaving but one case, the *U&I* matter, which Ritter stated he would assign to Christensen "if Anderson so requests."[51]

On December 20, 1971, the court of appeals ordered that Ritter vacate his order reassigning Christensen's cases. Ritter, Christensen, and Anderson "had responded in writing," the order declared, indicating "that a controversy does presently exist, and has existed as to the division of business and assignment of cases." "The stumbling block" in Ritter's position, the order declared, was another provision of the Judicial Code providing that the chief judge's authority to assign cases was only "so far as such rules and orders do not otherwise prescribe."[52] There was an outstanding order concerning division of cases between the chief judge and the associate judge. Christensen's successor had been appointed effective August 17, 1971, coinciding with the date of Christensen's termination of active service. Therefore, there was no vacancy in the office of associate judge, and Ritter was ordered to vacate his order reassigning cases to himself, the previous order on assignment of cases remaining in effect, and Ritter was required to assign those cases previously assigned to Christensen to Anderson.[53]

On June 5, 1972, the court of appeals rendered its opinion in the mandamus action filed in the *U&I* case. In granting the petition, the court summed up many years of experience in the District of Utah:

> It was therefore entirely proper for the Judicial Council to declare Ritter's order void.... His act of choosing which cases to keep and which to assign to Anderson did not comply with the Council's mandate that the assignment of civil cases be equal and random.... In sum then the Judicial Council was justified, first by reason of the fact that Ritter acted unilaterally and not in conjunction with Anderson; and second, because there was continued disagreement between the judges of the District. We find and conclude this writ of mandamus is essential to continuation of fair division of cases in the District of Utah and in implementation of prior orders of the Judicial Council.[54]

The order of mandamus against Ritter was issued. The campaign against Ritter begun by Watkins in 1950, and the decades-long strife between the two judges that followed, at last ground to an ambiguous but fruitless halt. Christensen withdrew to his retirement quarters in the new Federal Building, several blocks away, without the disputed cases, never having realized his and Watkins's goal of taking over administration of the District of Utah, while Ritter and new associate judge, Anderson, became respectful colleagues, one with another. The control over the court that Ritter enjoyed in 1950 had been reduced by the appointment of a second judge, but that effect was inevitable as the population of Utah expanded and, at the most, had merely been accelerated. Exposure of character flaws in both judges was the only discernible product of their decades-long dispute.

15

CONSTITUTION

> Holmes once said he could write all he knew on a half sheet of note paper; but that he would keep the other half so that he could write, "I'm not sure."
>
> —Willis W. Ritter

> Young feller, you will never appreciate the potentialities of the English language until you have heard a southern mule driver search the soul of a mule.
>
> —Oliver Wendell Holmes Jr.

In the fall of 1961, United States Attorney for the District of Utah William T. Thurman had a problem. The FBI had discovered a ring of automobile thieves, operating out of Ogden, who were smuggling high-priced, stolen cars to Mexico, where they were either sold on forged title documents or dismantled and sold in pieces. The case, being prosecuted by Thurman's deputy handling the criminal calendar, Assistant United States Attorney Gerald R. Miller, was scheduled to go to trial before Judge Willis W. Ritter. Key witness to the successful prosecution of the case was a prostitute who was privy to details of the criminal enterprise. The prostitute had been located by the FBI, in California, and she was willing to testify, but demanded that she be taken to Salt Lake City *now*! She was not willing to remain on call and come to Salt Lake City on short notice, when the case was eventually called on for trial.

The problem for Miller, and his superior, Thurman, was that Ritter refused to give them a firm setting for the trial. He had noticed the case for trial as part of one of his customary "trailing" calendars, which meant that it was set for trial along with a multitude of others, both criminal and civil, on the same hour of the same day. The attorneys in each of the cases, and their clients if they were civil disputes, together with their witnesses and other evidence, must be on hand, prepared to go to trial on a moment's notice, if and when Ritter determined to call their case on.

For Miller and the FBI, the trailing calendar presented a particular hardship—because of the demands of the prostitute, their star witness.

Miller was obliged to bring the prostitute to Salt Lake City, at government expense, and lodge her in the Hotel Newhouse—the very hotel where Ritter was a permanent resident, located directly across the intersection from the courts—also at government expense. All of the FBI agents working the case were also obliged to remain at hand, ready to present their case whenever Ritter's whim required. As it turned out, Miller's case was far down on the calendar, and the prostitute/witness was housed at the Newhouse for the better part of a month. Only she knows if she plied her trade while there, or with what success.

The hardship was not confined to government lawyers and the agencies they represented. Veteran Salt Lake City lawyer Nick Cotro-Manes appeared for one of Ritter's trailing calendars and found his civil damage claim far down on the cases scheduled for trial. He retired to his office, located directly across the street, a few short yards from the federal courthouse. When word finally came that his case had been called, the trial was already in progress. "I am not complaining," Nick explained to the court of appeals on his appeal from the eventual adverse result, "but he started the trial, and I was not even present. It's not that I am complaining," Nick reasoned further, "but he picked the jury, and I was not even there. Now mind you, I am not complaining, but opening statements were already concluded, and I never got a chance to address the jury."[1] The case was reversed, on procedural grounds, and a new trial directed.

It was not uncommon, lawyers being the procrastinators that they are, for Ritter to notice up such a calendar and find, unlike with the Miller and Cotro-Manes incidents, that every case had been settled and there was nothing left for him to either decide or present to a jury. If there were any cases left for trial, every lawyer in every case was expected to have his witnesses and other evidence ready for trial, at the same time, immediately upon the conclusion or settlement of the case ahead of them, at the risk of dismissal if they did not.

Difficult as that was for the lawyers, and however bizarre the result at times, in cases such as that of Cotro-Manes, the trailing calendar had its merits in the economy that resulted for the court and jurymen, for resources and time were not wasted when cases collapsed, as they frequently do, "on the courthouse steps." Ritter, whose empathy was usually with the lot of the masses rather than the privileged in society, frequently declared that the convenience to members of the public summoned to serve on juries was, to him, a more important consideration than any inconvenience to the lawyers and litigants not having the advantage of a firm time setting for their cases.

The incidents with Miller's stolen car ring case and Cotro-Manes's civil damage claim were not atypical. Critics complained that the Ritter judicial style exceeded his authority and brought disrespect to the federal courts. Critics also pointed to the language of the United States Constitution, article 3, section 1, that judges "shall hold their offices during good Behaviour," reasoning that his conduct violated that standard and he should be removed from office. Ritter's response was that "the 'during good behavior' provision...served not as a limitation on judicial tenure, but as a protection against judicial removal by the executive power," and he reminded them of the practice in common-law England of removal of judges by the king. "That is the way James I got rid of Sir Edward Coke," Ritter explained. "The Colonies had had their bellyfull of a judiciary that was appointed at the pleasure of the king, and the lack of judicial independence was one of the charges against British tyranny in the Declaration of Independence" that resulted in the "good behavior" clause in the Constitution.[2] Judicial independence was the object of the good-behavior clause, not disability from holding office, Ritter reasoned.

Permitting the actual or de facto removal of a federal judge other than by impeachment, such as for disregard of the good-behavior clause, would amount to a revival of the practice of removal of judges by "Address," in which judges are removed by the executive body for reasons not warranting impeachment, or by the common-law writ of scire facias, in which a judge is required to show cause why his authority should not be annulled or vacated. Ritter rebutted that contention, pointing out that "the Constitutional Convention expressly rejected Address as a means of removal" of a judge and "rejected" removal by means "other than by impeachment."[3]

Because of incidents like the Miller and Cotro-Manes cases, Willis W. Ritter became a controversial judge—perhaps as controversial as any who ever sat on the bench. The reasons for the controversy surrounding him were not confined to the trailing calendar, and stemmed from a variety of sources, most of which related to his application of the notion of independence of the federal judiciary. We have the good fortune of having a statement of the Ritter philosophy, in his own words, in the form of his brief in opposition to petitions for mandamus pending against him at the time of his death, filed with the United States Court of Appeals for the Tenth Circuit.[4] In it he explained his view that a district judge not only has the constitutional prerogative to decide matters brought before him, pursuant to his original jurisdiction, but also has the *obligation* to do so, and not to be directed in doing so by others.

Anyone who ever argued a case before Ritter knows that he frequently declared, and his conduct demonstrated, his regard for the Supreme Court and the Court of Appeals for the Tenth Circuit as his "superiors" in the sense of their correction of his decisions by judicial review. They were not, however, his "superiors in the *exercise* of his Constitutional responsibilities."[5] He was a firm believer in following precedent. "But the character of every act depends on the circumstances in which it is done," his judicial inspiration, Oliver Wendell Holmes had declared.[6] He was a follower of the Holmes philosophy and considered that the construction of precedent and determination of its application was a fact-finding process for the court of original jurisdiction, and thus his constitutional prerogative. It was not subject to mandate by any superior, for "no trial judge can maintain genuine independence if his continuation in office," which is what an order of mandate for his decision would amount to, "is subject to review."[7] Because an order of mandate would be a direction of certain conduct, or to refrain from certain conduct, if entered pursuant to appellate jurisdiction, any such order must be based on the facts of the particular case in which it was entered.

Those who argued cases before him were equally familiar with his frequent declarations, in response to argument that "the court of appeals thinks such-and-so" with respect to a line of reasoning urged, that "this court thinks otherwise." Critics claimed that his attitude was another abuse of his office, amounting to neglect of governing case law, and contempt for the judges of superior courts.[8] He rejoined that his approach was not an expression of disrespect for the superior court, but a mere expression that it was his constitutional duty to decide, and for the superior court to correct by review, if necessary. The prerogative of decision could not be dictated by the superior court, even if it could reverse that decision on appeal.

The Ritter philosophy merely recognized the logic of the constitutional language. The United States Constitution, article 3, section 1, provides that "the judicial power of the United States shall be vested in one Supreme Court, and such inferior Courts as the Congress may from time to time ordain and establish." Congress established district courts and gave them "original jurisdiction." Original jurisdiction, Ritter reasoned, relates to actions commenced in a lower court, raising issues of fact. Congress also established the courts of appeals, Ritter affirmed, but "the only jurisdiction Congress has entrusted to [them] with regard to the district courts of the United States is appellate and not original."[9]

"The test of appellate jurisdiction," as opposed to original jurisdiction,

Ritter pointed out, "was settled by the Supreme Court in *Marbury v. Madison,*" where Chief Justice John Marshall stated that "the essential criterion of appellate jurisdiction" is "that it revises and corrects the proceedings in a cause already instituted, and does not create that cause."[10] Facts determine the applicability of every legal precept, and the court of appellate jurisdiction must take the facts as given to it. Only the court of original jurisdiction can determine the facts. The court of appellate jurisdiction may determine that there was an error in the finding of the facts, in which event it must remand for further fact-finding. Thus, the superior court could correct, and even reverse, decisions, pursuant to its appellate jurisdiction, but it could not direct the decision of a district judge. To do so would be the exercise of original rather than appellate jurisdiction.

Many lawyers, including some in the Justice Department, did not appreciate the relation between Ritter's concept of the independence of the federal judiciary and the manner in which he dealt with citations of authority, particularly from other jurisdictions. They saw him as abusing his authority, or disrespectful of judicial precedent.

His philosophy, however correct according to a plain reading of the Constitution, inevitably made for trouble with the judges of the court of appeals, for it appeared to place him in disregard of, or as some thought contempt for, their directions on how business in his court should be conducted. "Circuit councils are not vested with judicial power to discipline or remove a district judge for misbehavior," he objected. The power to discipline or direct the conduct of a district court judge would require fact determinations, which is the exercise of original jurisdiction. Since only the district courts (or the Supreme Court, when a state, ambassador, or consul is a party) are vested with original jurisdiction, and the discipline of a judge would be an original judicial proceeding requiring resolution of issues of fact, recognition of such a power "would subject Supreme Court justices to removal by inferior federal courts."[11] Specifically, because district courts are the only courts other than the Supreme Court having original jurisdiction, Ritter pointed out, recognition of the power of discipline, and removal, of federal judges would require recognition of a power to remove a Supreme Court justice by a proceeding in the district court.

To Ritter, the issue was judicial independence. No one, including superior courts, could "invade judicial independence."[12] Superiors could review his action, pursuant to their appellate jurisdiction, correct errors, or reverse when they saw him as wrong, but could not intrude into the independence of his court.

A superior court could enter an order of mandamus, requiring certain conduct, and both the court of appeals and the United States Supreme Court did so from time to time. But mandamus is, by definition, "in aid of jurisdiction." So the jurisdiction exercised on mandamus was still appellate. Even if an order of mandamus was entered in a particular case, such as on refusal to call a grand jury, on the theory of a threat to eventual appellate review, the government might find itself confronted with similar actions in future cases. After all, appellate review was, at least according to his philosophy, a correction of his conduct in a particular case and not an interference in his judicial independence. Such an attitude led critics in the Justice Department to again claim "abuse of power," that Ritter was "a lawless federal judge," and "that [it is] our responsibility to attempt to foster the sound administration of justice in the federal courts." They claimed that his was a "chronic disregard for accepted legal norms," which may have been correct, but they failed to either recognize or acknowledge that such criticism represented a bald effort to direct his judicial administration. They even declared in one instance that "Judge Ritter belongs in an asylum rather than on the bench." The "abuse of power" they had in mind was "his conscious attempts to frustrate review of his decisions" and "his refusal to follow the binding decisions of higher courts"—in short, his refusal to allow mandamus in a particular case to control the administration of his court in subsequent cases.[13] He knew what the result in the court of appeals would be, they seemed to reason, and he should just comply.

No one who ever appeared before Ritter, we state with confidence, ever doubted his facility to get to the heart of a matter, never mind how complex, quicker than any judge ever. His mind was quicker than almost anyone's, and he usually showed little patience for those not equal to his mental acuity. That having been said, however, one must immediately recall the numerous times he responded generously, leading as if by the hand those who appeared incapable of the complexities of a trial or argument of a sophisticated legal question. One could never be sure, when entering his courtroom, which Ritter one would find there. Paul D. Viernieu, a thoroughly decent and likeable lawyer, was a notable example. He prevailed before Ritter in complex trade regulation and commercial claims many might have considered beyond his learning or experience, for the chief judge would "take him by the hand," much as he had done with marginal students when he was a law professor, presenting his evidence for him, then make the arguments for him that were appropriate to winning the case.

Those who suffered most at his demands were usually lawyers in the

United States Justice Department, like Thurman and Miller, or with the attorney general of Utah, with whom he brooked neither lack of preparation nor failure of support by the best authorities on the question. And however harsh it may have seemed at times, and however unjust when a case was dismissed or motion denied because a government or civil lawyer did not have the witness present or the correct document or citation of authority at hand, there was merit, nevertheless, in the exacting demands he imposed. The government, after all, had thousands of Justice Department lawyers and the awesome investigative resources of the FBI, United States Department of the Interior, or other interested agencies arrayed against the individual citizen claimant, often represented by a lone lawyer with no legal or investigative support. It was right, he thought, to impose high standards on those representing the sovereign—and he was not unfair to do so. High standards were expected of those in a position to deliver, and he demanded that they do so.

Still, his demands had their reverberations. It was said that there was a special table reserved at the Department of Justice in Washington, D.C., just for lawyers to commiserate after they had returned from Utah and an encounter with Ritter.

Control of his judicial prerogatives and the independence of his judicial style led to other problems for prosecutors and defense counsel alike in criminal cases. It became well known that Ritter would not accept plea bargains, and his refusal was cited as another abuse of judicial power. By overcharging, or threats to do so, or by unauthorized promises or assurances, Ritter reasoned, prosecutors could too easily coerce a plea that was essentially involuntary. He therefore allowed no such promises, or even assurances of influence or recommendation with the court. Once a charge of crime had been lodged, Ritter and no one else would be allowed to determine its disposition.

Law professor William J. Lockhart, during his tenure as acting United States Attorney for the District of Utah, "discussed the problem of plea-bargaining with Judge Ritter and frankly advised him that such negotiated pleas were frequently in the best interest of both the defendant and the Government." Ritter concurred, but repeated his concerns. Lockhart then agreed to formalize the plea-negotiation process in a written form, disclosing all of the considerations discussed by either party as a basis for the proposed guilty plea. Negotiated pleas were then sometimes accepted, but only after the defendant acknowledged to him in open court and on the record that the form reflected fully all of the prosecutor's representations.[14]

The Ritter judicial style was characterized by simplicity. The "trailing calendar" was one of his devices of simplicity. Another was his "law and motion" calendar. Long periods of time would go by, as criminal complaints accumulated and motions in civil cases for summary disposition or ruling on important legal questions remained undisposed of, usually for months at a time. Then Ritter would notice everything up for hearing, including arraignment of every person charged with a crime, sentencing of those who entered guilty pleas, and all motions pending in both civil and criminal cases, at the same hour on the same day. Because of the importance of business conducted in the federal court, virtually every lawyer of prominence in the state of Utah, or at least those regularly engaged in trial practice, would be in attendance—so much so that Ritter's rule days became known as "Ritter's Bar Convention."

Then the entertainment began! Ritter would dispose of the entire calendar, civil as well as criminal, usually consisting of hundreds of cases, and often do so before the noon recess. His critics, though they claimed to have other grievances, usually were upset over abuse, or perceived abuse, when they could not meet his intellectual demands. His stock response to sophisticated legal argument, and citation of authority in its support, was: "Give me your best case!"—and it had better be United States Supreme Court, or Tenth Circuit Court of Appeals at least, for if not bound by direct, superior authority, Ritter considered himself empowered, and competent, to decide for himself. Sophistry was not permitted. Lawyers must state their case precisely, and when they had done so his ruling was immediate and direct. His mind was quicker than almost anyone's, so much so that before statement of the controversy was even concluded, he usually had the essence of the dispute in mind and his ruling announced. And his ruling was usually the right one.

Critics said they were not questioning his honesty, but contended he had become a "law unto himself." They claimed, because of his intellectual demands and lack of patience with those who could not meet his demands, that he abused attorneys, abused witnesses, and was "a disgrace to the federal judiciary and a disgrace to the bar." Lockhart was of the opinion that some lawyers, notably his successor as United States Attorney for the District of Utah, Ramon Child, adopted an "openly confrontational" approach to Ritter's demands, "lock[ing] both sides into rigid positions," resulting in their differences with him becoming "a matter to be escalated rather than to be de-escalated."[15]

The best way to get at the heart of a problem, usually, was the most direct. His rulings, whether on law and motion or in trials on the merits, were usually oral and from the bench. The Ritter philosophy on the application of substantive law was explained during his law school days, and there is nothing to indicate that it changed after he assumed the bench. He quoted Holmes:

> The joy of life is living, is to put all one's powers as far as they will go; that the measure of power is obstacles overcome; to ride boldly at what is in front of you, be it fence or enemy; to pray, not for comfort, but for combat; to keep the soldier's faith against the doubts of civil life, more besetting and harder to overcome than all the misgivings of the battle field, and to remember that duty is not to be proved in the evil day, but then to be obeyed unquestioning; to love glory more than the temptations of wallowing ease, but to know that one's final judge is one's self.[16]

The young Professor Ritter explained his judicial philosophy in a newspaper article published in 1934. He did not subscribe to the notion of modern-day "strict constructionists," that lawyers merely apply the law:

> Much can be said for the tenacity of a doctrine which has withstood vicissitudes of the crowding centuries since the 1200's. Can as much be said for its ethics. Can anything be said for it if it is out of joint with our times? I am suggesting that the antiquity of legal habits should not be their only justification. I am by no means suggesting that the good should be discarded. The orgy of codification since the turn of the century, in discarding good common law and adopting poor codes, has done probably as much harm as it has accomplished anything beneficial.[17]

His progressive attitude, and the liberality that would typify his judicial decisions, was expressed in the same article:

> No doubt we shall always have a lag between advancing society on the one hand and the rules which govern us on the other. Architects plan, engineers build, business men advance, all pushing forward the frontiers of our civilization. Somewhere behind, the law is plodding along. It must not get so far behind that it retards our progress. It must not get so far behind that it does not serve the moral, social, economic and industrial needs of our times. The cases which arise mirror contemporary events.

> They should be decided with an eye to conditions which will be affected by the decisions.[18]

"What is the source of law, anyway?" Ritter queried. "Of course, legislatures impose some of it upon us. It has been said of legislatures that they generally change law for the worse and it is the business of courts to keep the mischief within the narrowest possible bounds. Most of our law comes to us from judicial decisions. Where do the judges find those rules?" he queried further, laying the basis for his progressive philosophy.

> You will say, of course, in the reports of decisions, in the precedents. But where did the first precedent for any doctrine of law have its origin? Was it handed down by divine dispensation? Did some judge evolve it through arm chair meditations in the field of abstract justice? The notion that the law is the product of revelation or is discovered by starting an expert's mind to working in the realm of abstract justice and then recording his reactions is to regard law as the "natural law" of the ancients.[19]

His philosophy was that facts determine the applicability of any legal precedent, and legal precedent, including statutory law, must be flexible enough to accord the needs of society:

> Dean [Roscoe] Pound's "sociological jurisprudence" re-introduced ethics and social cause and effect into the law. His work marks a revolt against case law positivism. But Pound's philosophy contains some of both the natural law based upon reason, and positivism as solely a recourse to precedents.
>
> The most recent development in legal philosophy is "realism." The "realist" wants the law to deal with things, with people, with tangibles, and not with words alone. He wants to know what the law does to people. What is its effect? He wants to know, too, what ought the law do to people?
>
> To make the law live in these stirring times of change, we need "a minimum of legal legerdemain and a maximum of data and logic."
>
> 1. We need to know what the law is.
>
> 2. We need to know what the law ought to be. We need improved conditions to be affected. We need similar machinery to make available to courts data showing the effects of rules in action.

> 3. We need courts which use the full freedom precedent affords in working toward conclusions that fact and data show to be desirable.
>
> 4. We need men of great character, of wide and careful training, of enlightened judgment in the judiciary, and at the bar. Our legal profession today is far from being a credit to us.[20]

"Law does change—sometimes for the worse, but in the main for the better," Ritter explained in one of his lectures at the Hotel Utah during his early years as a professor. "It is much more closely related to our social, economic and political thinking than we are in the habit of believing. It is not only shaped by us but it shapes us. We are what we are, and we do very much because of law. On the other hand, law conforms to community standards. It is what we make it. Much in it that is subject to criticism is merely a reflection of the law ideals of you and me and the community at large."[21]

He quoted Benjamin Cardozo: "The whole subject matter of jurisprudence is more plastic, more malleable, the molds less definitively cast, the bounds of right and wrong less pre-ordained and constant than most of us have been accustomed to believe." He also quoted Justice Oliver Wendell Holmes: "There is nothing I more deprecate than the use of the Fourteenth Amendment beyond the absolute compulsion of its words to prevent the making of social experiments that an important part of the community desires.... [E]ven though the experiments may seem futile or even noxious to me and to those whose judgment I most respect."[22]

"Statutes are to be viewed, not in isolation or in vacuo as pronouncements of abstract principles for the guidance of an ideal community, but in the setting and framework of present-day conditions as revealed by the labors of economists and students of the social sciences in our own country and abroad.... Holmes sounded the view of the law fifty years ago which is only now gaining ground," Ritter explained further, stating:

> The life of the law has not been logic, it has been experience. The felt necessities of the time, prevalent moral and political theories, intuitions of public policy avowed or unconscious, even the prejudices which judges share with their fellow men have had a good deal more to do than syllogism in determining the rules by which men should be governed. The law embodies the story of a nation's development through many centuries and it cannot be dealt with as if it contained only the axioms and corollaries of a book of mathematics.[23]

Many saw the Ritter approach as unacceptably liberal. "Law has in it the machinery for change, adaptation and growth. The very important function of the jury is in relation to ordinary, popular standards," he maintained. But he also believed strongly in the conservative tradition of the rule of law. "Common law principles have been made too rigid by logical extremists," he continued, but "disregard of legal principle and precedent…is worse than rigidity. It is chaos. Both stability and susceptibility to change are needed."[24]

The Ritter philosophy appears to have never changed. Virtually on the eve of his OPA days, he wrote to Senator Elbert Thomas complaining that the "philosophy of governmental non-interference with private enterprise has been too long read into our constitutional system" by a minority of the United States Supreme Court. "If our constitutions do not permit regulation of private initiative for the general good, they are not likely to endure very much longer," he declared. The Supreme Court has been a check against "mob-psychology-popular will," he asserted, explaining again the conservative need for the rule of law, "but when it stubbornly heads off changes which a considerable majority of people passionately want, the pent-up resentments may embroil us in something worse."[25]

Elsewhere, he explained: "The logical process of applying a principle to new cases can be made a rigid one. It can be so inflexibly applied as to leave no room for change. It has been so applied. But the whole life and vigor of the common law has been found in regarding those principles as sufficiently flexible to adjust to new conditions and demands."[26]

The Ritter procedure for resolving a case, after it had been tried and he had announced his decision, was also characterized by simplicity. Attorneys for the prevailing side, in civil cases, would be directed to prepare findings of fact and conclusions of law, to which their opponents could file objections and the court would settle any differences, typically on one of his rule-day calendars. That way, in the event of appeal, the prevailing party would have the issue framed in the manner it wished to defend, and the ruling of the court on both facts and law would be clear so a superior court could determine if there had been an error as to either fact or law. Critics who said he avoided review on appeal when the issue was his independence as a member of the federal judiciary may have had a point in that context, but were decidedly wrong with respect to his rulings on the facts and the law. It was right there, in plain view, for all—the reviewing court, in particular—to see. He did not mask his decisions, as some judges do, in an ambiguous written opinion taking both sides of every critical issue. There was no reticence to lay it out there, in a clear black-and-white ruling, even when he knew that the appellate court was of a different view and was likely to reverse him on appeal.

Jury trials, both civil and criminal, were submitted on general verdicts, that is, on a simple direction to determine liability or guilt or innocence. Instructions to the jury were framed by Ritter, and he was a master at that, often delivering them extemporaneously. Lawyers were free to submit written requests for instructions thought critical, but if he granted their requests they were also delivered in an extemporaneous style, not read from a prepared text. Even when working from written submissions of the lawyers, Ritter had the ability to deliver instructions in a manner convincing to jurors and spectators that he spoke extemporaneously, from his own Olympian knowledge.

All agreed, even his harshest critics, that Ritter presented a compelling case to those called upon to serve as jurors that he was both brilliant and fully in charge. His commanding style left him fully in control of the jury. He was so skillful in his instructions that it became legend among practitioners in and observers of his court that he, in effect, directed the determination of every jury. It was a rare event when a jury decided a case other than the way Ritter would have it decided. In one case, in which former prosecutor David K. Winder persuaded a jury to acquit, against Ritter's inclination of guilt, Ritter declared: "Well, you beat us on this one!"

Written opinions were sometimes issued, but few of them were published. Those that were, in cases like the controversy between Albert E. Price and Aboitiz and Company over the promissory notes issued in the Japanese prison camp, the Braasch and Sullivan case, or the airplane crash that took the life of William Kapel, were concerned with more sophisticated questions than presented in the usual commercial or criminal matters coming before the courts. Normally, the judge would come in just before ten o'clock on court days. During the night he had thought about the cases and made notes. All of his decisions were written in long hand.[27]

Ritter's judicial style was exemplified by the admonition of Justice Benjamin N. Cardozo that "historic liberties and privileges are not to bend from day to day.... A community, whose judges would be willing to give it whatever law might gratify the impulse of the moment, would find in the end that it had paid too high a price." It was also epitomized by Holmes, who once said, "The truth to me is what I can't help but believe; but I do not suppose that my can't-helps are compulsory for the universe" and that "every calling is great when greatly pursued."[28] Ritter believed in, and followed, the Holmes philosophy, perhaps like none other.

In criminal matters, Ritter's compassion for the common man and sensitivity to the lot of the underdog led him to temper the punitive aspects of the penal system, other than in cases of organized crime or where protection of society by incarceration was necessary. Prosecutor Miller, during his tenure as Assistant United States Attorney, observed that characteristic in a case involving a man with an extensive history of arrest whom he brought before the chief judge. The man was African American, although race was not a factor, other than as it identified a segment of the underclass of Salt Lake City at the time. Ritter displayed similar reactions to the underprivileged, without regard for ethnicity. "Tell me about this man," Ritter requested when the man came on for sentencing. Miller handed up the "rap sheet," which showed several pages of arrests for theft and related crimes, and numerous convictions and periods of imprisonment. "Why do you steal?" Ritter inquired. "Other black people in this community are fine, upstanding citizens, and they don't steal." The man replied, "Yes they do, judge. They just ain't been caught!" The judge thumbed through many pages of the arrest record, noting its indication of multiple periods of incarceration in both state and federal institutions. "I don't know what we are going to do with you," Ritter finally said. "It is obvious that prison doesn't work. Let's try probation." That was, of course, before the days of mandatory minimum sentencing. Similar flexibility and compassion would be difficult—perhaps impossible—under the tough sentencing regimen legislators have since imposed.

His attitude eventually provoked a petition for writ of mandamus by Ramon Child, who became United States Attorney for the District of Utah in 1975, when Ritter denied a government demand for a jury trial. The rules of criminal procedure provide that "cases required to be tried to a jury shall be so tried unless the defendant waives a jury trial in writing with the approval of the court and the consent of the government." "Well, the right by trial of a jury runs in favor of a defendant, not the government," Ritter declared in denying the request. "That rule is really not in point!"[29]

His attitude about the essential dignity of the common man mirrored the writings of James Truslow Adams, contained in his personal papers after his death. "We have a long and arduous road to travel," said Adams, "if we are to realize our American dream in the life of our nation, but if we fail, there is nothing left but the old eternal round. The alternative is the failure of self-government, the failure of the common man to rise to full stature, the failure of all that the American dream has held of hope and promise for mankind." Adams's vignette on the dignity of the common man declaimed, "That dream was not the product of a solitary thinker. It evolved from the hearts and burdened souls of many millions who have come to us from all nations. If some of them appear to us to have too great faith, we know not yet to what faith may attain."[30]

In April 1968 Ritter was involved in an automobile accident at the intersection of 300 South and West Temple streets in Salt Lake City while riding in a car driven by his secretary, Catherine Jensen. Afterward, he experienced "pain [that] moves up behind the ears...and moves right and left over the back of [his] head." He reported "never [being] entirely free of pain" and that it was "disabling in what I do both on and off the bench" and that it "interferes with concentration, attention to lawyers' statements...to a point where it is impossible to work." As a consequence, he had to leave the bench at times and was unable to work long periods writing opinions.[31] Through the latter part of 1974 and early 1975, Ritter acknowledged to acting United States Attorney for the District of Utah William J. Lockhart that he was suffering from considerable pain and found it physically difficult to work for sustained periods, and as a consequence he sometimes vacated calendars he had set.[32] The pain may have been related to the automobile accident or to the tumors he suffered during the last years of his life, but the effect on his judicial performance was significant in either event.

There can be little doubt that the model and inspiration for the judicial career of Willis W. Ritter was Justice Oliver Wendell Holmes Jr. He said as much during his confirmation hearings.[33] The personal papers of Ritter, and his public and private writings, are involved extensively with quotations, or epigrams, of Holmes, such as this one: "How silly it is for anyone to give way for vanity! No one knows very much anyway, so there's no excuse for fatuous self-satisfaction. Any two philosophers can tell each other everything they know in a few hours."[34]

16

CONTROVERSY

> The King of Brobdingnag gave it for his opinion that "whoever could make two ears of corn, or two blades of grass to grow upon a spot of ground where only one grew before, would deserve better of mankind, and do more essential service to his country, than the whole race of politicians put together." In matters of justice, however, the benefactor is he who makes one lawsuit grow where two grew before.... Questions of law or fact which would otherwise be tried over and over can by this means be determined once for all in a single proceeding. This avoidance of multiplicity of suits saves the parties from needless expense and vexation, economizes the time of judges and jurymen, and frees the dockets for the affairs of other litigants.
>
> —CHANCELLOR ZECCHARIAH CHAFFEE JR.

Willis W. Ritter put the wisdom of the chancellor to work when a mining prospector named Howard Balsley filed suit in Ritter's court, claiming that Union Carbide and Carbon Corporation and Vanadium Corporation of America conspired to control the price of uranium on the Colorado Plateau. "The avoidance of multiplicity of suits by every device, which is jurisdictionally possible and practically convenient, should be encouraged and should be one of the main objectives of procedural administration."[1] There was neither logic nor good sense in requiring another approximate 350 unnamed miners to file new suits, or to afford the companies a chance to contest liability, over and over, grinding miners with little means to conduct expensive litigation under with costs, and burdening the courts with redundant litigation. Liability had already been determined. After deciding the Balsley suit, Ritter entered an order declaring the case a "class action," appointed Calvin W. Rawlings special master, and gave the unnamed miners six months to appear, file claims, and participate in the judgment.[2]

Balsley's complaint centered on the facts, common to all miners, that carnotite and rosceolite ore, bearing vanadium used in the manufacture of alloy steel, was found in commercial quantities on the Colorado Plateau together with uranium. The uranium was of no value, other than perhaps a small amount used in making pottery, until 1939 when scientists learned how to split the atom. Thereafter, until June 1958, when Balsley's suit was filed, the two companies conspired to pay nothing for the value of the uranium content of the ore, while selling it to the government and keeping the additional profits for themselves. The United States entered into a contract to purchase vanadium-bearing ore at prices not to exceed fifty cents per pound, but the two companies, which controlled the market, kept the price paid to the independent miners at thirty-one cents per pound.

In a jury trial, Ritter determined that Balsley should have been paid fifty centers per pound. Invoking the class action meant that all of the miners, all 350 of them, would be granted similar relief, even though they had not been parties to the suit. Sensible as that may seem, a storm of controversy followed the order. Corporate defense lawyers characterized the decision as "one way intervention"—a pejorative coined to suggest that there is something improper about allowing the absent miners to win without also subjecting them to the expense and risk of losing. Ritter recognized that a lawsuit is not a sporting event, however, and that the judicial task is to dispense justice, and do so with economy. The court of appeals agreed with Ritter. "Defendants' liability and the extent thereof has been competently proven by the named plaintiffs and it would be grossly redundant to say that it must be proven again by the other 350 miners," the appellate court wrote.[3]

Other courts followed Ritter's example. It was not uncommon for them to rule, as Ritter had done, that "where litigants have once battled for the court's decision, they should neither be required, nor without good reason permitted, to battle for it again."[4]

"You see ugliness on that bench, terrible chilling evil," D. Frank Wilkins, a former trial judge and justice of the Utah Supreme Court, once said while speaking of matters like the "one way intervention" disparagement. A friend of Ritter, he said of such deprecation: "It's upsetting. If people understood. You have to exude and truly have a part of you be judicial temperament. The best judge is he who is sensitive to matters before him on a daily basis... has great sensitivity and affection for the legal tradition in the highest form. There is no substitute for brains tempered with strength. At times you stand against an ocean wave of all society, but you don't just stand there, you stand against it."[5]

Coauthor Nielson sat in his chambers, with lawyer Bryce Evans Roe, and heard Ritter declare his belief that it was his responsibility, as United States District Judge, to serve as a bulwark against those in authority—in that instance, when the issue was city officials allowing religious authority to present their doctrine on public grounds, in the form of a plaque of the Ten Commandments. He declared that it was the responsibility of all right-thinking persons in the community to stand against such misuse of public funds.

Paranoia seemed confirmed when, to public uproar, in February 1972 Ritter ordered the monolith inscribed with the Ten Commandments removed from the grounds in front of the Salt Lake City Metropolitan Hall of Justice. The monument was a gift to the people from the Utah state aerie of the Fraternal Order of Eagles. "The law that governs this case," Judge Ritter wrote on September 18, 1972, "is the U.S. Constitution, Amendment I: 'Congress shall make no law respecting an establishment of religion, or prohibiting the free exercise thereof.'" "By the use of his famous figure of speech," Ritter continued, the Constitution "thus build[s] a wall of separation between Church and State," and Thomas Jefferson verifies and confirms the inner logic of the establishment clause itself that is absolute and uncompromising—"Congress shall make no law respecting the establishment of religion."[6] Ritter declared, quoting James Madison, "Who does not see" that "the same authority which can force a citizen to contribute threepence only of his property for the support of any one establishment, may force him to conform to any other establishment in all cases whatsoever?"

Replying, in advance, to the inevitable criticism that his decision was antireligious, Ritter explained that the purpose of freedom of religion is "not only to keep the states' hands out of religion, but to keep religion's hands off the state, and above all, to keep bitter religious controversy out of public life." Therefore, "The purpose and primary effect" of his order, Ritter announced, "is the *advancement* of religion." He wrote, "The [city and county] commissioners have given affirmative and direct aid to this teaching in the form of a financial grant." The mayor of Salt Lake City, and one of the persons enjoined, was E. J. "Jake" Garn. Those of Garn's point of view, and they were the majority in Utah and perhaps in the entire nation, had the notion that the nation was founded on Christian ideals and that, therefore, Christian observances, including Christian symbols and prayers, should be part of our national life and public gatherings. Ritter received a flood of correspondence critical of his opinion on that basis.[7]

As controversy concerning Ritter swelled, it seemed that Salt Lake City was bound by two poles: the Mormon Temple and its environs and Ritter's domain, the United States Post Office and Courthouse and the Hotel Newhouse, four blocks south of the Mormon Temple. The business and commercial district during the Ritter years was in the center. Those seeming poles gave rise to ironic witticisms, some not so clever or apt, like that they also marked the centers of heaven and hell, conservatism and liberalism, and so on.

At approximately the center—neutral territory, so to speak—Lamb's Restaurant was situated. Some days Ritter took all of his meals there, others he might come in only for lunch. It was a rare day when he failed to come in at all, probably indicating that he was out of town. The look and feel of Lamb's Restaurant was decidedly masculine and clubby: uniformed workers, marble counter, polished dark wood, leather-upholstered chairs, plate-glass mirrors, white linen tablecloths and napkins. Pies, cakes, and other desserts were displayed under glass on the back counter. Men's food was the fare—meat and potatoes, bread, soup. It served a largely male clientele—white, in those days, and non-Mormon (though Mormons and persons of color were always welcome), persons of influence in law, commerce, finance, publishing, and broadcasting. Women seemed not to have a particular interest in spending time there. It was a social and gustatory center for non-Mormon men, founded by George Lamb in 1929. George was always there seeing that things were done right and that customers, especially regulars like Ritter, were properly greeted. Perhaps every city has a favorite gathering place for merchants and businesspeople. That is the kind of place Lamb's was and had been for decades.

George was like many prominent men Ritter had known in Park City—David Keith, Thomas Kearns, John Judge, Albion Emery, and James Ivers. He immigrated from Argos, Greece, in 1907 at the age of fifteen with a Greek man who had just purchased his mother's farm. George was not old enough to get a passport, so the man pretended that he was his son, but when they got to Salt Lake City on the train, at three in the morning, George was told, "This is where you get off," and George never saw the man again. Speaking little English, George found a Greek market and inquired where he could go to find more foreigners like himself. They sent him to Logan, where he lived for twenty-two years, saving his money until he moved to Salt Lake City in 1929 and opened Lamb's Restaurant.[8] George exemplified the American ideal of a self-made man. He learned passable English, rose from poverty, and opened a very nice restaurant in the heart of downtown Salt Lake City. He was Ritter's kind of man, and they became fast friends.

George took a partner, Ted Speros, in the 1950s. Speros met the judge for the first time on an evening when Ritter came in shortly before closing, was shown to a booth, and engaged the waitress in friendly conversation. He invited her to sit down and join him. "Oh no," the waitress answered, "I can't. Ted would fire me." "Ted," Ritter yelled in his big voice. "Who the hell is Ted?" "I'm Ted," said Speros, overhearing the conversation and rushing to the table. "Do you know who I am?" Ritter boomed, banging his fist on the table so hard the water glasses shook. "And do you know who I am?" Speros demanded, in the biggest voice he could muster, pounding his fist so that the water glasses shook even harder, drenching the tablecloth. "I'm the boss—she can't sit down."

The next day, Ritter came in at noon, as was his custom. He walked right up to George, ignoring Ted, standing next to him. "George, who's boss here?" George answered, "Ted," having already heard of the incident. "Ted's boss." "Goddam right! Ted's boss," Ritter agreed. Speros never had trouble with him again.[9]

Tough as his public image was, there was ever the empathetic side, usually concealed from public view. In 1965 he received a handwritten letter, captioned "an original [Richard D.] Ruckenbrod longhand manuscript," because "what I want to say is no business of any stenographers." Ruckenbrod, Ritter's former law student, was totally blind, so much so that it was necessary to lead him by the hand to the elevator when he entered or left a building. Yet Ritter had hired him as his law clerk, although it was obvious he could not perform the normal functions of that calling.

> You gave me this opportunity [as law clerk] at a time when my morale, my practice and my luck were at a low ebb because of the interruption for that [optic] surgery.... I was given the chance to put my practice on its feet...which I could never have done without that salary.
>
> I won't ever forget when we first talked about my coming to work for you, you saw to it that I didn't feel like a hat-in-hand job applicant. It was pretty damn nice. It...has been so generous.... In plain Anglo-saxon, you've sure been a good teacher and a good judge and a good friend.[10]

Ritter clearly had his admirers. Still, at least as many disapproved of or disliked him. Few were ambivalent. It was either love him or hate him. Among the former were those whose political and philosophical views fitted well with his own, or who numbered themselves among the forgotten or persecuted of society—ethnic or political minorities, the poor, and those connected with the labor side of labor-management. Few of his friends or supporters, with notable exceptions, were to be found among the remainder of the population.

When lawyers or community leaders who were his friends, like Wally Sandack or Cliff Ashton, would go to his chambers, he often wanted them to stay for a drink. Alcohol was prohibited on the premises by rules of the GSA, but Ritter ignored the regulations.

Ever the student of the law, Ritter would go to the Supreme Court Reporter and pick out decisions about free speech and liberty to read to his visitors in chambers—decisions by Holmes and Cardozo.[11] He knew them by heart, and when reading them aloud he sounded like Orson Welles.

Sandack also invited Ritter to his home sometimes—not often, but when there was a family gathering and they thought Ritter would enjoy it. Ritter was invited to Passover dinners, for the seder commemorating the Jews leaving Egypt and crossing the sea to the Holy Land. Each person had a section of the Haggadah to read. When Ritter read his, everyone agreed that he sounded like Moses on the mountain, thundering over Zion.

One night Sandack told Ritter he had something he wanted him to hear. It was a package of Roosevelt speeches from campaigns in 1932, 1936, and 1944. Ritter especially liked a speech delivered by the president in Boston criticizing Hamilton Fish, Republican National Chairman. "I'll bet no one in the whole United States of America is doing this tonight," Sandack's son Rick observed, amused at Ritter's fascination with his political alter ego and inspiration.[12]

Lawyers who appeared before Ritter were, without exception, impressed with his brilliance. Robert S. Campbell witnessed Ritter instruct a jury in a complicated antitrust case. "He did it without written material, all extemporaneous.... It was brilliant. He was one of the most articulate men I've known, one of the most fascinating."

While trying a large antitrust case in San Francisco in the 1960s, which had gone on for weeks, the evidence ended late, and Ritter sent the jury out to a restaurant. He went out for drinks with some of the local judges and forgot all about the jury. They found him in a bar on Market Street at about one o'clock, very much in his cups, the jury still waiting. He climbed on the bench, a little unsteady, and delivered instructions that were brilliant.[13] They became renowned among other federal judges, who requested copies of his charge.[14] "The more drunk he got the more articulate he would become.... [E]very other faculty left him except his rationality and his ability to speak. The more he drank the lower his voice and the more resplendent his ideas."[15]

The case-assignment system worked out between Ritter and Judge A. Sherman Christensen was put to another test in 1962, when approximately nineteen hundred separate cases, similar in nature, were filed by purchasers of electrical equipment in federal courts throughout the country alleging a conspiracy to fix prices in violation of the Clayton Antitrust Act. Some of the cases were filed in the District of Utah, the first one being assigned to Christensen.[16] Later cases were assigned to Ritter, who kept control of them.

Cal Behle, employed to represent the electrical company defendants, complained that it complicated the process for the court and wasted time and money for counsel and litigants to have substantially identical cases pending before two judges in the same district. "It was impossible," Behle explained. "Finally, I filed a writ with the Circuit....I asked that the cases all be assigned to one judge, either one."

The writ was presented to Judge Alfred ("Fish," as Ritter called him, claiming that he was formerly a heavy drinker) Murrah, during the judicial conference being held at Oklahoma City. Murrah was not pleased with Behle bringing such business before what was intended to be a friendly social session, and kept Behle waiting. During the wait, Behle attended a private party where he encountered Ritter. "Well Cal, it's good to see you over here," Ritter exclaimed. "What brings you here?" "I'm here about the Electrical Cases," Behle truthfully replied. "I brought a petition asking that they either be assigned to you or to Christensen. It is a matter of common sense. They should be handled together." "You son-of-a-bitch!" Ritter fumed, and threw his glass against the wall.

After the conference was over, Murrah went to Ritter and Christensen, put his arm around the two of them, and sidestepped issuing the writ by saying: "I've got something worrying me. Let's have an internal conference. There's a petition on this series of cases. Under your Utah rules, doesn't one judge have them all? Under that rule, who got the first? Wasn't it Christensen?"The two Utah judges agreed that it was. "Well, Judge Ritter, it seems they should go to Judge Christensen. We'll assign them to Judge Christensen. We won't tell Behle."

Behle learned about it through a clerk, then traveled back to Salt Lake City the following Friday with a pilot who was a common friend of himself and Ritter. "Why don't you go with me to have a visit with Judge Ritter," the pilot inquired. "He's having a few people up to his farm in Idaho. George Lamb is going to fry the fish." It was agreed, and they flew to Twin Falls together. Six or seven of Ritter's friends were there. He was so cordial. "Cal, I'm awfully glad you came. We're going to have a pleasant evening." They did, but as usual, Ritter was drinking. Near the end of the dinner, at the point when alcohol had robbed him of inhibition—the point anyone involved in drinking with Ritter learned to fear—in his thundering voice Ritter said: "Behle, stand up. What are you doing here? Get out! Go!" Behle walked the pipeline to the power station above Ritter's Island for about an hour. "What got into him?" Behle mused, but he was sure "he'll be fine in the morning. He'll come back and be a different man." Behle returned a half hour or so later, after Ritter had gone to bed. Nothing further was said.[17]

Public perception and experience of the legal community with his judicial temperament were thus mixed, but even his critics agreed that his handling of criminal matters with forcefulness and dispatch was often a redemption. One such incident was the case of Gary Stewart Buckley and James Woodward. William T. Thurman, United States Attorney for the District of Utah during the event, used it to make the point that Ritter demanded respect for the United States District Court, describing it as an assault on two Salt Lake attorneys by "mobsters."[18] The "attorneys represented the plaintiff in a securities fraud action before Judge Ritter," Thurman wrote, and after assaulting one of the attorneys at his home, "they went to the other attorneys [office] address [but] were unable to find him."[19]

Thurman's description of the event was correct, but omitted important details. Actually, it was Christensen's division where the securities-fraud action was pending. Ritter only learned of it while studying the local section of the daily newspaper, describing the incident of the previous day, just as Catherine Jensen was showing the two lawyer victims in. "It looks to me like someone is fooling around with my court," the always unpredictable Ritter growled. To Ritter, the dignity of the federal court was the issue, as Thurman noted, not whether it was his division or that of the associate judge. He considered it "my court," in either event.

The article Ritter was reading described how Buckley and Woodward had presented themselves at attorney A. Reed Reynolds's door, demanded that his wife get him out of his sickbed, then punched him in the nose without any warning as he extended his hand in greeting. "If you don't give up on this thing we'll kill you," Buckley declared, while Reynolds was picking himself up off of the floor and wiping the blood from his face. "I get the message," Reynolds replied, "but what thing do you mean?" "The Phoenix thing," Buckley replied. Then they left. "The Phoenix thing" told Reynolds all he needed to know. The defendant in their securities-fraud case lived in Phoenix! He was on the phone immediately, warning his associate counsel.

Before they got to the office of the other attorney, his secretary, Billie Karabatz, had the office door locked and Lieutenant Nicholas Morgan III of the Salt Lake County Sheriffs Department on the way. The two men fled to the Salt Lake International Airport, followed by attorney Phil Cowley, who had been observing their threatening behavior from an adjoining office. They had boarded a plane bound for Las Vegas, Cowley advised Morgan when he arrived, and Buckley and Woodward were arrested on the plane before takeoff, physically dragged off and manacled on the tarmac, in full view of incredulous passengers.

The evening of the day following the assault, after their visit with him in chambers, Ritter phoned the two attorneys at the jail, where they were attempting to question the two men. "I want you fellows to come back over here," Ritter explained, possibly recalling his own pronouncements on the requirements for questioning criminal suspects in cases such as Braasch and Sullivan. "I don't want you making any mistakes. And bring those two fellows with you."

When Buckley and Woodward arrived at about nine in the evening, escorted by the jailer, the clerk of court was in attendance, together with United States Attorney Thurman; U.S. marshal Royal Buttars; magistrate Ronald N. Boyce; Lucille Hallam, Judge Ritter's court reporter; and Spence VanNoy, his bailiff. No one knew why they were there, save that it related to Buckley and Woodward, until Ritter announced that "this is a proceeding on a warrant of arrest." Testimony on the events of the previous day was taken, and when that was concluded, Ritter announced that the facts amounted to the crime of "obstruction of justice." Perhaps recalling his own experience in Denver, dealing with the Smaldones in 1953, he directed the United States Attorney to prepare the complaint, arraigned Buckley and Woodward on the spot, and ordered them held on five hundred thousand dollars' *cash* bail.[20] Two torpedoes went nowhere, at least before their trial.

Buckley and Woodward then moved for Ritter to withdraw, reasoning that he had displayed an interest disabling him to act as judge. The motion was denied, Ritter explaining that he had no pecuniary interest.[21]

When the time of trial arrived, a woman by the name of Diane Brown was observed in the corridor, waiting to testify. She had come to Salt Lake City earlier, in the wake of Reynolds's assault, ostensibly to negotiate a settlement agreement between herself and a paramour, with Reynolds's co-counsel engaged to draft the document. The discussions were at her motel, after she refused to come to the lawyer's office, but the attorney came to his senses—just barely, and at the last moment. When he got to the motel, still not savvy that he was being "set up," he recognized the appearance of a compromising situation, telephoned the woman from the front desk, and asked that they meet in the lobby. No agreement was negotiated, and the woman disappeared.

The ever perceptive Reynolds recognized the incident as related to Buckley and Woodward. "I only got a punch in the nose," he teased his colleague, "but they sent you a sweetheart." Special agent Elmer Raper of the FBI, who was investigating Reynolds's assault, said, "You boys have been reading too many detective novels," and declined their request to look into the Diane Brown incident.

Ritter, with experience of his own over Senator Watkins's attempt to infer sex in his friendship with Phyllis Katz, directed the two attorneys to be present in the courtroom, even though the exclusion rule had been invoked, to listen to what Diane Brown said. That precognition saved the day, for Brown testified truthfully about the meeting, knowing she could not do otherwise with the two attorneys listening to what she said. She suggested untruthfully, however, that Reynolds was to act as her lawyer; hence, she presented an alibi, or the appearance of one, for she claimed to be from Phoenix, and the "Phoenix thing" Buckley referred to was herself, rather than the defendant in the securities-fraud suit.[22]

The jury rejected the fabricated defense, and Ritter had the two convicted, sentenced, and in the custody of the U.S. marshal for delivery to the Bureau of Prisons before they could even get out of the city.

Ritter had his admirers, and many, for tough handling, when appropriate, of incidents such as the Ten Commandments or Buckley and Woodward. He had been receiving mail from all over the country, from people he had never heard of. A lawyer with a defender association in Philadelphia wrote: "I've been reading about you. Good for you—you've still got the bastards on the run.... God Bless!" "I don't have any fancy paper," a woman wrote from Mountain View, California. "We heard on the news last night about you giving the heroin pusher a life sentence, the possibility of *no* parole.... Too bad there weren't [*sic*] more judges like you. Keep up the good work. Maybe it will catch on." And this: "Although I have never met you, Judge Ritter, I feel that I know you quite well," a lab supervisor at the University of Utah Medical Center wrote. "I salute you for your firm stand on issues that you believe in, in spite of occasional violent opposition. Often I find myself saying: 'Sock it to them, Judge! Give them Hell!'"[23]

A decision favoring academic freedom, against efforts of the Utah attorney general to restrict it, drew praise. "It is the decisions of judges like you who safeguard the rights of citizens from being trampled by men who get into positions of authority (as they think) and get carried away with their authority."[24]

Even David T. Lewis, who succeeded Murrah as chief judge of the Court of Appeals for the Tenth Circuit and had become a frequent critic of Ritter's judicial style, confessed that the Buckley-Woodward incident demonstrated the importance, at times, of having an "activist judge" like Ritter. He had thus avoided the appearance of bias that doomed his tough handling of the Smaldones, and the conviction and equally tough handling of Buckley and Woodward withstood a challenge on appeal.

The authors know the story well, for Phil Cowley, who pursued them to the airport, was married to coauthor Patricia Cowley, and the other attorney threatened by Buckley and Woodward, and to whom Lewis made his statement, was coauthor Parker Nielson.

However firm, and efficient, in his exercise of the power of the federal court in matters striking at the dignity of society, at the same time, law enforcement officers were frustrated by his refusal to entertain other matters that he considered petty. An FBI report in 1965 acknowledges that "since about 1949, we have been providing the Department of Justice with derogatory and unfavorable information regarding the personal conduct and decisions of Judge Ritter." It claimed that "he has been notorious for his arrogant conduct and flagrant abuse of authority for many years," and that "in 1960, the Department furnished to the Judicial Council of the Tenth Circuit information concerning Judge Ritter's conduct, but nothing appears to have come of this action." The FBI's efforts included attempts to draw assistant United States Attorney C. Nelson Day into critical comments over "remarks from the bench in open court [which] have been extremely abusive of members of the U.S. Attorney's office" and the bureau. Day laughed off the FBI's comments and said he "was used to it."[25]

By the late 1960s, the FBI intensified its attacks on Ritter. The FBI claimed that the reason convictions for fiscal year 1969 were 40 percent below those for the previous year "can be attributed principally to two factors, namely, the Court and the U.S. Attorney's Office." By 1970 Day had been elevated to United States Attorney for the District of Utah, after a term as state district court judge. "It would appear his taste of political life has dulled his interest in aggressive prosecutive [*sic*] action," the agent in charge of the FBI's office in Salt Lake City reported. "On two occasions USA Day has been advised the record of his office is under last year's performance and he has stated he is endeavoring to make progress but is hampered by the difficulties encountered in prosecuting cases in Judge Ritter's Court."[26]

The "difficulties" the FBI experienced with Ritter included that "he has often voiced his contempt for statistics." Ritter frequently stated openly and on the record his contempt for holding needless hearings for the sake of accumulating "brownie points" with court administrators. The FBI was determined to improve its "statistics," however, and indicated that his reduced conviction rate was also attributable to "refus[al] of guilty pleas from several Selective Service subjects...on the premise he is awaiting U.S. Supreme Court decisions on cases from other districts before proceeding further" and his "attitude that Indians who commit crimes against other Indians should not be prosecuted in the U.S. District Court."[27] The FBI was correct in that regard, for it was and had always been Ritter's attitude that matters such as stolen automobiles, insufficient-fund checks, and other matters including petty crimes on Indian reservations were essentially local matters that should not be handled in the federal courts where the severity of the offense was magnified unreasonably.

More fodder for his critics was generated in 1968 over a series of events that eventuated in hard-fought litigation between the American Gypsum Trust, which went back to Ritter's years as a law professor and was controlled by himself and his family, and Georgia-Pacific Corporation. The litigation included an antitrust claim against Georgia-Pacific and a contract claim by the Ritter interests.

A fifty-year lease of the gypsum property at Sigurd, Utah, had been entered into with Sid Eliason on November 6, 1946. American Keene Cement and Plaster Company was then dissolved, transferring the gypsum claims to the trust, initially consisting of Ritter, members of his family, and sixty residents of Sevier County. As additional shares became available, Ritter acquired them, for the benefit of his family. By the time of the litigation,

American Gypsum Trust was essentially the Ritter family, with Willis W. Ritter and his wife, Rita, alternating as trustee.[28]

The fifty-year lease, requiring payments to the trust of 11¢ per ton on all rock removed, $12,000 per year minimum rental, plus 7 percent of net profits, was assigned to Georgia-Pacific Corporation in 1965. A dispute developed in the Sixth Judicial District Court in Richfield, Utah, over the terms of the agreement and whether a "requirements provision" obligated the lessee to take all of its gypsum from the Sigurd property.

The lease stipulated that "all gypsum requirements" of Eliason "or his assigns" were to be supplied from the Sigurd property. Georgia-Pacific agreed that it was saddled with those provisions, but in 1967 it acquired a gypsum processing plant in Lovell, Wyoming, and the Pryor plant at Acme, Texas. Ritter and the trust claimed Georgia-Pacific "creamed" the market by diverting major portions of the historic Sigurd market to its plants in Lovell and Acme and engaged in creative accounting practices that reduced the trust to its $12,000 minimum rental. Georgia-Pacific "employed a brand new accountant" who adopted "an equally brand new, unilateral and different kind of bookkeeping that would and did eliminate rental income save for the minimum annual and tonnage rate, to the exclusion of the 7% net profit factor."[29] Ritter described the new creative accounting:

> Georgia-Pacific was entering into an inter-company transaction between the Georgia-Pacific Corporation and its wholly owned subsidiary, Pryor, the effect of which was that instead of using Pryor's costs for the manufacture of paper supplied to the Sigurd plant, what Georgia-Pacific was doing was going out in the market and taking a computed figure, ascertained in some way by looking at the market for paper such as Pryor manufactured and then instead of charging us the cost, Pryor's costs of manufacturing, they were charging us those costs plus a write-up to a figure that they regarded as what Georgia-Pacific would have to pay for it if they went out in the open market. Now that is not the terms of our lease.

The issue was how "net profits" should be calculated, for purposes of the 7 percent royalty. "I don't know what the hell they called it but it is phony accounting, that is what it is. As a matter of fact, at the end of the year they had to wash all that crap out of the accounting for Internal Revenue purposes but they never washed it out for the purpose of computing our royalty and so there you have it."[30]

The trust was represented in the suit by the Salt Lake City firm of VanCott, Bagley, Cornwall, and McCarthy, principally through Dennis McCarthy, Cliff Ashton, and C. Keith Rooker, partners in the firm. In addition, there were junior associates in the VanCott firm assisting, and Ken Chamberlain of the Richfield firm of Olsen and Chamberlain engaged as local counsel. Georgia-Pacific was represented by the firm of Ritter's friend and former student—sometimes critic—Cal Behle. The Parsons-Behle firm was also prominent, perhaps equally with VanCott. Because of the sensitivity of opposing a federal judge, before whom a significant portion of its litigation must be conducted, only one member of the Parsons-Behle firm was engaged—Keith E. Taylor, who was well liked by Ritter and had attended law school at Stanford with Bill Ritter. The Georgia-Pacific trial resulted in the loss of a substantial portion of Parsons-Behle's federal practice, however, for the firm perceived, whether correctly or incorrectly, that it must decline representation in Ritter's court to avoid the possibility of prejudice.[31] Taylor described the firm's motives: "Altruistically, [the firm's directors] reasoned that G-P was a good corporate citizen and was entitled to a defense," and therefore he was "volunteered" for the assignment.

Ritter was in total control of the trust. There was immediate talk about whether it was proper for a federal judge to be acting as plaintiff and taking counsel from persons practicing before him and being in an adverse position with others practicing before him.[32] Cliff Ashton prevailed upon Ritter to resign as trustee and substitute his son, John. Ritter was still a principal figure in the proceedings, for he had drafted the fifty-year lease and its royalty provisions.[33]

The trial was held in Richfield, Utah, and Ritter was the principal witness for the American Gypsum Trust. Ritter and all of the attorneys stayed at the only hotel in town and had breakfast, lunch, dinner, and drinks together. "Every morning he had a lemon and would peel it with great ceremony," Ashton recalled. "He loved food. It was a pure delight to see him eat."[34]

The trial before state court judge Ferdinand Erickson resulted in dismissal of the antitrust claims, but judgment in favor of the trust on its claims that Georgia-Pacific had breached terms of the lease. Georgia Pacific eventually paid more than $770,000.[35] The lease provided that "reasonable attorneys fees incurred in enforcing the terms and provisions of this lease shall be borne by the party who breaches the covenants, agreements, terms and provisions thereof," but Erickson denied the recovery of attorneys' fees, reasoning that the terms of the lease were fairly in dispute.

The incident marked the demise of the VanCott firm in Ritter's court as well, or at least of Cliff Ashton, for the unfavorable result of the antitrust claims resulted in Taylor refusing to pay the high costs of legal representation as an element of damages on the breach-of-contract claim. The contract portion of the case was only a one-lawyer issue, Taylor contended, and he refused to pay for the half-dozen or so lawyers necessary to represent Ritter on the antitrust claim, which Ashton's firm lost.

Meanwhile, controversy with the press was mounting. Starting in 1953, Ritter had barred photographers from the second floor of the United States Post Office and Courthouse. On May 8, 1969, he issued a formal order, prohibiting "the taking of photographs in any form, including the taking of television pictures, and making artists drawings or caricatures in any form, and the broadcasting [of them] by radio, television or other means, in the courtroom or its environs in connection with any judicial proceedings...at any place in the Post Office and Federal courthouse." By February 1973, Ritter had expanded his order, not only prohibiting drawings of proceedings in his court but also prohibiting *any* drawings, "whether the cartoons, artists' sketches, caricatures, or whatever they may be called, are made on these premises or elsewhere." The action was in response to a television station publishing sketches made by a reporter from memory, off the premises of the court. Ritter claimed that the ban was necessary and intended to secure "the process of getting a fair trial" and that he did not "want defendants badgered and harassed by photographers." His new order was humanitarian, he claimed further, for people have the right to come to court "without being held up to degradation by grotesque representations of their physical characteristics...and a constitutional right...to be free from being made a public display of." The news media pointed to the First and Fourteenth Amendments to the United States Constitution and claimed that the order was an interference with freedom of expression.[36]

Conflict with the press continued. When Joe Bauman, a *Deseret News* reporter, was observed taking notes in Ritter's courtroom, Ritter directed him to "come up here." Bauman was required to sit at a dais at the side of the room, next to where the bailiff was seated. "I want you to sit right there," Ritter explained, "where I can keep my eye on you." When Bauman left to cover another story and stepped over the felt rope bordering the dais, to avoid disrupting proceedings by walking around it, Ritter glared and said, "Well, I didn't tell you to jump rope, did I?"[37]

As criticism of him increased in volume and intensity, it attracted the attention of many who previously had only the slightest, if any, idea of who he was, what he did that had produced so much contention, or why it should be of any interest to them. Such attention resulted from the so-called Christmas tree case, in which a group of young men, many of them teenagers, were drawn into a conspiracy to cut Christmas trees illegally.[38] He tried them, back to back, over a day or so and held each young man in the courtroom after he was convicted and awaiting sentencing. The ring leader, an older man named Vernon Black, was convicted last. Ritter then brought them forward, in a group, and gave them all maximum sentences of a fine of ten thousand dollars and ten years in the penitentiary. One of the young men was dragged out, clawing at the furniture and crying that he had a wife and children, all of whom were in the courtroom, crying. Parents were crying. Jurors were crying.

Ritter retired to his chambers, reverted to his disposition of empathy, reduced the sentences to probation, and released all of the young men before they were taken out of the building lockup, other than the principal defendant and conspirator. The young men, and everyone connected with the case, were scared into respect for the seriousness of crimes against the environment and the national forest. The conviction of the principal defendant was reversed on appeal, there being insufficient evidence of the origin of the trees.[39]

The controversy surrounding Willis W. Ritter increased throughout the decade of the 1960s and into the 1970s and became the fodder for increasing assaults on him personally, and on his office, during the final years of his tenure. His best friends from university days, people like Dean Angleman, Myrtle Austin, and Dorothy Snow, were among those who observed that he had changed from the mannerly, good-looking, well-groomed, and entertaining law professor they had known. His character had deteriorated, as had his disposition. He had become cantankerous. Incidents such as arresting the mail clerks over operation of the elevator, conflicts with the press, and the Ten Commandments were well publicized and convinced his old university friends that he was a transformed person. Ritter was not the man they had known.[40] Ritter had become a very lonely man, and his reputation was further damaged in the process.

17

EXPIATION

> I won't say that the papers misquote me, but I sometimes wonder where Christianity would be today if some of those reporters had been Matthew, Mark, Luke and John.
>
> —Barry M. Goldwater

> The Senator might remember that the evangelists had a more inspiring subject.
>
> —Walter Lippmann

By the early 1970s, when Willis Ritter had been on the bench for just over twenty years, he had grown a vast paunch, the more noticeable, perhaps, for the white shirt that encased it. He had a head of hair many men of seventy would envy, but its salt-and-pepper gray in 1950 was now silver-white, and his hairline had receded slightly. He had developed jowls, and his face appeared more florid, partly because of the extreme light color of his hair. He perspired while on the bench, causing him to run the air-conditioning into October, keeping the room uncomfortably cold for attorneys and personnel, and he expectorated into tissues that accumulated in heaps before him on the bench and were removed by bailiff Spence VanNoy at every recess.[1]

The number of friends seen with any regularity was dwindling. The loss of friends made him a lonely, ever more difficult personality. His mother abandoned him when he was sixteen. His father died when he was twenty-six, Uncle Willis when he was thirty-three, and Aunt Mary when he was forty-three. Those losses, of course, other than abandonment, occur in most people's lives.

During his university years, his friends were truly distinguished people, with warmth of personality, conservative in their behavior, and socially conscious. After becoming a judge he seemed, increasingly as time went on, to be losing his old, stable friends. Elbert Thomas, his "best friend," died in 1953. His contact, more and more, was with the lawyers. In earlier years he had enjoyed gathering (or summoning, as some felt) friends to his chambers when court adjourned. Sometimes the drinking and talking would go on until seven or eight in the evening, and he would extend the session by suggesting that they all go to dinner together. Because they did not want to decline, fearing that it might offend, and did not want to be late getting home to their wives and families, many just found it easier to slip away before being asked. Persons of quality and social consciousness among his lawyer friends, more and more, became substituted with sycophants and drinking buddies. Employees of the clerk's office began to refer to him as a "petty alcoholic" and to the clique at his after-hours drinking sessions as "that bunch of alcoholics."[2]

The matter of alcohol abuse, in many respects, is in the eye of the beholder. In conservative and religious circles, the Mormon-dominated Utah scene in particular, many condemn *any* use. More liberal-minded persons, which would include Ritter and his friends, see a temperate use of alcohol as acceptable and perhaps even desirable as a release for tensions and anxieties surely associated with the trial process. William J. Lockhart, who was present at many of the drinking sessions, could not "recall any occasion...where the judge became anything more than vigorously gregarious." Still, there is little doubt that he did exceed that status on occasion, and even Lockhart conceded "not more than a few" occasions of excess.[3]

The decline in the number of friends, coupled with the increasing number who found convenient excuses to avoid drinking sessions with him in chambers, left Ritter there alone with greater frequency. The supervisor of the custodial staff at the courthouse complained to United States Attorney William T. Thurman that it was becoming regular for his phone to ring at ten thirty in the evening, with a request by Ritter that two custodians come to his chambers and assist him out of the building, across the street, and to his room at the Hotel Newhouse. And that was not worst part! When they got Ritter to his room, he would demand that they undress him and put him to bed. The problem was solved by the custodian refusing to answer when the phone rang at ten thirty.[4]

Probably he was tired more often than when he was younger. Tiredness can be cumulative. He had been—still was—tough as a boot, but his life was not easy. Being a judge thrust him, always, in the middle of contention, multiplied by the contention in his own life. He had to deal, day by day, with the graphic evidence of the worst of human behavior, and with the worst in lawyers.

He was irascible—who knows if more irascible than thirty years earlier. He had reason to be, given his disposition and the stressfulness of a life one-third of which had been dominated by all-out battle, first with Rube Clark in Tomie's political campaigns, then at the OPA, then over his own confirmation, and then by constant critics of his judicial style and personal behavior. Who wouldn't be weary? He had his first heart attacks in the 1950s and they continued in the mid-1960s. Hillman Castle, his principal physician, said that if Ritter lived five years it would be a miracle. He suffered from bladder tumors, too, and had to have them surgically removed. He could lie down and sleep between court sessions, however, and doing so restored him somewhat.[5]

His voice was still full and deep. He could still use it to great effect, when he chose—to charm a woman or rattle the doors of his courtroom, or at least the rattled nerves of staff and lawyers made it seem so. And he could still transfix and delight a courtroom of lawyers on law-and-motion days with his wit, displays of intellectual brilliance, and ability to capture, in a moment, the essence of a complex matter. He could do this as well as ever, and he could still have his way with a jury, so deftly that few ever realized he had done so. Nor had he lost his ability to stupefy a stammering young lawyer with a turn of his chair, a look, or by clearing his throat.

In 1950 Ritter could, and did, cover the several uphill blocks between his court and Lamb's Restaurant in a few minutes. By 1970 his gait was slower and his body less willing. In earlier times Ritter would have as many with him as would fit at his table. By 1970 the number at his table had dwindled. More and more, it got down to just Spence VanNoy, his bailiff.[6]

He dined out in the evenings, usually alone, at a series of restaurants he frequented. If he saw someone he liked, they would be invited to join him, and he would send his bailiff, if he was available, out for wine or his favorite tipple, Wild Turkey. On one such occasion Max Mercier, proprietor of the restaurant Le Parisien, one of his frequent stops, could not get Ritter and his party to depart, in spite of polite hints, at closing time. Mercier went over to Judge Ritter, handed him the key, and told him to lock up and put the key in the mailbox. "I felt I could trust him," Mercier explained.[7]

Hard life had taken its toll. Ritter's room at the Newhouse, where he lived, was bleak, like a lonely jail cell, and the farm and his personal appearance had become unkempt. His clothes were threadbare, and he would wear an old hat and worn shoes. He never had more than four suits at one time and usually wore only two of them. He always wore a white shirt, even at the farm, even though the family would buy him colored or print shirts that he left in their wrappings for years. Eventually, he took to wearing a blue denim shirt.[8]

Someone seeing Ritter for the first time, say in the 1970s when age and indulgence had combined to slow his pace and tax his lung power, someone passing him in the street at that stage in his life, as he crossed Fourth South, for instance, between the court and his hotel room at the Newhouse, or as he made his way up Main Street toward Lamb's, that person, knowing nothing of his position or intellect or accomplishments, likely would have paid him no more notice than any other worn, paunchy, bored, cantankerous old man.

But if one's first impression of him in those later years came in the courtroom, as he presided over, instructed, cajoled, and sometimes delighted with a wry wit those gathered there, one not only would notice him but also feel oneself in the presence of a man of great power—personal and judicial. He continued to dispense justice in the Old Testament tradition—sound and fury, thunder and lightning, with the clouds parting, like Cecil B. DeMille's portrayal of Moses on Mount Sinai. Critics aside, he usually made the right ruling.[9]

He had reached his seventieth year, the twentieth of his judgeship carrying the baggage of criticism from the battle over his confirmation, and having collected a lot more enmity and criticism along the way, not universally popular and most controversial. There was a store of antagonism in the hearts and bones of the lawyers he had scolded for poor preparation or a poorly calculated act. All but a handful of lawyers who had appeared before him had, at some time or another, fumed about such treatment, or adverse results in a case. He was loved by a few; respected, admired, and feared by most; and despised and reviled by many.

One custodial person alone was allowed to enter the chambers, and only when Ritter was there. Holding "chambers" became a necessary ritual, when Nancy would assist and oversee the cleaning.[10]

Sometimes the children, grandchildren, and their friends would gather at Willis's chambers. Ritter loved his grandchildren and was patient with them. They saw him from a different perspective than those who, as the controversy surrounding him was rising, wrote exaggerated, biased, and shortsighted critiques of him, at least from the children's point of view. "They" didn't know him, according to Puddy. The children were allowed to sit in his chair and pretend they were the judge, and Ritter would put on his robes—Ritter never wore robes, except on special occasions like when sitting on a special three-judge court—and have fun with them. He took them on long walks, like the ones he had shared with Willis Adams, and talked with them about animals, plants, and mother nature—doubtless learned in his own youth "walking the tracks" with Adams, or from Rita.[11]

His warmth for children was not confined to his own grandchildren. While visiting his friend Bill Lang's sister, Mary Blattner, in Walnut Creek, California, Ritter observed Lang's nephews, aged seven and nine, playing in cowboy outfits and wearing tin badges. "I'm going to have to get you boys some real Marshall's badges," Ritter remarked. True to his promise, Ritter obtained two real U.S. marshal badges dating from frontier days from the U.S. marshal for the District of Kansas. Lang and Ritter flew to San Francisco for an official "pinning-on" and "swearing-in" ceremony for two wide-eyed children.[12]

He was at his most fatherly with youthful offenders, almost always boys who stole cars, went AWOL, or stole a few bucks, with whom he was notoriously easy. "They were only on a joyride," he would say, and put them on probation. One such youth was required to bring the judge his report card every time he got one, and he turned out all right.[13] You can never be too lenient with the young seemed to be his attitude.

"Ladies and gentlemen, we must never forget in the courts we are dealing with human beings," he would instruct his juries, "in this case kids." He discharged the criminal law with compassion, eschewing the punitive:

> The time has long passed when the theory of the criminal law was punishment.... [T]he theory is simply to save a human being...because in most instances we find a sickness of some sort is involved, sickness of alcohol, nervous sickness, neurosis, sickness of drugs, sickness of sex...and particularly the children who find themselves in trouble with the law. We don't pursue them, we don't persecute them, we don't punish them. We try to help them.... What those kids need is counsel, advice, direction, and supervision in their own home town, in their families, in their churches, and in their schools.... The only time we treat offenders differently is when society needs protection from [bank robbers, drug pushers and such].[14]

"It isn't going to do [a] boy any good to send him to a federal penitentiary," he reasoned. "That is unspeakable, unthinkable."[15]

His rulings on the evidence presented against youth offenders were guided by the same empathy: "The FBI said he signed a waiver of his rights. This fifth grade kid doesn't know what a waiver is. He doesn't know what those great Constitutional guarantees of the Constitution are. He doesn't know that the right against self-incrimination entitles him not to say a word to them."[16]

Even if he found it necessary to impose punishment, his empathy for youth offenders continued. The young men placed on probation in Ritter's court, for crimes like draft evasion, stealing an automobile, or bad checks, were followed up on by chief of probation Bernie Rhodes to make sure they were working and staying out of trouble. Rhodes went to work for Ritter as an assistant probation officer in 1962. From the first day they met, Rhodes and Ritter were close. Before many years passed, Rhodes was made chief of probation.

Sometimes Ritter would go with Rhodes, riding "shotgun," when he was interviewing probationers living out of Salt Lake City. Utah is a large state, and it would take them several days. They would drive down Highway 89, to Nephi, where they would have dinner at Ray's Café and spend the night. The next day, they would drive on down Highway 89, to Mount Carmel Junction, then cross through Zion National Park to St. George, where they would have dinner at Dick's Café, spend another night, and return by way of Highway 91.

When Rhodes knocked on the door of his youth offenders, they and their parents "lost their breakfast" when they saw the chief judge who had sentenced them standing behind Rhodes in the doorway, hovering to dispense more of his sound and fury if they had not toed the line.[17]

And his compassionate approach often produced the desired result. The director of the United States Bureau of Prisons suggested that a young boy named Robert L. Stahl be returned to his court "since he respects you highly and is very anxious to please you.... I think your instructions and guidance and continuing contact with him would be most helpful," the director of prisons urged. "This is one of the most extraordinary cases I have encountered in almost 25 years... because he has found in a Federal Judge not only an understanding and sympathetic person but one willing and anxious to take of his own time and resources to come to his aid."[18]

While almost everyone who ever encountered him agreed, in some way or another, that he possessed extraordinary personal gifts and that his achievements were considerable—he knew the law and could do a whiz-bang job of running the court—the 1970s, for Willis Ritter, began with about the same degree of strife, dissension, and contention that had prevailed in the 1960s. Controversy over his judicial style was added to by contention in his personal life that developed starting in 1950, and if not the cause certainly contributed to both his physical decline and the loss of many high-quality friends.

Following his separation from Rita, Willis became a member of the University Club, a men's athletic and social club situated on South Temple Street, in the downtown business district of Salt Lake City.[19] The club was managed by Tad Bullen, a tiny man, scrupulously polite to members and guests, who was slightly disabled and walked with a noticeable limp.

The club had residence accommodations, and Ritter lived at the University Club for a time. Verl Ritchie, a former student of Ritter, was a member of the club and frequently socialized with Delbert Draper Jr., the son of Ritter's longtime political confederate in the Thomas campaigns. Ritter often invited himself to their table when on his "good behavior," and Ritchie became good friends with him in the process. Draper fell into disfavor, however, for when intoxicated he would throw napkins and popcorn at Ritter, taunting him: "Judge, you're a mental giant but an emotional idiot."[20]

Ritter's resentment erupted at a victory celebration following the election of President Lyndon B. Johnson in 1964, at the studio of George Hatch. Ritter brought a collection of campaign buttons with him going back to Woodrow Wilson. Draper pinned some of them on, only to have Ritter strip them off, one by one, throwing them on the floor. "You don't deserve to wear those," he declared.[21]

Ritter's residence at the University Club was cut short by events related to his excessive drinking. The club was closing at midnight on a Saturday in January 1963, as required by a state law prohibiting the serving of alcohol on the Sabbath. Ritter, who was at the bar drinking with his friend Phil Hansen, demanded that the club manager, Bullen, serve them another drink. When he refused, Ritter punched the smaller, crippled Bullen.[22] Bill Fowler came into the bar at about the same time and was insulted by Ritter, who compared him to "Lucky Legs Luciano" and declared that he would call the U.S. marshal and have Fowler arrested and taken to jail. Fowler, in the same loud voice Ritter was using, declared that he did not come to the club to be insulted by a drunken judge. Ritter spewed profanity, rolled up his sleeves, and approached Fowler with clenched fists held high. Three club members wrestled Ritter to the floor, took him out the back door, threw his hat and coat after him in the snow, and locked the door behind him.[23] Ritter's membership was revoked over the incident.[24] Bullen asked Verl Ritchie to file suit for him. Ritchie declined. Bullen was unable to get another lawyer to do so, and the incident died.[25]

It was after his eviction from the University Club that Ritter took up residence in a room at the Hotel Newhouse, located directly across the street to the south from the post office and courthouse, where he continued to live for the balance of his life.

He would work late in his chambers, and see lights on at prosecutor James Housley's office, rap on the door, and say, "Let's go get something to eat."[26] A regular stop on such occasions was the Manhattan Club, located conveniently across the intersection from the federal court, in the other direction from the Newhouse, in the basement of the New Grand Hotel and Apartments. Proprietor Tony Hatsis operated the Manhattan, as its name implied, in the style of a New York City nightclub, but within the strictures of Utah's peculiar liquor laws, which meant only members or their guests could be on the premises. Of course, sponsorship by a member could be arranged instantly, on the spot, for anyone deemed reputable, and that included about anyone other than officers of the liquor control agency.

The Manhattan Club featured good food, fine wine, and liquor by the drink. There was a large dance floor, and on weekends a provocative fashion show by Suzy McCarty's Models, accompanied by a live orchestra. On one occasion when Ritter was present, Hatsis arranged for the band to stay for an after-hours party, and for guests to play "strip spin the bottle" with Suzy's sensuous models. The girls knew, but Ritter did not, that there was a depression in the dance floor that caused the bottle to stop at one particular spot. Ritter was positioned at that spot, and the game ended with the chief judge prancing around the dance floor, "in the buff," to full orchestral accompaniment.

Ritter's conduct at the Manhattan Club generated ever more controversy. He urinated on the stanchion attached to one of the pillars at the entrance, before the patrons. Hatsis snapped his fingers, "Bring some towels! Hurry now, and bring towels." He could be crude and filthy, and gentle and kind, simultaneously. He and Tony would sing, "Some enchanted evening, you might meet a strange whore."[27]

One night Ritter walked east and urinated in the alley. Phil Hansen then took him to the Hotel Newhouse, and watched as he stood at the east entrance. Before going up to his room, the judge urinated in the gutter while facing the oncoming traffic. The urbane Professor Ritter of his university days, who emulated the sophistication of Willis Adams and entertained his intellectual friends with wit and charm, had become uncouth.

Catherine Jensen could get infuriated over the way he behaved, but she also could feel for him as a man and was saddened by the fact that he was alone on holidays. She frequently had James Ivers Jr., formerly president of the Silver King Mining Company during Ritter's adolescent years, to her home for dinner, in the early days perhaps once a week. She invited Ritter when Ivers was there so that he would not be alone, and always had others, usually her mother, who lived with her at the time, or one of her brothers or sisters over, and old cronies from Park City with whom Ivers had played cribbage daily for almost sixteen years. Ritter was usually there for the cribbage games and enjoyed the chance to visit with old friends from Park City.[28]

When his condition deteriorated in the 1970s to where he could not drive, it was necessary for Catherine's son, Jack, to meet him at his chambers and drive him to the Jensen home. Jack saw his chambers as a "fascinating world" where "there was that huge desk with that huge chair and that little man behind it. It was dreamlike," according to Jack. "It had a fairyland aspect, a lot of ivory and he had that huge Navajo rug collection—screens and rugs that went on forever. It was sort of its own little museum back there.... [H]is chambers were his home. He lived there."[29]

In early 1974, Ritter appointed Verl Ritchie clerk of the court. "I knew he was crazy," Ritchie declared, "but I thought I could control him a little bit" and decided to "give it a go." They had an understanding that they would remodel the courts, that Ritchie could attend the seminars of the federal judicial center on court management, and that he would not have to sit in Ritter's court "like a flunky." It was but a few months until there was trouble, however, and it all seemed to involve Vicki Jolley.

It became apparent that Ritter wanted Hana Shirata, who had long been the minute clerk in Ritter's court, out and Vicki in. He began making petty remarks about Hana, that she was officious and a difficult personality, and replaced her with Vicki.

Even before Ritchie became clerk of court, Ritter had arranged for a series of secret raises for Vicki, unknown to anyone else except the clerk of court. She had also been placed on sick leave for an extended period of time and was given raises while on leave. But Ritchie considered Vicki "a vicious little backbiter," and before long Vicki went on sick leave and Hana was back. "She was his girlfriend," according to Ruth Bailey, whom Vicki worked with in the clerk's office for three years. "She was *very* smart. She was *very* smart. She was just too smart. It wasn't right that he should hire his girlfriend in the office.... I got so mad—I went twice to [Ritter] and just really poured my heart out. She's a very smart girl, I said, why don't you promote her and give her some responsibility, and maybe she'll come to work."[30]

Then Ritter set up a special office for Vicki, part of the clerk's office but adjacent to Ritter's chambers, and saw that Vicki got expensive antique furniture for her office. Ritchie could see Ritter becoming insanely jealous about Vicki, who reported to Ritter if anyone looked "cross-eyed" at her, "not in the sense of making advances to her, but just giving her trouble." Assistant United States Attorneys who had to work with her on management of the calendar found themselves in that difficulty.[31]

Unbeknownst to Ritter and Vicki, there was a crawl space between the first floor, where the post office was located, and the second floor, where the courts and Ritter's chambers were located. Ritter's chambers were directly over the mail sorting rooms, and the crawl space was sometimes used by postal inspectors to maintain surveillance on postal employees suspected of pilfering mail in the sorting room. It could also be used for other purposes, including surveillance on the second floor.

Use of the crawl space was discontinued, for a time, when a postal inspector monitoring the second-floor men's room, to catch a transient who had been trashing it, inadvertently witnessed an attorney employed in the building masturbating. The incident was innocuous, the attorney merely obtaining a semen sample for analysis by his doctor, but the postal inspector didn't know that. It looked terribly bad and placed the postal inspector in an unacceptable position.

When surveillance was resumed, the postal inspectors found themselves in another embarrassing situation. Ritter was inadvertently observed in a compromising situation with Vicki in the private area of his chambers.[32] Use of the crawl space was finally ended, once and for all!

On September 8, 1975, Ritter telephoned Ritchie and asked for his resignation. Ritchie already saw Ritter's conduct toward Vicki as "strange," and said, "Fine, I'll give you my resignation." It was only a ploy, however, to get control over Ritchie, for Ritter then said, "Okay, now how about sitting in my court sometime?" Ritchie refused, saying that was not part of the deal he was hired under. Ritter telephoned Ritchie again, about eight at night, and said, "Oh, you're playing with me. Get [your resignation] to me in the morning or I'll discharge you!" Ritchie said, "Okay, here's my resignation. I'm getting out of here." Ritter wanted to "talk about it," to "get some communication going," but it was the end of their relationship.[33]

Ritter's capacity for vindictiveness, predicted by Grant Ivins at his confirmation hearings, was displayed in the years 1970-1976. By then Swede

Larson had left the FBI and had been elected sheriff of Salt Lake County. Ritter convened a grand jury to investigate Sheriff Larson, on information that the civil rights of prisoners in the county jail, administered by the sheriff, were violated by Larson cutting the amount expended for food and pocketing the difference.[34]

Larson was the FBI special agent whose reports first included the unsubstantiated rumors of an affair with Phyllis Katz, and from whose reports other possibly negative information is expurgated.[35] Knowledge concerning the report was necessarily gleaned by Ritter in the course of the hearings. Dean William H. Leary was interviewed by the FBI, testified concerning it, and presumably identified the interviewer. Details of the report's contents may have been obtained by Ritter from other sources. It became clear in later years that Ritter believed, and perhaps had positive knowledge, that Larson was the author of the report and the source of negative information that came into the hands of Senator Arthur V. Watkins.

There was a factual basis, nevertheless, for the grand jury investigation of Larson. Aldo Richins, an officer at the jail, testified that twenty-three cents per meal was budgeted for each prisoner, but the amount actually spent was in the range of eighteen to twenty cents, and Larson applied the difference to his personal account, for flowers or other personal items. The actual amounts involved were documented by "meal cards," which Richins described as work sheets and which he destroyed after the grand jury was convened.[36] Larson confirmed Richins's testimony, but justified himself by saying that chief deputy county attorney Leon Halgren had "directed" him "to destroy" the meal cards.[37]

The grand jury returned indictments against them all, including Halgren, for "impeding the due administration of justice" by concealing evidence from the grand jury when the meal cards were destroyed, and for conspiracy to deny civil rights and denial of civil rights. The indictments charged that the average cost of meals was less than twenty-three cents and that Larson pocketed a profit of fifty-three thousand dollars in 1967-1969.[38]

After the indictments were returned, the new United States Attorney, C. Nelson Day, on instructions from the United States Department of Justice, refused to sign them, claiming the grand jury was improperly constituted, thus preventing them from becoming effective. Day informed the grand jury on February 9, 1971, that there were "legal reasons" he would not sign the proposed indictments. By letter dated February 13, 1971, the Department of Justice informed Ritter that "anything further would be inappropriate." The "legal reasons" stated were that the "procedure by which special grand jurors were selected...constitutes a 'substantial failure' to comply with" the Criminal Code, because "selection of names for the master jury wheels [must be] from voter registrations lists from all counties in the division." Ritter had supplemented the voter registration lists with names from telephone directories, city directories, and other sources. According to assistant Utah attorney general Robert B. Hansen, Ritter handpicked the grand jury, and handpicked the foreman, Maurice Warshaw, who had served on a previous grand jury empaneled by Ritter.[39] It is likely that bad feelings toward Larson were also a factor.

The indictments never became effective. But Ritter reasoned that, in addition to its authority to indict, the grand jury was empowered to hand up a "presentment" dealing with "public affairs, in this instance the operation and management of the county jail." He was also persuaded that the grand jury, "a group of [twenty-three] interested freeholders [was] empowered, as occasion may demand, to voice the conscience of the community." He released them to the press, nevertheless, on February 26, 1971. He considered, and so instructed the grand jury, that "you are free to exercise your own judgment without fear or favor, and [are] not to be deterred or influenced by the criticism of the public, the prosecutor [*viz.*, the Department of Justice], or even the court." A "presentment" had been returned, Ritter explained, that was to be "sent to such public bodies and officials as may be concerned."[40]

There was solid precedent for Ritter's action and rejecting the stance of the Department of Justice. The grand jury is "a kind of people's watchdog, to search out and disclose governmental imperfections, corruption, or matters needing legislative reform." There is a long tradition of acting on their own initiative, in face of opposition from the prosecuting attorney. Ritter had the contemporary example of the Watergate grand jury issuing a report naming President Richard M. Nixon an "unindicted co-conspirator" as part of an effort to root out corruption in government—an example generally applauded. His files also include reference to a grand jury indictment of a New Jersey sheriff for corruption, over objections of the prosecutor.[41] After the Swede Larson incident, Ritter was fond of threatening defendants, and even lawyers whose performance was seen as inadequate, with "those 23 cent meals" served by the Salt Lake County sheriff.

If not already evident in the Swede Larson affair, the negative side of Ritter's personality perceived by men of integrity, Grant Ivins in particular, and testified to at the confirmation hearings—the tendency or capacity of Ritter to be arbitrary, tyrannical, and abusive—was on display, for anyone to see, when in 1976 the case of Richard Cardall came before him.[42]

Cardall, the very person who, as administrative assistant to Arthur Watkins, had plotted the campaign against Elbert Thomas and who Ritter believed had leaked the derogatory information alleged in the FBI report prepared by Swede Larson to the news media during his own confirmation proceedings, was charged by the Securities and Exchange Commission (SEC) criminally with securities fraud. If "payback" was not a motive in the Utah Farm Bureau case of 1952, when Ritter held the "communist" and "fellow traveler" smear used against both himself and Elbert Thomas libelous, or when he caused the grand jury to investigate Swede Larson, it plainly appears to have been a motivation when Cardall came before him.

Cardall and his business confederates claimed to have a process for extracting magnesium from the brine of the Great Salt Lake. They put the process and a corporation named International Chemical Corporation into a shell corporation and began selling stock. The price went from 24¢ per share to $8.50, and they raised $12–$15 million, only about $250,000 of which went into mineral-extraction operations. Cardall put the rest into other business ventures.

The SEC criminal prosecution was assigned to Ritter, who did not recuse himself as other judges might have done. Ritter assigned Paul Badger, the former administrative assistant to Elbert Thomas at the time of the confirmation hearings, to represent the corporation. Cardall retained Dean Mitchell, a Salt Lake City lawyer with a reputation for success before Ritter in criminal matters. Badger warned Mitchell that he must get Ritter to recuse himself. Mitchell was already aware of the Ritter-Cardall problem, but was of the opinion that a recusal motion would mean that he could never go before Ritter again, and refused.[43]

Mitchell recalled that Ritter was a model of judicial decorum during the preliminary stages, never raising his voice until the jury was seated. Then trial became a brutal affair. Mitchell made a peremptory challenge. Ritter screamed at him, and it went downhill from there. Badger was also worked over unmercifully, as if to remove any suspicion that he was favored because of his former association with Thomas. The judge interjected himself relentlessly. By the tone of his voice and his facial expressions the jurors were plainly told that Cardall was guilty, long before the case was submitted to them. The jury convicted quickly, as they had virtually been directed to do.

If ever a man was entitled to be vindictive or to carry a grudge—and it must be agreed that if men are sublime, they are not so entitled—Ritter had that right because of what Arthur Watkins, Ernest Wilkinson, John Boyden, and their ilk had done to him, Rita, and their family in the confirmation process, with the help of Cardall. For all of his strengths, Ritter was far from an ideal man, and never pretended to be. All of his imperfections came out, as he sentenced Cardall to five years on each of the counts, to run consecutively, which amounted to forty-five years in the federal penitentiary, together with a $150,000 fine. Cardall was in shock. Ritter threatened to increase the penalty for Cardall's "audacity of staring at the Judge," and said: "You see, I was right about you all along."[44] The Cardall sentence was far in excess of that imposed in similar cases, none of which exceeded two years. Judicial discretion and the compassionate side of Ritter came through, somewhat, several weeks later when Ritter reduced the sentence to eighteen years. The conviction was affirmed on appeal, but further reduced to the two and a half years already served.

Following the sentencing of Cardall, Ritter invited Badger to his chambers and appointed him to the office of clerk of court, then vacant because of the resignation of Verl Ritchie.[45]

His opponents and critics were definitely on the rise, and now ever more increasing in influence. They had come to include most public officials, city, county, and state, and now members of the press, who had editorialized approvingly of his appointment, were about to become opponents. With the resignation of Ritchie, Ritter was left ever more isolated and lonely. Other events of the 1970s, including his empathy toward youth offenders that did not sit well with tough sentencing advocates, and his behavior toward Vicki, added fuel to the opposition. The Swede Larson and Dick Cardall incidents seemed to confirm the critics. The controversy surrounding Willis W. Ritter was about to increase, and ever more powerful adversaries were soon to join in mounting a campaign against the man and his office.

18

ISOLATION

Wisdom has taught us to be calm and meek,
To take one blow, and turn the other cheek;
It is not written what a man shall do,
If the rude caitiff smite the other too!

—Oliver Wendell Holmes Jr.

In courts across the United States, at every level, sessions begin with the bailiff's direction, "All arise." The judge then enters the chamber, decked out in a splendid, flowing black robe. The bailiff makes an announcement, to this general effect: "Hear ye! Hear ye! The Honorable Justice Court of Local County, the Honorable Judge Pretentious presiding, is now in session. All ye with business before this Honorable Court draw near, and ye shall be heard. God save this Honorable Court and the United States of America. Be seated." It is merely tradition, dating back to the courts of common-law England. In remote jurisdictions of the former British Empire the ritual may be carried further, even to the extreme of powdered wigs.

There was no such pomp in the court of Willis W. Ritter. Bailiff Spence VanNoy would enter, followed by Ritter, dressed in a plain blue business suit—the same one he always wore—conservative cut, white shirt, and dark tie. Those in attendance would rise, not by command but out of custom and respect. Ritter took the bench, and VanNoy announced: "This court is in session."

The conduct of Ritter's court was decidedly egalitarian. Ritter would ask the marshal to bring in the prisoners. "Are the prisoners in manacles?" he would ask. If they were, he would ask, "Why are they?" and order the manacles removed.[1]

When a middle-aged man charged with auto theft appeared before him on a cold, snowy day, Ritter asked: "Where's your coat?" "Don't have no coat." Ritter inquired further, "What did you wear coming here from the county jail?" The county jail was several blocks away. "What I'm wearing." Ritter asked, "Were you cold?" The man said yes. Ritter then requested the marshal who transported the prisoners to come forward. "Was it you who brought this prisoner to court? Did you wear a coat?" The marshal said yes. "Well, when you go back, he will wear your coat, and the next time on a day like this when you bring someone from the county jail, and he doesn't have a coat, he will wear yours." There was the person Nancy had seen bringing failing students home for counseling, still caring now that he was United States District Judge.[2]

Judge David K. Winder, who prosecuted criminal cases before Ritter as Assistant United States Attorney, never knew of anyone who commanded the total power Ritter exercised.

> There was some undefinable thing that guy had. He ran this place so totally and completely.... His arraignments were the most entertaining things I have ever seen. There would be 65 or 70 [defendants] in a morning or an afternoon.... [H]e would seize on anything he could to get rid of them. Someone would make the mistake of saying something like, "Your Honor, I don't know why they brought this into the court today"—then Ritter would mimic him and seize on anything that would lead to the quickest way of handling it.[3]

Willis Ritter was always watching, listening, and alert to what was going on around him. He observed people and fathomed their motives. Usually he read them as if he had them charted. With his keen insight, though not infallible, he was right enough of the time to give pause to would-be manipulators and create an aura of clairvoyance about him.

United States Attorney William T. Thurman received a teletype from the Department of Justice requesting that someone ask Ritter for an extension of time in a sensitive antitrust case. The United States Supreme Court had reversed Ritter several times, and there was a record of delays by the United States. Specific reasons for the request were spelled out by Justice, but the memo said, "Don't let Ritter know the real reason we want the continuance but get him to continue." It was given to Winder, who enjoyed good rapport with Ritter, and he was sent to persuade the judge. Winder knew Ritter would be cantankerous. He must approach the subject just right. Otherwise, he wouldn't have a chance. He put the Justice memo on a clipboard and held it close to his body for easy reference while making the request, conscious of its contents and taking care that Ritter could not see it as he entered his chambers. Ritter's uncanny intuition alerted him immediately. He snatched the memo and read it, just as his telephone was ringing. It was Cliff Ashton. "Do you know what this fellow came in here and did?" Ritter roared profanely and appearing almost frothing, and told Winder to get out and never come back. The next time Winder saw the chief judge, the incident was not an issue. He was cordial. His anger appeared feigned or forgotten.[4]

He demanded high performance out of lawyers appearing before him. If he did not get it, he might stop the trial. "Get out! Go home! Get some help if you need it, but hurry up about it." It was not uncommon for him to order lawyers not to appear in his court, when he found their performance wanting or their demeanor irritating. He ordered Lewellin O. Thomas, who represented the BLM in the Indian pony case, not to come back in his court, and when asked why said, "Because he talks too loud." On June 22, 1967, he sent a memorandum to United States Attorney Thurman declaring, "I hope I made myself clear the other day in court that I cannot any longer tolerate having [Assistant United States Attorneys] Walker Anderson or Ralph Klemm make any further appearances in my court." Klemm maintained that, as a duly licensed lawyer qualified as a member of the court, he had a right to appear and that Ritter could not disenfranchise him. Thurman requested a meeting with Ritter, to discuss the memorandum, but was ignored.[5] Klemm was therefore proud when at the calling of the next trial calendar Ritter asked if the United States was ready to proceed, and Thurman said, "Yes, and the first case will be handled by Assistant United States Attorney H. Ralph Klemm." Ritter directed, "If that's the case it will be stricken," and he continued to strike it from every trial calendar thereafter until Klemm eventually left the office to engage in private practice.

When he held arraignments of persons charged with crimes, Ritter would turn to the Assistant United States Attorney and say, "Tell me about him, Mr. Winder." The prosecutor was expected to give a concise, accurate summary of the facts leading up to the alleged crime so that Ritter could determine whether to accept a plea, order a trial, or require other proceedings.

Chief of probation Bernie Rhodes, and his staff, had to do presentence reports on those convicted or who entered guilty pleas in Ritter's court. Without the reports, Ritter would be unable to deal with his criminal calendar with the dispatch for which he became famous. The probation staff would work to put together background information, which Rhodes was expected to digest and report to Ritter succinctly, even in complicated cases.

Rhodes would take the reports home at night and memorize everything in them so he would be prepared to give Ritter what he wanted the next day. Ritter would then say, as he had done to the prosecutor at the time of arraignment: "Mr. Rhodes, tell me about this man," and expect a recitation of all that was necessary to an appropriate sentence. If not sufficiently succinct, or precise, Ritter might throw the front page of the report at Rhodes. "Take this back," Ritter would direct. "I'm an old man and I'm not going to go through all this." "He just scared the best out of people," Rhodes recalled, "and he got the best.... We'd go down there with a stack of files, thinking 'we can't do it.' There'd be a half a dozen bandits waiting to be sentenced. And we'd do it!"

There were periods of levity, and Ritter's keen sense of humor was frequently on display. One day when the court was packed with high-priced lawyers, Rhodes was giving his report on a kid who brought a camper in from Mexico with a false top packed with marijuana valued at a half-million dollars. "And it wasn't his first offense," Rhodes explained to the judge. "He's been arrested for controlled substances, was a user and had experimented with LDS." There was muffled laughter in the courtroom behind him. Rhodes recognized his mistake. *LDS* was the acronym for the dominant religious faith, the Church of Jesus Christ of Latter-day Saints. "Excuse me," Rhodes apologized. "He's experimented with LDS," repeating the mistake. "That's okay," Ritter shot back. "Too much of either one can act as a hallucinogen."[6]

Peter Billings Sr. had grown up on Butler Avenue, near the Ritter home on University Street and on Ritter's route when he walked to the law school. Willis always stopped to talk with Pete when he saw him in the yard and encouraged him to go to Harvard Law School. Billings rose to prominence as an antitrust lawyer in Salt Lake City and was engaged as local counsel, or "spear bearer," for a number of high-priced lawyers from San Francisco, Chicago, and New York City.[7] They had associated him because of his prominence and known friendship with the judge. Billings introduced his distinguished out-of-town colleagues, and moved their admission "for this case only." Ritter graciously admitted them all, after hearing recitation of their standing and accomplishments, then turned to Billings. "But counsel, who are you?" Billings, deflated before a courtroom packed with lawyers who knew of Billings's prominence, was nevertheless amused with his antic.

Ritter's interest in objects d'art continued. He collected and kept them at his judicial chambers in Salt Lake City, as well as at the Thousand Springs farm, including plates that belonged to Kaiser Wilhelm, Venetian hand-blown eggshell porcelain, Navajo weavings, and four hundred paintings, mostly by Willis Adams. He gathered FDR memorabilia, and always displayed a framed letter of warm greeting to him from Justice Learned Hand.

He increasingly became more difficult, in ways born, perhaps, of his loneliness. During periods when he had retired to the farm, Assistant United States Attorney Gerald R. Miller telephoned him concerning routine orders he needed to present regarding management of the criminal calendar. Rather than direct a minute entry, which could easily be done by telephone, Ritter would say, "Well, Jerry, I'm up here and you are down there. You will have to come up here if you want me to sign that order." The object, it seems, was relief from his loneliness by a forced visit from one of the more entertaining members of the courthouse family.

Others subjected to such requests who knew of the chief judge's volatile nature, including coauthor Parker Nielson, contrived reasons they could not make the trip, such as conflicts in domestic life, and awaited his return for the signing of their orders. They were deprived, no doubt, the opportunity to socialize with Ritter in the setting of the farm, away from the rigors of the legal vocation, but spared the risk of an unexpected explosion of the mercurial Ritter personality.

As the decade of the 1970s wore on, there was ever more criticism of him. On February 27, 1973, Ritter issued an order requiring the United States Department of Interior "to remove all waters which have already intruded from Lake Powell and the Glen Canyon Unit from the Rainbow Bridge National Monument and to prevent the waters from Lake Powell and the Glen Canyon Unit from entering the boundaries of the Rainbow Bridge National Monument at all times in the future."[8] The order had the effect of isolating him from most of the government support that remained, after the decades of sniping by FBI, state, and local officials.

Ritter's order, in favor of Friends of the Earth, David S. Brower, the Wasatch Mountain Club, and river guide Kenneth G. Sleight, implemented a provision of the 1956 Colorado River Storage Project Act (CRSP) prohibiting any water from backing up into a national monument. Brower and his fellows, represented by James B. Lee and Utah law professor Owen Olpin, pursued a clever strategy of merely asking for an order limiting the elevation of the waters behind the dam, thus avoiding controversy over congressional appropriations, separation-of-powers problems, or the need to ask the secretary of the interior to drain the lake.

Ritter's opinion gave expression for his intellectual abilities as well as his conservationist ethic and feeling for the marvels of nature. He wrote that "Rainbow Bridge is a majestic sandstone arch...the world's largest natural arch...far and away the most spectacular in all nature and...a national treasure." He quoted geologist Herbert E. Gregory's United States Geological Survey Professional Paper 93 of 1913: "Its symmetry and graceful proportions, as well as its size and beauty of color, give this arch a commanding position among the natural bridges of the world." Then he quoted Joseph E. Pogue, who first described Rainbow Bridge for *National Geographic* in 1910: "'The Great Rainbow Natural Bridge of Southern Utah'...surpasses any structure of its kind known to man....It is not the size alone, though this far exceeds the greatest masonry arches constructed by engineering skill; nor is it solely the graceful lines or curvature of maximum stability, but rather all of these, that combine to make this the most remarkable single arch known. It would easily span, with room to spare, the dome of the Capitol at Washington.'"

Many, including Cliff Ashton, felt that Ritter went overboard on the Rainbow Bridge issue, and on the Christmas tree case and every issue that came before him involving wildlife, nature, or conservation, because of Rita's influence, she being an environmentalist.[9] To Ritter, however, the law was clear: no waters were to enter a national monument. He thought it sufficient that President Taft, in his presidential proclamation of May 30, 1910, establishing Rainbow Bridge as a national monument, also reserved "as much land as may be needed for its protection." Moreover, the language of CRSP section 1 directed the secretary of the interior to "take adequate protective measures to preclude impairment of the Rainbow Bridge National Monument," and section 3 declared "the intention of Congress that no dam or reservoir...shall be within any national park or monument."[10] The two provisions were a promise by Congress to conservationists, Brower included, who had successfully blocked construction of the proposed Echo Park dam because its waters would encroach on the Dinosaur National Monument. The same objections were withheld as to Glen Canyon, proposed as a substitute for Echo Park, in exchange for the promises. Ritter found that after section 1 was included, both conservationists and government officials "continued to observe that Section 3 would apply to limit the height of Lake Powell," and therefore appropriations by Congress to build the dam, cited by Interior officials to justify their actions, could not be understood as abandoning the restrictions of CRSP sections 1 and 3, or waiving their effect as to Glen Canyon. "The longer I am on the bench the more I believe that it is a district judge's responsibility to protect citizens from their government," he declared, in another context.[11] His order protecting the Rainbow Bridge was of that flavor. The issue, at least to Ritter, was a simple one. Solemn promises, particularly by officials as high as the Congress and the secretary of the interior, should be honored and given effect. The more so when enacted into law.

Senator Frank E. Moss, who had been Ritter's sometime supporter, was now isolated from and opposed to Ritter. Moss called for a meeting of senators and representatives of the upper Colorado River basin states, together with the secretary of the interior, on the "Rainbow Bridge crises." Senator Wallace F. Bennett wrote to Senator Henry M. Jackson (D-WA), chairman of the powerful Senate Interior Committee, asking him to schedule hearings at the earliest possible date on a bill deleting the provisions of CRSP preventing waters from entering a national monument. "If the Ritter decision is allowed to stand," Moss declared, "and it becomes necessary to draw down Lake Powell by 4 million acre feet the economic basis upon which the Colorado River Act rests will be undermined."[12] The harm Moss had in mind was that Utah, and the other upper-basin states, would be impaired in their ability to use their share of the Colorado River waters stored behind the dam.

On March 28, 1973, a hearing was held before Ritter on a request by the secretary of the interior, Rogers C. B. Morton, and Ellis L. Armstrong, commissioner of the Bureau of Reclamation, that Judge Ritter stay his Rainbow Bridge order. "The bridge is beautiful and you can't replace it," Brower testified, and he affirmed that the provision of the CRSP was a promise made to conservationists by Congress.

Ritter considered the religious significance of the "Great Bridge" to the Navajos.[13] "Whitehorsebegay," the Paiute guide to the original United States Geological Survey (USGS) party that discovered it, at least for non-Indians, "would not go beneath the arch [believing] one who passed under could not return without a certain prayer. Evidently Whitehorsebegay had forgotten this prayer and feared vengeance should he break the legendary prohibition." Nearly beneath the arch the original USGS party found "the remains of an ancient altar," thus confirming its religious significance.

"I am 68 years old," Billy Yellow testified in the hearings before Ritter, and "the medicine men hold these prayer services and ceremonies and... they put medicine in the water flowing from the little springs coming out of the foundation of Rainbow Bridge," praying for "protection from the white man." Ritter asked what was the disadvantage of an order keeping the waters out of the national monument. John W. Mueller, regional supervisor of power for the Bureau of Reclamation, conceded that the power-generation turbines at Glen Canyon Dam would work efficiently at 3,606 feet, or at 5,643 feet that would be reached without the order. "There is not a great deal of difference. The turbines are efficient at both elevations. I would say 3,606 is a good area of efficiency," Mueller agreed. "I suggest this as an alternative," Ritter proposed. "Maybe we can work this problem out so that Powell can be kept at 3606 [feet]," which was the elevation of the monument boundary, "which is pretty close to filling it." Ritter refused to stay his order.[14]

On March 12, 1973, Moss introduced another bill to repeal the provisions of CRSP prohibiting waters from entering a national monument. Before the bill could be acted upon, the United States Circuit Court of Appeals for the Tenth Circuit reversed Ritter's order, reasoning that failure to appropriate funds to protect Rainbow Bridge amounted to repeal, by implication, of the section of CRSP providing for its protection.[15] But Ritter had already exposed the fallacy of that rationale. He found that, in the intervening years after adoption of CRSP, it was recognized that the consequence of a barrier dam below the bridge keeping waters out of the monument, "*whether a barrier dam is constructed downstream or not*" (emphasis by Ritter), would be "flash floods com[ing] roaring down the steep gradient of Bridge Creek, with a load of 4-5 foot quartzite boulders, cobbles, logs and driftwood," with "explosive force." That was the reason Interior had not requested funds to construct the barrier dam, rather than intent to repeal the promise to keep the waters out. Ritter reasoned that "implied repeals are disfavored, and will not be found unless the intent of the legislature to repeal is manifest" and that "the judgment of the court will not be substituted for that of the legislature. Where the intent of the legislature has been made explicit, judicial construction ends."

Chief judge David T. Lewis dissented from the opinion of the court of appeals and agreed with Ritter. "The judicial words 'repealed by implication,' by very definition, carry heavy overtones of erosion into the doctrine of separation of powers," Lewis warned. "Eight different bills have been presented to the United States Congress [including the two recent ones by Moss]...to amend the limiting language in sections 1 and 3." It was not "through inadvertence" that Congress failed to repeal, and it must be assumed that it intended the two sections to remain in effect.

Meanwhile, the controversy generated by the Georgia-Pacific matter, the prominent lawyers engaged in it, as advocates for and in opposition to

Ritter, became more fodder for the Ritter critics, of whom there were an increasingly larger number. The controversy resulted in allegations against Ritter's integrity and another series of investigations by the FBI and the Justice Department.

A disgruntled litigant before Ritter by the name of Julius Petrofsky picked up on it. He got wind of the Georgia-Pacific matter, went to the offices of the clerk of court for the District of Utah numerous times during 1972, verbally abused the clerks, refused to confine himself to the public working area, and removed papers from the court files.[16] Andrew John Brennan, clerk of court, was directed to "advise each of your deputies that [Petrofsky] is not to be given or shown anything from our files."[17] After Petrofsky went to the clerk's office with an attorney, Gerald Kinghorn, Ritter modified his direction by instructing each deputy clerk, by name, to allow any attorney for Petrofsky to examine any records but said that the U.S. marshal was to prevent any disturbance.[18]

Petrofsky took note of the law firm representing the American Gypsum Trust, reviewed the docket sheets from Ritter's court to see how Cliff Ashton and other lawyers from the firm of VanCott, Bagley, Cornwall, and McCarthy had fared, and concluded that Ritter was paying for his expensive legal representation by dispensing favors in his court, in the form of biased and dishonest adjudication of cases before him. "The lawyers connected to Judge Ritter during the period 1970-74 were involved in 40-some cases before him (not including those involving the state or federal government)" Petrofsky calculated, "and they didn't lose one of them."[19] He never took into account, or considered, that there was an entirely logical and innocent explanation for that result, including the probability that lawyers of such prominence could, and usually did, handpick only cases that were winners. Cal Behle and Keith Taylor fueled Petrofsky's charges, wittingly or unwittingly, with allegations that they had formerly been recipients of favored treatment by Ritter, but that he had effectively "disbarred" Taylor and "our whole firm, including Behle," over their opposition to Ritter in the Georgia-Pacific matter.[20]

Petrofsky reasoned that Ritter, though no longer trustee, had testified in the case and had been the original trustee. A Public Report of Extra-Judicial Income filed by Ritter for the period January 1–June 30, 1970, in which Ritter wrote "none" under all sections, was therefore false, according to Petrofsky, for "there's serious conflict there. Ritter leaves a gap of four months, from January to April, unaccounted for. His testimony and the official report conflict."[21]

The accusations by Petrofsky may have been the most intense and pervasive, but his claims illustrated that as the general public became aware of Ritter and his rulings, there were those who became ever more watchful. Among them were a group of religious and political ideologues who saw his every judicial act as libertine, antireligious, and dangerous. In April 1972 Salt Lake City, through Mayor Jake Garn, filed an affidavit alleging that Ritter was "personally biased and prejudiced" against the city and its officials, and in favor of one of the attorneys for the plaintiff in a suit against the city. The affidavit also alleged bias and prejudice in favor of the attorney for the plaintiffs in the suit over the Ten Commandments.[22] Another affidavit was filed by Salt Lake City public safety commissioner James L. Barker Jr., alleging "personal bias and prejudice" against the city and the police in a suit over civil rights of persons arrested in a drive to clean up prostitution in the city's West Second South area. Ritter denied the two motions on April 19, 1972, and ordered stricken as being without basis a statement in the city's affidavit that Robert S. Campbell Jr., counsel for the plaintiff in one of the cases, "implied that he and his firm did enjoy a favored status before Judge Ritter and would be available to assist the city." Garn and Barker claimed that their suspicion was confirmed by the alleged statement and Ritter's order striking it. The court of appeals affirmed Ritter on the issue. "It is not necessary to consider" the evidence, the court of appeals ruled, "for the reason that Mr. Barker is not personally involved in the suit. There is no showing, of course, that Judge Ritter is prejudiced against the City."[23]

In May 1973, deputy Utah attorney general Robert B. Hansen filed another affidavit, citing "personal bias or prejudice" in a civil rights case against Dixie College officials. It was alleged by the college president that Ritter had made a "biased and prejudiced statement in which he called me a tyrant" in a related case, and that Ritter had failed or refused to have the statement transcribed. Hansen alleged that the failure of Ritter "to make [an] appointment [with Hansen] to discuss the matter" indicated "personal animosity, bias and prejudice against me."[24] Hansen failed to recognize, or acknowledge, that the court of appeals had already ruled that such affidavits did not state bias and prejudice, "for the reason that Mr. [Hansen] is not personally involved in the suit."

As the decade of the 1970s wore on, the chief judge's formerly regal opinions were, more and more, replaced by the trivial. The unpredictable and sometimes eloquent Ritter could be as capricious in one direction as he was discerning in the other. On a Friday afternoon in May 1973, in an act most ordinary citizens oppressed from time to time by meter maids might applaud, he issued a ten-day restraining order preventing Salt Lake City from issuing parking tickets. The parking ordinance was unconstitutional, the plaintiff alleged in a suit against Mayor Garn and the city commissioners, because of a provision presuming the owner of the vehicle guilty rather than innocent. A parking ticket dispute was poor stuff for the federal court, under any circumstances, and the city attorney tried to explain that the proceeding was unnecessary for the ordinance had been repealed, but Ritter ignored him. Mayor Garn called the action "very dangerous," citing the loss of parking revenues during the ten-day period and the possibility of vehicles being parked in troublesome places or obstructing fire hydrants while the order was in effect. The restraint lasted only a few days, and he knew he was wrong, magistrate Ronald N. Boyce laughed, but he "delighted in throwing a dead rat in the center of the floor."[25] Making as much mischief as possible for Garn and the city officials on short notice seemed the only consequence.

In another pronouncement sports fans would cheer, Ritter entered an order restraining the National Collegiate Athletic Association from preventing a local television station televising a basketball game between the University of Utah and University of Nevada at Las Vegas. The court of appeals reversed the order, citing irreparable injury from loss of gate receipts.[26]

In 1975 Catherine Jensen, Ritter's trusted secretary since 1957, discovered a mass in her abdomen. It was ovarian cancer. Ritter went with Catherine to the hospital at the time of her surgery. He informed the doctors that they must do everything for her, for she was so important to him. Afterward, she applied for early retirement, and Ritter assisted her in getting the maximum benefits possible. He then wrote a long note to her on court stationery, in his own hand, praising her for the excellent work she had done for him, enclosing a check, signing the note, "Affectionately." Catherine declined the check, but treasured the note.[27]

Gone was the principal, and perhaps only, tempering influence against his extreme and destructive biases and dispositions. The loss of Catherine compounded his feelings of isolation. Ritter replaced her with Vicki Jolley, while leaving Vicki on the payroll of the clerk's office in a vain attempt to prevent her from being fired if something happened to him. Vicki was not the tempering influence Catherine had been, and may actually have had the contrary effect. Ritter was, increasingly, ever more isolated.

Whether Catherine could have returned to work is problematic. The last six years she worked for Ritter, she felt that her integrity was being challenged. Jack Jensen saw his mother as turning her back on Ritter. There were her "no-nonsense" rules, according to Jack, and Willis wasn't behaving by them. One of them had to do with Vicki, and Catherine viewed her own scruples as being compromised by staying with Ritter. Even after she resigned, however, Catherine continued to take care of his personal finances until he died, and continued to have him over occasionally for dinner.[28] But she never returned.

The case of convicted murderer Gary Gilmore revived the controversy of the Braasch and Sullivan case and exemplified those in which Ritter attracted public criticism, and it placed him in another controversy with Robert B. Hansen. Gilmore, possibly because of frustration over life in incarceration, possibly because of a clever strategy to put the State of Utah to the burden of carrying out his execution, had discharged his lawyers and stated that no one was to petition on his behalf to prevent his execution. The American Civil Liberties Union (ACLU) avoided the direction by presenting a petition for a restraining order to Ritter in the form of a taxpayers' suit, claiming that the Utah death penalty statute was unconstitutional and that it would be an improper expenditure of public monies on an execution and the wrongful death action that might be its consequence. The State of Utah, through Hansen, and assistant attorney general Earl F. Dorius, urged that the death penalty statute had withstood all previous challenges and that "an expenditure of tax monies to pay off any judgment for wrongful death was nothing but sheer speculation; any chances of recovery on a wrongful death theory in such a case were slim." Ritter convened his court after midnight on the morning Gilmore was to be executed and heard arguments by the ACLU and Dorius. "He conducted court in a very judicious manner," Dorius recalled, "allowing both sides to present their argument with no interruption." After a brief recess to consider the matter, Ritter announced his opinion, from the bench at 1:05 AM on July 17, 1977, declaring, "The Utah death penalty statute has not been held constitutional by any courts." Ritter then noted that Justices White, Brennan, and Marshall had all emphasized that there were serious doubts about the statute in a petition filed by Bessie Gilmore, Gary's mother. "Until the State courts and the United States Supreme Court have resolved these doubts and have held the Utah Death Penalty Statute constitutional, there can be no lawful execution. The consent of a convicted defendant in a criminal case gives the state no privilege to impose a punishment forbidden by the 8th Amendment." In the state of the United States Supreme Court cases at the time, no one could say the Utah statute was constitutional. "There is too much uncertainty in the law."[29] Ritter therefore issued an injunction against the execution scheduled later that morning.

Hansen and Dorius were determined that the execution be carried out. Dorius, "angered and fatigued," flew to Denver in the early hours following Ritter's ruling with an application for a writ of mandamus and prevailed upon the Court of Appeals for the Tenth Circuit to convene an extraordinary session at 7:30 AM to review Ritter's order. It was nothing against Ritter personally, according to Hansen; they were simply upholding judicial dignity and the law. The appeals court issued an order at 7:35 AM declaring that "1. The writ of mandamus is granted. 2. The temporary restraining order entered at about 1:05 this morning by Honorable Willis W. Ritter... is set aside and held for naught" and that Ritter "is ordered to take no further action in any manner nor of any kind involving Gary Gilmore unless such matter is presented by a duly accredited attorney for Gary Gilmore or by Gilmore himself." Dorius remembered, "I immediately raced out of the courtroom, banging into newsmen, yelling at them to get out of my way so that I could get to the telephone. Go ahead with the execution," Dorius instructed the warden of the Utah State Penitentiary, after giving the prearranged code, "Eudora from Park Hill calling," that Dorius had devised to identify himself, James Bond style. After giving the instructions to kill a fellow human, Dorius recalled that "I was relaxed and felt a very warm feeling, one of gratification."[30]

With the loss of Catherine Jensen, and her restraining influence, followed by the execution of Gilmore, the final assault on Ritter's office as chief judge, amounting to virtual besiegement by the Utah State Bar, the United States Justice Department, both U.S. senators from the state of Utah, and the Utah attorney general, which would dominate his final year, was about to begin.

19

SIEGE

[Ralph Waldo] Emerson said to [Oliver Wendell] Holmes [Jr.], "Young man, have you read Plato?"

Holmes said he hadn't.

"You must. You must read Plato...."

So off he went and read Plato for a few months or a year, and then wrote a piece doing in Mr. Plato in one of those ephemeral literary things at Harvard. He laid this, as it were, at the feet of Mr. Emerson....Holmes didn't see him again for about a year. When he saw him...Emerson said, "Oh, by the way, I read your piece on Plato. Holmes, when you strike at a king, you must kill him."

—Felix Frankfurter

As the decade of the 1970s reached the midpoint, the strife and dissension increased to a point where, looking back, Willis W. Ritter's life in the 1960s looks to have been a party. Critics of Ritter were frustrated by him—frustration that led them to want to be free of the authority he exercised in their work and in their lives. The FBI's effort to discredit him continued and became more active.[1] He was frustrating the life out of them and, especially, the judges on the United States Court of Appeals for the Tenth Circuit, when he refused to knuckle under to their edicts on assignment of cases or evaded them, and the United States Attorney for the District of Utah and other Justice Department officials, because he would not accommodate them or give them special consideration and, at times, seemed openly hostile in a very personal way. Their frustration, in some cases, bordered on outright hatred.

The existing rules, and those directed at Ritter in particular, would have brought ordinary judges into line, but may as well have been written on a cloud for all the effect they seemed to have on him. They began, individually and collectively, looking for ways to remove him, or at least mitigate his power and influence.

Impeachment is the constitutional device for removing a judge. But soft on crime, on criminals, and on capital punishment, or controversial on religion, or stringent with law enforcement officers, government officials, and lawyers—the true grievances, or assumed grievances, of the Ritter critics, do not rise to the level of impeachable conduct. At the same time, those working closest with him, even his staunchest defenders, agreed that the combination of his physical deterioration and perception of collected injustices in the attacks by his critics, along with drinking, led him to sometimes injudicious behavior. He would increasingly deal with his criminal calendar, formerly current but now way behind, by merely sweeping it away.[2]

His critics began looking about for other means to secure relief, any relief. On February 2, 1972, the Judicial Conference of the United States, chaired by Justice Warren Burger, had asked Congress to repeal the grandfather clause. They jumped on that, making their bandwagon a campaign to curb his powers by rescinding the grandfather clause.[3]

By the mid-1970s those who were trying to get rid of him, or stymie him, came to include the United States Department of Justice, the Judiciary Committee of the United States House of Representatives, and a couple of subcommittees of the United States Senate, in addition to long-standing critics in the FBI and state and local officials of the state of Utah. Their battle cry, "rescind the grandfather clause," like "down with tuna sandwiches on Wednesday," seemed wan. Ritter was the only district judge over seventy who was still serving as chief judge, and the lone remaining judge affected by it.[4] There were thirty when the clause was enacted in 1958, but within the preceding year the only other two, in North Dakota and Nebraska, had retired.[5] His chief judge status, moreover, was already diluted by the orders of the Judicial Council removing his control over assignment of cases. There was no explanation of, and seemingly little thought given to, what effect his removal as chief judge would have, for that would have no effect on his powers as a judge. It would merely dilute the prestige of his office, or serve as a gratuitous insult, which seemed to be the real goal of his critics. Nevertheless, the siege was on.

A major indication that his opponents were becoming bolder in their attempts to curb his powers was a resolution introduced in the summer of 1973 to the convention of the Utah State Bar Association in Provo by the bar president, Ritter's former student Calvin L. Behle. The resolution was one more request that Congress rescind the grandfather clause. Behle contended that, in 1969 when Ritter turned seventy, his behavior took a definite, noticeable change for the worse and that in 1972, while serving as a Utah delegate to the ABA and as a member of its board of governors, he was "approached from several sources" concerning Ritter, including because of his "refusal to establish court rules pertaining to such matters as assignment of cases.... A written resolution was submitted by me for action whereby the Utah State Bar...was to request Congress to repeal the Grandfather Clause." Behle reasoned that Ritter "was an outstanding example of just why mandatory [retirement] age had been passed."[6]

Ritter said, in response, that divesting him of his chief judge status would be a useless exercise. Unlike other United States District Court chief judges, he reminded his adversaries, he was essentially without any say in the assignment of cases in his district. They were assigned by lot. What Ritter said was true, but not quite accurate. The Judicial Council had ordered Ritter to cease assigning cases to himself on several occasions—1958, 1963, 1968, and 1972—but he was notorious for circumventing the orders.

Behle's resolution was adopted by the bar convention, but nullified by the board of bar commissioners as "not well conceived and appears to be prompted by motives which disparage the dignity of the federal judiciary and of this bar." Those attending the meeting where it was presented were far less than a majority, and fewer than one hundred of the more than a thousand members voted for it, at a meeting without notice that it was to be considered and in a forum improper for its presentation. "Neither the procession of the calendar nor the resolution of cases has been mismanaged by the judge," the petition leading up to nullification of the resolution stated, and it "in effect, is a direct challenge not only to the office of Judge Ritter, but to the internal workings of the federal judiciary system."[7]

Deputy Utah attorney general Robert B. Hansen, then an announced candidate for the Republican nomination for U.S. representative, picked up on the issue and made it a part of his political campaign. Speaking to members of the Davis County Bar on September 28, 1973, Hansen urged his audience "to write their congressmen and support the State Bar Resolution [to repeal the Grandfather Clause and curb Ritter's power] when it is re-submitted."[8]

A written ballot was submitted to the full Utah State Bar membership. For what purpose, it is unclear, for United States District Judge do not serve, nor are they removed, by majority vote of members of the bar. In February 1974, the bar released the ballot, or poll, of its sixteen hundred members, a majority of whom supported action to strip Ritter of his status as chief judge.

Other powerful groups and individuals—the United States Department of Justice, the Utah attorney general and E. J. "Jake" Garn, mayor of

Salt Lake City—gradually added their voices and their ideas for curbing Ritter's power. Garn declared that "Ritter has also displayed an obvious, strong bias against Salt Lake City in cases that have appeared before him. We feel that we cannot get a fair hearing in his court."[9]

On March 8, 1974, the Judicial Conference of the United States, for the third time in four years, called for mandatory retirement of all district judges at age seventy. The resolution asked Congress to repeal the grandfather clause.[10]

In the 1974 election, Mayor Garn was elected to the United States Senate. He then employed his new office in the campaign against Ritter he was already engaged in. In May 1975, he secured the appointment of Ramon Child, his prominent political supporter, as United States Attorney for the District of Utah.

The appointment, considering Garn's politically motivated attacks, caused Ritter concern about the potential danger of a similarly motivated prosecutor with power to manipulate the grand jury sitting at the time Child assumed office. Legal scholars of the time concluded that the grand jury was archaic. Rather than a protection of the accused, it "has a far greater potential as an instrument of oppression," for it "is really nothing more than a review of the prosecutor's predigested evidence and a ratification of his conclusions."[11]

Ritter was apprehensive because of the relentless attacks on his character and judicial style then being led by Garn, and before that by Arthur Watkins and his confederates dating from the hearings on his confirmation, and mindful of the potential for "use of the grand jury for political purposes," which had "evoked critical responses from the courts."[12] In the hands of an improperly motivated prosecutor, the grand jury could become "an instrument of oppression" or be used "to pry into beliefs and associations of dissident and unpopular" persons or groups, including himself.[13] He also knew that, arguments to the contrary aside, a prosecutor could get a grand jury to indict anyone, for anything. He had the Richard M. Nixon and Swede Larson grand jury experiences to attest that the grand jury may be used for an investigation and report, which might even extend to the campaign Garn had entered into against his discharge of the role of chief judge. But the grand jury is an adjunct of the courts, whose duty it is to prevent such abuse. He therefore discharged the grand jury.[14]

Later, in 1975, Garn introduced two bills aimed, directly or indirectly, at Ritter. First, he cosponsored a "judicial tenure act," United States Senate Bill 1110, to establish a judicial tenure council and a procedure for retirement of a disabled judge and allowing removal of a judge whose conduct was inconsistent with good behavior required by the Constitution. Second, he individually sponsored a measure to "rescind the grandfather clause," affecting Ritter and no other member of the federal judiciary, United States Senate Bill 1130, under which Ritter would retain his office as United States District Judge.

Hansen attempted to enlist the support of the Utah State Bar for Garn's two bills. Using the research of Julius Petrofsky, Hansen presented to the board of commissioners of the bar a compilation of cases appealed from Ritter's court, purporting to show that a high percentage of criminal cases and 60 percent of civil cases were overturned on appeal.[15] Based in part on his "statistics," Hansen presented six resolutions at a meeting of the commissioners on January 9, 1976, aimed at removing Ritter from the bench or curtailing his powers.

The following day, Hansen presented his resolutions to the membership of the Utah State Bar at its midyear meeting held at the Hilton Hotel in Salt Lake City. Hansen claimed that Petrofsky had been denied access to court records while trying to document favoritism toward certain attorneys. Harold Christensen, who had succeeded Behle as president of the bar, explained that the commissioners opposed the resolutions and considered them unprofessional and accusatory rather than factual. "The issue before the Bar is not whether Ritter is a good judge," Christensen reasoned. "The issue is the independence of the judiciary. [The resolution proposed by Hansen] is an unwarranted interference with the independence of the judiciary and probably unconstitutional." "Let's not make fools of ourselves," partner to Behle and Bar commissioner James B. Lee added, explaining that there was no evidence supporting Hansen's proposals. The members of the bar in attendance then voted, by heavy majorities, to reject the resolutions, but did vote in favor of support for the judicial tenure act and endorsed repeal of the grandfather clause.[16]

The bar resolutions, including their rejection of the major resolutions proposed by Hansen, were directed by the bar commission to be delivered to Ritter by Christensen as bar president. He did so, and was met with an affidavit of bias and prejudice filed by the United States in an antitrust case against four egg producers and two of their executives. The affidavit, by C. Robert Disharoon of the United States Department of Justice, Antitrust Division, San Francisco, alleged that Ritter had "a personal bias and prejudice in favor of Harold G. Christensen, counsel for Olson Farms, Inc.," because he had delivered the bar resolutions to Ritter.[17]

The Disharoon affidavit signaled that the Justice Department had joined in the campaign against Ritter. Ritter denied the affidavit because it was not timely, not made by a party, did not state facts indicating bias, and Disharoon was not a member of the bar of Ritter's court. "Mr. Christensen's actions were, and the court hereby finds them to have been proper, professional and in conformity with the highest standards of conduct befitting the office of president of the Utah State Bar," Ritter concluded, and "such conduct creates no prejudice."[18]

The court of appeals agreed. "No one could ever accuse Judge Ritter of being in league with the Utah Bar," the appellate court reasoned. "There is no indication that Christensen acted unfairly or unethically," the appeals court wrote, and "there is no bias to be gleaned from Judge Ritter's ruling in favor of the defendants." The court of appeals nevertheless ordered that the "interests of justice" required that Ritter be removed, and the case assigned to another judge from another district.[19] The decision marked a change in the attitude of the court of appeals.

By February 1976, the campaign against Ritter was building up steam. Garn claimed in a February 1976 statement that while mayor of Salt Lake City and testifying about placing tablets of the Ten Commandments on public grounds, "when I said I saw nothing wrong in placing them there he threatened to hold me in contempt of court." In fact, Ritter made no such statement during the proceedings.[20] Finally, a new president of the Utah State Bar, LaVar Stark, signed a formal resolution reciting that in a secret poll 77.7 percent of the lawyers polled were in favor of repeal of the grandfather clause and 23 percent were against, and that those in favor constituted 50.8 percent of the active bar membership.

Ritter said he didn't "care two bits" about the bar action. "For almost 200 years since the Constitution of the United States was adopted, in 1789, in fact, it has been a tradition of the federal judiciary that judges do not respond to any criticism. I prefer to follow that tradition," Ritter explained. "This is a fumbling, bumbling political tactic by [Hansen,] a poor chap who is trying to make a political name for himself and has no other issue."[21]

"I have known this Judge and generally favorably since...law school more than 45 years ago," Behle wrote to Garn, in support of the bill to rescind the grandfather clause. "No one can fault him for not having a brilliant mind. However, a lack of judicial temperament (which on candid occasion he freely admits) has made things difficult for everyone....But personally I do not know of anything in his conduct that would justify impeachment. . . . The situation seems to have become aggravated to an almost impossible point now that his normal retirement age from that position was achieved," Behle concluded. On February 25, 1976, Senator Garn issued a statement in support of and endorsing both the judicial tenure act and the bill to rescind the grandfather clause, claiming that Ritter was "a disgrace to the federal judiciary" and that the bills would allow his "remov[al] from office without the agony of impeachment."[22]

On May 6, 1976, Senator Quentin N. Burdick (D-ND), chairman of the Judiciary Committee, wrote to University of Utah College of Law professor William J. Lockhart, inviting his views on the bill to rescind the grandfather clause. Lockhart's views were important, for he had served as acting United States Attorney for the District of Utah following the death of C. Nelson Day, from November 22, 1974, until May 5, 1975, when Child was appointed. He responded on May 13, 1976, with a formal written statement. "I view this bill as a heavy-handed and poorly-disguised effort to use the US Senate as a political forum for certain elements of the Utah political spectrum who wish to strike back at a federal judge who has generally been recognized as a stout protector of civil rights and civil liberties in Utah," Lockhart's seven-page written statement advised. "The politically-motivated nature of this proposal is clearly revealed by the irrelevancy of the arguments offered in its support. Although the proposal is designed solely to strip Judge Ritter of his title of Chief Judge by repealing a narrow Grandfather Clause, virtually none of the arguments bandied about in Utah have anything to do with the functions of a Chief Judge."[23]

When the Senate Judiciary Committee convened on May 18, 1976, to consider efforts to curb Ritter's power by rescinding the grandfather clause, it had become clear that Congress was confronted with an open assault on the autonomy of the federal court. His critics, including Garn, Child, and Hansen, were looking for something to curb Ritter's authority that would work. They were emboldened by the bill and on the offensive as the hearings on repeal of the grandfather clause opened. Ritter's unpopularity would present the senators with a severe test of the doctrines of separation of powers and independence of the judiciary. "What kind of cockamamie reasoning is it which argues that a special one-man exemption should be continued after it has been shown that the only man still serving under the exemption abuses both his administrative and regular judicial duties?"

Garn queried, in advocating for his bill. "Must we continue to reward intemperate and injudicious behavior with a special exemption? I certainly hope we do not."[24]

Child testified in support of the bill, reciting problems his office had with Ritter, including that he did not hold rule days on a regular basis, his refusal to convene a grand jury, and delays in ruling on pretrial motions in criminal cases until after a jury was sworn and jeopardy had attached. Chairman Burdick, who had personal experience practicing before Ritter as cocounsel with Rick Lamoreaux in their 1951 trial before Ritter of the "communist dominated" libel of the Farmers Union, interrupted. "Just a minute, Mr. Child," Burdick challenged. "Much of your testimony...deals with the actions of Judge Ritter as a trial judge," repeating the point made by Lockhart in his written statement, "and do you understand that this subcommittee would have no authority to do anything about his actions as a trial judge?" Child was forced to agree.

Hansen testified, and referred to opinion polls of the Utah State Bar members showing that high percentages rated Ritter's record and temperament poor, and that 77 percent wanted him to step down as chief judge. "Do you really think this Committee should take into consideration opinion polls?" Burdick challenged. Then he cornered Hansen. "You and I are both lawyers.... Do you use opinion polls in your prosecution of cases?... Well, this Committee wants evidence."[25]

Lockhart was in attendance and then testified. "Proponents of this bill seek to use [this] forum...as a launching platform," Lockhart charged, pointing out that Hansen has been "posturing for political office ever since he began his harassment program more than two years ago." To Hansen's claim that Ritter was arbitrary, Lockhart agreed that "Judge Ritter has been a controversial judge, and I think he would agree to be characterized as sometimes crotchety. It is clear that he does not tolerate fools gladly in his courtroom, and often assists them in recognizing their true identity. But the proper way to deal with these conflicts is to recognize that our legal system is designed to accommodate and resolve the inevitable conflicts between administrative and judicial branches," Lockhart reasoned. "So long as efforts to resolve these inevitable conflicts remain within the legal process, strongly held viewpoints will be expressed, but the issues will be resolved on principal and without damage to our institutions. But when politicians begin to suggest the use of political institutions to punish or chastise federal judges, Constitutionalists are obligated to speak out for the independence of the federal judiciary."[26]

Garn's bill and the controversy generated by Hansen and the other critics of Ritter were "unwarranted attacks or attempts to make political gain from unfounded attacks upon the Judiciary," John J. Flynn, professor of law at the University of Utah College of Law testified. The only legitimate question before the committee, Flynn pointed out, was whether Judge Ritter was performing the administrative duties of chief judge, and all would agree that "the Court personnel and the dispatch of its business are outstanding." Flynn continued, "The major criticisms by some of Judge Ritter have not been with his performance as Chief Judge, but with his performance as a Judge," going right to the nub of the controversy generated by Garn and Child, with the help of Behle, Hansen, Petrofsky and others, but "such matters are not only beyond the subject matter of these Hearings .... [T]hey are constitutionally beyond the authority of the Senate.... I am confident that the members of this Committee do not subscribe to such a casual disregard for the Constitutional requirements nor will the Committee tolerate such an abuse of the Senate's appropriate role in our scheme of government."[27]

Ritter did not have many defenders at the time—not in the media, the law offices, or in the streets of his town. Perhaps the most vocal and articulate were Lockhart and Flynn. Without them there might have been no debate at all, at least not at the public level. "My views represent the views of a substantial number of experienced attorneys who are appalled, disgusted, and deeply disturbed at these efforts to politicize a federal court," Flynn asserted, but they could not testify because they feared recusal motions would be filed in cases they were handling before Ritter, as they had been against Christensen. Flynn also pointed out that, because Ritter was the only remaining federal judge "grandfathered" in as a chief judge and the only person who would be affected by the legislation, "if this Committee passes a bill to remove Judge Ritter from the office of Chief Judge without a factual basis for doing so it will be recommending a law which clearly smacks of a Bill of Attainder." Flynn acknowledged that "on occasion I have personally witnessed an arbitrary attitude on the part of the Judge with certain classes of attorneys. [They] have generally consisted of attorneys who are unprepared, incompetent attorneys, attorneys utilizing delay by excessive motion practice, or attorneys making arguments or claims the Judge believed irrational." In the latter category, according to Flynn, were Hansen,[28] and many others who were extremely conservative, "while Ritter was liberal on issues such as civil liberties, labor legislation, minority rights and the Bill of Rights guarantees of the federal Constitution." As an example, Flynn referred to "rather bizarre actions of the conservative Utah Supreme Court," supported by Hansen, in which they refused to follow binding decisions of the United States Supreme Court interpreting the Bill of Rights, claiming that the Fourteenth Amendment applying such rights to the states was unconstitutionally adopted.[29] "Such a startling holding...rejected by every other court I know of, indicates the depth of the ideological split in the State [of Utah] and the intellectual 'quality' of the conservative side of that split in the legal profession," Flynn concluded. "They simply do not subscribe to his view of the law; a view generally in accord with interpretations elsewhere in the country. I leave to this Committee's judgment who is irrational, arbitrary, or wrong on the law because of this bizarre state of the law in the state courts."

Discussion then turned to Child's specification of failure to call a grand jury as one of the reasons for repeal of the grandfather clause. The *Salt Lake Tribune,* in an editorial of May 14, 1976, reported that Ritter "explained to a new Grand Jury on Monday that the prosecutor shapes and guides Grand Jury proceedings." The *Tribune* explained, "As a result, Grand Juries have become, in many instances, little more than tools of government inquisition conducted in secret," in a proceeding in which "virtually all Constitutional rights are suspended or ignored."

> Judge Ritter, in refreshing contrast to many of his colleagues on the federal bench, has taken the trouble to instruct a Grand Jury in its right to protect as well as indict, and in the past he has attempted through refusing to approve immunity grants to witnesses and by terminating the Grand Jury itself to preserve citizen's rights.
>
> How many, for instance, know that no law or right requires that a citizen be notified that he is a target of a Grand Jury investigation? Called before the jury the same individual (and all other witnesses) leaves his Sixth Amendment right to counsel at the jury room door. And, once he has answered even the most innocent question from the prosecutor (or in rare instances, a jury member) he can thereafter be compelled to incriminate himself and never mind the Fifth Amendment.
>
> If so-called use immunity is granted the witness, he can also be forced to testify against himself or others. And even though he (or she) may be guilty of no crime, refusal to talk can result in imprisonment for contempt.[30]

The problem, according to Lockhart, was Child himself, and his open hostility to the chief judge. Ritter in fact seemed to have acted in contravention of his own precept, familiar to anyone who ever appeared before him in a criminal case: "In this Court, if you want a Grand Jury, you get a Grand Jury." His maxim was but a reflection of the clause in the Fifth Amendment to the Constitution that "no person shall be held to answer for a capital, or otherwise infamous crime, unless on a presentment or indictment of a Grand Jury." In 1976 he had recoiled from that rule and was refusing to call a grand jury. His refusal tied Child's hands, for unless a defendant waived indictment by a grand jury he could not proceed. "There is reason for the prosecutor to be concerned about his need for the investigative and charging power of the Grand Jury," Lockhart explained. "But there is equally good reason for a responsible judge to be concerned about the prosecutor's easy control of the Grand Jury or the possible misuse of grants of immunity." The problem is one "on which there is a reasonable basis for differences of opinion."[31] The threat of such abuse, according to Lockhart, was the reason for Ritter's refusal to call a grand jury, at least with the regularity Child would have liked.

> It is true that Judge Ritter occasionally expressed what I considered unfounded hostility toward Mr. Ramon Child, my successor as U.S. Attorney. Judge Ritter was fully aware that Mr. Child had been an important political supporter of Senator Jake Garn, who has constantly sought to obtain media attention through unrestrained public and personal attacks on the judge. The judge's comments about that appointment left no doubt that he regarded Mr. Child's appointment as highly political in origin and purpose. For that reason he expressed great concern about the potential danger of a politically-motivated prosecutor with power to manipulate a sitting grand jury. It was clear to me that those concerns were the primary reason for Judge Ritter's later discharge of the Grand Jury that was sitting at the time Mr. Child assumed office.[32]

While the hearings on repeal of the grandfather clause, and events leading up to them, were in progress, a campaign against Ritter was developing in the office of Child and in the Justice Department. Though he admitted during the Senate hearings that the only way to remove a U.S. judge under the Constitution was by impeachment, Child embarked upon a campaign to restrict his powers. Brent Ward, formerly legislative assistant to Senator Wallace F. Bennett and trial lawyer in the Department of Justice, arrived in

January 1976 to work in Child's office and found himself in the midst of the first two of what were to become a series of attempts at mandamus against Ritter in the United States Court of Appeals for the Tenth Circuit.

The first was filed January 19, 1976, with the support of solicitor general Robert H. Bork, asking for mandamus against Ritter's practice of deferring consideration of pretrial motions filed by defendants in criminal cases until after a jury had been sworn, thus ensuring that jeopardy attached if the motion was granted. The court of appeals granted the request, ordering that such motions be disposed of at least ten days before trial. The second, filed April 20, 1976, asked for mandate against Ritter's discharge of a grand jury, Ritter believing that use of a grand jury as an investigative tool of the prosecutor, rather than as a protection of the accused, was improper. The second petition was denied, but the court retained jurisdiction. Ward was of the opinion that the retention of jurisdiction was a continuing threat that, if Ritter "stepped out of line," a writ would be issued.[33]

While the first two petitions were pending, Ward developed a "Ritter strategy," with the knowledge, approval, and participation of Child. They proposed on February 3, 1976, that the United States Department of Justice petition the court of appeals to remove Judge Ritter from "trials of criminal matters, and possibly even civil matters, involving the federal government." The Justice Department refused, and suggested that petitions be filed "piecemeal," or on a case-by-case basis, for any abuse that might occur. Benjamin Civiletti, assistant attorney general, Criminal Division; George Gulinsky, chief of the Appellate Section; and Victor Stone of the Appellate Section staff were of the opinion that "there [was no] legal support for the course of action the United States Attorney seeks to pursue here, as compared with, for example, impeachment."[34]

Child and Ward took the "piecemeal" directive as an invitation to petition the court of appeals "every time an abuse occurred," and according to their own perception of what an "abuse" consisted of. Throughout 1976 and early 1977 they filed a chain of petitions for mandamus to require Ritter to permit nonresident attorneys of the Justice Department not members of the bar of his court to appear before the grand jury, to delay criminal trials when Child claimed he did not have sufficient time to prepare, to prohibit scheduling cases on a trailing calendar, to remove him from a particular case, to require that petty offenses be tried in the federal court, to require consent of the United States to waiver of jury trial by criminal defendants, to require the use of a magistrate for minor offenses, and to require him to produce certain transcripts. "Well, ladies and gentlemen of the jury, the

U.S. Attorney, Mr. Ramon Child, didn't like the way I was running this Court," Ritter explained when it became necessary to send a jury home because a case collapsed with a guilty plea. He was prohibited from scheduling a trailing calendar, which would have economized the time of the jury, because "he got the Circuit Court to impose this calendar on me, one case a day. Now my system has always been to have a case standing by so that when we bring you in, 50 or 60 jurors, we have something for [you] to do when the cases go off.... [W]hen that happens we waste the time of the jurors because the U.S. Attorney has nothing for you to do." Ritter explained to the jurors that Child had "never been in my courtroom, never practiced in the federal court," but "now he's busying himself embarrassing me, embarrassing the Court [and] imposing on the time of the jurors by this sort of business." He proclaimed that "this is a strange way to run a railroad, or a court or anything else. When we get through we'll summarize this whole thing and I'll have something very strong to say about it."[35]

By late 1976, Child and his assistants were nigh insolent to Ritter. He had nullified Child's petition seeking delay in the criminal trials scheduled the preceding October by indicating that his calendar was "too hastily prepared by me and not artfully drawn" and that a new calendar would begin on November 8, 1976. Assistant United States Attorney Steven Snarr appeared on that date. "You folks understand when we call the calendar, we start the cases?" Ritter inquired of Child's deputy. "No, I didn't," Snarr replied. He added that he understood that was the practice, but that it was the subject matter of the mandamus petitions filed with the circuit court. "Methinks there is a viper in it. And I am proceeding to deal with it," Ritter declared.[36]

On July 11, 1977, solicitor general Wade McCree, in a letter to Judge David T. Lewis, asked the court of appeals to consider certifying Judge Ritter as mentally or physically disabled, for purposes of the judicial tenure act, and removing him as being unable to discharge the duties of his office.[37] Lewis, an essentially good, fair-minded man, refused. Moreover, Lewis was still feeling the rebuke of the United States Supreme Court a few years earlier when the Judicial Council, consisting of all active judges of the Tenth Circuit Court of Appeals, en banc, took similar action against Stephen S. Chandler, chief judge of the Western District of Oklahoma. "What the Judicial Council did when it ordered [Judge Chandler] to 'take no action whatsoever in any case or proceeding now or hereafter pending' in his court was to do what [only the United States Senate, sitting as a] Court of Impeachment can do," Justices William O. Douglas and Hugo S.

Black warned the Judicial Council. They cautioned further that "an independent judiciary is one of this Nation's outstanding characteristics," and echoing Ritter's letters to Judge Christensen during their dispute over administration of the District of Utah, "once a federal judge is confirmed by the Senate and takes his oath, he is independent of every other judge. He commonly works with other federal judges who are likewise sovereign. But neither one alone nor any number banded together can act as censor and place sanctions on him. Under the Constitution the only leverage that can be asserted against him is impeachment, where pursuant to a resolution passed by the House, he is tried by the Senate, sitting as a jury."[38]

Judge Lewis, recognizing that an attack on the least of judges was an attack on them all, was unwilling to suffer further rebuke by taking even more aggressive action against Ritter. "The wise authors of our Constitution provided for judicial independence because they were familiar with history," Justice Black explained in the *Chandler* case. "They knew that judges of the past—good, patriotic judges—had occasionally lost not only their offices but also sometimes their freedom and their heads because of the actions and decrees of other judges."[39] Bork, Garn, Child, Ward, Hansen, and their claque of critics were unaware of the lessons of history. Their attacks on Ritter continued.

Frank H. Easterbrook of the solicitor general's office telephoned Ward with instructions to prepare a petition for a writ of mandamus preventing Ritter from handling cases involving the United States. Easterbrook and Bork had been in favor of such action since early 1977 but had been unable to overcome objections of Civiletti, Gulinsky, and Stone that the move was illegal and ill-advised. Ward swept aside the constitutional objection. He dismissed their protest as "nothing more than a flimsy bureaucratic self-justification reflecting a reluctance to depart from an original position, once expressed."[40]

By late 1977, perhaps because of Burdick's chiding during the grandfather-clause hearings, Child had a change of heart. He no longer cooperated in Ward's proposals, but Ward and Assistant United States Attorney Jim McConkie went "behind his back" and continued lobbying the Justice Department in favor of filing the petition. The most they could persuade Child to do was sign a letter backing a move by Senator Orrin Hatch, the new junior senator from Utah, to add a third judge to the District of Utah. A proposed draft was prepared by Ward, and the broad-based petition against Ritter was finally filed on October 5, 1977,[41] over the objections of Civiletti, Gulinsky, and Stone.

Lockhart again came forward. Based on presence at rule days in which the United States had any significant business, and "frequent and extended conferences with Judge Ritter in chambers attempting to work out procedures for resolving problems or differences... [regarding] issues which the government's petition suggests as indicative of Judge Ritter's bias against the government," Lockhart saw "no evidence [of] bias or general animus against the government." Lockhart declared that, "To the contrary," Ritter "frequently expressed great pride in our system of government, particularly in its adherence to Constitutional limitations." And he "frequently expressed concern about failure of the government to assume a more active or aggressive posture" in securities enforcement or police misconduct cases. Lockhart conceded that Ritter "frequently expressed strong views about particular litigating positions taken by the government in cases of public interest such as the government's claim of authority for warrantless electronic surveillance... [and] possible conduct of some government attorneys" before the grand jury, but his statements were "frequently balanced with explicit expressions of approval of other government attorneys," including Assistant United States Attorney Max Wheeler, a member of Child's staff.[42]

On October 11, 1977, the by then ancient charges of womanizing were revived when columnist Jack Anderson appeared on ABC's *Good Morning America* and claimed that twenty-eight years earlier, when he was "an investigative reporter for the late Drew Pearson, I found out that Judge Willis Ritter had stuck the Government with the bills for a long-distance romance with a girlfriend in Albuquerque" and that "he charged the taxpayers for his long-distance telephone calls to the girl and for a cross-country trip to visit her." Revival of those charges was clearly inspired by Child, for Anderson went on to say that "the Justice Department is investigating allegations that Judge Ritter was involved in some payroll shenanigans... detailed in a confidential letter from U.S. Attorney Ramon Child... rais[ing] the possibility that Ritter secured salary payments for his personal secretary while she was supposed to be on leave without pay."[43]

The House Judiciary Committee met in late October 1977. The proposed repeal of the grandfather clause was disapproved. Garn renewed his assault on Ritter by proposing an amendment to the omnibus judgeship bill, United States Senate Bill 11, to create a third judge in the District of Utah as proposed by Hatch.[44] Hatch had been elected in 1976 to the seat formerly occupied by Frank E. Moss, and secured for himself a seat on the Judiciary Committee. Hatch was instrumental in causing the subcommittee of the Judiciary Committee to adopt the amendment proposed by Garn, this time without any notice to Ritter or opportunity for him or other opponents to be heard.[45]

Thus, Garn, now with the collaboration of Hatch, seized on the same tired old tactic pursued by Arthur Watkins since 1954: dilution of Ritter's office by the appointment of another United States District Judge. A third judge was not needed, just as a second judge was not needed when A. Sherman Christensen was appointed in 1954, but now the tactic had a different effect. Conversion of the District of Utah into a three-judge court had the effect of eliminating Ritter's status as chief judge under the grandfather clause, for the clause, by its terms, applied only to two-judge courts. There was no change in Ritter's power or authority. He remained the senior judge of the District of Utah. He was merely subjected to the gratuitous insult of being stripped of his authority, without notice to him or the opportunity of hearing, to hire and fire personnel and otherwise control the administration of affairs of the District of Utah. The vice in the ploy had implications beyond Ritter's status as chief judge. The entire balance of the federal judiciary was upset, for there were other districts with far greater need for additional judges, based on the prescribed criteria of the number of assigned cases per federal judge.[46] There was no reason for a third judge in the District of Utah other than as an attack of Ritter.

On November 9, 1977, the House Judiciary Committee approved by voice vote Garn's amendment. The Ritter critics realized, at least in part, their vengeful designs by the political maneuver of Garn and Hatch, smacking as it did of a bill of attainder warned by Professor John Flynn. The separation-of-powers problem and independence of the judiciary principle were finally ignored.

There was no longer any doubt that Willis W. Ritter's judgeship was under full siege.[47] Neither can there be any doubt that the entire object of the siege was circumvention of the Constitution vis-à-vis impeachment. The internal memorandum of the Justice Department in fact acknowledges that securing "means for disciplining and removing an unfit judge short of impeachment" was "worthwhile" and had "always been in mind" from the time when the siege was launched.[48] It was clear that critics in his home state of Utah were not just critical of his compassionate dealing with youthful offenders, minorities, and victims of what he saw as inequities in the criminal system. Those who complained about him often cited what they saw as his soft attitude toward murderers, thieves, and muggers as reasons he should never have been confirmed and should be removed. Criticism had been building for all of his adult life, certainly dating from the confirmation hearings and extending throughout his judicial tenure. Nevertheless, by the end of 1977, the campaign to repeal the grandfather clause came to an end, after the appointment of a third judge. The final scene in the lifelong saga that was the life and career of Willis W. Ritter was now set to begin.

20

CONSUMMATION

> This is life and all there is to life; to play the game, to play the cards we get; play them uncomplainingly and play them to the end. The game may not be worth the while. The stakes may not be worth the winning. But the playing of the game is the forgetting of self, and we should be game sports and play it bravely to the end.
>
> —Clarence Darrow

WILLIS W. RITTER'S THOUGHTS ABOUT LIFE, and its abolition, death, were collected in his personal papers, in these "Last Words" of the inspiration of his legal career, Oliver Wendell Holmes.[1]

> There is time to hear the kind voice of friends and to say to one's self: "The work is done."
>
> But just as one says that, the answer comes: "The race is over, but the work is never done while the power to work remains."
>
> . . . .
>
> For to live is to function. That is all there is in living.
>
> And so I end with a line from a poet who uttered the message more than fifteen hundred years ago: "Death plucks my ears and says, Live—I am coming."

On one of their trips together checking on probationers, Ritter and Bernie Rhodes took their usual route from Mount Carmel Junction on Highway 89 through Zion National Park to St. George. Ritter had been drinking and began explaining his ideas about death, religion, and God. They stopped for pie and coffee at a place just outside the park called Bumbleberry Inn where there was a collection of horse-drawn carriages, stage coaches, and similar vehicles, arranged in a circle for tourists to view. Rhodes drove around the display and Ritter spied two horse-drawn hearses, one macabre black and in poor repair and the other white. Ritter had seen such things growing up in Park City. "Get out of here! Get out! Oh, my

God," Ritter pleaded. Rhodes had also been drinking and, emboldened by the alcohol, was just enough under the influence to stop, light a cigarette, then drive around the display again. He drove around again and watched Ritter put his hands over his eyes, realizing how afraid of death Ritter was.[2]

In retrospect, many, perhaps most, of the controversial aspects of Ritter's career seem to have had their origin in, or were the product of the contention produced by, his confirmation hearings. The Cardall case was a notable example. The incidents with Pratt Kesler and Swede Larson were of the same flavor. Jack Gallivan, publisher of the *Salt Lake Tribune* and his friend and confidant during their frequent trips back to Park City, believed that the wounds inflicted by the confirmation process damaged Ritter's personality in a way he could never overcome. Certainly, the disruption of the Ritters' marriage, which before then had been a happy one, and perhaps ideal, at least until the time of his OPA service, was directly caused by spreading unsubstantiated rumors of marital misconduct on the public record and in the news media.

Incredibly, according to the FBI, it was not Senator Arthur V. Watkins, or his administrative aid, Richard Cardall, but Senator Elbert Thomas who disregarded confidentiality and leaked damaging information to the news media. The FBI concluded, more incredible still, that Thomas did so in a conspiracy with Ritter:

> During the course of the political battle over [Ritter's] confirmation…the reports of our investigation were read to an executive session of the Judiciary Committee of the Senate at which session the then Senator Elbert Thomas was present. There was also a leak of information to Drew Pearson, and in view of the fact that when we subsequently were investigating Senator Thomas…there was a definite leak/information (all of it false) from Thomas, to Drew Pearson, there is little doubt as to where Pearson got his information about our investigation of Ritter.[3]

What motivation Thomas, or Ritter, would have had to leak negative information, destructive of the Ritter home and family, "all of it false," is impossible to conceive.

It is clear that something in Ritter changed after his confirmation hearings. Before then, during his recess appointment, if not a model of judicial temperament his demeanor was at least sufficiently subdued to satisfy his most ardent critics. Knox Patterson is a prominent example. It is unlikely that Ritter was putting on a show, knowing that his conduct was under scrutiny, for doing so for the entire period would be improbable. Even on that assumption, however, the period of his recess appointment illustrates the judicial capacity Ritter was capable of.

Always difficult, because of the combination of his superior intellect and impatience with those not up to his own mental acuity, he became more crotchety as time went by. Most noticeable was the turnaround after the confirmation hearings, but he became even more difficult during the final years of his judicial tenure. It is possible that the combination of loneliness and drinking broke down his earlier restraint, for the trait was also displayed from time to time during his teaching career.

Was Willis W. Ritter mentally unbalanced, as Verl Ritchie and Bernice Gibson suggested? We leave that to those with the skills to make such an evaluation. If so, it is clear that his intellect was never affected. It is also clear that if unbalanced, it was at an early period while still a law professor and that something stripped away his ability or willingness to control his destructive impulses as his judicial career progressed. That something may have been triggered by his unrelenting anger, which he was clearly capable of, over the injustice of attacks during his confirmation, or it may have been the effect of alcohol abuse in later years.

On January 26, 1977, Ritter conducted a proceeding for the admission of recent law school graduates to the bar of the United States District Court for the District of Utah. "There are some who are talking about bringing my term of office to an end," he declared in the course of the proceedings, apparently alluding to the "siege" then in progress. "Forget it. I'm going to be here. That is a decision that I am going to let the Lord make. That is one decision I'm not going to make. I'm going to let the Lord make that decision. I'm going to be around. My work isn't finished here."[4]

During 1977 he had a falling-out with Spence VanNoy, his bailiff for many years, and fired him. Royal Buttars assumed the duties of bailiff, in addition to U.S. marshal. VanNoy offered to "tell all" for five thousand dollars to CBS's *60 Minutes,* which VanNoy knew had already interviewed Ritter and was preparing to do a story.

During mid-1977, Ritter, Bernie Rhodes, and Vicki Jolley went to the Room at the Top, a bar at the Hilton Hotel in Salt Lake City. Ritter had a leather valise filled with bottles of his favorite liquors—Chevis Regal, Wild Turkey, Beefeaters, Cognac, and so on. After several hours of drinking, they decided to go to Elko or Jackpot, Nevada. Rhodes went to the telephone but reported back that no charter flight was available. Ritter was drunk by then and launched into derisive discourse on all of the people at the court he had fired. "I fired Spence VanNoy," he blustered, and Verl Ritchie, and Andrew John Brennan, who had preceded Ritchie as clerk of court, followed by denunciations of each of them as disloyal. "And you're not immune, Rhodes. I'll fire you! And you're not either," he declared, turning to Vicki. "I'll fire you!" "And I'll fire you!" Vicki answered back. Ritter staggered off to relieve himself. While he was gone, Rhodes put all of the liquor back in the leather valise, took it, and left with Vicki. He drove Vicki home, then went to his own home. His wife, Judy, told him that the judge had been calling every ten minutes. Rhodes ignored the calls and went to bed.

It was the end of any effective relationship between Ritter and the last two of his intimates at the court. There was no amorous encounter between Rhodes and Vicki that night, but Rhodes knew Ritter would believe that there was. The next day Rhodes saw Vicki in the corridor and asked how much trouble they were in. "I think I will be able to keep my job," Vicki explained, "but I am not sure about you." Vicki in fact was fired, but not until after Ritter's death.[5] Rhodes went to Ritter's chambers, to try to make amends. The judge refused to see him. "It is not a big thing, and does not merit discussion," he declared.

At the next rule day, when the first criminal defendant was to be sentenced and it was time for Rhodes to make his report, he just stood there, saying nothing. Ritter looked the other way, away from Rhodes. There was silence. After about ten minutes, Ritter said, "Bernie, are you going to tell me about this man or do I have to guess?" Rhodes still said nothing, resolved that if Ritter would not address him respectfully, as "Mr. Rhodes," he would not report. Their relationship was never repaired, although Rhodes continued in the office of chief of probation until Ritter's death, and beyond.[6]

Ritter never revealed himself to others. He never complained when not feeling well, never allowed others to see any weakness in him. By the end of 1977, however, the specter of death overcame him. On December 14, 1977, Ritter was in the middle of a criminal trial. Sensing that he needed to go the hospital, he excused the jury, dismissed court, and made his way to the elevator on the second floor near his chambers. It was about two o'clock and was to be his last time at the courthouse, and his final exit from the building. He stepped into the elevator. Before he could push the button for the ground floor, two young men, apparently Native Americans, got in the elevator and pushed the button for the fourth floor, taking the elevator up instead of down. Ritter protested, and one of the youths "bumped the jurist in an abusive manner." Royal Buttars detained the two men for about two hours, then released them. Ritter got himself to the University of Utah Medical Center, where he was admitted for an undisclosed ailment.[7] He stayed for a few days, then received outpatient treatment for several days longer for what was diagnosed as fluid in the lungs.

He suffered a relapse very quickly, and was admitted to Holy Cross Hospital. Rita rushed to see him, and they evidently reconciled their differences. She said that they were closer in feeling, if not in words, than ever before.[8]

He remained the gourmand, even on his deathbed. Tired of hospital food, he asked Nancy to bring some Dover sole, which he was particularly fond of, from La Parisien. Max Mercier prepared the meal himself and had it ready for Nancy to rush to the hospital, piping hot, on fine china and with the linen napkins Ritter always preferred. Ritter was dying, but uncovered the dish, surveyed the lovely dinner, and with fork poised, looked at his daughter and demanded to know: "How much did he charge you for this?"[9]

Nancy telephoned Wally Sandack, informing him Ritter was in the hospital with prostate cancer and cancer of the bladder. He had it for some time, but the doctors would periodically clean him out and he would leave the hospital. "My father, the great lawyer and tax expert that he is, does not have a will!" "Who is his lawyer?" Sandack inquired. "Who took care of his matters on the farm?" It was Don Holbrook, Nancy informed Sandack, who was not available, but George Larsen did his tax work. Sandack got Larsen, and the two of them went to Ritter's private room at the hospital. When they arrived, Ritter was smiling—he was always smiling—but it was evident he was in pain. "We understand you haven't got a will." Sandack said. "Yeah, I should have done that a long time ago," Ritter admitted, and they offered him their services. Ritter wanted to leave half of everything to Rita, his "beloved, beautiful and wonderful wife," among many other generous superlatives he used to describe her. The rest, he wanted to go to his four children.

Larsen went with Sandack to his office, dictated a will, and brought it back to the hospital about four thirty. An intern and a doctor at the hospital witnessed the execution of Ritter's will. He ordered up a bottle of champagne he had on ice, and they toasted the occasion. "His mind was always there," Sandack recalled. "I never knew him, whether well or not well, to show any flagging of his mental ability. He had a mind like a trap. He loved stories, especially Jewish stories. He would roar!"

The first week in January 1978, Ritter lay on his deathbed at Holy Cross Hospital in Salt Lake City. It was the first month of his seventy-ninth year. His heart was failing due to a sclerotic major artery.

On Sunday evening, January 8, 1978, as he lay ill in the hospital, "The USA vs. Judge Ritter" was broadcast on CBS's *60 Minutes.* Brent Ward claimed that it was instigated, or influenced, by Bob Hansen, Ramon Child, Ward, and the Justice Department, and Hansen admitted that he gave numerous documents to CBS in an effort to get them to do a story critical of Ritter.[10] His friends and supporters would have thought no better of the segment had Ritter been in prime condition that night, sitting in an easy chair with friends around him and his favorite Wild Turkey in his hand. To those who counted him a good judge, a brilliant man, a powerful ally of the powerless, or a sentry keeping the establishment honest, of whom there were many, the broadcast was the more offensive for the coincidence of its timing.

Ritter had become notorious among lawyers in general and government lawyers from Washington, D.C., in particular, and to a considerable extent among the general public, as a maverick—for protecting Indians and their ponies, for banning photographers from the courthouse, or interrupting a trial to have an artist making sketches in the back of the courtroom expelled, for ordering removal of a monument bearing the Ten Commandments from public grounds, for ordering workmen or postmen brought before him when they made too much noise, for ordering the waters out of a national monument, for staying the execution of convicted murderers at the last minute, for imposing harsh prison sentences for cutting Christmas trees, or singing "Some Enchanted Evening" in his powerful bass voice at any restaurant or club he chose. He had become a painful thorn in the collective side of those of propriety and conservative political and social views, which included most public officials and lawyers. If the measure of a man be taken by the quality of his enemies, Ritter's were a corps to be proud of. "I love my enemies," he said on occasion, and those hearing his words knew they were meant not just in the biblical sense.

Commentator Mike Wallace began the broadcast by describing the efforts to remove Ritter, or curtail his power, as an attempt to "resolve" a dilemma brought on by an "erratic" and "tyrannical" federal district court judge. Federal judges, Wallace said, are "the most powerful men in the nation," and can be removed only by impeachment. But if one turns out not to be criminal, but only "erratic" or "tyrannical," what is to be done? "You will not hear from him on this broadcast," Wallace continued, "because he refuses public comment...would not even approve our taking pictures of him, but you will hear a good deal of criticism of him, criticism he sneers at, for...[they will have to] 'take me off the bench feet first,'" Ritter had declared.

Wallace then summarized the venom accumulated against Ritter for almost three decades, beginning with the scandal of his confirmation hearings, running through the Gary Gilmore execution and the claims of attorney general Griffin Bell and United States Attorney Ramon Child that Ritter was biased against the United States. He repeated their claims that Ritter brought the judicial process into "disrespect." An unnamed adversary was quoted as saying he was "arbitrary, tyrannical, arrogant and abusive," and "his prejudices so violent, his respect for others so lacking, his integrity so questionable as to make him unfit for calm objectivity and absolute honesty." The phraseology was so similar to that of the 1949 confirmation hearings, and of Garn, Hansen and Child who repeated those charges, as to leave little doubt of the source.

The trailing calendar, Child's pet peeve, was Wallace's next point. It puts pressure on the prosecutor or plaintiff's lawyer, and the expense of keeping witnesses waiting multiplies his or her costs. "We had been preparing cases, filing cases, criminal matters, for many months and getting very little activity," Child told Wallace. "But all of a sudden, in a panic situation, they were all put on the calendar at once. We were told on the 12th of December to be ready with every case on the 18th of December....We didn't have all of our witnesses there, and in those cases where we didn't have the witnesses present, the cases were dismissed." Defenders of such scheduling, it was pointed out, claim that it is more efficient and results in economic use of judicial staff and facilities, saving expense and promoting expeditious resolution of the public business. When trials end early, or cases are resolved "on the courthouse steps," there is not the loss of time, space, and money resulting from firm settings.

Following Child's whining complaints, Robert Hansen, by then Utah attorney general, aired his complaints. "When have you last sat down and talked to this man?" Wallace queried. "He won't talk to me," Hansen explained. "He does not like me, and whatever chance the State had would be totally lost were I to appear personally in that courtroom." Hansen then restated the "statistics" gathered by Julius Petrofsky and asserted that Ritter favored firms representing him in the dispute over the islands in the Snake River or in other matters such as Georgia-Pacific. Hansen confessed that he hired those same firms to represent the State of Utah, but denied that he did so because they were the best lawyers. He said it was necessary to get "a fair hearing."

Wallace then summarized the "siege" of 1977. In October 1977 the United States Justice Department filed a petition with the United States Court of Appeals for the Tenth Circuit requesting that Judge Ritter be removed from their cases. Four days later, the State of Utah petitioned that the same be done with regard to its cases. The reasons advanced by both were the same, and appear to have been coordinated. "And…the House Judiciary Committee," Wallace said, "which has for years been hearing about…'a judicial nightmare' in Utah, recently voted to add a third federal judge in Ritter's territory." The segment was closed, following similar complaints by Lynn Packer, a reporter for the Mormon Church–owned television station, by saying that *60 Minutes* had been trying for six months to get the judge to appear on the program, but he had refused on grounds that it would be improper for a sitting judge to comment publicly.

He did talk to Wallace privately, however—for three hours. "Scoundrels!" Ritter called his critics, and worse. "I would like to report in some detail—and in the judge's colorful language—just what he told me," Wallace concluded, "but about 10 minutes into our conversation he said his remarks were off the record."

CBS appears to have been nosing around Albuquerque, trying to confirm allegations in the 1949 confirmation hearings of an affair, for a card was delivered to Ritter's chambers from Mrs. Phyllis K. Heikkila, postmarked December 19, 1977. Mrs. Heikkila was the former Phyllis Katz. Ritter may have never seen her card, for it was delivered after he had gone to the hospital, and he never returned to his court. Vicki Jolley may be the only person who saw it, and its significance would be unknown to her. In it, Phyllis said that "on the 12th" she "talked with" George Taylor, for whom she was secretary at the OPA in 1944, "by phone." "He's…on your side," Phyllis assured, possibly with reference to the coming *60 Minutes* segment, "even tho he doesn't know the whole story."[11]

What "whole story" Taylor did not know was not explained. It is clear that, even after thirty-three years, Phyllis and Ritter, whom she referred to as "My Dear Bill," remained in communication with one another. "For auld lang syne," Phyllis concluded. Being personal in nature, unrelated to business of the court, the note may not have been there for inspection had it been delivered to or seen by Ritter.

None of Ritter's defenders, of whom there were many, were interviewed. People from all over the country, many of whom had never heard of him, sent him letters of support. One was found, after his death, from Stephen S. Chandler, dated January 24, 1977—the same chief judge of the United States District Court for the Western District of Oklahoma who had been the victim of an attempt to limit his own judicial powers during the "siege" on Willis W. Ritter. It was on official court letterhead, but with the word *Chief* crossed out before the title *Judge.* "Greetings and blessings on your birthday," the letter read. "I revere you as a judge and person," Chandler affirmed, and "consider you the finest judge in the 10th Circuit or anywhere else for that matter.... You have made a great contribution to mankind through the wise administration of your trust, meting out justice, love and divine fearlessness. So few nowadays seem to know what a judge *is,* what he should be, what he *must* be. But you know, my dear friend.... God will continue to go before you making the crooked road straight," the letter concluded. It was signed "With sincere respect and affection, Steve."[12]

"It was a bit biased, to put it mildly," Mary Blattner wrote of the *60 Minutes* segment, from Reno, Nevada, "but it brought back memories," including "when you swore in Bobby and John as your deputies, and when you found you couldn't give them current badges, sent away for those Dodge City ones, which they still have and treasure." "I have been praying for you and I hope you will be well soon," read a "missed your birthday" card from Sister Marie Camille received during the last week of January 1978. It was signed "Marie McDonough." Another "get well" card dated January 13, 1978, was from Bill Dye, son of Joseph Dye, brother to Ritter's aunt Mary.[13]

The end was near. Ritter knew it. The last twenty-one of his Navajo weavings, "the things I'm most proud of...a treasure, all of it, a trove of western Indian cultural history" that had adorned his judicial chambers, were donated to the Utah Museum of Fine Arts, located on the University of

Utah campus. They included a Two Grey Hills tapestry woven by Annie Redwiskers that was selected grand winner of all crafts at the 1950 Gallup, New Mexico, Intertribal Ceremonial. He had already made two separate gifts of the artifacts to the museum in 1973 and 1975. A special exhibit of Indian textile craftsmanship, to begin March 5, 1978, was titled "The Navajo Weaver: The Judge Willis W. Ritter Collection." It included more than 130 rugs, blankets, and items of Indian dress either held by the museum or on loan to the museum expressly for the exhibit. He would never live to see the exhibit. "You have at all times recognized the intrinsic frailties of human nature," one of his admirers wrote, "and have made allowances.... [I]f there is anything to this hereafter business you will receive and merit everything the Deity has to offer."[14]

The petitions of the Justice Department and of the State of Utah to remove him from consideration of their cases were never to be decided.[15] The brief of Ritter, discussing the constitutional and jurisdictional questions presented by the petitions, was nevertheless filed with the court of appeals for their "historical significance" and to make his "analysis of these matters of public record."[16] Two days before Ritter died, Joseph Rosenblatt, his former client and then chairman of the hospital Ritter was in, visited him in the intensive care unit. He was as alert and sound of mind as he had ever been. As Rosenblatt was leaving, Ritter was warm in his expressions of friendship and gratitude. "The tragedy is not what he was, but what he might have been," Rosenblatt astutely remarked.[17] He was a contradiction, truly great in both big and small ways.

Among the last of his friends and supporters to see him alive was Utah governor Scott M. Matheson, who had served as Ritter's law clerk during the Braasch and Sullivan proceedings. Ritter was always proud that "one of my law clerks became governor." Learning that he was in the hospital, Matheson went to see him and was told "the Judge was receiving no visitors." Matheson told the head nurse who he was and asked her to find out if he felt up to seeing him for a few minutes. The storied judge said yes, then didn't want Matheson to leave, although he was heavily sedated and sinking fast.[18] He died March 4, 1978, at Holy Cross Hospital. The autopsy, summarized by C. Hilman Castle, Ritter's long-standing physician, attributed death to "severe sclerosis and narrowing of all coronary arteries, which produced insufficient blood supply to the heart and ischemia and infarction of the left ventricle." There was no residual evidence of the kidney tumor that had been removed and had spread to the bladder, although the right kidney had been removed and there was scarring in the bladder secondary to the surgery.

News of Ritter's death came to Catherine Jensen as she was returning from a trip to Mexico. Ritter had been in the hospital when she left, and she was informed by the cab driver en route from the Salt Lake International Airport that he had died. Her phone rang at seven o'clock the next day, the morning of the funeral, with Nancy confirming the fact and advising of the funeral arrangements.

Rita and the family members decided that the funeral should be private, at the hospital chapel, with only members of the immediate family, other than Catherine, invited to attend. But Rita told her cousin Marjorie, the wife of Joe Jones, of the arrangements. Marjorie told Joe, and he told George Lamb. Jones and Lamb showed up at the funeral and burial, unannounced and uninvited. Rita was disconsolate over the breach in the agreed-upon arrangements for a family interment.[19] Willis W. Ritter was buried in the family plot at Charleston, Heber Valley, Utah, alongside his grandfather William Ritter and Emma Chamberlain, his grandmother and the former wife of William Ritter. An honorary rite was held for Willis W. Ritter later. Governor Scott M. Matheson and attorney John Snow both eulogized him.

After he had died, there was remorse among Ritter's intimates over the harsh treatment the chief judge had dispensed. Rhodes recalled how Ritter had abused Dick Hammer, proprietor of Dick's Café, during one of their trips to St. George. Hammer presented Ritter with a gift of a huge set of mounted steer horns, but he had walked out and left them. When Lang Foremaster, a local attorney, came to their motel to deliver the steer horns, Ritter refused them, declaring that he would not have such rubbish.

Nancy knew not only of her father's affront to Dick Hammer but also of others he had offended. She went to Bernie and prevailed upon him to write the letters of thanks and appreciation her father might have—should have—written during his lifetime, using the skills he had developed while working as chief of probation to write in Ritter's voice. Nancy then affixed Ritter's signature stamp, which was in her possession, to the letters and mailed them, together with her own letter pretending that she had found the letter in her father's personal effects, unmailed, and was sending it to carry out Ritter's wishes.

On Bernie's next trip to St. George, and his next stop at Dick's Café, the letter Bernie had composed was on display. "We have lost a dear friend," Hammer gushed. "What do you mean?" Rhodes inquired. "Why, the Judge," Hammer replied, proudly showing Bernie the words in the letter saying the steer horns were treasured and inviting Hammer to a banquet and stay at the Thousand Springs farm in honor of the gift.[20]

While Ritter was undergoing change, the farm had also been subjected to change. Offers to purchase the farm were made from time to time. "I am not too interested in selling my place," he indicated in 1959. "However, I am either going to sell it or lease it one of these days because I find myself increasingly unable to spend any time up there....My asking price is $500,000.00."[21]

The offer prompted Willis, no doubt influenced by Rita and her naturalist ethic, to decide to convert the farm to a wildlife refuge. On December 28, 1959, Willis approached the United States Fish and Wildlife Service with a proposal. "I should like to know what the mechanics of designating my property may be, as I am now presented with the problem of what to do with the place and I am considering some other possibilities."[22]

A lease to the Fish and Wildlife Service was executed on July 14, 1962, apparently tentative and as a precaution, for it was never implemented. On February 20, 1963, there was a public announcement that "subject to state approval" the "Thousand Springs in Gooding...would be made available under lease without cost by the owner, Federal Judge Willis W. Ritter of Utah." On September 27, 1963, he advised Oren Hutton that "I have made a wildlife and wild fowl refuge covering all of Thousand Springs Farms, Thousand Springs Island, Bonnyview, and all of my land above the rimrock...effective September 1, 1963....We hope to encourage the wildlife that has already come to live with us so that they may bring their families and friends."[23]

After Ritter's death, Rita lived on at the Thousand Springs farm. She continued to live at the green house and never lived in the block house. She died in November 1980 in the Twin Falls, Idaho, hospital from injuries in an automobile accident. Her grandson had been driving her big Cadillac when they were hit head-on by a drunk driver. Nancy and her sister stayed in a motel room and took twelve-hour shifts watching her. She was put on life support, from which she begged to be released. "Let me go," Rita pleaded, but there was a debate within the family, and the decision was to do everything possible to keep her alive.[24]

In March 1986, the probate court ordered Judge Ritter's estate to sell the farm. Several developers had designs on it, but the estate entered into a contract with the Nature Conservancy. The Idaho Board of Water Conservation approved an immediate application to protect the minimum stream-flow rights in the big spring, also being eyed by developers. The Nature Conservancy now operates the farm as the Thousand Springs Preserve, effectuating the preservationist designs of the Ritter family and Minnie Miller before them. The block house is maintained, with Ritter's furnishings, and the green house has been remodeled and restored.[25]

"If you want to see justice do well," Robert S. Campbell observed after Ritter's death, "it would be with two strong trial lawyers, well prepared, and with Ritter as the judge."[26] His harshest critics, if they had the willingness or capacity to be rational about it, would have to agree. For all the flaws in his character, of which there were many, he was still an unyielding, tireless bulwark against oppression by those in power, secular or religious. He was a friend of the masses and the downtrodden of the sort not often seen.

The *Salt Lake Tribune* received letters mourning his passing: "Judge Willis Ritter may have been controversial and disliked by some, but if ever there were a decent, honest, learned federal judge who loved his country, his state and his people, it was he. Truly he was a great man to match your mountains.... It will be a long time before you find another to match his impeccable honesty, courage and individuality. Melvin Belli."[27]

A letter from Robert Owings dated February 16, 1979, in his personal papers, evidently received after his death, expresses "appreciation for your handling of my case" and "reach[ing] out." Owings enclosed a study on drug abuse he had done, apparently as a term of probation imposed by Ritter, concluding, contrary to the attitude of harsh sentencing advocates, that "the expense of a multitude of years of incarceration is too much for society to pay if these young people can be given direction early in their addictions"—direction such as Ritter had provided Owings.[28]

After he was gone, and his successor appointed, Ritter's name was removed from the building directory at the north end of the Frank E. Moss U.S. Courthouse. Traces of the letters remained, however, still outlining his name. Perhaps that gave rise to the ghost stories circulated in the classical revival–style building constructed in 1902. "On weekends, a low, resonant sound goes through the building," said United States Magistrate Judge Ronald N. Boyce. "Kind of like how his voice sounded." U.S. marshals began to notice inexplicable beeps in the metal detector, and claimed that the elevator door would close, go to the second floor, and return. They took to shouting out greetings to the ghost of Chief Judge Willis W. Ritter.

"We've got to show respect," they explained. "Even if he's dead, he's still the judge."[29]

Not to worry. His Navajo rugs had been transferred to the Utah Museum of Natural History at the University of Utah shortly before his death. Where they were Willis W. Ritter's spirit would be also. Many of his paintings and personal artifacts had been sold at public auction by then.[30]

Bernie Rhodes now takes periodic trips to the little cemetery in Charleston, just to be sure he is still there and "not just in recess."

EPILOGUE

It seems as if the Department [of Justice] sees the value of the Bill of Rights as no more than an obstacle to be overcome.

—Sanford H. Kadish

Before Willis W. Ritter's minacious foreboding came to pass, he was to have the satisfaction of seeing the most controversial of his decisions, if not his judicial style, vindicated. He was clearly ahead of his time, for his opinions on criminal justice, police interrogation, and the right to counsel in particular have now become accepted standards in jurisprudence. They are, indeed, so universally accepted that few, if any, viewers of televised police court dramas would even question them.

FBI director J. Edgar Hoover did not welcome reformative views, however, and reacted to Ritter's criticism of the taking of "confessions" without affording the right to legal counsel by asking, "Just what is back of Ritter's hostility?" The "hostility" Hoover perceived was Ritter's insistence that the two drifters who murdered Howard Manzione, or juvenile defendants, such as those accused of car theft in the Denver proceedings he presided over, be informed of their right to and provided with an attorney if they so requested. Special agent Rosen, to whom Hoover's question was directed, responded that "the answer to the Director's inquiry is that Ritter is unworthy to be a Federal Judge."

Verne Alfred Braasch and Melvin LeRoy Sullivan were put to death by firing squad subsequent to the FBI memorandum. The United States Supreme Court declined consideration of the petitions in their behalf filed by Wally Sandack asserting that the pattern of law enforcement and judicial practices leading up to their arrest and conviction, the source of Ritter's "hostility," were unconstitutional.

Any United States Supreme Court practitioner can attest that denial of certiorari does not indicate that the decision of the lower courts, in this instance the Utah Supreme Court and the United States Court of Appeals for the Tenth Circuit, is correct. Neither does the granting of certiorari indicate that the lower court is wrong. Denial of the writ more often indicates, in normal circumstances and without more, that the Supreme Court merely has no space on its crowded calendar to consider the questions presented, or that for reasons of judicial politics the time has not yet come to do so. The time for consideration of when, and under what circumstances, denial of the right to counsel or refusal to appoint counsel for a defendant without the means to hire a lawyer was unconstitutional had simply not yet come.

That time came very quickly after the execution of Braasch and Sullivan. The ways the issues developed when they reached the High Court demonstrate that Ritter was ahead of the time, by more than a decade. On January 15, 1963, the United States Supreme Court considered the refusal of the State of Florida to appoint counsel for a defendant by the name of Clarence Earl Gideon, who was charged with the felony of breaking and entering a poolroom with intent to commit a misdemeanor. Gideon was indigent and asked the court to appoint counsel. The judge stated, much as the justice of the peace did in the Braasch and Sullivan case: "Mr. Gideon, I am sorry, but I cannot appoint counsel to represent you. Under the laws of the State of Florida, the only time the Court can appoint Counsel to represent a Defendant is when that person is charged with a Capital offense." Gideon replied, "The United States Supreme Court says I am entitled to be represented by Counsel." Gideon was right, his reply an astute one. The Supreme Court had ruled, many times, that the Sixth Amendment guaranteed a defendant the right to be represented by counsel, and in the federal courts persons charged with a felony were provided counsel if they could not hire their own lawyer. The question Gideon's request posed that had *not* been decided was whether the right to counsel was a right so fundamental that its denial by a state, rather than in a federal proceeding, was a disregard of due process of law guaranteed by the Fourteenth Amendment.

Gideon was compelled to act as his own lawyer, and was convicted, after which he filed a petition for a writ of habeas corpus, still acting as his own lawyer. The Supreme Court appointed Abe Fortas, prominent Washington lawyer, later a Supreme Court justice himself, to assist Gideon in presentation of his writ and advise the Court on the important constitutional questions it presented. Speaking through Justice Hugo Black, the Supreme Court ruled that the provision of the Sixth Amendment to the Constitution that "in all criminal prosecutions, the accused shall…have the assistance of counsel for his defense" was "made obligatory upon the States by the Fourteenth Amendment," and requires that "every person accused of a crime, whether state or federal, is entitled to a lawyer at trial." Ritter had so concluded as to Braasch and Sullivan, but they were already executed. "Reason and reflection require us to recognize," Black wrote further, "that in our adversary system of criminal justice, any person haled into court, who is too poor to hire a lawyer, cannot be assured a fair trial unless counsel is provided for him."[1]

On April 29, 1964, the Supreme Court considered the second aspect of Ritter's ruling in *Braasch and Sullivan:* that an accused is entitled to counsel at the time of police interrogation. The question was presented in the case of Danny Escobedo, a twenty-two-year-old Mexican with no prior criminal record and no experience with the police, who was arrested in Chicago for the murder of his brother-in-law during the commission of a crime. An accomplice told the police that Danny was the killer. When the police told him he "might as well admit to this crime," Danny said, "I am sorry but I would like to have advice from my lawyer." Danny's lawyer was right outside the room where he was being interrogated. They even waved to one another through the door, but the police would not allow Danny to talk to his lawyer until they were through questioning him. After questioning him for four hours, the police confronted Danny with the accomplice. Danny blurted out: "I didn't shoot Manuel, you did it." That declaration was exculpatory in the mind of the youthful, unsophisticated Danny Escobedo, but it led to his conviction, for he did not realize that being implicated in a crime that resulted in a homicide, even if he was not the shooter, made him guilty of murder by reason of what is known in the law as the "felony-murder" rule.[2]

Ritter ruled in *Braasch and Sullivan* that the right to counsel applied at the critical stage when incriminating statements were taken. Justice Goldberg, writing for the Court in the *Escobedo* case, made Ritter's ruling the law. Goldberg observed, and the Court agreed, that "no system worth preserving should have to *fear* that if an accused is permitted to consult with a lawyer, he will become aware of, and exercise, these rights."

The justice of the peace told Braasch and Sullivan that they could have counsel at the time of trial, but Ritter cautioned the Utah Supreme Court that counsel was necessary at every critical stage, for if not required when a suspect is initially questioned, and when a confession or admission is secured, "one can imagine a cynical prosecutor saying: 'Let them have the most illustrious counsel now. They can't escape the noose. There is nothing that counsel can do for them at the trial.'" The Danny Escobedo facts and circumstances demonstrated to the Supreme Court that Ritter was right. Justice Goldberg quoted Ritter's admonition as justification for his conclusion.[3]

In addition to counsel at the time of trial, the Supreme Court ruled that where "the investigation is no longer a general inquiry into an unsolved crime but has begun to focus on a particular suspect," counsel must be provided. If "the suspect has been taken into police custody [and] the police carry out a process of interrogations that lends itself to eliciting incriminating statement," the suspect has been denied the right to counsel if "the police have not effectively warned him of his absolute constitutional right to remain silent...and that no statement elicited by the police during the interrogation may be used against him in a criminal trial."[4]

The final question decided by Ritter in relation to Braasch and Sullivan, the youthful and inexperienced Sullivan in particular, namely, whether police may question criminal suspects of obvious limited ability without advising them of their right to counsel, was presented in 1966, when the Supreme Court considered the case of Ernesto Miranda, a seriously disturbed indigent Mexican found guilty of kidnap and rape. He had been identified by the complaining witness and questioned by police officers for two hours, without an attorney, after which the police emerged with a confession. Unlike Gideon and Escobedo, Miranda did not request counsel.

Justice Earl Warren, writing for the Supreme Court, issued the opinion resulting in the renowned and much debated "Miranda Warning," now familiar to every police officer, every criminal in the street, and virtually every member of the public. It is so familiar, and accepted, that most law enforcement officers carry cards imprinted with the warning prescribed by the Miranda case: "HE MUST BE WARNED PRIOR TO ANY QUESTIONING THAT HE HAS THE RIGHT TO REMAIN SILENT, THAT ANYTHING HE SAYS CAN BE USED AGAINST HIM IN A COURT OF LAW, THAT HE HAS THE RIGHT TO THE PRESENCE OF AN ATTORNEY, AND THAT IF HE CANNOT AFFORD AN ATTORNEY ONE WILL BE APPOINTED FOR HIM PRIOR TO ANY QUESTIONING IF HE SO DESIRES." That is "but an explication of basic rights that are enshrined in our Constitution," Justice Warren wrote, "that 'No person...shall be compelled in any criminal case to be a witness against himself,' [United States Constitution, amend. 5] and that 'the accused shall...have the Assistance of Counsel [United States Constitution, amend. 6.].'"[5]

On November 9, 1966, after his opinion on police interrogation without the benefit of legal counsel was vindicated, on all three grounds, Ritter dismissed an indictment against a defendant charged with interstate transportation of a stolen motor vehicle because agents of the FBI interrogated him in the jail, out of the presence of his lawyer, after Ritter had appointed counsel to represent him. Ritter's rebuke of the FBI, which was the subject of Hoover and Rosen's charge of "hostility" making him "unworthy," was in the flavor of and incorporated the essence of the "Miranda Warning," then being adopted. "Now, I made that appointment, and I don't intend to have my appointments of counsel circumvented in that sort of fashion. Certainly that is a circumvention of the Court's appointment. When I appoint counsel for him, I mean for him to be represented by counsel. I mean for counsel to be present at every state of the proceeding, and particularly interrogation of him in the jail house while he is in custody."[6]

Was Willis W. Ritter arbitrary, or incorrect, to order a delay in the execution of Gary Gilmore in November 1976, as attorney general Robert Hansen and his assistant, Earl Dorius, claimed? After Ritter died, among his papers was found a U.S. government office memorandum to Ritter dated April 19, 1976, by Larry Stepan summarizing the results of the *Braasch and Sullivan* litigation. "Your first opinion (discussing the constitutional questions) was cited by Justice Black, dissenting, in *In re Groban,* 352 US 330, 334 (1957), and by Justice Goldberg in *Escobedo v. Illinois,* 378 US 478 (1964) (opinion of the Court)." Ritter's handwritten note was attached to the memorandum, apparently prepared while he was considering the Gilmore case and documenting his thinking in ordering the delay. It stated:

> The Utah death penalty statute has not been held constitutional—not by the Utah State courts nor by the United States Supreme Court.
>
> Mr. Justice White, Mr. Justice Brennan and Mr. Justice Marshall emphasize that there remains "obvious serious doubts" about the validity of the statute [and] until the state courts and the United States Supreme Court have resolved those doubts and have held a Utah death penalty statute constitutional there can be no lawful execution.
>
> The consent of a convicted defendant in a criminal case gives the state no privilege to impose a ["cruel and unusual"] punishment forbidden by the 8th Amendment. The defendant has no power to agree to be executed under an unconstitutional statute.
>
> In the present state of Supreme Court decisions no one can say with assurance that the statute is constitutional.
>
> Too much uncertainty.
>
> Too much haste.[7]

The qualities of mental brilliance and dedication to the law possessed by Chief Judge Willis W. Ritter are not unique. Many judges, at all levels of the judiciary, are endowed with those qualities, in varying degrees. His independence; courage; sensitivity to the lot of the common people, outcasts, and disenfranchised of society; and in particular his disdain for the abuses of those in political or religious authority and his willingness to champion commoners against such abuses, however, are more unique and may not be seen again any time soon. A person having those qualities could ascend to the bench only under the "spoils system," in which a loyal friend like Elbert Thomas could insist on the appointment of one like Willis Ritter, over the opposition of the likes of Arthur Watkins, Ernest Wilkinson, John Boyden, and leaders of the Mormon Church or persons in authority like J. Edgar Hoover, Swede Larson, Bob Hansen, Jake Garn, and Ramon Child. The advent of judicial selection committees, which is the norm in judicial selection as the twenty-first century begins, has the effect of screening persons of controversy out of the process, yet they are the very ones required to do justice in cases of controversy. There are many who believe that a desirable result. Surely, it is true that many outstanding judges have been produced by the selection committee system, and certainly many, perhaps most of them, fit the stereotype of a silver-haired, gracious jurist.

Utah's celebrated former governor J. Bracken Lee, himself controversial, an opponent during Ritter's confirmation proceedings, and surely one from the opposite end of the political spectrum, summed it up well in a letter to Ritter on the occasion of Lee's retirement: "One thing I have admired most about you is that you have been outspoken as well as honest and considerate." All right-thinking persons, whatever their political persuasion, would, or surely should, join in Lee's affirmation that "I particularly want you to know that I appreciate what you have done to try to make this a better country."[8]

NOTES

CHAPTER I. BEGINNINGS

The personal papers of Willis W. Ritter, including those related to his judicial administration, are collected in the Willis W. Ritter Papers, Manuscripts Division, J. Willard Marriott Library, University of Utah (cited as RP).

1. George A. Thompson and Fraser Buck, *Treasure Mountain Home: A Centennial History of Park City,* 2-3; Eugene E. Campbell, *Establishing Zion: The Mormon Church in the American West,* 36; Frances M. Gibbons, *Brigham Young: Modern Moses, Prophet of God,* 166-67.

2. Carter Eldredge Grant, *The Kingdom of God Restored,* 495-96.

3. Allan Kent Powell, ed., *Utah History Encyclopedia,* 112-13, 199. Colonel Connor himself made the first silver discovery in the Wasatch Range in 1864, the Emma mine in Little Cottonwood Canyon, across the ridge from Park City. Nothing much was done with it because of the expense of hauling ore out of the rugged area by wagon, until completion of the transcontinental railroad in 1869 made possible the transportation at economical prices of large quantities of ore. Thompson and Buck, *Treasure Mountain Home,* 3.

4. Thompson and Buck, *Treasure Mountain Home,* 3.

5. Willis W. Ritter, statement to Parker Nielson, ca. April 30, 1968, in *Mitchell v. Texas Gulf Sulphur Co.,* 309 F. Supp. 548 (D Utah 1970). See Powell, *Utah History Encyclopedia,* 414. Ritter's account varies slightly from the commonly accepted version at Thompson and Buck, *Treasure Mountain Home,* 5-7, 18, which relates that "late in the fall of 1868," three of Connor's troops made their way over the ten thousand–foot pass above Bonanza Flats, above Parleys Park. "Being experienced prospectors, it was inevitable that they should find the black galena and green copper that stained the rock. Taking samples to Col. Connor they erected a dead pine pole with a bandana tied to its top as a flagstaff to mark their discovery and in doing so gave their find its name, the Flagstaff."

6. Campbell, *Establishing Zion,* 283, 312.

7. *U.S. Code,* vol. 30, secs. 22, 26; David Hampshire, "Mining Leaves Its Mark on Park City," 18. Park City was named by 150-odd inhabitants of a mining camp located there on July 4, 1872. Thompson and Buck, *Treasure Mountain Home,* 19.

8. Thompson and Buck, *Treasure Mountain Home,* 42-44; Powell, *Utah History Encyclopedia,* 451. The Utah Eastern Railroad completed a narrow-gauge line between Coalville and Park City in 1880, parallel to the Summit County Railway, which was shut down in December 1883 after Union Pacific gained control of it.

9. Thompson and Buck, *Treasure Mountain Home,* 10-17, 21.

10. Powell, *Utah History Encyclopedia,* 299.

11. Thompson and Buck, *Treasure Mountain Home,* 91, 94, 98-99.

12. Willis W. Ritter, Testimony, May 5, 1950, in Senate Subcommittee of the Committee on the Judiciary, *Hearings on the Nomination of Willis W. Ritter, of Utah, to Be United States District Judge for the District of Utah,* 204 (hereafter cited as *Denver Hearings*).

13. U.S. Bureau of the Census, *Twelfth Census of the United States;* gravestone, Charleston, Utah.

14. Emma died at thirty-five. William lived to about sixty-five. Both are buried at the family grave site in Charleston.

15. James W. Hulse, *The Silver State: Nevada's Heritage Reinterpreted,* 67-113.

16. Thompson and Buck, *Treasure Mountain Home,* 167.

17. Minnie May Ritter Halbert interview.

18. U.S. Bureau of the Census, *Thirteenth Census of the United States.*

19. Halbert interview.

20. Thompson and Buck, *Treasure Mountain Home,* 65, 192.

21. Powell, *Utah History Encyclopedia,* 452.

22. U.S. Bureau of the Census, *Twelfth Census.*

23. Salt Lake County, Recorder, Book 64, C2, Block 72, Plat A, Salt Lake City Survey, January–February 1902. Cf. James W. Beless Jr., "Episcopal Church in Utah," 80. The Episcopal Church and mine operators, associated with doctors at Camp Douglas, "formed an early day 'Medicare' program, to which ... the individual miners contributed $1.00 each month to entitle them to full hospital care, such as was available." By 1899 the program had established St. Mark's Hospital.

24. Halbert interview.

25. William James Mortimer, ed., *How Beautiful upon the Mountains,* 593.

26. Ibid., 591-92.

27. Ibid., 593.

28. Ibid., 592.

29. "Preserving the Heritage of the Homestead," author unknown, box 110, folder 18, RP.

30. Mark Smith and Jess McCarrell were the first non-Indians on record to have explored the hot pots. The hot pots were homesteaded in 1875 by Samuel Thompson, Tom Mantle, and Hyrum Shelton. Simon Schneitter purchased the property in 1878 for a farm. The purchase price was said to have been an Indian saddle horse and a secondhand sewing machine. When Park City developed into a mining center, and Park City residents began visiting to see the hot pots and craters, Schneitter decided to make it a resort. A two-story brick hotel, called Virginia House, still standing, and swimming pool supplied with warm water piped from a hole drilled at the base of the large hot pot were built in 1886. On March 10, 1888, Andrew Luke and John Busby purchased the property for six hundred dollars and renamed it Luke's Hot Pots. Thomas Monks then leased the property until Jacob Schneitter purchased it from his father, and "Dutch" Pete Kraller acquired it from Schneitter. Mortimer, *How Beautiful,* 591-96.

31. Halbert interview.

32. Ibid.

33. "Preserving the Heritage of the Homestead."

34. Halbert interview.

35. Currently, and for many years, its name has been the Homestead.

36. Halbert interview.

37. "Preserving the Heritage of the Homestead."

38. Powell, *Utah History Encyclopedia,* 623; Arthur V. Watkins, *Enough Rope: The Inside Story of the Censure of Senator Joseph McCarthy by His Colleagues,* 6-7.

CHAPTER 2. PARK CITY II

1. The population of Park City at statehood, January 4, 1896, was more than seven thousand. Thompson and Buck, *Treasure Mountain Home,* 83, 145.

2. Ibid., 42-44, 149; Powell, *Utah History Encyclopedia,* 451.

3. Thompson and Buck, *Treasure Mountain Home,* 149-50, 113, 180; Powell, *Utah History Encyclopedia,* 395.

4. Thompson and Buck, *Treasure Mountain Home,* 160-70; David Hampshire, "Remembering Park City's Great Fire," 234-38.

5. Margaret Mawhinney interview.

6. Thompson and Buck, *Treasure Mountain Home,* 176.

7. Ibid., 174, indicates that Dr. Monahan maintained "a small hospital for emergency cases at his home on Park Avenue." Directories of the day list no Dr. Monahan, but the Ritter home was on Park Avenue.

8. See Chapter 1, note 23.

9. Thompson and Buck, *Treasure Mountain Home,* 21, 33-40, 62-64, 67, 70, 92, 106-7, 134-35.

10. Ibid.

11. Ibid., 21, 120,176-77.

12. U.S. Bureau of the Census, *Thirteenth Census;* Sister Marie Camille interview.

13. Thompson and Buck, *Treasure Mountain Home,* 134-35, 177-78, 192, 204.

14. Ibid., 28-31.

15. Later, a girl scout camp was located there.

16. Mawhinney interview.

17. Ibid.

18. Halbert interview.

19. Thompson and Buck, *Treasure Mountain Home,* 197, 204.

20. Hampshire, "Mining Leaves Its Mark," 18.

21. Thompson and Buck, *Treasure Mountain Home,* 140-41; Hampshire, "Mining Leaves Its Mark," 18.

22. Thompson and Buck, *Treasure Mountain Home,* 28, 86.

23. Ibid., 170, 177.

24. Jack Gallivan interview.

25. Halbert interview; Sister Marie Camille interview.

26. Halbert interview; Nancy Ritter interview. May was carried as Willis's beneficiary of government life insurance issued during his military service.

27. Jack Green interview.

28. Thompson and Buck, *Treasure Mountain Home,* 170, 177.

29. Ida Norton and Joe Norton interview; William H. Leary, Testimony, May 2, 1950, in Senate Subcommittee of the Committee on the Judiciary, *Hearings on the Nomination of Willis W. Ritter, of Utah, to Be United States District Judge for the District of Utah,* 823 (hereafter cited as *Salt Lake City Hearings*).

30. Halbert interview. Mary and Willis Adams had moved to Sugarhouse, a suburb of Salt Lake City, on the edge of Fairmont Park.

31. Myrtle Buck interview.

32. The California Supreme Court, overall, was "considered the nation's most aggressive and progressive state court.... [Traynor was] named Chief Justice in 1964 [and] wrote more than 900 opinions, many of which boldly abandoned precedents and, especially in expanding criminal defendants' rights, anticipated later federal court rulings" ("Milestones").

33. Camille interview.

34. Park High, 1918, Graduation Program, box 1, folder 1, RP; D. Frank Wilkins interview.

35. Principal B. A. Fowler wrote of Willis W. Ritter: "In the art gallery of the White House I saw a life size photograph of the present President.... I asked a bystander whose work it was, and he said that it was done by the President's official photographer, a western man named Ritter—Willis Ritter."

36. Willis Adams was one of a group of gifted and accomplished Utah painters of the late nineteenth century. He knew, and was a personal friend to, most of the leading Utah artists of his time, including John Harwood who had studied the European masters in France, with whom Adams traded paintings. Robert S. Olpin, *Dictionary of Utah Art,* 3-4; Vern G. Swanson, Robert S. Olpin, and William C. Seifrit, *Utah Painting and Sculpture,* 97-98.

37. Craig Smay interview; "Preserving the Heritage of the Homestead," author unknown, box 11, folder 18, RP.

38. W. A. Adams, "League of Nations," March 30, 1920, box 115, folder 14, RP.

39. Halbert interview.

40. Ritter interview.

41. Pete Davies, *The Devil's Flu: The World's Deadliest Influenza Epidemic and the Scientific Hunt for the Virus That Caused It,* 45, 63. The pandemic is generally understood to have begun in the spring of 1918, with possibly the first cases in the United States at Forty Riley, Kansas, during the first week of March.

42. Thompson and Buck, *Treasure Mountain Home,* 213, 52.

43. Gallivan interview.

44. Judicial Conference of the United States, Questionnaire, n.d., 5, box 138, folder 11, RP.

45. Thompson and Buck, *Treasure Mountain Home,* 104-6, 110-13; Judy Dykman and Colleen Whitley, *The Silver Queen: Her Royal Highness Suzanne Bransford Emery Holmess Delitch Egalitcheff,* 29-49, 140.

46. Thompson, *Treasure Mountain Home,* 99, 123, 145.

47. Ibid., 104-6; Powell, *Utah History Encyclopedia,* 291-92, 299; Leonard J. Arrington and Heidi S. Swinton, *In the Utah Tradition: A History of the Governor's Mansion,* 4-6.

48. Thompson and Buck, *Treasure Mountain Home,* 210-13.

49. Ibid., 68.

50. Ritter interview.

51. Willis W. Ritter, quoted in Halbert interview.

CHAPTER 3. FRIENDS

1. See *Who's Who in America.*

2. Thompson and Buck, *Treasure Mountain Home,* 174; Halbert interview; Judicial Conference of the United States, Questionnaire, n.d., 2, box 138, folder 11, RP; Roger Pusey, "Being Chief Judge Is No Snap, Either." Davies, *Devil's Flu,* 83-86, 90, describes treatment of the day, including "universal wearing of masks" and "putting sulphur in their shoes."

3. Questionnaire; Leary, Testimony, *Salt Lake City Hearings,* 820.

4. Donald N. Zillman, "The University of Utah College of Law: An Analytical History, Part II," 10-16.

5. Ibid.; Ritter interview; Norton and Norton interview; Questionnaire, 5.

6. Ritter to Willis and Mary Adams, October 31, 1924, RP.

7. Ibid.

8. Ibid.

9. Box 115, folder 3, RP.

10. William Kixmiller and Arnold R. Baar to University of Utah, September 8, 1941, box 121, folder 4, RP; Bill Lockhart and Lois Lockhart to Ritter, Christmas card, ca. 1968, box 125, folder 7, RP.

11. Ritter, Application, September 7, 1944, box 17, folder 4, RP.

12. Zillman, "College of Law, Part II," 15.

13. Ritter, "Jurisdiction of Board of Tax Appeals under Act of 1926," *National Income Tax Magazine* (April 1926), 128, box 109, folder 4, RP.

14. Lockhart and Lockhart to Ritter; Frankie to Ritter, 1926, box 115, folder 4, RP.

15. Federal Bureau of Investigation, "Willis W. Ritter," July 19, 1949, 4.

16. Don Lloyd, Ireta Memorial Services, February 27, 1981, 7.

17. Bowler interview; Nature Conservancy, memorandum from Chris to Fredda, "Chat with Aldrich Bowler," July 17, 1997. The primitive condition of the highway to California of the era is detailed at Edward Leo Lyman, "The Arrowhead Trails Highway: The Beginnings of Utah's Other Route to the Pacific Coast."

18. Norton and Norton interview.

19. Lloyd, Ireta Memorial Services.

20. Algie B. Ballif, *Salt Lake City Hearings,* 497, 502; George S. Ballif, Testimony, *Salt Lake City Hearings,* 487-89.

21. Lloyd, Ireta Memorial Services; Norton and Norton interview.

22. Leary, Testimony, *Salt Lake City Hearings,* 821.

23. Zillman, "College of Law, Part II," 14-15.

24. A. LaDrue Jensen interview.

25. Norton and Norton interview.

26. Halbert interview; Frankie to Ritter.

27. Ritter interview; A. L. Jensen interview.

28. Joe Jones interview; Norton and Norton interview.

29. Trustees Deed, August 30, 1935, box 75, folder 19, RP.

30. Norton and Norton interview.

31. Myrtle Austin interview.

32. Charles Wilkinson, *Fire on the Plateau: Conflict and Endurance in the American Southwest,* 325, 329.

33. Don Lloyd interview; Ritter interview; Cliff Ashton interview. "He would do anything she wanted," Ashton claimed.

34. Lloyd interview; and "Memorial Services, Judge Willis W. Ritter" attached, March 9, 1978.

35. Harold Schindler, "Ritter Navajo Collection Highlights Exhibition."

36. Ibid.

37. Kohlberg's, 429 Seventeenth Street, Denver, receipt, ca. 1953, box 119, folder 7, RP; "Judge Gives Indian Weaving to U. Museum of Fine Arts," in box 207, folder 11, RP; Berlant Associates, Inc., appraisal, box 207, folders 6-11, RP.

38. Harold W. Bentley, ed., *The University of Utah: A History of Its First Hundred Years, 1850 to 1950,* 371-73.

39. Dorothy Snow interview.

40. Austin interview.

41. Lloyd interview; Lloyd, Ireta Memorial Services.

42. Dean R. Brimhall to Warren G. Magnuson, October 7, 1949, Brimhall Papers; Robert H. Hinckley and JoAnn Jacobsen Wells, *"I'd Rather Be Born Lucky than Rich,"* 24-25, 29, 32.

43. Hinckley and Wells, *"Lucky than Rich,"* 33; Marriner S. Eccles, *Beckoning Frontiers: Public and Personal Recollections,* 81.

44. *Salt Lake City Hearings,* 29-30; Ritter interview; W. Barton Leach to Ritter, January 17, 1939, box 9, folder 1, RP.

45. George Thomas, Testimony, *Salt Lake City Hearings,* 769.

46. Donald N. Zillman, "The University of Utah College of Law: An Analytical History, Part III," 8, quoting *Utah Chronicle,* May 11, 1932, 1 col. 1; Ritter, lecture, "What the Law Is in a Changing World," box 13, folder 15, RP.

47. Zillman, "College of Law, Part III," 8; Lee Nebeker and eight others, ca. spring 1929, box 12, folder 3, RP.

48. Nebeker et al., spring 1929, box 12, folder 3, RP.

49. Ritter, lecture notes, box 125, folder 7, RP.

50. Willis W. Ritter, "Lifting Law," box 211, RP.

51. Calvin Rampton interview; Joe McCarthy interview; Herschel Saperstein interview.

52. Ritter, Notes, n.d., box 1, folders 2-7, RP; ibid., 1938-1939, folders 9-13; box 2, folders 1-17, RP; A. Wally Sandack interview.

53. Ritter interview.

54. McCarthy interview; Bill Lang interview.

55. Board of Regents, Minutes, February 16, 1932, George Thomas Presidential Records, 32; Zillman, "College of Law, Part II," 10; Ritter to Thomas, December 20, 1932, Thomas Presidential Records, box 117.

56. Ibid.; Board of Regents, Minutes, November 11, 1932, 30; January 13, 1933, 44; February 10, 1933, 51; June 15, 1934; Zillman, "College of Law, Part III," 10.

57. Box 67, folders 7, 8, 9, RP.

58. *American Gypsum Trust v. Georgia-Pacific Corporation,* 512 P2d 658, Abstract of Record, 207.

59. Ibid., 208.

60. The case in the federal court before Judge Johnson was after an appeal to the Utah Supreme Court, *Golden v. American Keene Cement & Plaster Co.*

61. *American Gypsum Trust v. Georgia-Pacific Corporation,* 512 P2d 658, Abstract of Record, 208.

CHAPTER 4. RIVALS

1. Fawn M. Brodie, *No Man Knows My History: The Life of Joseph Smith, the Mormon Prophet,* 131-41, 208, 225-26, 258, 262-74, 286-88, 353-54.

2. Frances M. Gibbons, *Heber J. Grant: Man of Steel, Prophet of God,* 199.

3. D. Michael Quinn, *Elder Statesman: A Biography of J. Reuben Clark,* 64.

4. Calvin A. Behle interview.

5. James H. Moyle, speech, November 4, 1944, box, 73 folder 14, RP.

6. Lang interview.

7. Powell, *Utah History Encyclopedia,* 303.

8. Rick Lamoreaux interview.

9. Powell, *Utah History Encyclopedia,* 616.

10. George McMillan interview.

11. Lamoreaux interview.

12. Quinn, *Elder Statesman,* 22, 35-36.

13. Ibid., 37-39.

14. Ibid., 35.

15. Kristen Smart Rogers, "'Another Good Man': Anthony W. Ivins and the Defeat of Reed Smoot," 73. Rogers quotes Ivins: "I have never told anyone how to vote, not my own sons and daughters, my only counsel has been to investigate and vote as they desired."

16. Ivins's role in keeping the Mormon Church neutral, whether in favor of Democrats or Republicans, is detailed at ibid., 61-73.

17. Elbert D. Thomas, "The Challenge of Trusteeship," NBC University of the Air, March 22, 1947, box 72, folder 2, RP; Thomas, "Women's Debt to Roosevelt," November 2, 1944, KLO, ibid., box 73, folder 14.

18. Box 73, folders 14, 21, RP.

19. "Quick Action Helped Utah Survive Drought of 1934, Lecturer Says."

20. Brimhall Papers; "Dean R. Brimhall Dies—Noted Utahn, Educator"; *Ogden Standard-Examiner,* May 16, 1972, 2C; *Provo Herald,* May 17, 1972.

21. Eccles, *Beckoning Frontiers,* 48-50, 81, 131, 165-66; Powell, *Utah History Encyclopedia,* 152.

22. Powell, *Utah History Encyclopedia,* 152; Eccles, *Beckoning Frontiers;* Sidney Hyman, ed., *Marriner S. Eccles: Private Entrepreneur and Public Servant;* Jonathan R. T. Hughes, "Marriner Eccles: Logician in Wonderland."

23. Quinn, *Elder Statesman,* 74-75; Robert Gotlieb and Peter Wiley, *America's Saints: The Rise of Mormon Power,* 69, 70.

24. Ritter, "Law and Social Progress," February 11, 1932, box 12, folder 4, RP.

25. *Utah Chronicle,* November 16, 1933; February 20, 1936; Ritter, lecture notes; Ritter, "Lifting Law."

26. Ritter, "Lifting Law"; Ritter, lecture notes.

27. Ritter, lecture notes.

28. Ritter, "Contemporary Affairs," ca. 1936, 16, box 4, folder 6, RP.

29. Ritter, "Government in Our Times," lecture 5, "Political Parties," ca. February 1936, box 8, folder 5, RP.

30. Box 72, folder 2, RP. Ritter's handwritten notes on Mark Ethridge, "For What the Hell Should We Apologize?" (Democratic National Committee, May 15, 1944), indicate his philosophy.

31. Ritter to E. Thomas, March 3, 1937, box 12, folder 1, RP.

32. Gotlieb and Wiley, *America's Saints,* 67, 69, 70; Gibbons, *Heber J. Grant,* 198-200.

33. Gotlieb and Wiley, *America's Saints,* 70; Gibbons, *Heber J. Grant,* 3. In that short period four thousand bushels of wheat, thirteen thousand pounds of beans, and twenty-three thousand pounds of dried fruit had been raised and stored, along with many other grains and vegetables. The sisters of the Relief Society had made more than twenty-three thousand articles of clothing and more than two thousand quilts. Gibbons, *Heber J. Grant,* 2-3.

34. Gotlieb and Wiley, *America's Saints,* 70; Brian Q. Cannon, "Mormons and the New Deal: The 1936 Presidential Election in Utah."

35. "Harris Enters GOP Race for Governor"; Ritter to Brimhall, November 10, 1944, Brimhall Papers.

36. Box 73, folder 21, RP.

37. Pratt Kesler interview.

38. W. Barton Leach to George Thomas, September 12, 1941, box 121, folder 1, RP.

39. William Kixmiller and Arnold R. Baar to Thomas, September 8, 1941, box 121, folder 4, RP.

40. Board of Regents, Minutes, September 17, 1941, Thomas Presidential Records.

41. Bentley, *University of Utah,* 475-77.

42. Ritter interview; box 180, folder 2, RP.

CHAPTER 5. ASPIRATIONS

1. Frank W. Fox, *J. Reuben Clark: The Public Years,* 382-84.

2. Lang interview; United States Navy, *The Story of the* Bennion, 3-4; NBC's *Pearl Harbor: Legacy of Attack.*

3. Leary, Testimony, *Salt Lake City Hearings,* 19-20.

4. Lynn S. Richards, Testimony, ibid., 159-66; H. Grant Ivins, Testimony, ibid., 173-74.

5. George C. Taylor, Testimony, *Denver Hearings,* 73, 127.

6. Grant McFarlane, Testimony, *Salt Lake City Hearings,* 647-49, 654.

7. "Rent Official Rouses Ire of Probers."

8. "Fight Widens on Nation's Food Policy."

9. Federal Bureau of Investigation, "Willis W. Ritter," August 17, 1949.

10. Neither Thomas nor Ritter meant for that promise to get out. It became known only because years later, in 1949, his friend at OPA told an FBI investigator that Ritter confided in him about the promised appointment. Federal Bureau of Investigation, "Willis W. Ritter," June 20, 1949, 4.

11. Ibid., June 13, 1949, March 14, 1950.

12. Box 19, folder 14, Hinckley Papers.

13. O. N. Malmquist interview; McMillan interview; Paul Badger interview; Lang interview.

14. Board of Regents, Minutes, March 10, 1944, Thomas Presidential Records, 74.

15. Ritter interview.

16. Box 115, folder 4, author unknown, RP.

17. Mary Lynn (Ritter) Kramer, letter to Patricia Cowley, July 15, 1986; Badger interview. Badger was at the Ritter home when Willis refused to allow his children to go to MIA, the Mormon youth organization, for that reason.

18. Badger interview.

19. Ibid.

20. Box 85, folders 1-3, RP.

21. Joseph Rosenblatt, Testimony, *Salt Lake City Hearings,* 790-95.

22. Ritter, transcript of admission ceremony, United States District Court for the District of Utah, box 84, folder 12, RP.

23. Rosenblatt, Testimony, *Salt Lake City Hearings,* 792.

24. Box 67, folders 1-6, 9, RP; Lloyd interview; Lloyd, Ireta Memorial Services, February 27, 1981, attached.

25. Box 72, folder 3, RP; Arthur Wooley, Testimony, *Salt Lake City Hearings,* 786.

26. Ritter, Testimony, in *American Gypsum Trust v. Georgia-Pacific Corporation,* 512 P2d 658, Abstract of Record, 208-9.

27. Ibid., 186.

28. Ibid., 179.

29. *American Gypsum Trust v. Georgia-Pacific Corporation,* 512 P2d 658.

30. Keith Taylor interview; Max B. Knudson, "S.L. Law Firm Enjoys 100th—Despite Judge Ritter"; *American Gypsum Trust v. Georgia-Pacific Corporation,* 539 P2d 1040.

31. Quentin Cannon, Testimony, *Salt Lake City Hearings,* 310; Ritter interview.

32. Cannon, Testimony, *Salt Lake City Hearings,* 307. Cannon became an investigator for OPA in August 1942, and later was OPA chief of investigation for the State of Utah, and later still, an assistant district enforcement attorney. Ibid., 333.

CHAPTER 6. DEFERRAL

1. Willis W. Ritter, Official Application, April 16, 1949, in "Judgeship," Elbert D. Thomas Papers.

2. "Democrats Back Thomas for Vice President."

3. Jack Lawrence, address on KSL, November 1, 1944, box 73, folder 14, RP.

4. Richard Norton Smith, *Thomas E. Dewey and His Times,* 403-4, 409-10.

5. "Utahn Gains Favor for Vice President."

6. "Democrats Row over No. 2 Spot on Ticket." "Tired old men" was a mockery of the slogan supporters of Thomas E. Dewey had coined to discredit Roosevelt's ability to conduct the war.

7. The CIO Political Action Committee reportedly said they would gladly give Thomas some votes except for the fact that they were "engaged in a grim fight to save Vice President Wallace and in no position to engage in political amenities." O. N. Malmquist, "Utahns Adhere to Plan to Enter Thomas' Name."

8. "Democrats Nominate Roosevelt."

9. Rogers, "'Another Good Man,'" 64-73, quoting James H. Moyle; Quinn, *Elder Statesman,* 74.

10. Quinn, *Elder Statesman,* 28, 36, 42, 57, 67, 95; Gotlieb and Wiley, *America's Saints,* 69-72; Cannon, "Mormons and the New Deal," 8-9.

11. Brimhall to John Fitzpatrick, February 29, 1944; Brimhall to Ritter, June 30, 1944, box 33, folder 12, Brimhall Papers; J. Reuben Clark Jr., excerpts from address before a special annual Church Welfare Plan meeting, January 31, 1944, box 33, folder 12, Frank E. Moss Papers, as reported in *Deseret News,* church ed., February 12, 1944, 7.

12. "Rube" Clark was Ritter's disrespectful appellation for the Honorable J. Reuben Clark Jr. Ritter to Brimhall, July 14, 1949, box 19, folder 24, Brimhall Papers.

13. Julia Brixen Bertoch, "Rhetorical Theory and Practice of Adam S. Bennion," 20-31.

14. Fox, *J. Reuben Clark,* 383.

15. Quoted at Smith, *Thomas E. Dewey,* 423-24.

16. Ibid., 433-34.

17. "Dewey Readies Blast at FDR Denial of Reds"; "Roosevelt Delays War at Huge Cost in Lives"; Cannon, "Mormons and the New Deal," 12-17.

18. "Rallies End Appeals to Utah Voters"; Jack Lawrence, speech, November 1, 1944, box 73, folder 14, RP; ibid., address on KSL.

19. Bertoch, "Rhetorical Theory," 33.

20. James H. Moyle, speech, November 4, 1944, box 73, folder 14, RP.

21. Box 73, folder 13, RP.

22. Ibid.

23. Ritter, radio address, November 3, 1944, box 73, folder 17, RP.

24. Ritter, radio speech, November 4, 1944, in ibid.

25. Ibid.

26. Ibid.

27. Gotlieb and Wiley, *America's Saints,* 72.

28. Ibid., 69. There is little question that the Mormon leadership influences politics in Utah. The debate—an endless one—most often centers on whether the influence is a result of the predominance of Mormons (never less than 60 percent in the decade of the 1940s) whose views on most matters, sacred and profane, tend to be the same, or if the church authorities directly or indirectly manipulate the members to achieve a desired result.

29. "Senatorial Candidates Debate at Women's Council Meeting."

30. Ruth Bailey interview; Lucille Hallam interview.

31. Brimhall to Ritter, June 30, July 19, 1944; Ritter to Brimhall, September 23, 1944, box 33, folder 24, Brimhall Papers.

32. George Gallup, "Survey Gives GOP Chance to Win House"; "GOP Chief Sees Vote Tide Running to Gov. Dewey"; O. N. Malmquist, "Utah Remains Democratic Vote Samples Indicate"; Malmquist, "Election Interest Grows in Final Days of Campaign"; Ritter to Brimhall.

33. "Rallies End Appeals to Utah Voters."

34. "Maw, Lee Race Close"; Ritter to Brimhall, November 10, 1944, box 33, folder 24, Brimhall Papers.

35. Frank H. Jonas, ed., *Political Dynamiting,* 78.

36. "Late Returns Raise Lead Past 2,000,000 Mark."

CHAPTER 7. VACILLATION

1. United States Constitution, art. 2, sec. 2.

2. Richard J. Richardson and Kenneth N. Vines, *The Politics of Federal Courts: Lower Courts in the United States,* 56-79.

3. University of Utah Board of Regents, Minutes, August 3, 1945.

4. Ibid., August 10, 1945.

5. Bentley, *University of Utah,* 512-13.

6. Joseph Rosenblatt interview.

7. Hinckley and Wells, *"Lucky than Rich";* Robert Hinckley to Abe Glassman, Telegram, October 19, 1945, box 29, folder 11; Hinckley to Glassman, n.d., box 38, folder 16, Hinckley Papers. Born June 8, 1891, in Fillmore, Utah, Hinckley established Dodge dealerships in Mount Pleasant, Salt Lake City, and Ogden, Utah; developed the Ogden airport and Utah Pacific Airways with Dean Brimhall; and was an executive with Sperry Corporation, among other civic and commercial accomplishments.

8. Ritter to Brimhall, January 3, 1946, Brimhall Papers; "500 at Reception Honor Senator Thomas, Bride."

9. Watkins, *Enough Rope,* 9-10.

10. Gary A. Donaldson, *Truman Defeats Dewey,* 8, quoting Joseph C. Goulden, *The Best Years: 1945-1950* (1976), 226.

11. Donaldson, *Truman Defeats Dewey,* 8.

12. Ibid., 222n11, citing *Life,* November 4, 1946.

13. Thomas to Ritter, October 31, 1947, box 71, folder 4, RP.

14. *U.S. News,* July 21, September 13, 1946; Donaldson, *Truman Defeats Dewey,* 7-8, 222n8.

15. Powell, *Utah History Encyclopedia,* 230; McMillan interview.

16. David J. Wilson, Brief, 1-2; "Rep. Granger Asks Dismissal of Wilson Ballot Contest."

17. *Salt Lake City Hearings,* 512, 740-42; House Committee on House Administration, *Contested Election Case of Wilson against Granger, First Congressional District of Utah,* 1.

18. Brimhall to Ritter, November 24, 1945, box 19, folder 24, Brimhall Papers.

19. University of Utah, Budget, 1946-1947, in Minutes of Board of Regents, 61; Zillman, "The University of Utah College of Law: An Analytical History, Part I"; Bentley, *University of Utah,* 264. Spencer L. Kimball was appointed dean in 1950, Daniel J. Dykstra in 1954.

20. Donaldson, *Truman Defeats Dewey,* 6.

21. Ritter to Thomas, November 20, 1947, box 72, folder 4, RP; Jack Goodman to John Oakes, Telegram, November 22, 1947, box 71, folder 4, RP: "Utah State Democratic Committee meeting here Saturday pledging support of Senator Elbert D. Thomas for Vice President in 1948. Anyone want any wordage on this for Sunday?"

22. "Lawyer of S.L. Enters Race for Congress."

23. "It's Bosone vs. Leavitt in Primary."

24. Donaldson, *Truman Defeats Dewey,* 12-16.

25. Ibid., 5-16.

26. Ibid., 17-19.

27. Ibid., 214-20.

28. Ritter to Brimhall, December 15, 1948, box 19, folder 24, Brimhall Papers. David Lawrence was a widely syndicated columnist whose views tended to be conservative.

29. Ritter to Thomas, December 3, 1948; Thomas to Ritter, December 29, 1948, Thomas Papers.

30. Bernie Rhodes, letter to Nielson, June 21, 1999.

31. Lynn Packer and Robert Hansen, "Judicial Mania," photocopy; Ritter interview.

32. Ritter interview.

33. See Haydie (Mrs. Gus) Rinehart to Ritter, December 9, 1966, box 84, folder 1, RP.

CHAPTER 8. RESOLUTION

1. Fisher Harris to Ritter, January 24, 1949, box 185, folder 3, Thomas Papers.

2. Ritter to Thomas, February 3, 1949, box 185, folder 3, Thomas Papers.

3. Thomas to Ritter, December 29, 1948, in ibid., folder 2.

4. United States Constitution, art. 2, sec. 2.

5. Thomas Papers.

6. Thomas to Lucille Greenwood, December 30, 1948, box 185, folder 3, Thomas Papers.

7. Ritter to Thomas, December 3, 1948, box 185, folder 3, Thomas Papers; box 72, folder 5, RP.

8. Thomas to Ritter, December 29, 1948, box 138, folder 2, Thomas Papers.

9. Ibid.

10. Ritter to Thomas, January 12, 1949, box 185, folder 4, Thomas Papers.

11. George C. Hatch to Hinckley, January 10, 1949, box 29, folder 17, Hinckley Papers.

12. There were only three others in Utah's congressional delegation, one of whom, Senator Arthur V. Watkins, was a Republican. Rosenblatt may have referred to the two Democratic congressmen and the Utah Democratic Party leadership.

13. Morris Rosenblatt to Thomas, December 29, 1948, box 185, folder 3, Thomas Papers.

14. Abe Glassman to Thomas, January 15, 1949, box 185, folder 3, Thomas Papers.

15. Quentin Cannon to Thomas, January 14, 1949, box 185, folder 3, Thomas Papers.

16. McMillan interview.

17. John S. Boyden to Thomas, December 29, 1948, box 185, folder 3, Thomas Papers.

18. Chiyo Telford is Thomas's daughter.

19. Kendall Thomas to Thomas, December 17, 1948, box 185, folder 3, Thomas papers.

20. Scott M. Matheson Sr. to Thomas, December 29, 1948, box 185, folder 3, Thomas Papers.

21. Mrs. Scott M. Matheson to Thomas, December 1948, in ibid.

22. Hatch to Hinckley.

23. See, generally, Parker M. Nielson, *The Dispossessed: Cultural Genocide of the Mixed-Blood Utes.* Boyden's influence in Washington is explained at ibid., 213, and at Stephen G. Boyden, Brief (to BIA) in Support of Agreed Fee, August 9, 1972, 9, box 51, John S. Boyden Papers.

24. Mrs. William Everett (Frances) Boyden to Thomas, December 15, 1948, box 185, folder 3, Thomas Papers.

25. Cal Rawlings interview.

26. Thomas to the president, June 3, 1949, box 185, folder 4, Thomas Papers.

27. "Senator Thomas Recommends Willis Ritter for Judge"; "Selection for Federal Bench Vacancy Meets with General Approval."

28. Thomas to Ritter, June 6, 1949, box 185, folder 4, Thomas Papers.

29. Ritter to Brimhall, July 14, 1949, box 19, folder 24, Brimhall Papers.

30. Hinckley to Hatch, Telegram, August 2, 1949; Hinckley to Hatch, August 8, 1949, box 29, folder 18, Hinckley Papers.

31. George Hatch to Thomas, October 1, 1949, box 185, folder 3, Thomas Papers; "Truman Names Ritter Utah Federal Judge."

32. "Ritter Looms as Judge Post Choice."

33. Brimhall to Ritter, July 1, 1949, box 19, folder 24, Brimhall Papers.

34. Ritter to Brimhall.

35. Petition for Rehearing, No. 4933, Court of Appeals for the Tenth Circuit, box 122, folder 8, RP, lists Bill Hatahley, Widow Sleepy, Charley Burk, Lucy Harvey, Shorty Smiles, Natona Begay, Mark Tootsonian, Mary Jay, John Jay, Frank Joe, Dany Jones, Jim Antez, Cyrus Begay, Allen Ben, Willie Harvey, Tom Jones, Hosteen Sakezzie, Fred Johnson, Jim Hatahley, Billy Antez, Little Wagon, Tom Mustash, Slim Todachennie, Mary's Boy, Eddie Nocki, Susie Sleepy, Mrs. Lillie Thomas, Jim Harvey, Tom's Father, and Tom Belatso.

CHAPTER 9. SUSPENSION

1. Federal Bureau of Investigation, "Willis W. Ritter," July 19, 1949, 2.

2. Harold Chase, *Federal Judges,* 25, 20-26.

3. Senate Subcommittee of the Committee on the Judiciary, *Hearings on the Nomination of Willis W. Ritter, of Utah, to Be United States District Judge for the District of Utah,* 5 (hereinafter cited as *Washington Hearings*). The record of the 1949 ABA House of Delegates Proceedings indicates that a number of other nominees for federal district and circuit court judgeships were "recommended." Less enthusiasm for Ritter's nomination, which was "not opposed," may have been implied.

4. Watkins to Harley M. Kilgore, September 20, 1949, in *Salt Lake City Hearings,* 35-37, referred to at *Washington Hearings,* 12.

5. Knox Patterson to Pat McCarran, September 12, 1949, in *Salt Lake City Hearings,* 133, quoted at *Washington Hearings,* 6-7.

6. *Washington Hearings,* 4.

7. Ibid., 6.

8. E. Thomas to McCarran, April 6, 1950, in *Salt Lake City Hearings,* 66-71; *Washington Hearings,* 7.

9. "Not believing in the Constitution" was a "favorite whipping boy of conservatives" used to attack the New Deal of Franklin Delano Roosevelt and its supporters. For example, see editorial, "The Constitution." Cannon, "Mormons and the New Deal," states that the charge was rooted in a "spontaneous comment [of Roosevelt] in a press conference on May 31, 1935, four days after the Supreme Court had ruled against the National Recovery Act, a key piece of New Deal legislation. In its decision the Court had narrowly interpreted the interstate commerce clause in the Constitution, ruling that the clause conferred upon the federal government only the right to regulate the actual shipment of goods between the states. Roosevelt complained, 'The country was in the horse-and-buggy age when that clause was written.' Now, in an era when the nation's economic and political spheres were far more integrated and when a broad interpretation of that clause was needed in order to permit the federal government to 'administer laws that have a

bearing on, and general control over, national economic problems and national social problems,' Roosevelt had lamented, 'we have been relegated to the horse-and-buggy definition of interstate commerce.'" Ibid., citing *The Public Papers and Addresses of Franklin D. Roosevelt* (New York: Random House, 1938), 4:200-222. Discussion of that conflict by Ritter would be natural, and perhaps necessary, in lectures about the Supreme Court during the era.

10. Patterson to *Salt Lake Tribune,* box 185, folder 3, Thomas Papers.

11. *Washington Hearings,* 8-9.

12. Ibid., 45.

13. Ibid., 9-10.

14. Ibid., 10.

15. Ibid., 10-12.

16. L. M. Cummings to Kilgore, Telegram, October 8, 1949, box 185, folder 3, Thomas Papers; George S. Ballif to Thomas, October 7, 1948, in ibid.

17. *Washington Hearings,* 13-14.

18. "Ritter Passes U.S. Senate Loyalty Test"; box 185, folder 3, Thomas Papers.

19. Box 185, folder 3, Thomas Papers.

20. Ritter, "Democracy—Has It a Future?" ca. 1938, box 12, folder 6, RP; Ritter, "You and Your Government: Present Day Significant Political Movements," February 1936, box 8, folder 3, RP.

21. *Washington Hearings,* 15.

CHAPTER 10. SMEAR

1. Wilkinson to Ritter, October 11, 1945; Ritter to Wilkinson, October 13, 1945, box 17, folder 15, RP.

2. Powell, *Utah History Encyclopedia,* 639; Richard T. Cardall, Testimony, *Salt Lake City Hearings,* 483-84.

3. Boyden Papers.

4. "Ritter Hearing Goes Back to Committee."

5. Federal Bureau of Investigation, Mr. Rosen, Memorandum to Mr. Ladd, "Willis W. Ritter," June 18, 1952; "United States Senate News," ca. 1950, charging that Thomas was a communist "puppet" and that "Commies use [his] book to raise dollars," box 74, folder 19, RP.

6. *Salt Lake Tribune,* October 10, 1949; *Washington Hearings,* 27.

7. Watkins to McCarran, January 19, 1950, in *Salt Lake City Hearings,* 31; E. Thomas to McCarran, April 6, 1950, in ibid., 66.

8. *Salt Lake City Hearings,* 131-32.

9. Rosen, memorandum to Ladd; "One Man's Justice"; Robert B. Hansen, Statement, Senate Subcommittee on Improvement in the Judicial Machinery, *Hearings on S. 1130,* 95; box 147, folder 12, RP; Jack Anderson, "Judge vs. Sheriff."

10. Watkins to Magnuson, October 5, 1949, in *Salt Lake City Hearings,* 37-42. Watkins appears to have been ignorant of, or chose to ignore, the protocol with regard to FBI reports, which precluded himself or Thomas from having access to the document.

11. Compare, transcript, ABC, *Good Morning America,* October 10, 1977, box 148, folder 4, RP. But see also John A. Carroll, Testimony, *Washington Hearings,* 23.

12. "Ritter Is Opposed by Governor."

13. *Washington Hearings,* 20-21.

14. Ibid., 22.

15. Ritter categorically denied the accusation, and stated that the only trouble he had with an expense account was on telephone calls, which were turned down by the General Accounting Office because such calls were not approved as expenses. "Ritter, Welker Clash in Jury Bribe Case."

16. *Washington Hearings,* 21-23.

17. J. Lambert Gibson to Magnuson, October 3, 1949, in ibid., 63.

18. *Washington Hearings,* 25; Hatch to Hinckley, October 15, 1949; Hinckley to Hatch, October 18, 1949, box 29, folder 18, Hinckley Papers.

19. *Washington Hearings,* 46.

20. Ibid., 26.

21. Ibid., 28-29.

22. Ibid., 36.

23. Ibid., 45.

24. Ibid.

25. Ibid., 46.

26. *Salt Lake Tribune,* October 14, 1949.

27. Hinckley to Hatch, October 13, 1949, Hinckley Papers; E. Thomas to Calvin S. Rampton, October 14, 1949, Thomas Papers.

28. Compare, Jack Anderson, statement on ABC's *Good Morning America,* October 11, 1977, transcript in box 148, folder 4, RP.

29. Hatch to Hinckley, October 15, 1949, box 29, folder 18, Hinckley Papers; Hatch to Ritter, October 6, 1949, box 185, folder 3, Thomas Papers.

30. Magnuson to Truman, October 19, 1949.

31. Katherine Johnson, "Solon Seeks Bar to Recess Naming."

32. Hinckley to Hatch, October 26, 1949.

33. Johnson, "Solon Seeks Bar." A second recess appointment was promised if Watkins "succeeds in staying committee action and confirmation." E. Thomas to Ritter, June 8, 1950, box 72, folder 10, RP.

34. "Ritter Takes Oath."

35. "Ritter Proves Mild during Opening Case."

36. Hinckley to Hatch, November 17, 1949, Hinckley Papers.

37. Cannon, Testimony, *Salt Lake City Hearings,* 341-43, 347.

38. H. Grant Ivins, Testimony, ibid., 257-62.

39. Ibid., 263-64.

40. Watkins, Statement, ibid., 348, 485; "Utahn Praised for Action on Irrigation," box 212, RP.

CHAPTER 11. WATKINS' FOLLY

1. Byron Mock interview; Milt Oman interview; "Navajos Camp Out in S.L. to Wait Court's Decision," box 213, RP.

2. *United States v. Hosteen Tse-kesi.*

3. Dan B. Shields to E. Thomas, January 23, 1950, in *Salt Lake City Hearings,* 10-13.

4. "President Backs Judge Ritter for Permanent Court Seat," *Salt Lake Tribune,* January 6, 1950, 1, box 214, RP.

5. Watkins to McCarran, January 19, 1950, in *Salt Lake City Hearings,* 31-35.

6. Ibid.

7. *Salt Lake City Hearings,* 140-41.

8. McCarran to Watkins, March 30, 1950, in ibid., 47-49; February 10, 1950, in ibid., 45; Watkins to McCarran, March 13, 1950, in ibid., 45-47.

9. Watkins to McCarran, March 13, 1950, in ibid., 45-47.

10. Rawlings to Hinckley, March 16, 1950, box 38, folder 16, Hinckley Papers; Rawlings interview.

11. McCarran to Watkins, March 30, 1950, in *Salt Lake City Hearings,* 47-49. Hearing was scheduled for April 18, 1950, in the committee room, and Watkins was requested, again, to furnish the names and addresses of his proposed witnesses. McCarran to Watkins, April 5, 1950, in ibid., 50.

12. McCarran to Watkins, April 11, 15, 1950, in ibid., 50-53.

13. Ibid., April 15, 1950, 51-53.

14. Ibid., April 20, 21, 1950, 53-56.

15. Watkins to McCarran, April 24, 1950, in ibid., 56-64.

16. Thomas to McCarran, April 6, 1950, in ibid., 66-77.

17. *Salt Lake City Hearings,* 416, 433-34, 445-46, 843-57. Ritter explained that "Mr. Boyden wanted to know what my policy would be and I said, 'I have no policy about anything. Each one of these cases is handled as I hear the evidence and then we decide from the Bench and no commitments are made and then that plea was decided on the evidence.' When that plea was presented to me on the basis of the record, twenty pages of it, I thought if I accepted a nolo contendere plea I felt it was indicating I thought the fellow ought to be given some leniency and I therefore, when the fellow came up to sentence, would have prejudiced my own independence of position, my own thought on what the sentence should be. On a plea of nolo contendere, it seems to me, when they come up for sentence you have already committed yourself and I didn't want to be committed" (ibid., 854).

18. Ibid., 416.

19. Ibid., 1.

20. Ibid., 6. The ABA had previously submitted a telegram to the Judiciary Committee stating that it "begs to inform you that it does not oppose the nomination of Willis W. Ritter as district judge for the district of Utah" (*Washington Hearings,* 5). The change in the ABA recommendation was not explained.

21. Samuel D. Thurman, Testimony, *Salt Lake City Hearings,* 682-89.

22. Chase, *Federal Judges*, 125. Chase describes the role of the ABA during the period and Senate reaction to it: "As Professor Joel Grossman pointed out in his very fine book on the [ABA] committee: 'Although the ABA Committee did contribute to the rejection of four judgeship nominations during this period, it was unable to do much to promote the nomination of high-quality judges.' Actually, as Grossman indicates, the committee opposed ten nominations to the federal courts, only four of which were subsequently rejected by the Senate. The partial success that the committee had achieved with the Senate Judiciary Committee can be attributed to events as well as personalities. In the election of 1946, the Republicans won control of the Senate and Senator Wiley became chairman of the Judiciary Committee. Rightly or wrongly, Republicans have tended to be more sympathetic to ABA efforts to involve itself in the selection process and to pay more mind to ABA ratings than Democratic senators who have tended to regard the ABA as a Republican-oriented organization. As Grossman reports: 'The Democratic Committee Chairman from 1949-1953 did not hold the ABA in the same affection as had Senator Wiley.' Although Senator Pat McCarran of Nevada continued the practice of formally requesting an ABA opinion on each nominee, he declared that he was 'firmly resolved that the bar associations shall not choose the judiciary of the country'" (ibid., 124-25; footnotes omitted). Grossman attributes the failure of the committee to establish a liaison with the Justice Department at this time to President Harry Truman's hostility to the ABA. But it was not a matter of the president standing alone. His hostility was reinforced and fed by partisan Democrats who headed the Department of Justice and who constituted a good number of the members of the Senate. In any case, the committee did make recommendations to the attorney general when it learned of judicial vacancies, but these recommendations were not given any special weight, nor did the attorney general take up the committee's offer to investigate and report upon candidates other than its own.

23. *Salt Lake City Hearings*, 131-32.

24. Ibid., 138.

25. Ibid.

26. Ibid., 22-23; *Washington Hearings*, 30-40.

27. *Salt Lake City Hearings*, 143, 146-47.

28. Ibid., 631-33.

29. Ibid., 176-76.

30. Ibid., 180-209.

31. John S. Boyden, Testimony, in ibid., 428, 417, 429.

32. Ibid., 424-26.

33. Leary, Testimony, May 2, 1950, in ibid., 822-24.

34. Robert L. Cranmer to Ritter, April 25, 1950, in ibid. 80; Darrell Greenwell to Hinckley, February 18, 1950, box 19, folder 14, Hinckley Papers.

35. G. Edward White, *Oliver Wendell Holmes Jr.*, 40-48.

36. *Denver Hearings*, 204.

37. Ibid., 221.

38. Ibid., 207.

39. Ibid., 239.

40. Ibid., 235.

41. Ibid., 127.

42. Ibid.

43. Ibid., 14.

44. Ibid., 244.

45. Ibid.; Lynn Richards interview.

46. *Denver Hearings,* 244.

47. "McCarran Asks U.S. to Seek Ritter Witness"; "Judge Ritter Ballot Due Monday."

48. "Full Committee Okehs Ritter as Utah Judge."

49. *Congressional Record,* 81st Cong., 2d sess., 1950, vol. 96, pt. 7: 9441.

50. Ibid., 9444; Lang interview, 5; *Congressional Record,* 9588-89, box 930, RP.

51. *Congressional Record,* 81st Cong., 2d sess., 1950, vol. 96, pt. 7: 9443-45.

52. *State v. Braasch;* "Congress Tiff Looms on Recess Judges."

53. *U.S. Statutes at Large,* 65 (1848): 922, *Treaty of Guadalupe-Hidalgo.*

54. *Pelt v. Utah,* 1538, recites the history of the Tse-kesi group of Navajo: "At the time of the United States' entry into the Southwest in the 1840's, the Navajo culture was characterized by a scattered settlement pattern and lacked any centralized form of tribal government. Aubrey W. Williams, Jr., *Navajo Political Process* 4 (1970). In 1864, United States conflicts with the Navajo people had culminated in the decision to relocate them to Bosque Redondo in New Mexico territory, away from their homelands. Gerald Thompson, *The Army and the Navajo* 27 (1976). By March of 1865, over 9,000 Navajos had been relocated by Kit Carson and were forced to live communally at Bosque Redondo, [Frederick Webb Hodge, ed., *Handbook of American Indians North of Mexico,* 2d ed.], 51, thus fostering a sense of tribal unity in the Navajos who were there. Thompson, *supra.* at 164. However, a number of Navajo clans refused to be relocated and fled north into areas in present-day Utah; one such area is the Aneth Extension. [Senate Committee on Indian Affairs,] *Addition to the Western Navajo Indian Reservation: Hearings on S. 3782,* 71st Cong., 2d Sess. 2, 13 (1930); *see also Handbook, supra,* at 514."

55. "This varied history has led to an alleged divergence in the interests of the residents of the Aneth Extension and the [Navajo Nation]. In fact, until the 1933 Act was passed, the majority of residents of Aneth had never lived on the Navajo Reservation. *Hearings on S. 3782, supra,* at 13." *Pelt v. Utah,* 1538.

56. See James M. Aton and Robert S. McPherson, *River Flowing from the Sunrise: An Environmental History of the Lower San Juan,* 75-76, 95.

CHAPTER 12. TOMIE'S AUTUMN

1. D. Worth Clark, "Idaho Made the Desert Bloom," 680; "Are the Thousand Springs Going Down the Drain?"

2. "Proceedings and Remarks at the Installation of Hon. Willis W. Ritter as United States Judge for the District of Utah—August 1, 1950," *Utah Bar Bulletin* (July–August 1950): 69, 77-78; transcript, August 1, 1950, 7-10, in box 84, folder 12, RP.

3. Bernie Rhodes interview (1983); Rhodes to Nielson, June 21, 1999.

4. Catherine Jensen interview; Jack Jensen interview.

5. Bailey interview.

6. Greenwell to Hinckley, March 22, 1950, box 19, folder 14, Hinckley Papers.

7. Jonas, *Political Dynamiting,* 48. McCarthy's initial charges were on February 9, 1950.

8. "The 'prime targets' in 1950, [Drew Pearson] said [the speaker was Ab Herman, assistant to Guy Gabrielson, National Republican Committee chairman in 1950], were Scott Lucas in Illinois, Francis Myers in Pennsylvania, Elbert Thomas of Utah, and Millard Tydings of Maryland. Turning to Frank Smith, assistant to Senator John M. Butler, who defeated Tydings, Herman continued: 'We did a beautiful job in Maryland and Utah, Frank. I don't see why the Democrats yelled so much about the composite picture in your campaign, when, by comparison with the anti-Thomas newspaper in Utah, your publicity was like a country gentleman's'" (ibid., 106).

9. Paul Robeson, the famous singer, would be considered distinguished company as the twentieth-century closes, and has since been lionized as a champion of liberty, but in the witch-hunting days of 1950 was vilified as a communist or sympathizer.

10. Jonas, *Political Dynamiting,* 3; Pratt Kesler, quoted in ibid., 50; Kesler interview.

11. Ibid., 91.

12. Kent Shearer interview.

13. Sandack interview.

14. Jonas, *Political Dynamiting,* 97.

15. Box 72, folder 10, RP.

16. Clegg quoted in Jonas, *Political Dynamiting,* 106. Jonas provides a description of the 1950 campaign in some detail.

17. Thomas to Ritter, December 20, 1950, box 72, folder 5, RP. Thomas's reference is obscure, but Wilkinson's "big case" was the claim for the Ute Indians for loss of the west slope of the Rocky Mountains in 1880. A special Ute jurisdictional act of June 28, 1938, was necessary to waive the bar of the statute of limitations and confer jurisdiction on the United States Court of Claims. *U.S. Statutes at Large* 52 (1938): 1209-11.

18. *Congressional Record,* 73d Cong., 3d sess., 1938, vol. 83, pt. 8: 8997, box 73, folder 1; box 110, folder 19, RP. Thomas's letter stated, "He was the first man I recommended to President Roosevelt for a job at the recommendation of Walter Moyle. The position he sought in 1933 was a member of the tax court."

19. Thomas to Ritter, August 15, 1951, box 72, folder 6, RP.

20. *Salt Lake Tribune,* January 2, 1953; "Thomas Dies at Home in Honolulu"; "Friends, Colleagues Eulogize Thomas as Great Statesman"; Memoriam, *Micronesian Monthly,* February 1953, box 73, folder 1, RP.

21. Kesler interview.

22. Box 121, folder 12, RP.

23. Lula E. Bachman, Little Resume, April 23, 1953, box 118, folder 13, RP.

24. Lamoreaux interview.

25. *Utah State Farm Bureau Federation v. National Farmers Union Service Corp;* Bachman, Resume, 23.

26. *Aboitiz and Co. v. Price.*

27. Ibid., 608.

28. Ibid., 621.

29. Ibid., 622-23.

30. Lamoreaux interview.

31. Charles P. Larrowe, "Notches on a Chair."

32. "U. Professors Say Killers' Trials Legal."

33. Larrowe, "Notches on a Chair."

34. Ibid., 293-94; *State v. Braasch.*

35. Attorneys Reid Nielson and Allan Moll were appointed to represent Braasch, and made the same arguments.

36. Federal Bureau of Investigation to director, "Willis W. Ritter," June 9, 1952, December 15, 1956.

37. "Icy Reception Given Ritter Slayer Ruling."

38. "U.S. Judge Grants 2 Killers 45-Day Stays of Execution," quoting Mrs. Manzione.

39. *State v. Sullivan,* 513; *Braasch v. Utah;* "2 Killers Lose Third Plea to Top Tribunal."

40. Similar respect was paid to attorneys Reid Nielson and Allan Moll.

41. "U. Professors Say Trials Legal"; Ritter to Donald A. Wine, box 89, folder 4, RP.

42. Nature Conservancy, "Chat with Aldrich Bowler."

43. Ritter interview; Minnie W. Miller to Ritter, May 12, 1954, box 176, folder 1, RP.

44. Ritter to Arthur Watson, January 10, 1961, box 175, folder 12, RP; Don Holbrook interview.

45. Glen Hanson, proprietor of the West Point Store and Service Station, Wendell, Idaho, sometimes assisted at the farm. Ritter to Hanson, June 25, 1958, box 175, folder 8, RP.

46. Holbrook interview.

47. Jones interview.

48. Nature Conservancy, "Chat with Aldrich Bowler;" Norton and Norton interview; Lloyd interview.

49. Hammer Galleries, Auction, November 12–December 3, 1951, box 121, folders 5, 6, RP; Ritter interview. The exhibition and sale of these items were held at the Hammer Galleries in New York between November 12 and December 3, 1951. Nancy said Ritter went to New York prior to the sale to mark the items he wished to buy.

50. Notice of Award, September 13, 1959, box 179, folder 12, RP; registration certificate, box 180, folder 2, RP; Idaho State Brand Inspector, No. 23434-A, July 1, 1969, box 187, folder 4, RP.

51. Ritter to Gladys T. Keel, February 16, 1961, box 188, folder 9, RP; Ritter to Virgin Likely, October 24, 1960, in ibid., folder 2; Orval Beads and Jenny Beads interview.

52. Jack Goodman and Marge Goodman interview, 4; Ritter to Orval Bradley, November 19, 1976, box 186, folder 9, RP.

CHAPTER 13. TRANSFORMATION

1. "Judge Ritter Clamps Silencer on Mail, Delays Postal Processing One Hour"; Federal Bureau of Investigation to director, "Willis W. Ritter," November 18, 1952; Goodman and Goodman interview.

2. Bill Miller, "Smaldones Guilty," box 213, RP.

3. "Checkers' Bond Forfeited; Judge Orders Him to Stand U.S. Trial," box 213, RP.

4. *Smaldone v. United States;* "Checkers' Tax Trial Delayed: Jurors, Witnesses Face Quiz," box 213, RP.

5. "Checkers' Tax Trial Delayed"; Robert H. Hansen and Charles Roos, "U.S. Indicts Flip Flop Too," box 213, RP; "Smaldone Jailed on Charge of Jury Tampering," box 213, RP; "Smaldones Guilty"; *Calvarisi v. United States.*

6. Palmer Hoyt to Ritter, January 6, 1954, box 73, folder 4, RP; collected correspondence, box 117, folder 10, RP.

7. "Ritter All Set to Testify at Probe of FBI," box 213, RP.

8. Ashton interview; *Smaldone v. United States; Calvarisi v. United States.*

9. Rampton interview.

10. Rhoda Ramsay interview.

11. Box 115, folder 4, RP, from Dr. F. Alexander Magoons, "Love and Marriage," published by *Harper.*

12. Peggy Swenson interview; Norton and Norton interview.

13. Rampton interview; Shearer interview.

14. Willis W. and Ireta O. Ritter, Agreement, June 1, 1959, box 117, folder 14, RP.

15. Ritter interview.

16. A. L. Jensen interview.

17. W. W. Dawson to Ritter, n.d., box 117, folder 11, RP.

18. Rose Dunaway Allen, article, n.d., box 175, folder 5, RP.

19. Beads and Beads interview.

20. Ibid.

21. Di Bowler interview.

22. Robert Swenson interview.

23. George Templar to Ritter, October 10, 1964, box 86, folder 6, RP: "I especially enjoyed the trip to Park City, meeting your old friend 'Henie' [*sic*]. . . . "

24. Green interview.

25. Ritter to Neal D. Nelson, March 10, 1955, box 181, folder 1, RP.

26. *Ritter vs. Fritz,* A-27755, Opinion, December 22, 1958, box 181, folder 1, RP; section 17, Township 8 South, Range 14 East, Boise base and meridian, Gooding County, Idaho.

27. H. W. Langton to Harry LeMoyne, September 28, 1955, box 177, folder 2, RP.

28. Ritter to Clair M. Senior, March 1, 1959, box 176, folder 6, RP; *U.S. Statutes at Large* 76 (1962): 89.

29. Raymond T. Senior to Ritter, February 10, 1964, box 176, folder 6, RP.

30. *Ritter vs. Morton,* et. al., civ. no. 1-70-74 (USDC D Idaho 1972), Judgment and Decree, box 181, folder 9, RP; *Ritter v. Morton,* 513 F2d 942.

31. Packer and Hansen, "Judicial Mania."

32. Federal Bureau of Investigation to director, "Willis W. Ritter," July 3, 1958, and attached Administrative Inquiry, July 1, 1958.

33. Federal Bureau of Investigation, Callan to Rosen, "Willis W. Ritter," July 9, 1958.

34. J. Lambert Gibson to Magnuson, in *Washington Hearings*, 63.

35. Fannie eventually married Leslie R. Samuels, of Ogden, Utah, who founded the L. R. Samuels Company department store in Ogden, purchased in 1968 by the Auerbach Company of Salt Lake City ("Leslie R. Samuels Dies").

36. *Halmos v. British Commonwealth Pac. Airlines, Ltd.*, No. 34123, NDCal, March 9, 1959, cited at *Berner v. British Commonwealth Pacific Airlines, Ltd.*, 539.

37. At the time, case assignment was by the chief judge, with no necessity for random assignment, as is the practice today. Chief Judge Sylvester J. Ryan to Ritter, August 2, 1960, box 74, folder 1, RP, states that "you may have your choice as to any type of case you desire to have referred to you." There is no indication of a request. It is therefore probable that the chief judge in the Southern District of New York assigned the case to Ritter as a matter of judicial economy, he already being familiar with the facts and legal issues. Austin P. Magnem and Charles G. Parker, Petition, March 13, 1961, *British Commonwealth Pacific Airlines, Ltd. vs. Willis W. Ritter*, 6, state that "counsel for Plaintiff... eagerly sought and actually procured the assignment" to Ritter (box 74, RP).

38. *Berner v. British Commonwealth Pacific Airlines, Ltd.*, 294.

39. President, Proclamation.

40. Article 25(1) reads: "(1) Le transporteur n'aura pas le droit de se prevaloir des dispositions de la presente Convention qui excluent ou limitent sa responsibilite, si le dommage provient de son dol ou d'une faute qui, d'apres la loi du tribunal saisi, est considerée comme equivalent au dol.

"(2) Ce droit lui sera egalement refuse si le dommage a éte causé dans les memes conditions par un de ses preposes agissant dans l'exercice de ses fonctions."

One of the Netherlands delegates to The Hague Conference of 1955, Huibert Drion, translates art. 25 as follows: "The carrier shall not be entitled to avail himself of the provisions of this Convention which exclude or limit his liability, if he has caused the damage intentionally and wrongfully or by such fault as, in accordance with the law of the Court seized of the case, is considered equivalent thereto.

"Similarly he shall not be entitled to avail himself of the said provisions, if the damage was caused as aforesaid by one of his servants or agents acting within the scope of his employment. ("Limitation of Liabilities in International Air Law." The Hague, Holland, 1954, 195).

41. Translation of "faute lourde du transporteur assimilee au dol...," box 89, folder 6, RP.

42. 219 FSupp 322, citing Kreindler, "Aviation Accident Law" (1963) vol. 1, 342.

43. The translation into English is at *U.S. Statutes at Large* 49 (1934): 3020: "(1) The carrier shall not be entitled to avail himself of the provisions of this convention which exclude or limit his liability, if the damage is caused by his *wilful misconduct or by such default on his part as, in accordance with the law of the court to which the case is submitted, is considered to be equivalent to wilful misconduct.*

"(2) Similarly the carrier shall not be entitled to avail himself of the said provisions, if the damage is caused under the same circumstances by any agent of the carrier acting within the scope of his employment [emphasis added]."

44. 219 FSupp 322-23.

45. Ritter to Mostecky, December 5, 1961, box 74, folder 1, RP.

46. 219 FSupp 321 (all emphasis by Ritter).

47. Ibid., 324.

48. Ibid.

49. Ibid., 297; Ryan to Ritter, July 3, 1963, box 74, folder 2, RP.

50. *Berner v. British Commonwealth Pacific Airlines, Ltd.,* 537.

51. 93 FSupp 745 (D. Utah 1950). Action was initiated by the white livestock men against the Navajo to enjoin their use of the range without permits under the Taylor Grazing Act. The Utah Supreme Court held that it could "not go behind a treaty which has been ratified to inquire whether an Indian tribe was properly represented by its head men." *Young v. Felornia.*

52. Mock interview.

53. "Navajo Camp Out," box 213, RP.

54. "Ritter to Visit Indian Area in Navajo Suit," box 213, RP.

55. Goodman and Goodman interview.

56. Dennis McCarthy interview; Mock interview; Oman interview.

57. *Pelt v. Utah,* 1538, quoted at Chapter 11, notes 53-54.

58. *Taylor Grazing Act, U.S. Code,* vol. 43, secs. 315-315r (1952). But see *U.S. Statutes at Large* 43 (1924): 253, *Indian Citizenship Act.*

59. Oman interview. See also Powell, *Utah History Encyclopedia,* 487; and *United States v. Morrell,* one of a series of cases filed by Oman for white livestock operators.

60. The first non-Indian entry in the area, of any consequence, was the Bluff Mission of the Mormon Church in 1880. Before that there were approximately eighteen families at Aneth, established in 1878. Powell, *Utah History Encyclopedia,* 488.

61. Oman interview.

62. *United States v. Hatahley,* 257 F2d 920, 925; 79 SCt 751.

63. Mock interview.

64. *United States v. Hatahley,* 220 F2d 666; *Hatahley v. United States.*

65. Robert S. McPherson, ed., *The Journey of Navajo Oshley,* 132-33nn127-28, discusses the "feeling of helplessness and despair that Navajos [in the Montezuma Creek area] felt during stock reduction" of the BIA during 1933-1946, and explains that "although it is difficult for a white person to understand, the Navajos' connection to livestock was as much psychological as economic. Each animal had its own personality and was recognized ... as a contributor to life." Destruction of livestock "was an attempt at enslavement similar to the Fort Sumner years."

66. *Hatahley,* 257 F2d 926.

67. Gallivan interview.

CHAPTER 14. A "LITTLE HELPER"

1. Lang interview.

2. Hansen, Statement, Senate Subcommittee on Improvement of the Judicial Machinery, *Hearings on S. 1130,* 95, box 147, folder 12, RP: "Four years [after Ritter's appointment] Utah got its second federal judge ... created to offset Judge Ritter."

3. A. Sherman Christensen, Statement, ca. December 1970, box 101, folder 15, RP.

4. Christensen to Watkins, February 13, 1957, box 120, folder 4, RP.

5. Polk, Provo City Directory, 1929. The firm, Christensen, Watkins, and Dunford, was at 32 West Center, Provo. After his defeat for reelection as Utah State District Judge in 1932, Watkins practiced at 4 Roundy Building, Orem, Utah, through 1946.

6. Christensen to Alfred P. Murrah, April 15, 1970, 5-7, box 101, folder 19, RP; Christensen to Ritter, February 9, 1960, box 102, folder 2, RP; Christensen to Ritter, Memos, August 23, 1955, May 14, 1957, box 120, folder 4, RP.

7. Ritter to Christensen, June 28, 1961, box 102, folder 6, RP. See dissent of Justices Black and Douglas in *Chandler v. Judicial Council of the Tenth Circuit of the United States,* 136: "An independent judiciary is one of this Nation's outstanding characteristics. Once a federal judge is confirmed by the Senate and takes his oath, he is independent of every other judge."

8. Ritter to Warren Olney III, May 18, 1961, box 102, folder 10, RP.

9. Christensen, Memorandum Decision, December 6, 1965, box 101, folder 10, RP, citing *U.S. Code,* vol. 28, secs. 631(a), 751, 755 (emphasis added); Christensen to Joseph F. Spaniol Jr., October 24, 1969, box 101, folder 10, RP; Christensen to Samuel G. Bratton, November 20, 1957, box 73, folder 2, RP.

10. Christensen to Ritter, Memo, February 4, 1960, box 102, folder 2, RP; Ritter to David T. Lewis, May 11, 1970, box 101, folder 18, RP.

11. Christensen to Bratton, December 27, 1957, box 73, folder 2, RP; Judicial Council, United States Court of Appeals for the Tenth Circuit, Order, January 20, 1958, box 81, folder 1, RP; Senate Subcommittee on Improvement in the Judicial Machinery, *Hearings on S. 1130,* 7.

12. Transcript, January 17, 1957, box 120, folder 3, RP.

13. Ritter, *In the Matter of: Assignments of the Clerk of the Court and Deputy Clerks to Courtroom Duty,* Order, April 29, 1970, box 101, folder 19, RP.

14. Hatch to Ritter, Memo, June 13, 1958, box 134, folder 3, RP; Hatch to Ritter, Memo, July 11, 1967, box 134, folder 3, RP.

15. Box 102, folder 1, RP.

16. Wayne Christopherson, Statement, May 8, 1961, box 102, folder 10, RP.

17. Ritter, *In the Matter of: Assignments.*

18. Christensen, Order, February 2, 1970, box 101, folder 13, RP; Transcript, February 2, 1970, box 101, folder 15, RP.

19. Bernice Gibson to Cowley, January 2, 1983.

20. Transcript, February 2, 1970, 42, box 101, folder 15, RP.

21. *United States v. Woolsey,* Ncr. 41-69, Transcript, box 101, folder 17, RP; Ritter to Christensen, Memo, April 23, 1970, in ibid.

22. Christensen to Murrah, February 4, 1970, box 101, folder 14, RP; Christensen to Ritter, April 23, 1970, in ibid.

23. Transcript, February 2, 1970, box 101, folder 15, RP.

24. Christensen to Ritter, Memo, February 25, 1970, box 101, folder 18, RP; Christensen to Murrah, April 15, 1970.

25. *Corporation of the President of the Church of Jesus Christ of Latter Day Saints v. Jolley,* 167 P2d 984 (Utah 1970), box 101, folder 19, RP; Bill Fowler interview; Verl Ritchie interview; Christensen to Murrah, April 15, 1970, 2-3.

26. Ritter, *In the Matter of: Assignments.*

27. Box 101, folder 8, RP. The request is in ibid., box 7.

28. Order to show cause hearing, Transcript, October 7, 1968, box 101, folder 13, RP.

29. Box 101, folder 9, RP.

30. Vicki Jolley, statement to Nielson, ca. 1973.

31. *United States v. Atwood,* Cr. 29-61, United States District Court, District of Utah, Order, box 102, folder 7, RP.

32. Fowler interview.

33. Ritter to Christensen, June 28, 1961, box 102, folder 6, RP.

34. Box 101, folder 5, RP.

35. Ritter to Robert F. Kennedy, February 13, 1962; Ritter to John F. Kennedy, February 13, 1962, box 101, folder 5, RP.

36. Ibid.

37. Ritter to Raymond H. Farrell, January 16, 1962, box 103, folder 18, RP.

38. Christensen to Murrah, January 9, 1962, Ibid; Olney to Murrah, February 6, 1962, ibid.; Christensen, Memorandum decision, January 22, 1962, ibid., folder 20.

39. Ritter to Murrah, February 9, 1962, ibid. folder 19.

40. Judicial Council of the Tenth Circuit, Order, April 20, 1962, ibid. folder 21.

41. Act of August 6, 1958, *U.S. Statutes at Large* 72 (1958): 497.

42. Lang interview.

43. *U.S. Statutes at Large* 72 (1958): 497.

44. Ritter to Wayne L. Black and David K. Watkiss, January 13, 1971, box 87, folder 3, RP: One such attempt was S. 3055, February 28, 1968, box 87, folder 1, RP, unadopted, providing that no judge shall be chief judge after reaching the age of sixty-five.

45. Lang interview.

46. Christensen, to E. J. "Jake" Garn, May 11, 1976, quoted at Senate Subcommittee on Improvement in the Judicial Machinery, *Hearings on S. 1130.*

47. *U.S. Code,* vol. 28, sec. 294(c).

48. Ritter to Aldon J. Anderson, October 4, 1971; Anderson to Ritter, October 12, 1971, box 140, folder 2, RP.

49. William J. Lockhart, personal handwritten notes in *Utah Idaho Sugar Co. v. Willis W. Ritter,* Nos. 71-1686 and 72-1236, United States Court of Appeals for the Tenth Circuit; ibid., No. 71-1686 (10th Cir., filed June 5, 1972).

50. *Kerr-McGee v. Ritter,* No. 71-1681 (United States Court of Appeals for the Tenth Circuit), Answer to Order to Show Cause on Petition for Extraordinary Writs in the Nature of Mandamus and Prohibition.

51. Ritter to Lewis, ca. January 1972, box 139, folder 3, RP.

52. *U.S. Code,* vol. 28, sec. 137; Judicial Council, United States Court of Appeals for the Tenth Circuit, Order, December 20, 1971, box 64, folders 5, 6; box 119, folder 13; box 140, folder 2, RP.

53. *In the Matter of the Division of Business and Assignment of Cases in the United States District Court for the District of Utah.*

54. *Utah Idaho Sugar Co. v. Ritter;* "Court Names New Judge in U-I Case."

CHAPTER 15. CONSTITUTION

1. Nick Cotro-Manes, statement to Nielson.

2. *United States v. Willis W. Ritter,* No. 1829, Brief in Support of Motion to Dismiss Petitions and Answer of the Honorable Willis W. Ritter, 5, 18.

3. Ibid., 15.

4. Ibid.

5. Ibid., 9.

6. Quoted in *Schenk v. United States,* 249 U.S. 52 (1919).

7. Brief in Support.

8. Ibid., 6.

9. *U.S. Code,* vol. 28, sec. 1331; Brief in Support, 32, 31.

10. 1 Cranch 137; Brief in Support, 32.

11. Ibid., 19, 29-30.

12. Ibid., 9, 18, 30.

13. Ward to file, Memorandum, *The Ritter Project,* 6-8, 34.

14. *United States v. Willis W. Ritter,* No. 77-1829, Affidavit of William J. Lockhart, 7.

15. Carol Green, "History-Shaping Debate Focuses on Embattled Judge," 31.

16. Ritter, Quotations from lecture "A Liberal Philosophy of Living," ca. 1936, box 12, RP.

17. Ritter, "Lifting Law," box 211, RP.

18. Ibid.

19. Ibid.

20. Ibid; Ritter, "What the Law Is," box 13, folder 15, RP.

21. Ritter, "Our Changing Social World," box 12, folder 4, RP.

22. Ritter, Quotations from Lecture "A Liberal Philosophy of Living."

23. Ritter, "Contemporary Affairs," ca. 1936, box 4, folder 16, RP.

24. Ibid.

25. Ritter to Thomas, March 15, 1937, box 12, folder 1, RP.

26. Ritter, "What the Law Is."

27. C. Jensen interview.

28. Box 12, folder 2, RP.

29. *U.S. Code,* vol. 28, Federal Rules of Criminal Procedure, Rule 23(a); *United States v. Willis W. Ritter,* No. 77-1240, Petition.

30. Box 12, folder 2, RP, citing James Truslow Adams, "Epic of America." Adams continued that his epic "may hearken to the words of one of them, Mary Antin, a young immigrant girl who came to us from Russia, a child out of the 'Middle Ages,' as she says, into our twentieth century. Sitting on the steps of the Boston Public Library where the treasures of the whole of human thought had been opened to her, she wrote, 'This is my last home, and it invites me to a glad new life. The endless ages have indeed throbbed

through my blood, but a new rhythm dances in my veins. My spirit is not tied to the monumental past, any more than my feet were bound to my grandfather's house below the hill. The past was only my cradle, and now it cannot hold me, because I am grown too big; just as the little house in Polotsk, once my home, has now become a toy of memory, as I move about at will in the wide spaces of this splendid place, whose shadow covers acres. NO! It is not I that belongs to the past, but the past that belongs to me. America is the youngest of the nations, and inherits all that went before in history. And I am the youngest of America's children, and into my hands is given her priceless heritage, to the last white star espied through the telescope, to the last great thought of the philosopher. Mine is the whole majestic past, and mine is the shining future.'"

31. Ritter, statement, box 74, folder 16, RP.

32. Lockhart, Affidavit, 8.

33. See *Denver Hearings,* 204.

34. For example, see box 12, folder 2, RP.

CHAPTER 16. CONTROVERSY

1. Zeccharia Chaffee Jr., *Some Problems of Equity,* 183.

2. Notice of proposed settlement, June 5, 1962, box 86, folder 14, RP, hearing on approval scheduled June 20, 1962; *Union Carbide and Carbon Corp. v. Nisley:* "It is likewise sophistic to argue that mutuality of estoppel operates to prevent the unnamed miners from intervening after rendition of the verdict. For one is not precluded from claiming the benefits of a favorable judgment to which he was not a named party, simply because he would not have been bound by an unfavorable judgment rendered against named parties who did not adequately represent his interests."

3. A wholesale revision of the federal rules of procedure was adopted, to prevent another such result. See Rule 23, *Federal Rules of Civil Procedure.*

4. Judge Henry Friendly, in *Sdanok v. Glidden Co.,* 954-56.

5. Wilkins interview.

6. Lance S. Gudmundsen, "Ritter Reaffirms Monument Ruling," 19.

7. Box 146, folder 1, RP; emphasis in original.

8. George Lamb interview.

9. Jennifer Falk, "Ritter Dines Out."

10. Richard D. Ruckenbrod to Ritter, ca. 1965, box 84, folder 1, RP.

11. Ritter, notes, n.d., box 134, folders 9, 10, RP.

12. Sandack interview.

13. See also McMillan interview.

14. Louis Rosenberg to Ritter, May 17, 1963, box 86, folder 14, RP.

15. Robert Campbell interview.

16. *Clayton Antitrust Act, U.S. Code,* vol. 15, sec. 15; *Brigham City Corp. v. General Electric Co.*

17. Behle interview.

18. William T. Thurman Sr., "Vignettes of the Late Chief Judge Willis W. Ritter."

19. "The FBI conducted an extensive search for the two mobsters and eventually they were captured, transported to Salt Lake, and brought to trial in his court," Thurman wrote, where they "were found guilty and sentenced" (ibid.). The event occurred, but Thurman has the facts wrong. There was no "extensive search" conducted by the FBI, and they were not "eventually... captured [and] transported to Salt Lake." On the contrary, they never got out of the city until after Ritter had them convicted, sentenced, and in the custody of the U.S. marshal for delivery to the Bureau of Prisons.

20. *Buckley v. United States.*

21. Ritter, handwritten notes, box 137, folder 10, RP.

22. Your authors—both of them—know the story well, for Phil Cowley, husband of Patricia Cowley, was instrumental in the arrest and capture of the two mobsters, and Parker Nielson was the second of the two lawyers Thurman referred to. When they came to Nielson's address they most decidedly were able to find him, for he was seated at his desk waiting—with a loaded revolver in hand. They tried to escape, but Cowley followed them to the Salt Lake International Airport. Nielson arrived in pursuit, accompanied by Deputy County Sheriff Nicolas G. Morgan III, and Phil led them to an airliner bound for Las Vegas they had just boarded. These "mobsters" were physically dragged off the plane, arrested and manacled on the tarmac in plain view of the incredulous passengers, after which they were dealt with every bit as coarsely, as Thurman recalled.

23. Britt Adams to Ritter, July 25, 1974, box 125, folder 7, RP.

24. *Smith v. Lossee,* Opinion, October 1971, box 142, folder 10, RP; Brian Asher Evans to Ritter, February 5, 1972, box 125, folder 7, RP.

25. Federal Bureau of Investigation, "Willis W. Ritter," April 9, 1965, October 17, 1957, 6.

26. Ibid., January 27, 1970, 1, 3.

27. Ibid., 5, 1-2.

28. Box 151, folder 2, RP; Taylor interview; *American Gypsum Trust v. Georgia-Pacific Corporation,* Abstract of Record, 178-87.

29. *American Gypsum Trust v. Georgia-Pacific Corporation,* 660.

30. Ibid., Abstract of Record, 201.

31. Taylor interview.

32. Ritter's counsel was Dennis McCarthy, Clifford L. Ashton, and C. Keith Rooker, of the firm Van Cott, Bagley, Cornwall, and McCarthy. Counsel for Georgia-Pacific was Keith Taylor, of the firm Parsons, Behle, and Latimer. Cal Behle also acted as counsel in the trial proceedings.

33. Taylor interview.

34. Ashton interview.

35. Taylor interview; Don Tibbs, Judgment, box 151, folder 5, RP; Dennis McCarthy to Ritter, November 11, 1975, box 151, folder 1, RP; *American Gypsum Trust v. Georgia-Pacific Corporation.*

36. "U.S. Judge Ritter Bars Press Photographers"; "How Far, Your Honor?"; Ritter, Order, May 8, 1969, box 80, folder 1, RP; M. Dallas Burnett and Nelson Wadsworth, "Ritter: Paranoia and Paradox on the Federal Bench"; "KSL Gets Back TV Camera from

Ritter," 29; "Marshalls Seize Camera"; Bonneville International Corporation, Motion and Brief, United States Court of Appeals for the Tenth Circuit, No. 77-1791, December 29, 1977, box 73, folder 10, RP.

37. Joe Bauman interview.

38. "Appeals Court Dismisses Case in Theft."

39. Ibid.; Max Wheeler interview; *U.S.A. v. Vernon Black,* No. 75-1766 (United States Court of Appeals, 10th Cir., District Court No. Cr. 75-24), box 136, folder 7, RP.

40. Snow interview.

CHAPTER 17. EXPIATION

1. Robert Bryson interview.

2. Bernice Gibson to Cowley, January 2, 1983.

3. William J. Lockhart to Lynn Packer, comments on his manuscript about Judge Ritter, n.d.

4. H. Ralph Klemm interview.

5. Ritter interview.

6. Behle interview.

7. Falk, "Ritter Dines Out."

8. Ritter interview.

9. Shearer interview.

10. Ritter interview.

11. Mary Lynn (Ritter) Kramer to Cowley, July 15, 1986.

12. Lang interview.

13. C. Jensen interview.

14. *United States of America v. James Stanton Perry,* jury charge, August 20, 1968, box 125, folder 12, RP.

15. Ibid.

16. Ibid.

17. Rhodes interview (1983).

18. James V. Bennett to Ritter, January 7, 1957, box 86, folder 2, RP.

19. Lang interview.

20. Ritchie interview; Saperstein interview; Delbert M. Draper Jr., apology, February 26, 1962, box 125, folder 2, RP; Draper, apology, ca. 1966, box 125, folder 3, RP.

21. Saperstein interview.

22. Snow interview.

23. Fowler interview. The incident was days earlier or later, but during the same period of time. Cf. Allan D. Johnson to Ritter, March 17, 1965, concerning "some scuttlebut at the University Club," box 74, folder 2, RP.

24. Credibility of the incident was confirmed when Bernie Rhodes, chief probation officer, witnessed Ritter punch Arthur Allen during a conference with Allen in Ritter's chambers. Allen, who was a member of the Board of Directors of the University Club, represented that he had voted against the expulsion. Ritter responded that the vote was a sham to provide cover for themselves, and that Allen and the other directors held another

vote in which they all voted his expulsion. Ritter then struck Allen. Rhodes to Nielson, June 21, 1999.

25. Ritchie interview.

26. James Housley interview.

27. Phil Hansen interview.

28. J. Jensen interview; C. Jensen interview.

29. J. Jensen interview.

30. Bailey interview.

31. Ritchie interview; Housley interview.

32. Ritchie interview (telephone).

33. Ritchie interview.

34. Anderson, "Judge vs. Sheriff."

35. Senate Subcommittee on Improvement of the Judicial Machinery, *Hearings on S. 1130,* 95, box 147, folder 12, RP.

36. Aldo Richins, Testimony, July 15, 1970, box 138, folder 2, RP.

37. C. Nelson Day to Maurice Warshaw, August 17, 1970, 3, box 139, folder 11, RP.

38. *U.S. Code,* vol. 18, secs. 1503, 241, 242; *USA vs. Delmar L. Larson, Leon A. Halgren, Edward D. Scherer and Aldo Richins,* CR-8-71, Indictment, box 95, folder 3, RP.

39. Day to Warshaw; Jerris Leonard to Ritter, February 13, 1971, box 95, folder 6, RP; Leonard to Ritter, February 9, 1971, box 135, folder 8, RP; Hansen, Statement, Senate Subcommittee on Improvement of the Judicial Machinery, *Hearings on S. 1130,* 95, box 147, folder 12, RP.

40. *In re Presentment by Camden County Grand Jury,* 89 Atlantic 2d 416, 444 (New Jersey 1952), box 73, folder 6, RP, quotation highlighted by Ritter; James L. Barker Jr., to Warren E. Burger, March 9, 1971, box 135, folder 8, RP; Ritter, Grand Jury charge, in ibid.; Maurice Warshaw, Grand Jury Report, September 2, 1971, box 95, folder 2, RP.

41. Marvin E. Frankel and Gary P. Naftalis, *The Grand Jury: An Institution on Trial,* 3, 15, 32, 91, 95; *Presentment by Camden County Grand Jury.*

42. *United States v. Richard T. Cardall, et. al,* CR 74-53 (USDC D Utah 1974).

43. Badger interview.

44. Ibid; Dean Mitchell interview.

45. Bernie Rhodes, Statement.

CHAPTER 18. ISOLATION

1. David Novelle interview. Federal Bureau of Investigation to director, "Willis W. Ritter," June 9, 1952, states that while holding court in Denver in May 1952, "the United States Marshall brought all five defendants into Court and did not remove their handcuffs until all five had entered the door to the Court Room. Judge Ritter openly criticized these acts on the part of the United States Marshall to the jury, and made scathing remarks concerning the efficiency of the U.S. District Attorney's Office and the U. S. Marshall's Office in permitting these acts."

2. Norman Johnson interview.

3. David K. Winder interview.

4. Ibid.

5. Ritter to William T. Thurman, Memorandum, June 22, 1967, box 86, folder 14, RP; Thurman to Ritter, Memorandum, June 28, 1967, in ibid., folder 6.

6. Rhodes interview (1983).

7. Peter Billings Sr. interview.

8. Frank Hassell, *Rainbow Bridge: An Illustrated History,* 135-37; *Friends of the Earth v. Armstrong.*

9. Ashton interview.

10. *Colorado River Storage Project, U.S. Code,* vol. 43, secs. 620, 620b.

11. *Friends of the Earth v. Armstrong,* 189; Pusey, "Being Chief Judge."

12. Frank Hewlett, "Moss Asks West Solons to Meet on 'Rainbow Bridge Crises.'"

13. Box 89, folder 7, RP.

14. Billy Yellow, statement, ca. 1972, box 84, folder 5, RP; Bryson, "Judge Studies Proposal to Lift Own Order on Rainbow Bridge"; Transcript, March 27, 1973, 63, box 144, folder 2, RP; Ritter, Opinion, April 21, 1973, box 89, folder 11, RP.

15. *Friends of the Earth v. Armstrong,* 485 F2d 1.

16. Ritter, Order, June 7, 1976, box 80, folder 5, RP.

17. Ritter to Brennan, Memorandum, December 8, 1972, box 80, folder 4, RP; James S. Lowrie, Statement, January 16, 1974: "The ACLU of Utah concluded that Mr. Petrofsky's visits did in fact constitute a continual threat to the good order of the office of the clerk of court," and "Judge Ritter's order was a proper order . . . ensuring that Mr. Petrofsky would not be denied his right of access to the court records" (box 105, folder 11, RP).

18. Ritter to deputy clerks, Memorandum, July 19, 1973, box 80, folders 5-18; box 111, folder 7, RP.

19. "One Man's Justice," 14-15.

20. Behle interview; Taylor interview. Taylor claimed that he "was one of his fair haired boys" until the *Georgia-Pacific* case, and that "he would go in my favor in court and humiliate the lawyers, well-prepared, good lawyers, on the other side when I was there." But "I felt a lot better" after he fell from favor; "that was fine." But see *Reynolds v. Texas Gulf Sulphur Co.,* in which Calvin E. Behle and Keith E. Taylor—both of them, together with Orison S. Marden, president of the American Bar Association—acted as counsel against coauthor Nielson, and lost. Claims of bias in their favor prior to their involvement in *Georgia-Pacific,* of similar bias in favor of other lawyers, must therefore be taken advisedly.

21. "One Man's Justice," 15.

22. "Attorney Files Prejudice Affidavit against U.S. Judge in Lands Suit."

23. "Judge Ritter Denies Two Motions to Disqualify Him in Civil Cases." The refusal was affirmed on appeal. "City to Appeal Ritter's Stand on 2 Suits"; "Court Refuses Plea by S.L. to Bar Judge in Case"; United States Court of Appeals for the Tenth Circuit, No. 72-1313, Order, May 23, 1972, box 77, folder 10, RP.

24. "Court Action Asks for New Judge." See also Brian Asher Evans to Ritter, April 5, 1972, box 125, folder 7, RP: "I recoil with distaste at the instinctive reaction of

Utah's Attorney General to fight every judgment in which the rights of the individual over the corporate state prevail."

25. Rose, "No Parking Tickets for 10 Days, Ritter Says"; Ronald N. Boyce interview.

26. Box 81, folder 2, RP.

27. C. Jensen interview.

28. J. Jensen interview.

29. Earl F. Dorius, "Personal Recollections of My Involvement and the Involvement of the Attorney General's Office Staff with the Gary Gilmore Case between November 1, 1976, and January 17, 1977," 52, 53; Ritter, Transcript, January 16, 1977, box 135, folder 15, RP.

30. Dorius, "Personal Recollections," 53, 61-62, 64.

CHAPTER 19. SIEGE

1. Federal Bureau of Investigation to attorney general, "Willis W. Ritter," April 9, 1965.

2. William J. Lockhart interview.

3. *Act of August 6, 1958, U.S. Statutes at Large* 72 (1958): 497.

4. Quentin N. Burdick to Ritter, April 27, 1976, box 147, folder 12, RP: "As the last of the 32 judges who were exempted from the age limitation, you are the sole chief judge who would be affected by such a repealer."

5. "Panel Action Threatens Ritter Status."

6. "Bar Halts Action on Ritter"; Calvin Behle to Jake Garn, May 13, 1976, in Senate Subcommittee on Improvement of the Judicial Machinery, *Hearings on S. 1130,* 30.

7. "Bar Halts Action on Ritter."

8. "Hansen Criticizes Owens on Judicial Issue."

9. Burnett and Wadsworth, "Ritter: Paranoia and Paradox," 6.

10. "Resolution Asked Congress to Repeal Grandfather Clause."

11. Melvin P. Antell, "The Modern Grand Jury: Benighted Supergovernment," *American Bar Association Journal* 51 (February 1965): 153, box 110, folder 19, RP.

12. David Rothman, "The Grand Jury vs. You," *Saturday Evening Post,* November 1974, 40, box 109, folder 16, RP, extensively noted by Ritter.

13. Frankel and Naftalis, *Grand Jury,* 52-59.

14. *United States v. Ritter,* No. 77-1829; Affidavit of William J. Lockhart.

15. Burnett and Wadsworth, "Ritter: Paranoia and Paradox," 11. Such statistics are misleading. Cases appealed are a small fraction of those decided, and many of those reversed are decided on procedural grounds having no relationship to the merits of the decision.

16. Nelson, "Bar Derails Action to Remove Judge Ritter."

17. Box 137, folder 20, RP; Bryson, "Remove Self? Ritter Kills Action."

18. Transcript, January 30, 1976, box 145, folder 7, RP; Bryson, "Judge Ritter Refuses Bid to Give Up Case."

19. Bryson, "Circuit Court Takes Ritter Off Case."

20. "Records Show No Contempt Threat."

21. Burnett and Wadsworth, "Ritter: Paranoia and Paradox," 46.

22. Hewlett, "Sen. Garn Assails Ritter in Statement."

23. William J. Lockhart, Statement, in Senate Subcommittee on Improvement of the Judicial Machinery, *Hearings on S. 1130.*

24. E. J. Garn, Statement, in ibid.

25. Quintin R. Burdick, Statement, in ibid., 96-155.

26. Lockhart, Statement, in ibid., 158, 162; Frank Hewlett, "Panel Hears Views on Ritter Case," *Salt Lake Tribune,* May 19, 1976, B1 at 5.

27. John J. Flynn, Statement, in Senate Subcommittee on Improvement of the Judicial Machinery, *Hearings on S. 1130,* 221.

28. Coauthor Nielson was personally present in Judge Ritter's chambers, at an attorney's conference in connection with the Ten Commandments case, when Judge Ritter stated that Utah attorney general Robert Hansen had filed "another" affidavit of prejudice in a case involving the State of Utah. "I am prejudiced against him, and I don't want the [SOB] in my court, but I am going to deny that affidavit," Ritter declared, "because his client is the State of Utah, and I am not prejudiced against the State of Utah."

29. *State v. Phillips.*

30. "Judge Ritter Condemns Grand Jury System Failings."

31. Frankel and Naftalis, *Grand Jury,* 3; box 133, folder 5, RP; Lockhart to Burdick, May 13, 1976, in Senate Subcommittee on Improvement of the Judicial Machinery, *Hearings on S. 1130.*

32. *United States v. Ritter,* No. 77-1829, Affidavit of William J. Lockhart; *In re Presentment by Camden County Grand Jury,* 169 Atlantic 2d 465 (New Jersey 1961), box 73, folder 5, RP.

33. *United States v. Ritter,* No. 76-1011; Bryson, "Order Ritter to Comply, U.S. Asks"; *United States v. Ritter,* No. 76-1331; box 95, folder 17, RP; Ward, Memorandum, "The Ritter Project."

34. Ward, Memorandum, "The Ritter Project," 3-4, 10.

35. Ibid., 4; *United States v. Ritter,* No. 76-1331; "Appeals Court Delays Trials"; *United States v. Ritter,* No. 76-1917; *United States v. Ritter,* 540 F2d 459; *In the Matter of the Trial and Sentencing of Minor Offenses, etc.,* No. 77-1208; *United States v. Ritter,* No. 77-1240; box 144, RP; *In the Matter of Transcripts Withheld from the United States by the Honorable Willis W. Ritter,* No. 77-1491; Ritter, Statement, in *United States v. Doiron.*

36. Bryson, "Specific Court Dates Set for 25 Cases."

37. *U.S. Code,* vol. 28, sec. 371, provides: "Any judge of the United States appointed to hold office during good behavior who is eligible to retire under this section who does not do so and a certification of his disability signed by a majority of the members of the Judiciary Council of his Circuit in the case of a circuit or district judge... is presented to the President and the President finds that such judge is unable to discharge efficiently all the duties of his office by reason of permanent mental or physical disability and that the appointment of an additional judge is necessary for the efficient dispatch of business, the President may make such appointment by and with the consent of the Senate."

38. *Chandler v. Judicial Council of the Tenth Circuit of the United States,* 136, Justices Douglas and Black in dissent, citing United States Constitution, art. 1, secs. 3 and 8. The

majority affirmed the action of the Judicial Council, based upon a number of cases under submission to Judge Chandler that were delayed in their decision, as a valid exercise of the power under the Judicial Code to regulate "the effective and expeditious administration of the business of the courts," but rejected the power of the Judicial Council to remove Judge Chandler from cases on the basis of there being a "disagreement" between the judges as to the assignment of cases.

39. 398 U.S. 129.

40. Ward, Memorandum, 6-12.

41. Ibid., 17; *United States v. Ritter,* No. 77-1829.

42. Ibid., Affidavit of Lockhart.

43. ABC, *Good Morning America,* October 11, 1977, transcript in box 148, folder 4, RP.

44. Ward, Memorandum, 17-20.

45. John A. Young to Ritter, June 9, 1977, box 141, folder 10, RP.

46. Young to Ritter.

47. "Anti-Ritterites took a major step last week by filing a unique petition with the 10th Circuit Court of Appeals... unprecedented in U.S. legal history, ask[ing] that Ritter be barred from hearing any new civil or criminal cases in which the federal government is a party" (Chicago Tribune Service, "Turning the Tables: Opponents Attempt to Muzzle Outspoken, Aging Federal Judge").

"Now, however, a determined posse of federal and state officials have mounted a strenuous effort to rein in the free-wheeling Ritter.... In Washington, the Senate has authorized an admittedly superfluous third federal judge for Utah, and a House subcommittee has approved repeal of a grandfather clause, which could also cost Ritter his power to assign cases" ("Feet-First Ritter under Siege").

"Like the Bermuda Triangle, the courtroom of Federal Judge Willis W. Ritter continues to be the scene of strange and unexplicable events.... [T]he chorus of nay-sayers to the 77-year-old judge is rising" (Jeff Williams, "Ritter under Siege [a Melodrama] with Phil Hansen as Court Jester.")

48. Ward, Memorandum, 36.

CHAPTER 20. CONSUMMATION

1. Radio talk, March 1931, box 149, folder 7, RP; White, *Oliver Wendell Holmes Jr.,* 3.

2. Rhodes interview (1983); Rhodes to Nielson, June 21, 1999.

3. Federal Bureau of Investigation, Mr. Rosen, Memorandum to Mr. Ladd, "Willis W. Ritter," June 18, 1952.

4. "Proceedings of Admission to the Federal Bar," Transcript, January 26, 1977, RP.

5. Ritchie interview.

6. Rhodes interview (2001).

7. Bauman interview; "Pair Freed after Arrest for Assault on Ritter."

8. Norton and Norton interview.

9. Falk, "Ritter Dines Out."

10. Robert Hansen interview.

11. Phyllis K. Heikkila to Ritter, card, ca. December 19, 1977, box 157, folder 12, RP.

12. Stephen S. Chandler to Ritter, January 24, 1977, box 157, RP.

13. M. M. Blattner to Ritter, ca. January 1978; Sister Marie Camille to Ritter, January 25, 1978; Bill Dye to Ritter, January 13, 1978, RP.

14. Schindler, "Ritter Navajo Collection"; Sandack interview; C. Robert Wagner to Ritter, ca. 1961, box 89, folder 6, RP.

15. "Judge Ritter of Utah Granted More Time for Ouster Defense."

16. Bryson, "Ritter's Answer to Charges Filed in Court."

17. Rosenblatt interview.

18. Scott Matheson interview.

19. C. Jensen interview; Ritter interview.

20. Rhodes interview (2001).

21. Ritter to Ed M. Bryan, December 15, 1959, box 177, folder 6, RP.

22. Ritter to Leo L. Laythe, December 28, 1959, box 184, folder 1, RP.

23. Willis W. Ritter and Ireta O. Ritter to Fish and Wildlife Service, Agreement for Lease and Option to Purchase Lands, July 14, 1962, box 182, folder 6, RP; Ritter to Oren Hutton, letter, September 27, 1963, box 184, folder 2, RP.

24. Ritter interview.

25. Aldrich Bowler interview.

26. Campbell interview.

27. *Salt Lake Tribune,* March 17, 1978.

28. Robert M. Owings to Ritter, February 16, 1979, in box 207, RP.

29. House, "Judge's Ghost Keeps Courthouse Memories Alive."

30. Rolly, "Ritter Auction Draws 'Special' Audience."

EPILOGUE

1. *Gideon v. Wainwright,* 344.

2. *Escobedo v. Illinois,* 483.

3. Ibid., quoting from *Ex parte Sullivan,* 517-18; *Escobedo v. Illinois,* 488.

4. *Escobedo v. Illinois,* 490-91.

5. *Miranda v. Arizona,* 479, 442.

6. Federal Bureau of Investigation, "Willis W. Ritter," December 15, 1966.

7. Ritter, memo for filing, n.d., box 125, folder 7, RP.

8. Lee to Ritter, December 15, 1971, box 78, folder 10, RP.

GLOSSARY OF LEGAL TERMS

This glossary is intended for nonlawyers. Where deemed appropriate or helpful, a descriptive phrase formulating the intent is set in quotation marks. For precise legal definitions, consult *Black's Law Dictionary.*

Address. Removal of judges deemed unworthy, by decree of the executive or legislature. *Not* provided for in the United States Constitution.

Affidavit. "I swear that this *written* statement is true and correct." Distinguished from *oral* testimony given out of court. *See* deposition.

Amicus curiae. To "remind the court" of the interest of those not engaged in the litigation, which the lawyers for the parties may not otherwise explain, such as for lack of interest of themselves or those they represent. Literally, a "friend of the court."

Arraignment. "Stand before the court and answer if you are guilty or not." The initiation of judicial proceedings against one who has been arrested or charged with crime.

Bailiff. One who superintends (that is, has charge of) the courtroom.

Bill of Attainder. "The legislature declares, by this law," that a "named or designated person is liable as follows."

Burden of proof. "This is how I think it happened," according to the evidence.

Certiorari. "Bring the record on that case before us. We want to have a look at it." Literally, a common-law writ of review or inquiry directed to an inferior court, not available as a matter of right, in cases or circumstances where an appeal is not allowed, to determine if justice has been served. The most common method by which matters are presented to the United States Supreme Court.

Class action. "Come along and share in my judgment." A proceeding, subject to rules of equity, in which one claimant declares himself "representative" of numerous others having claims with the same characteristics.

Common law. "Blackstone's decision has stood too long to change it now." The body of usages confirmed by judicial decisions, distinguished from statutory law, enacted by the legislature or by regulations of the executive.

Deposition. To take one's testimony, other than in court.

Duces tecum. "Bring these papers, documents, or things with you."

En banc. All judges serving on a particular court participating jointly.

Enjoin (restraining order or injunction). "I command you" to do, or refrain from doing, some act. "Don't do that!"

Felony-murder rule. If someone is killed while a serious crime is in progress (as in one subject to imprisonment), the perpetrators are deemed guilty of a species of murder, even if the killing was not intended.

Grand jury. A "grand inquest, [by] a body [of 25 persons] with powers of investigation and inquest [indictment], the scope of whose inquiries is not to be limited narrowly by questions of propriety or forecasts of the probable result of the investigation, or by doubts whether any particular individual will be found properly subject to an accusation of crime." *Blair v. United States,* 350 US 273, 282 (1919).

Habeas corpus, writ of. "Why am I restrained, and release me if you have not followed proper procedures." Literally, "why do you have the body." The common-law writ to question restraint of liberty or due process.

Impeachment. To proceed against the "President, Vice President and all civil officers of the United States" for "Treason, Bribery, or other high Crimes and Misdemeanors," by articles adopted by the United States House of Representatives, and trial by the United States Senate, presided over by the chief justice of the United States, under the United States Constitution, art. 2, sec. 4.

Jurisdiction. The authority of a court to act, created by constitutional or legislative grant, including authority over a person as by service of legal process upon him or over property or things brought before the court. Pertinent to the Willis W. Ritter saga, jurisdiction may be original, referring to a proceeding being initiated before a court that receives evidence and determines facts and law, or appellate, in which a superior court reviews the proceeding for correctness, on a record compiled elsewhere.

Libel. Words, published (not merely spoken) in writing or broadcast as by radio, that are false and injure the character or reputation of any person, including an artificial person such as a corporation, unless there is a legally sufficient "privilege" to do so (as in reporting a crime).

Mandamus, writ of. "We command you to perform your duty! Do it the way we said; or, don't do it at all, if that is what we said." An order by a superior court to do, or refrain from doing, some particular thing, usually of a ministerial nature, such as convening a grand jury or conducting a jury trial, where required by law.

Minute clerk. One who keeps notes, in a book, of court proceedings.

Nolo contendere. "I do not admit I am guilty, but will not defend against the charges." The same legal effect as pleading guilty, but is not an admission for the purpose of another proceeding.

Peremptory challenge. "My right to challenge that (juror, document, and so on) is absolute, without question." Positive, absolute, conclusive right to some objection or proceeding.

Probation. "Either stay out of trouble, or 'bring your toothbrush.'" A form of sentence in lieu of incarceration, contingent on good behavior.

Pro se. "I need no lawyer." Proceedings by a person acting for himself.

Rule day. In practice, a day on which a court hands down rulings on pending legal questions, usually in joint or common proceedings with other litigants.

Scire facias. "Why should I not have the advantage of changing, or revoking, the record of your authority?" A common-law writ to vacate or annul a record, such as a deed or conveyance, or revive a judgment or other legal proceeding. Sometimes applied to question judicial authority.

Subpoena. Process, or order, to "lay aside all pretenses and excuses and appear" before a court or body, legislative or administrative, "at a time mentioned to testify or produce records."

Temporary restraining order. A form of injunction, or order preventing certain conduct, for a short period of time, usually ten days, until the court can determine the merits of the dispute. *See* enjoin.

Trailing calendar. "Wait outside in the hall, or sit in court, and be ready."

Use immunity. Immunity from prosecution for a specific purpose only. The device for requiring a person to testify who will not otherwise waive, or abandon, his privilege against self-incrimination.

Writ (of attachment, entry, error, mandamus, possession, review, and so forth). "You are ordered to give the bearer, or applicant, his due." Process, dating from common law, essentially mandating certain conduct, proceedings, or results.

BIBLIOGRAPHY

MANUSCRIPT COLLECTIONS

Boyden, John S. Papers. Accession 823, Manuscripts Division, J. Willard Marriott Library, University of Utah, Salt Lake City.

Brimhall, Dean R. Papers. MS 114, Manuscripts Division, J. Willard Marriott Library, University of Utah, Salt Lake City.

Dorius, Earl F. "Personal Recollections of My Involvement and the Involvement of the Attorney General's Office Staff with the Gary Gilmore Case between November 1, 1976, and January 17, 1977." 1978. Utah Historical Society, Salt Lake City.

Federal Bureau of Investigation. "Willis W. Ritter."

Hinckley, Robert H. Papers. MS 102, Manuscripts Division, J. Willard Marriott Library, University of Utah, Salt Lake City.

Moss, Frank E. Papers. MS 146, Manuscripts Division, J. Willard Marriott Library, University of Utah, Salt Lake City.

Nature Conservancy. "Chat with Aldrich Bowler," July 17, 1997.

Ritter, Willis W. Papers. Accession 930, Manuscripts Division, J. Willard Marriott Library, University of Utah, Salt Lake City.

Salt Lake County. Recorder. Book 64, C2, Block 72, Plat A, Salt Lake City Survey, January–February 1902, Salt Lake City.

Thomas, Elbert D. Papers. Utah State Historical Society, Salt Lake City.

Thomas, George. Presidential Records. Accession 017, University Archives, University of Utah, Salt Lake City.

University of Utah Board of Regents. Minutes. J. Willard Marriott Library, University of Utah, Salt Lake City.

Ward, Brent. "The Ritter Project—a Two Year History." United States Department of Justice, February 22, 1978, Salt Lake City.

LEGAL CASES

Aboitiz and Co. v. Price. 99 F. Supp. 602 (USDC D Utah 1951).

American Gypsum Trust v. Georgia-Pacific Corporation. 512 P2d 658 (Utah 1973).

American Gypsum Trust v. Georgia-Pacific Corporation. 512 P2d 658, Abstract of Record in Abstracts and Briefs, vol. 513.

American Gypsum Trust v. Georgia-Pacific Corporation. 539 P2d 1040 (Utah 1975).

Berner v. British Commonwealth Pacific Airlines, Ltd. 219 F. Supp. 289 (USDC SDNY 1963).

Braasch v. Utah. 350 U.S. 973 (1956).

Brigham City Corp. v. General Electric Co. 210 F. Supp. 574 (D Utah 1962).

Buckley v. United States. 382 F2d 611 (10th Cir. 1967).

Calvarisi v. United States. 348 U.S. 961 (1955).

Chandler v. Judicial Council of the Tenth Circuit of the United States. 398 U.S. 74 (1970).

Escobedo v. Illinois. 384 U.S. 440 (1964).

Ex parte Sullivan. 107 F. Supp. 514 (D Utah 1952).

Friends of the Earth v. Armstrong. 360 F. Supp. 165 (USDC D Utah 1973).

Friends of the Earth v. Armstrong. 485 F2d 1 (10th Cir. 1973).
Gideon v. Wainwright. 372 U.S. 335 (1963).
Golden v. American Keene Cement and Plaster Co. 95 P2d 755 (Utah 1939).
Hatahley v. United States. 76 SCt 745 (1965).
In re Presentment by Camden County Grand Jury. 89 Atlantic 2d 416 (New Jersey 1952).
In re Presentment by Camden County Grand Jury. 169 Atlantic 2d 465 (New Jersey 1961).
In the Matter of Sullivan. 126 F. Supp. 564 (D Utah 1954).
In the Matter of the Division of Business and Assignment of Cases in the United States District Court for the District of Utah (Judicial Council of the Tenth Circuit, November Session, 1971).
In the Matter of the Trial and Sentencing of Minor Offenses, etc. No. 77–1208 (10th Cir. Judicial Council, filed March 28, 1977).
In the Matter of Transcripts Withheld from the United States by the Honorable Willis W. Ritter. No. 77–1491 (10th Cir. Judicial Council, filed March 5, 1977).
Kerr-McGee v. Ritter. 461 F2d 1104 (10th Cir. 1972), Answer to Order to Show Cause on Petition for Extraordinary Writs.
Miranda v. Arizona. 384 U.S. 436 (1966).
Pelt v. Utah. 104 F3d 1534 (10th Cir. 1996).
Public Service Co. of New Mexico v. General Electric Co. 315 F2d 306 (10th Cir. 1963).
Reynolds v. Texas Gulf Sulphur Co. 309 F. Supp. 548 (D Utah 1970).
Ritter v. Morton. 513 F2d 942 (9th Cir. 1975).
Sdanok v. Glidden Co. 327 F2d 944 (2d Cir. 1964).
Smaldone v. United States. 211 F2d 161 (10th Cir. 1954).
State v. Braasch. 229 P2d 289 (Utah 1951).
State v. Phillips. 540 P2d 936 (1975).
State v. Sullivan. 227 F2d 511 (10th Cir. 1956).
Union Carbide and Carbon Corp. v. Nisley. 300 F2d 561, 589 (10th Cir. 1961).
United States v. Cardall. CR–74–53 (USDC D Utah 1974).
United States v. Doiron. CR–76–31 (USDC D Utah, November 24, 1976).
United States v. Hatahley. 220 F2d 666 (10th Cir. 1955).
United States v. Hatahley. 257 F2d 920 (10th Cir. 1958).
United States v. Hosteen Tse-kesi. 93 F. Supp. 745 (D Utah 1950).
United States v. Morrell. 331 F2d 498 (10th Cir. 1964).
United States v. Ritter. No. 76–1331 (10th Cir., filed April 20, 1976).
United States v. Ritter. No. 76–1331 (10th Cir., mandamus denied April 29, 1976).
United States v. Ritter. No. 76–1011 (10th Cir., mandamus issued May 20, 1976).
United States v. Ritter. No. 76–1917 (10th Cir., mandamus issued November 6, 1976).
United States v. Ritter. 540 F2d 459 (10th Cir. 1976).
United States v. Ritter. No. 77–1240 (10th Cir., writ denied with precatory instructions, April 22, 1977).
United States v. Ritter. No. 77–1829 (10th Cir., filed October 5, 1977).
Utah Idaho Sugar Co. v. Ritter. 461 F2d 1100 (10th Cir. 1972).
Utah State Farm Bureau Federation v. National Farmers Union Service Corp. 198 F2d 20 (10th Cir. 1952).
Young v. Felornia. 244 P2d 862 (Utah 1952).

GOVERNMENT DOCUMENTS

Congressional Record. 81st Cong., 2d sess., 1950. Vol. 96, pt. 7.
President. Proclamation. "Convention and Additional Protocol between the United States of

America and Other Powers Relating to International Air Transportation: Concluded at Warsaw, October 12, 1929." *U.S. Statutes at Large* 49 (1934): 3000. *Warsaw Convention.*
Rule 23, *Federal Rules of Civil Procedure* (1966).
U.S. Bureau of the Census. *Twelfth Census of the United States,* 1900. *Population.* Washington, DC: 1900.
———. *Thirteenth Census of the United States,* 1910. Washington, DC: 1910.
U.S. Code. Vol. 15, sec. 15. *Clayton Antitrust Act.*
———. Vol. 18, secs. 241, 242.
———. Vol. 18, sec. 1503.
———. Vol. 28, sec. 137.
———. Vol. 28, sec. 294(c).
———. Vol. 28, secs. 631(a), 751, 755. *Judicial Improvements and Access to Justice Act.*
———. Vol. 28, sec. 1331.
———. Vol. 43, secs. 315-315r. *Taylor Grazing Act.*
———. Vol. 43, secs. 620, 620b. *Colorado River Storage Project.*
U.S. Congress. House. Committee on House Administration. *Contested Election Case of Wilson against Granger, First Congressional District of Utah.* 80th Cong., 2d sess., 1948. H. Rept. 2418. Washington, DC: GPO, 1948.
U.S. Congress. Senate. Committee on Indian Affairs. *Addition to the Western Navajo Indian Reservation: Hearings on S. 3782,* 71st Cong., 2d sess. Washington, DC: GPO, 1930.
———. Subcommittee of the Committee on the Judiciary. *Hearings on the Nomination of Willis W. Ritter, of Utah, to Be United States District Judge for the District of Utah.* 80th Cong., 2nd sess., September 29, 1949. Washington, DC: GPO, 1949.
———. *Hearings on the Nomination of Willis W. Ritter, of Utah, to Be United States District Judge for the District of Utah.* 81st Cong., 1st sess., May 2, 1950, Salt Lake City. Washington, DC: GPO, 1950.
———. *Hearings on the Nomination of Willis W. Ritter, of Utah, to Be United States District Judge for the District of Utah.* 81st Cong., 1st sess., May 5, 1950, Denver. Washington, DC: GPO, 1950.
———. Subcommittee on Improvement in the Judicial Machinery. *Hearings on S. 1130.* 94th Cong., 2d sess., May 18, 1976. Washington, DC: GPO, 1976.
U.S. Statutes at Large 43 (1924): 253. *Indian Citizenship Act.*
———. 49 (1934): 3020.
———. 52 (1938): 1209-11.
———. 65 (1848): 922. *Treaty of Guadalupe-Hidalgo.*
———. 72 (1958): 497.
———. 76 (1962): 89.
Wilson, David J. Brief. In *Contested Election Case of Wilson against Granger, First Congressional District of Utah.* House of Representatives of the United States. 80th Cong. (1947). Washington, DC: GPO, 1948.

INTERVIEWS

Transcripts of interviews are in the possession of Parker M. Nielson.
Ashton, Cliff. Interview by Cowley. March 16, 1983.
Austin, Myrtle. Interview by Cowley. March 1, 1984.
Badger, Paul. Interview by Cowley. November 29, 1983.
Bailey, Ruth. Interview by Cowley. May 30, 1984.
Bauman, Joe. Interview by Cowley. February 29, 1984.
Beads, Orval, and Jenny Beads. Interview by the Nature Conservancy. May 26, 1996.

Behle, Calvin A. Interview by Cowley. August 29, 1983.
Billings, Peter, Sr. Interview by Cowley. November 16, 1983.
Bowler, Aldrich. Interview by Fredda. July 17, 1997.
Bowler, Di. Interview by Cowley. Ca. 1983.
Boyce, Ronald N. Interview by Cowley. December 12, 1983.
Bryson, Robert. Interview by Cowley. January 5, 1983.
Buck, Myrtle. Interview by Cowley. August 16, 1983.
Camille, Sister Marie. Interview by Cowley. April 26, 1983.
Campbell, Robert. Interview by Cowley. February 2, 1984.
Fowler, Bill. Interview by Cowley. November 23, 1983.
Gallivan, Jack. Interview by Cowley. November 15, 1982.
Goodman, Jack, and Marge Goodman. Interview by Cowley. June 20, 1983.
Green, Jack. Interview by Cowley. October 20, 1983.
Halbert, Minnie May "Min" Ritter. Interview by Cowley. July 17, 1983.
Hallam, Lucille. Telephone interview by Cowley. July 9, 1984.
Hansen, Phil. Interview by Cowley. September 29, 1983.
Hansen, Robert. Telephone interview by Cowley. June 20, 1989.
Holbrook, Don. Interview by Cowley. September 16, 1983.
Housley, James. Interview by Nielson, July 29, 1998.
Jensen, A. LaDrue. Interview by Cowley. Ca. July 1983.
Jensen, Catherine. Interview by Cowley. November 18, 1982.
Jensen, Jack. Interview by Cowley. August 24, 1984.
Johnson, Norman. Interview by Cowley. November 15, 1983.
Jones, Joe. Interview by Cowley. February 18, 1983.
Kesler, Pratt. Interview by Cowley. June 23, 1983.
Klemm, H. Ralph. Interview by Nielson, April 18, 2000.
Lamoreaux, Rick. Interview by Cowley. March 10, 1983.
Lang, Bill. Interview by Cowley. June 27, 1983.
Lloyd, Don. Interview by Cowley. February 27, 1981.
Lockhart, William J. Interview by Cowley. April 20, 1983.
Malmquist, O. N. Interview by Cowley. August 8, 1983.
Matheson, Scott. Interview by Cowley. April 26, 1983.
Mawhinney, Margaret. Interview by Cowley. November 4, 1983.
McCarthy, Dennis. Interview by Cowley. January 19, 1983.
McCarthy, Joe. Interview by Cowley. September 1, 1983.
McMillan, George. Interview by Cowley. Ca. 1982 and January 6, 1983.
Mitchell, Dean. Interview by Cowley. December 15, 1983.
Mock, Byron. Interview by Cowley. January 5, 1984.
Norton, Ida, and Joe Norton. Interview by Cowley. February 3, 1983.
Novelle, David. Interview by Cowley. October 20, 1983.
Oman, Milt. Interview by Cowley. January 31, 1984.
Rampton, Calvin. Interview by Cowley. July 28, 1983.
Ramsay, Rhoda. Interview by Cowley. September 16, 1985.
Rhodes, Bernie. Interview by Cowley. January 13, 1983.
———. Interview by Nielson, June 21, 2001.
Richards, Lynn. Interview by Cowley. February 24, 1984.
Ritchie, Verl. Interview by Cowley. January 31, 1984, and January 23, 1984 (telephone).
Ritter, Nancy. Interview by Cowley. November 12, 1982.
Rosenblatt, Joseph. Interview by Cowley. July 19, 1983.
Sandack, A. Wally. Interview by Cowley. Ca. 1983.

Saperstein, Herschel. Interview by Cowley. January 30, 1984.
Shearer, Kent. Interview by Cowley. December 9, 1983.
Smay, Craig. Interview by Cowley. January 30, 1984.
Snow, Dorothy. Interview by Cowley. March 7, 1983.
Swenson, Peggy. Interview by Cowley. April 28, 1983.
Swenson, Robert. Interview by Cowley. March 22, 1983.
Taylor, Keith. Interview by Cowley. January 19, 1984.
Wheeler, Max. Interview by Cowley. March 7, 1984.
Wilkins, D. Frank. Interview by Cowley. December 20, 1983.
Winder, David K. Interview by Cowley. May 17, 1984.

OTHER SOURCES

Anderson, Jack. "Judge vs. Sheriff." *Washington Post,* July 20, 1971, B11.
"Appeals Court Delays Trials." *Salt Lake Tribune,* October 8, 1976, C1.
"Appeals Court Dismisses Case in Theft." *Salt Lake Tribune,* August 27, 1977, B8.
"Are the Thousand Springs Going Down the Drain?" *Idaho (Boise) Statesman,* August 23, 1970, B1.
Arrington, Leonard J., and Heidi S. Swinton. *In the Utah Tradition: A History of the Governor's Mansion.* Salt Lake City: Governor's Mansion Foundation, 1987.
Aton, James M., and Robert S. McPherson. *River Flowing from the Sunrise: An Environmental History of the Lower San Juan.* Logan: Utah State University Press, 2000.
"Attorney Files Prejudice Affidavit against U.S. Judge in Lands Suit." *Salt Lake Tribune,* April 6, 1972, B9.
"Bar Halts Action on Ritter." *Salt Lake Tribune,* July 15, 1973, B1.
Beless, James W., Jr. "The Episcopal Church in Utah: Seven Bishops and One Hundred Years." *Utah Historical Quarterly* 60, no. 1 (Winter 1968): 80.
Bentley, Harold W., ed. *The University of Utah: A History of Its First Hundred Years, 1850 to 1950.* Salt Lake City: University of Utah Press, 1960.
Bertoch, Julia Brixen. "Rhetorical Theory and Practice of Adam S. Bennion." Master's thesis, University of Utah, 1971.
Brodie, Fawn M. *No Man Knows My History: The Life of Joseph Smith, the Mormon Prophet.* New York: Alfred A. Knopf, 1966.
Bryson, Robert. "Circuit Court Takes Ritter Off Case." *Salt Lake Tribune,* July 17, 1976, D1.
———. "Judge Ritter Refuses Bid to Give Up Case." *Salt Lake Tribune,* March 30, 1976, B1.
———. "Judge Studies Proposal to Lift Own Order on Rainbow Bridge." *Salt Lake Tribune,* March 28, 1973, B1–B2.
———. "Order Ritter to Comply, U.S. Asks." *Salt Lake Tribune,* January 28, 1976, 24.
———. "Remove Self? Ritter Kills Action." *Salt Lake Tribune,* January 31, 1976, B3.
———. "Ritter's Answer to Charges Filed in Court." *Salt Lake Tribune,* March 12, 1978.
———. "Specific Court Dates Set for 25 Cases." *Salt Lake Tribune,* November 9, 1976, 25.
Burnett, M. Dallas, and Nelson Wadsworth. "Ritter: Paranoia and Paradox on the Federal Bench." *Utah Holiday,* February 10, 1976, 4-6.
Campbell, Eugene E. *Establishing Zion: The Mormon Church in the American West.* Salt Lake City: Signature Books, 1988.
Cannon, Brian Q. "Mormons and the New Deal: The 1936 Presidential Election in Utah." *Utah Historical Quarterly* 67, no. 1 (Winter 1999): 4-22.
Chaffee, Zeccharia, Jr. *Some Problems of Equity.* Chicago: Foundation Press, 1946.
Chase, Harold. *Federal Judges.* Minneapolis: University of Minnesota Press, 1972.
"Checkers' Bond Forfeited; Judge Orders Him to Stand U.S. Trial." *Denver Post,* June 3, 1953, 1.
"Checkers' Tax Trial Delayed: Jurors, Witnesses Face Quiz." *Denver Post,* September 21, 1953, 1.

Chicago Tribune Service. "Turning the Tables: Opponents Attempt to Muzzle Outspoken, Aging Federal Judge." *Houston Post,* October 9, 1977.

"City to Appeal Ritter's Stand on 2 Suits." *Salt Lake Tribune,* April 26, 1972, B20.

Clark, D. Worth. "Idaho Made the Desert Bloom." *National Geographic* 85, no. 6 (June 1944): 641, 680.

"Congress Tiff Looms on Recess Judges." *Salt Lake Tribune,* October 23, 1949, A4.

"The Constitution." *Deseret News,* October 31, 1936, 1.

"Court Action Asks for New Judge." *Salt Lake Tribune,* May 10, 1973, B8.

"Court Names New Judge in U-I Case." *Salt Lake Tribune,* June 9, 1972, A34.

"Court Refuses Plea by S.L. to Bar Judge in Case." *Salt Lake Tribune,* May 25, 1972, A19.

Davies, Pete. *The Devil's Flu: The World's Deadliest Influenza Epidemic and the Scientific Hunt for the Virus That Caused It.* New York: Henry Holt, 2000.

"Dean R. Brimhall Dies—Noted Utahn, Educator." *Salt Lake Tribune,* May 16, 1972, 25.

"Democrats Back Thomas for Vice President." *Salt Lake Tribune,* May 28, 1944, A1.

"Democrats Nominate Roosevelt." *Salt Lake Tribune,* July 21, 1944, A1.

"Democrats Row over No. 2 Spot on Ticket." *Salt Lake Tribune,* July 20, 1944, A1.

"Dewey Readies Blast at FDR Denial of Reds." *Salt Lake Tribune,* October 7, 1944, A4.

Donaldson, Gary A. *Truman Defeats Dewey.* Lexington: University Press of Kentucky, 1999.

Dykman, Judy, and Colleen Whitley. *The Silver Queen: Her Royal Highness Suzanne Bransford Emery Holmess Delitch Egalitcheff.* Logan: Utah State University Press, 1998.

Eccles, Marriner S. *Beckoning Frontiers: Public and Personal Recollections.* Edited by Sidney Hyman. New York: Alfred A. Knopf, 1951.

Falk, Jennifer. "Ritter Dines Out." *Bar and Bench* (ca. Fall 1991).

"Feet-First Ritter under Siege." *Time,* November 7, 1977, 63.

"Fight Widens on Nation's Food Policy." *Salt Lake Tribune,* June 16, 1943, 1.

"500 at Reception Honor Senator Thomas, Bride." *Salt Lake Tribune,* November 7, 1946, 13.

Fox, Frank W. *J. Reuben Clark: The Public Years.* Provo: Brigham Young University Press, 1980.

Frankel, Marvin E., and Gary P. Naftalis. *The Grand Jury: An Institution on Trial.* New York: Hill and Wang, 1975.

"Friends, Colleagues Eulogize Thomas as Great Statesman." *Salt Lake Tribune,* February 12, 1953, 8.

Gallup, George. "Survey Gives GOP Chance to Win House." *Salt Lake Tribune,* October 1, 1944, A8.

Gibbons, Francis M. *Brigham Young: Modern Moses, Prophet of God.* Salt Lake City: Deseret Book, 1981.

———. *Heber J. Grant: Man of Steel, Prophet of God.* Salt Lake City: Deseret Book, 1979.

"GOP Chief Sees Vote Tide Running to Gov. Dewey." *Salt Lake Tribune,* October 28, 1944, A2.

Gotlieb, Robert, and Peter Wiley. *America's Saints: The Rise of Mormon Power.* New York: Putnam's, 1984.

Grant, Carter Eldredge. *The Kingdom of God Restored.* Salt Lake City: Deseret Book, 1955.

Green, Carol. "History-Shaping Debate Focuses on Embattled Judge." *Denver Post,* October 23, 1977, 31.

Gudmundsen, Lance S. "Ritter Reaffirms Monument Ruling." *Salt Lake Tribune,* September 18, 1972, 19.

Hampshire, David. "Mining Leaves Its Mark on Park City." *Beehive History: Living on the Land* (Utah State Historical Society) 26 (2000): 18-21.

———. "Remembering Park City's Great Fire." *Utah Historical Quarterly* 66, no. 3 (Summer 1998): 225-42.

Hansen, Robert H., and Charles Roos. "U.S. Indicts Flip Flop Too." *Denver Post,* September 24, 1953, 1.

"Hansen Criticizes Owens on Judicial Issue." *Deseret News,* September 29, 1973, A3.
"Harris Enters GOP Race for Governor." *Salt Lake Tribune,* April 4, 1948.
Hassell, Frank. *Rainbow Bridge: An Illustrated History.* Logan: Utah State University Press, 1999.
Hewlett, Frank. "Moss Asks West Solons to Meet on 'Rainbow Bridge Crises.'" *Salt Lake Tribune,* March 25, 1973.
———. "Sen. Garn Assails Ritter in Statement." *Salt Lake Tribune,* February 26, 1976, C1.
Hinckley, Robert H., and JoAnn Jacobsen Wells. *"I'd Rather Be Born Lucky than Rich."* Provo: Brigham Young University Press, 1977.
Hodge, Frederick Webb, ed. *Handbook of American Indians North of Mexico.* 2d ed. 2 vols. Washington, DC: GPO, 1912.
House, Dawn. "Judge's Ghost Keeps Courthouse Memories Alive." *Salt Lake Tribune,* July 15, 1991, B1.
"How Far, Your Honor?" *Deseret News,* October 16, 1953, A18.
Hughes, Jonathan R. T. "Mariner Eccles: Logician in Wonderland." In *The Vital Few: The Entrepreneur and American Economic Progress.* New York: Oxford University Press, 1986.
Hulse, James W. *The Silver State: Nevada's Heritage Reinterpreted.* 2d ed. Reno: University of Nevada Press, 1998.
Hyman, Sidney, ed. *Beckoning Frontiers: Public and Personal Recollections.* New York: Alfred A. Knopf, 1951.
———. *Marriner S. Eccles: Private Entrepreneur and Public Servant.* Stanford: Graduate School of Business, Stanford University, 1976.
"Icy Reception Given Ritter Slayer Ruling." *Salt Lake Tribune,* September 26, 1952, B1.
"It's Bosone vs. Leavitt in Primary." *Salt Lake Tribune,* July 31, 1948, 1.
Jarvik, Elaine. "Judge Ritter: The Man and the Myth." *Utah Holiday,* February 10, 1976, 7-11.
Johnson, Katherine. "Solon Seeks Bar to Recess Naming." *Deseret News,* October 21, 1949, B1.
Jonas, Frank H., ed. *Political Dynamiting.* Salt Lake City: University of Utah Press, 1970.
"Judge Gives Indian Weaving to U. Museum of Fine Arts." *Salt Lake Tribune,* January 7, 1975.
"Judge Ritter Ballot Due Monday." *Salt Lake Tribune,* June 10, 1950, 1.
"Judge Ritter Clamps Silencer on Mail, Delays Postal Processing One Hour." *Salt Lake Tribune,* November 13, 1952, 18.
"Judge Ritter Condemns Grand Jury System Failings." *Salt Lake Tribune,* May 14, 1976, 22.
"Judge Ritter Denies Two Motions to Disqualify Him in Civil Cases." *Salt Lake Tribune,* April 19, 1972, D8.
"Judge Ritter of Utah Granted More Time for Ouster Defense." *Los Angeles Times,* January 19, 1987.
Knudson, Max B. "S.L. Law Firm Enjoys 100th—Despite Judge Ritter." *Deseret News,* December 3-4, 1982, D9.
"KSL Gets Back TV Camera from Ritter." *Salt Lake Tribune,* February 23, 1977, 29.
Larrowe, Charles P. "Notches on a Chair." *Nation,* April 14, 1956, 291.
"Late Returns Raise Lead Past 2,000,000 Mark." *Salt Lake Tribune,* November 8, 1944, A1.
"Lawyer of S.L. Enters Race for Congress." *Salt Lake Tribune,* July 8, 1948, 1.
"Leslie R. Samuels Dies at 84, Former Utah Businessman." *Salt Lake Tribune,* July 21, 1984.
Lyman, Edward Leo. "The Arrowhead Trails Highway: The Beginnings of Utah's Other Route to the Pacific Coast." *Utah Historical Quarterly* 67, no. 3 (Summer 1999): 242-64.
Malmquist, O. N. "Election Interest Grows in Final Days of Campaign." *Salt Lake Tribune,* November 5, 1944, A1.
———. "Utahns Adhere to Plan to Enter Thomas' Name." *Salt Lake Tribune,* July 20, 1944, A7.

———. "Utah Remains Democratic Vote Samples Indicate." *Salt Lake Tribune,* October 29, 1944, A1.

"Marshalls Seize Camera." *Salt Lake Tribune,* July 13, 1977, C8.

"Maw, Lee Race Close." *Salt Lake Tribune,* November 8, 1944, A1.

"McCarran Asks U.S. to Seek Ritter Witness." *Salt Lake Tribune,* June 7, 1950, 1.

McPherson, Robert S., ed. *The Journey of Navajo Oshley.* Logan: Utah State University Press, 2000.

"Milestones." *Time,* May 30, 1983, 88.

Miller, Bill. "Smaldones Guilty." *Rocky Mountain News,* October 30, 1953, 1, 6.

Mortimer, William James, ed. *How Beautiful upon the Mountains: A Centennial History of Wasatch County.* Wasatch County: Daughters of Utah Pioneers, 1963.

Murphy, Bruce Allen. *Fortas: The Rise and Ruin of a Supreme Court Justice.* New York City: William A. Morrow, 1988.

"Navajos Camp Out in S.L. to Wait Court's Decision." *Deseret News,* November 17, 1953, 1B.

Nelson, Angelyn. "Bar Derails Action to Remove Judge Ritter." *Salt Lake Tribune,* January 11, 1976, B1.

Nielson, Parker M. *The Dispossessed: Cultural Genocide of the Mixed-Blood Utes.* Norman: University of Oklahoma Press, 1998.

Olpin, Robert S. *Dictionary of Utah Art.* Salt Lake City: Salt Lake Art Center, 1980.

"One Man's Justice." *Utah Holiday,* February 10, 1976, 12-15.

"Output Controls Wait Slash after Nazi Fall." *Salt Lake Tribune,* October 1, 1944, A8.

"Pair Freed after Arrest for Assault on Ritter." *Salt Lake Tribune,* December 16, 1977, B5.

"Panel Action Threatens Ritter Status." *Salt Lake Tribune,* February 2, 1972, 18.

"Panel Hears Views on Ritter Case." *Salt Lake Tribune,* May 19, 1976, B1.

Powell, Allan Kent, ed. *Utah History Encyclopedia.* Salt Lake City: University of Utah Press, 1994.

"The President Has Named a Native Son as Judge." *Salt Lake Tribune,* October 23, 1949, A8.

"Proceedings and Remarks at the Installation of Hon. Willis W. Ritter as United States Judge for the District of Utah—August 1, 1950." *Utah Bar Bulletin* (July–August 1950): 69-78.

Pusey, Roger. "Being Chief Judge Is No Snap, Either." *Deseret News,* October 23, 1964, B4.

"Quick Action Helped Utah Survive Drought of 1934, Lecturer Says." *Salt Lake Tribune,* April 24, 1965, T5.

Quinn, D. Michael. *Elder Statesman: A Biography of J. Reuben Clark.* Salt Lake City: Signature Books, 2002.

———. *J. Reuben Clark: The Church Years.* Provo: Brigham Young University Press, 1983.

"Rallies End Appeals to Utah Voters." *Salt Lake Tribune,* November 5, 1944, B1.

"Records Show No Contempt Threat." *Salt Lake Tribune,* February 27, 1976, B1.

"Rent Official Rouses Ire of Probers." *Salt Lake Tribune,* May 21, 1943, 17-1.

"Rep. Granger Asks Dismissal of Wilson Ballot Contest." *Salt Lake Tribune,* January 21, 1947, 1.

"Resolution Asked Congress to Repeal Grandfather Clause." *Salt Lake Tribune,* March 9, 1974, 13.

Richardson, Richard J., and Kenneth N. Vines. *The Politics of Federal Courts: Lower Courts in the United States.* Boston: Little, Brown, 1970.

"Ritter, Welker Clash in Jury Bribe Case." *Salt Lake Tribune,* December 13, 1953, A6.

Ritter, Willis W. "Lifting Law." *Deseret News,* February 6, 1934.

"Ritter All Set to Testify at Probe of FBI." *Denver Post,* December 10, 1953.

"Ritter Hearing Goes Back to Committee." *Salt Lake Tribune,* October 4, 1949, B13.

"Ritter Is Opposed by Governor, Report." *Deseret News,* October 15, 1949, B1.

"Ritter Looms as Judge Post Choice." *Salt Lake Tribune,* June 4, 1949, 1.

"Ritter Passes U.S. Senate Loyalty Test." *Salt Lake Tribune,* September 30, 1949, 21.
"Ritter Proves Mild during Opening Case." *Salt Lake Tribune,* October 29, 1949, 20.
"Ritter Takes Oath as Third Federal Judge for Utah." *Salt Lake Tribune,* October 25, 1949, 1.
"Ritter to Visit Indian Area in Navajo Suit." *Deseret News,* November 20, 1953, 1B.
Rogers, Kristen Smart. "'Another Good Man': Anthony W. Ivins and the Defeat of Reed Smoot." *Utah Historical Quarterly* 68, no. 1 (Winter 2000): 55-75.
Rolly, Paul. "Ritter Auction Draws 'Special' Audience." *Salt Lake Tribune,* September 11, 1986.
"Roosevelt Delays War at Huge Cost in Lives." *Salt Lake Tribune,* November 5, 1944, A10.
Rose, Tim. "No Parking Tickets for 10 Days, Ritter Says." *Deseret News,* May 5, 1973, A3.
Rothman, David. "The Grand Jury vs. You." *Saturday Evening Post,* November 1974.
Ruotsila, Markku. "Senator William H. King of Utah and His Campaigns against Russian Communism, 1917-1933." *Utah Historical Quarterly* 74, no. 2 (Spring 2006): 147.
Schindler, Harold. "Ritter Navajo Collection Highlights Exhibition." *Salt Lake Tribune,* February 12, 1978, E4.
"Selection for Federal Bench Vacancy Meets with General Approval." *Salt Lake Tribune,* June 5, 1949, A12.
"Sen. Garn Assails Ritter in Statement." *Salt Lake Tribune,* February 26, 1976, C1.
"Senatorial Candidates Debate at Women's Council Meeting." *Salt Lake Tribune,* October 3, 1944, B11.
"Senator Thomas Recommends Willis Ritter for Judge." *Ogden Standard-Examiner,* June 5, 1949, A6.
"Smaldone Jailed on Charge of Jury Tampering." *Rocky Mountain News,* September 22, 1953, 5.
Smith, Richard Norton. *Thomas E. Dewey and His Times.* New York: Simon and Schuster, 1982.
"Solon Seeks Bar to Recess Naming." *Deseret News,* October 21, 1949, B1.
Swanson, Vern G., Robert S. Olpin, and William C. Seifrit. *Utah Painting and Sculpture.* Salt Lake City: Gibbs Smith, 1991.
Swift, Jonathan. *Gulliver's Travels.* In *Great Books of the Western World,* edited by Maynard Hutchins, vol. 36. Chicago: Encyclopaedia Britannica, 1952.
Thomas, Elbert D. *The Four Fears.* New York: Ziff-Davis, 1944.
"Thomas Dies at Home in Honolulu." *Salt Lake Tribune,* February 12, 1953, 1.
Thompson, George A., and Fraser Buck. *Treasure Mountain Home: A Centennial History of Park City.* Salt Lake City: Deseret Book, 1968.
Thurman, William T., Sr. "Vignettes of the Late Chief Judge Willis W. Ritter." *Utah Bar Journal* 7 (1994): 12-15.
"Truman Names Ritter Utah Federal Judge." *Salt Lake Tribune,* August 26, 1949, 1.
"2 Killers Lose Third Plea to Top Tribunal." *Salt Lake Tribune,* February 28, 1956, 17.
"U. Professors Say Killers' Trials Legal." *Salt Lake Tribune,* April 9, 1952, 21.
United States Navy. *The Story of the* Bennion. Salt Lake City: Utah State Historical Society, 1947.
"U.S. Judge Grants 2 Killers 45-Day Stays of Execution." *Salt Lake Tribune,* February 24, 1952, B1.
"U.S. Judge Ritter Bars Press Photographers." *Deseret News,* October 14, 1953, B1.
"Utahn Gains Favor for Vice President." *Deseret News,* November 26, 1943, 5.
"Utahn Praised for Action on Irrigation." *Salt Lake Tribune,* May 3, 1950.
Watkins, Arthur V. *Enough Rope: The Inside Story of the Censure of Senator Joseph McCarthy by His Colleagues.* Englewood Cliffs, NJ: Prentice-Hall, 1969.
White, G. Edward. *Oliver Wendell Holmes, Jr.* New York: Oxford University Press, 2006.
Who's Who in America. Chicago: Marquis, 1952-1953.

Wilkinson, Charles. *Fire on the Plateau: Conflict and Endurance in the American Southwest.* Washington, DC: Island Press / Shearwater Books, 1999.

Williams, Jeff. "Ritter under Siege (a Melodrama) with Phil Hansen as Court Jester." *Utah Holiday,* December 1977.

"Willis W. Ritter Named to Utah Federal Bench." *Salt Lake Tribune,* August 27, 1949, 8.

Zillman, Donald N. "The University of Utah College of Law: An Analytical History, Part I." *Res Gestae* 5, no. 2 (1982): 18.

———. "The University of Utah College of Law: An Analytical History, Part II." *Res Gestae* 5, no. 3 (1983): 10-16.

———. "The University of Utah College of Law: An Analytical History, Part III." *Res Gestae* 6, no. 1 (1984): 8-11.

INDEX